Supply Chain Excellence

Third Edition

Supply Chain Excellence

A Handbook for Dramatic Improvement
Using the SCOR Model

Third Edition

**Peter Bolstorff
and Robert Rosenbaum**

AMACOM

American Management Association
New York • Atlanta • Brussels • Chicago • Mexico City
San Francisco • Shanghai • Tokyo • Toronto • Washington, D.C.

Bulk discounts available. For details visit: www.amacombooks.org/go/specialsales or contact special sales:
Phone: 800-250-5308 • Email: specialsls@amanet.org
View all the AMACOM titles at: www.amacombooks.org

This publication is designed to provide accurate and authoritative information in regard to the subject matter covered. It is sold with the understanding that the publisher is not engaged in rendering legal, accounting, or other professional service. If legal advice or other expert assistance is required, the services of a competent professional person should be sought.

Various names used by companies to distinguish their software and other products can be claimed as trademarks. AMACOM uses such names throughout this book for editorial purposes only, with no intention of trademark violation. Individual companies should be contacted for complete information regarding trademarks and registration.

SAP, AcceleratedSAP, and R/3 are the trademark(s) or registered trademark(s) of SAP AG in Germany and in several other countries; SCOR is a registered trademark in the United States and Europe; DCOR and CCOR are trademarks of the Supply Chain Council; ProcessWizard is a trademark of Xelocity Limited; Microsoft, Excel, Access, Office Communicator, and Lync are registered trademarks of the Microsoft group of companies; Minitab is a registered trademark of Minitab, Inc.; GoToMeeting is a registered trademark of Citrix Online, LLC; and Cisco is a registered trademark of Cisco Systems, Inc.

Library of Congress Cataloging-in-Publication Data

Bolstorff, Peter.
  Supply chain excellence : a handbook for dramatic improvement using the SCOR model / Peter Bolstorff and Robert Rosenbaum.—3rd ed.
    p. cm.
  Includes bibliographical references and index.
  ISBN 978-0-8144-1771-3 (HC : alk. paper)
  ISBN 978-0-8144-3753-7 (PB : alk. paper)   1. Business logistics—
  Management.   I. Rosenbaum, Robert (Robert G.)   II. Title.
HD38.5.B64   2012
658.7—dc23

                                  2011026467

About AMA

American Management Association (www.amanet.org) is a world leader in talent development, advancing the skills of individuals to drive business success. Our mission is to support the goals of individuals and organizations through a complete range of products and services, including classroom and virtual seminars, webcasts, webinars, podcasts, conferences, corporate and government solutions, business books, and research. AMA's approach to improving performance combines experiential learning—learning through doing—with opportunities for ongoing professional growth at every step of one's career journey.

Printing number

10   9   8   7   6   5   4   3   2   1

Dedications

Peter:

To my wife, Cary, with whom
I have spent 25 amazing years!

Bob:

To my wife, Barb, a source of partnership,
support, and so much more.

Contents

The Active Executive Sponsor
  Educate-for-Support Behaviors of the Active Executive Sponsor
  Planning and Organizing Behaviors of the Active Executive Sponsor
  Measures and Strategy Behaviors of the Active Executive Sponsor
  Design Solutions Behaviors of the Active Executive Sponsor
Establishing Core Team Buy-In
  Collective Experience
  Attitude
  Effective Communication Skills
  Ability to Cope Well in Chaos
Picking the Project Design Team
  Problem-Solving Experience
  Personality Factors
  Dedication: Discipline to Tasks
  Access to Data

Preface

Using experience gained from 35 supply chain improvement projects, the first edition of *Supply Chain Excellence* (AMACOM, 2003) was an instruction manual for anybody who sought a rigorous and proven methodology for systematic improvement in supply chain performance, using a cross-industry reference called the Supply Chain Operations Reference (SCOR®) model.

The second edition (AMACOM, 2007) updated the method and approach based on an additional 30 engagements with companies that completed multiple projects and integrated deliverables and analytical concepts in continuous improvement methods using Six Sigma and Lean. The second edition also expanded the process scope to encompass the entire value chain—including product design and customer sales processes. This was done with addition of two new frameworks: the Design Chain Operations Reference (DCOR) and Customer Chain Operations Reference (CCOR) models.

The third edition (AMACOM, 2012) updates the tips and techniques based on experience with 30 more projects—a majority of which were completed by companies that have not only used the approach multiple times but also extended its application in three areas: global alignment, small business schedule, and utilization of SAP® software. As with previous editions, updated and expanded key concepts, steps, tasks, outcomes and behaviors are illustrated in the context of a composite case: Fowlers Inc. Specific additions for this third edition include:

- ◆ A refined, more efficient project timeline conducive to global and small business use
- ◆ Simplified deliverables that better utilize resources and sharpen focus on performance
- ◆ Integration of SAP functionality and system implementation processes into the Fowlers examples
- ◆ A section on effective global supply chain strategy
- ◆ SCOR Level 4 examples of sales and operations planning and master scheduling
- ◆ Updating to SCOR 10.0

Acknowledgments

We would like to acknowledge those companies and individuals who have directly (and indirectly) contributed to this book. First and foremost, we would recognize Ralph Maltese. Ralph has been a colleague on past projects, a subject matter expert for SAP functionality and implementation methodology and business practices in general, and a great friend. Without his insight, contributions, and energy, this edition would have been nearly impossible. Second, we would recognize our supply chain colleagues at Amway, the United States Air Force, the Diverse Manufacturing Supply Chain Alliance (DMSCA), Kohler Co., McCormick and Co., and Nortech Systems, who again committed themselves to the approach—bringing ideas and suggestions that challenged us to make *Supply Chain Excellence* easier, more effective, and more relevant. This third edition is another tribute to them. Specific thanks are in order to George Calvert and his team, as well as to Gerry Phillips, Jane McCarthy, Jeff Akers, David Burton, Jim Radin, Denise Layfield, Mike Degen, Pete Kucera, Davor Grgic, Joe Hnilicka, Gerrard Gallenberger, Oliver Kaestner, and the Supply Chain Operating System (SCOS) team.

Third, we would like to recognize Xelocity, eKNOWtion, and SCE Africa, who as partners have adopted the approach, added their expertise and regional perspectives, and successfully delivered project after project—including the application of the ProcessWizard tool—

to all but one continent on the planet. Specific thanks go to Ikhlag Kashkari, Michael Diver, Douglas Kent, and Jolanda Pretorius.

Fourth, we would thank the Supply Chain Council. Its dedication to improving SCOR (introducing 10.0) and to introducing new tools, like DCOR 2.0, CCOR 1.0, the SCORmark survey, and a SCOR People section, has provided the platform from which all of us experiment. Thanks are in order for the Council's permission to use the process models in this project and for its commitment to education through the SCOR Implementation Workshop. We would particularly like to recognize Joe Francis and Caspar Hunsche.

Fifth, we would acknowledge those who have translated *Supply Chain Excellence* into Korean (collaborated work by Northeast Asia Logistics Innovation Cluster, Bumhan Publishing, 2007); German (Dr. Rolf Poluha, Springer Verlag Berlin Heidelberg, 2007); and Japanese (Japan Business Create Co., Ltd., Japan Institute of Plant Maintenance).

Supply Chain Excellence

Third Edition

Introduction

During dinner at a recent supply chain conference, a senior executive asked me about the latest thinking on how to improve global supply chain performance. Without hesitation I whispered, "Have you tried the sardine strategy yet?" Anticipating the puzzled look, I continued: "For schooling fish, staying together is a way of life. Fish in a school move together as one."

Photo by Ihoko Saito/Toshiyuki Tajima/Dex Image/Getty Images.

For schooling fish, the "move as one" trait is innate. Separation means likely death. For global supply chains, misalignment—failure to move as one—means poor service, high inventory, unexpected costs, constrained growth and profits, and loss of market share.

The purpose of this book is not to convince anyone of the importance of supply chain management (SCM). That case has been well made many times in many industries since the first edition of *Supply Chain Excellence* was published in 2003. Even then, only the first two paragraphs of the book's introduction argued the "why" of SCM. The rest was about the "how."

While using the methodology of this book on roughly 100 supply chain projects around the world, "how" has been further refined into a series of processes to achieve the highest levels of supply chain alignment: moving as one.

Here are the 15 most common contributors to supply chain misalignment. Which ones are relevant to you?

Fifteen Common Causes of Misalignment

1. Lack of a Technology Investment Plan

A chief information officer deflected pressure to install the latest and greatest advanced planning system—making the case that simply having state-of-the-art tools was not a good enough reason to put her entire company into the kind of upheaval that such implementations create. As she watched the rapid evolution of web-based applications, event management tools, and demand-driven advanced planning systems, she found herself without a clear technology investment plan that supported the company's business strategy.

2. Little or No Return on Investment (ROI)

A company bought its Enterprise Resource Planning (ERP) package during the vendor's end-of-quarter push to meet sales goals. The deal included all the latest add-ons—things like customer relation-ship management, transactional processing, advanced supply chain planning, event management, and web portals providing self-service for customers and suppliers. Now the executive team is looking for an answer to a deceptively difficult question: When will a return on investment start to show up in the earnings statement?

3. Isolated Supply Chain Strategies

Three executive vice presidents—for sales, marketing, and opera-tions—assembled their own well-articulated strategies for developing supply chain competence within their departments. Then they invested in application technology, manufacturing processes, and product devel-opment—all with measurable success. Now what's missing is a compre-hensive blueprint that combines their individual efforts to drive profit and performance across the entire company.

4. Competing Supply Chain Improvements

A company's top executive for SCM assembled a dozen of his brightest managers for a structured brainstorming process—resulting in a list of 45 high-priority projects. But when the managers began implementation, the results were not encouraging. General manag-ers were being asked to support multiple initiatives that used many of the same financial, human, and technical resources. Goals seemed in conflict. They needed to align their objectives and prioritize proj-ects to make good use of the available resources.

5. Faulty Sales and Operations Planning

The vice president of operations for one of the companies had seri-ous cash-to-cash problems and declining customer satisfaction—all resulting from raw materials shortages, mismatched capacity, poor forecasting, and inventory buildup. The challenge was to address the planning and forecasting issues and put the balance sheet back in shape.

6. Failure to Meet Financial Commitments

A company's CEO promised the board of directors that he would improve earnings per share. An analysis of competitors' balance sheets and income statements indicated that the company's direct and indirect costs were out of line, and that its cash-to-cash cycle was too long. The leadership was charged with identifying the right mix of improvements to obtain a predictable result that would satisfy shareholders. The CEO's credibility then was at stake.

7. Lack of Support and Specialized Expertise

The director of a new supply chain solutions team needed a proven method for evaluating and implementing projects. That meant being able to show documented examples of its use, and evidence that it was both scalable and repeatable. Then she would have to sell the method throughout the organization—which would require executive references and easy, low-cost access to the method itself. Finally, she would have to develop a team that could use the model to deliver early successes.

8. Mismatch Between Corporate Culture and ERP

As the ERP implementation wore on and business processes were increasingly automated at one of the organizations, things suddenly started to go wrong. The project leader had a pretty good idea why: The company was organized in rigid, vertical functions that directed AS IS practices. But the ERP system was essentially horizontal, organized by transaction flow for purchase orders, sales orders, forecasts, master data, and so on. How could the corporate culture shift from functional management to process management?

9. Underutilization of Existing Technology

A vice president of administration was being pressured by her colleagues to replace a two-year-old transactional system with a new, name-brand system offering advanced supply chain planning. But the ROI analysis just wasn't adding up. A more detailed investigation revealed that not all of the business leaders were complaining. In fact, the vice president found a direct correlation between a business leader's satisfaction and the effort he or she had exerted to learn the system. Those who were least satisfied didn't handle implementation very well and as a consequence were utilizing few of the available modules. The challenge was to motivate business leaders to use existing functionality better.

10. Vaguely Defined Goals

The executive team achieved consensus that it would differentiate the company through a strategy of operational excellence. The other choices had been customer intimacy and product innovation. Now that the decision was made, the team had to define—at more tactical levels—the characteristics of an operationally excellent supply chain.

11. Impact of Mergers and Acquisitions

The executive teams from companies that had been acquired or were purchasing others needed the acquisition to go smoothly and yield short-term synergies. The challenge was how to leverage efficiencies in material flow, technology platforms, work and information flow, and capacity in the due diligence, integration, and stabilization stages of the merger.

12. Mismanagement and Poor Standardization of Business Processes

Five years after a "successful" ERP implementation, a company found pieces of chaos at different levels of its organization. Fifteen plants opted to turn off select pieces of the system functionality in the name of continuous improvement and leaning out their processes. Three business units independently opted to redefine how date fields were used by customer service to promise-date orders for their customers. Corporate logistics added a transportation optimization tool that subordinated the promised ship date to efficient truck load. And finally, business rules to manage planning master data were changed, ignored, or forgotten by new employees, who did not have the benefit of the original training.

The net result was poor delivery performance, extended order cycle times, and seemingly routine feast-or-famine capacity mismatches to demand. After a disastrous performance review by the company's largest retail account, the executive team members finally realized that they needed to get a handle on defining and managing supply chain process performance . . . at their level.

13. Extension from Supply Chain to the Value Chain

One company's operating committee issued the difficult directive to simultaneously improve quality and reduce cost in manufacturing. It challenged the supply chain executive with some equally difficult improvement pairings: support the increased pace of new-product rollouts while making material acquisition more efficient; support increased sales productivity while making presale and postsale customer service more effective; make global distribution more flexible while increasing the efficiency of warehouse and transportation costs; and implement planning for customer supply chains while improving internal planning efficiency. The challenge with competitive global manufacturing and sophisticated information exchange is that the improvement pairings move beyond the four walls of the company and include more than just supply chain processes. Executives need to define the concept of "value chain" processes and figure out how to improve them.

14. Running Out of Ideas for New Improvement Projects

After five years of using the annual "brainstorming" technique, a company's Lean Sigma executive steering team concluded that corporate impact on operating income had peaked. With all efforts seemingly aimed at inventory, many project scopes were competing for the same resources and had conflicting metric impact (supply chain cost versus service level improvement). Projects were moving further and further away from having legitimate strategic impact, and the proximity of the projects still seemed to be manufacturing. The steering team's challenge was to more effectively and efficiently identify and scope projects to solve more than just manufacturing issues.

15. An Organization That Defies Effective and Efficient Supply Chain

"We've got five business units, six high-level profit and loss statements, two headquarters, four global regions, 26 regional distribution centers, 18 plants, the requirement to implement collaborative planning, forecasting, and replenishment with our largest accounts, and about 5,000 active suppliers. We need a buildup to one unit forecast that supports the corporate financial plan *and* a set of supply chain plans to support the regional service levels and cost commitments. How do we staff this thing?" There is no more to be said about the challenge here.

Why Supply Chain Excellence?

Ultimately, one or more of these performance issues will inflict enough pain that the enterprise takes action. The question is how to do that without disrupting other areas where things are going well—how to move globally as one. Put another way, how to act like a school of sardines.

The content of the third edition of *Supply Chain Excellence* is refined by 30 additional project experiences (now more than 90 in total). It also has been enriched with more practices that have helped global supply chains move as one, with special emphasis on processes and practices in the SAP environment, including:

- Effective integration with global supply chain strategy
- Techniques for global organizational supply chain design
- Effective cross-references with software tools
- Project implementation case studies
- Quick assessments focused solely on smaller-scale performance analysis

As with the first and second editions, this book follows the progress of one company, Fowlers Inc., toward supply chain excellence. It is intended as a working handbook for using SCOR (the Supply Chain Operations Reference model) as a tool to help leaders at every step as they undertake supply chain initiatives. It is structured on a week-by-week project timetable, providing achievable action plans to navigate through the steps of a SCOR project.

Specifically, each chapter focuses on a week's worth of work conducted in face-to-face, remote, or classroom meetings with follow-up assignments (or "homework," which many clients have learned to love). Included are sample deliverables, summaries of tasks, tables, and figures to illustrate the step-by-step processes. An important note about Fowlers Inc.: It is not a real company, and the Fowlers employees are not real people. Fowlers is a compilation of circumstances found in a variety of projects. The purpose was to provide a textbook case study that addresses the broadest range of issues, while maintaining continuity to help readers follow the logic of the SCOR approach from beginning to end.

CHAPTER 1

The Supply Chain Operations Reference Model

▶ **The Cross-Industry Standard for Supply Chain**

Peter Bolstorff was introduced to the Supply Chain Operations Reference (SCOR) model in the fall of 1996 when he became part of a newly formed corporate "internal consulting" team for Imation, which had just been spun off from 3M. He's been using the SCOR model in supply chain improvement project work ever since. He was a delegate at the first conference of the Supply Chain Council, and has remained active in the Council, involved in the process of improving SCOR and teaching others how to use it. In fact, the Supply Chain Council adopted *Supply Chain Excellence* as the core text for its SCOR Project implementation workshops globally.

So he's heard all the questions. Among those most frequently asked are these: What is the Supply Chain Council? What is SCOR? How do I use SCOR? What is the value to my organization? How do I learn more about SCOR?

The Supply Chain Council

The Supply Chain Council (www.supply-chain.org) is an independent not-for-profit corporation formed in 1996 as a grassroots initiative to develop a supply chain process model. Among those involved at the start were individuals from such organizations as Bayer; Compaq; Procter & Gamble; Lockheed Martin; Nortel; Rockwell Semiconductor; Texas Instruments; 3M; Cargill; Pittiglio, Rabin, Todd & McGrath (PRTM); and AMR Research, Inc. In all, 69 of the world's leading companies participated in the council's founding. Its mission today is to perpetuate use of the SCOR model through technical development, research, education, and conference events. By the end of 2010, the council's technical community had released nine subsequent versions of SCOR, providing updates to process elements, metrics, practices, and tools. SCOR 10.0 also incorporates a "People" standard for describing skills required to perform tasks and manage processes.

The council has about 1,000 corporate members worldwide, with chapters in Australia/New Zealand, Latin America, Greater China, Europe, Japan, Southeast Asia, and South Africa. Membership is open to any organization interested in applying and advancing principles of supply chain management. In 2010 there were four tiers of membership: global, standard, small business, and nonprofit.

The SCOR Framework

SCOR combines elements of business process engineering, metrics, benchmarking, leading practices, and people skills into a single framework. Under SCOR, supply chain management is defined as the integrated processes of PLAN, SOURCE, MAKE, DELIVER, and RETURN—from the supplier's supplier to the customer's customer (Figure 1-1). The Supply Chain Council Web site, www .supply-chain.org, has an online overview of the model that can be viewed both by members and nonmembers.

Here's what's included in each of the SCOR process elements:

> **PLAN:** Assess supply resources; aggregate and prioritize demand re-
> quirements; plan inventory for distribution, production, and ma-

Figure 1-1. The SCOR Framework.

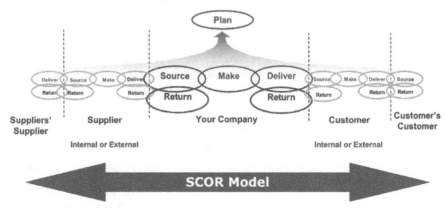

terial requirements; and plan rough-cut capacity for all products and all channels.

SOURCE: Obtain, receive, inspect, hold, issue, and authorize payment for raw materials and purchased finished goods.

MAKE: Request and receive material; manufacture and test product; package, hold, and/or release product.

DELIVER: Execute order management processes; generate quotations; configure product; create and maintain customer database; maintain product/price database; manage accounts receivable, credits, collections, and invoicing; execute warehouse processes including pick, pack, and configure; create customer-specific packaging/labeling; consolidate orders; ship products; manage transportation processes and import/export; and verify performance.

RETURN: Defective, warranty, and excess return processing, including authorization, scheduling, inspection, transfer, warranty administration, receiving and verifying defective products, disposition, and replacement.

In addition, SCOR includes a series of ENABLE elements for each of the processes. These processes focus on management around performance, information, policy, inventory strategy, capital assets, transportation, physical logistic network, regulatory, and other management processes to enable the planning and execution of supply chain activities.

SCOR spans all customer, product, and market interactions surrounding sales orders, purchase orders, work orders, return authorizations, forecasts, and replenishment orders. It also encompasses material movements of raw material, work-in-process, finished goods, and return goods.

The SCOR model includes three levels of process detail. In practice, *Level 1* defines the number of supply chains, how their performance is measured, and necessary competitive requirements. *Level 2* defines the configuration of planning and execution strategies in material flow, using standard categories such as make-to-stock, make-to-order, and engineer-to-order. *Level 3* defines the business processes and system functionality used to transact sales orders, purchase orders, work orders, return authorizations, replenishment orders, and forecasts. *Level 4* process detail is not contained in SCOR but must be defined to implement improvements and manage processes. Advanced users of the framework have defined process detail as far as *Level 5*, software configuration detail.

Value Chain Processes

In 2004, the Supply Chain Council introduced two new frameworks that help piece together more of the detailed mosaic of enterprise value chains (Figure 1-2). The Customer Chain Operations Reference (CCOR 1.0) model defines the customer part of the value chain as the integration of PLAN, RELATE, SELL, CONTRACT, SERVICE, and ENABLE processes.

The Design Chain Operations Reference (DCOR 2.0) model

Figure 1-2. Value Chain frameworks.

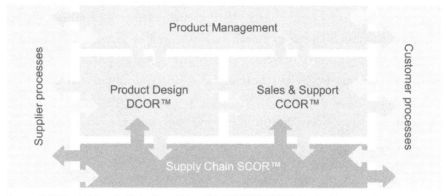

defines the design part of the Value Chain as the integration of PLAN, RESEARCH, DESIGN, INTEGRATE, AMEND, and ENABLE processes.

Chapter 19 will discuss how these process models can be used with SCOR to drive overall value chain performance improvement.

Using SCOR to Drive Supply Chain Improvement

For all its power and flexibility, the SCOR model is still essentially a series of definitions for processes, metrics, and leading practices. Simply having the "dictionary" doesn't do any good for a business. To use SCOR, it is necessary to add effective change management, problem-solving techniques, project management discipline, and business-process engineering techniques. *Supply Chain Excellence* is a handbook on how to use SCOR with a refined five-step formula that has been tested and proven in the course of more than 100 projects on six continents, in ten languages and with six enterprise software systems, incorporating Lean and Six Sigma, growing sales and profits, improving inventory turns, increasing productivity, and making customers happier.

The phases of the *Supply Chain Excellence* approach, as detailed in this third edition of the book, have been refined to support global projects in which units operate more like small business. The refinements have helped reduce the resource and time requirements to develop a project list by 50 percent and have eliminated non-value-added analysis by shifting material, work, and information flow analysis to implementation. We use the same analytical tools but focus only on the scope of each project. The refined steps are as follows:

1. Build organizational support
2. Define project scope
3. Analyze performance
4. Develop project portfolio
5. Implement projects

Build Organizational Support

Chapter 2 examines how to build organizational support for a SCOR project. The chapter explores four important roles: the "evangelist," the person in the company who has the passion, experience, and talent to lead a supply chain project; the "active executive," the individual who is accountable as sponsor of a supply chain project through modeling, influence, and leadership; the "core steering team," which has the champion role to review and approve recommendations and ultimately lead the implementation efforts; and the "design team," which analyzes the supply chain from end to end and assembles recommendations for change.

Define Project Scope

Chapter 3 helps to define and prioritize the organization's supply chains using a combination of data and strategic assessment. One of the primary outcomes from the discovery step is a Project Charter, which helps define a project's scope, approach, objectives, schedule, milestones, deliverables, budget, organization, measures of successes, and communication plan.

Analyze Performance

The analysis stage (Chapters 4 through 7) is where the metrics are defined, data are collected, defects are analyzed, benchmarks are tallied, and performance gaps are calculated. Frequently used SCOR metrics include cash-to-cash cycle time, inventory days of supply, perfect order fulfillment, order fulfillment cycle time, total supply chain management cost, and upside supply chain flexibility. This phase also helps the team to prioritize and balance customer metrics with internal-facing metrics: delivery, reliability, flexibility/responsiveness, cost, and assets.

Develop Project Portfolio

Chapters 8 through 10 describe the analytical steps required to identify a company's preliminary project list. Tasks in this phase include further analysis of metric defects; conducting a brainstorming session; using problem-solving tools such as fishbone diagrams, run charts, and affinity grouping; and working with finance to validate both financial and customer-service improvement commitments.

Implement Projects

Chapters 11 through 18 describe the thirteen steps necessary to implement a project identified in the portfolio. Analytic techniques for this phase include process and geographic mapping, transactional data analysis, leading practice assessment, "staple yourself to an order" interviews, storyboarding, design and test solutions, and the final rollout to the enterprise. This section also discusses effective supply chain strategy as a means to sustain gains and build momentum for future years.

Extend to the Greater Value Chain

Chapter 19 introduces a Value Chain Excellence project roadmap that can be used with any combination of DCOR, CCOR, and/or SCOR process frameworks. Although every project follows the same five steps, the deliverables have been tweaked to accommodate the broader scope of value chain issues, such as product development, sales, postsale service, or engineering changes and product life cycle management.

The Value of a SCOR Initiative

The *Supply Chain Excellence* approach is reliable and predictable with respect to project duration, cost, and benefits. Implementation results across the 100-plus projects for which this approach has been used are consistent:

- ♦ Operating income improvement, from cost reduction and service improvements in the initial SCOR project portfolio, averaging 3 percent of total sales; depending on how your company compares with benchmark data, it could be as high as 4.5 percent or as low as 1.5 percent. Return on investment of two to six times within twelve months—often with cost-neutral quick-hit projects under way on a six-month timeframe.

- ♦ Full leverage of capital investment in systems, improving return on assets for fixed-asset technology investments.

- ♦ Reduced information technology operating expenses through reduced need for customization and improved use of standard system functions.

- ♦ Ongoing profit improvement of 0.5 percent to 1 percent per year, using continuous supply chain improvement.

CHAPTER 2

Phase 0: Build Organizational Support for Supply Chain Improvement

➤ **Finding the Tipping Point for Change**

Brian Dowell called out of the blue after getting my name from a Google search; his keywords included SCOR, Supply Chain, Metrics, Operational Excellence, and Value Chain. He was looking for some direction for his company, Fowlers Inc., and had enough motivation within the company to justify a visit.

We showed up a week later, and Brian, the company's chief operating officer, gave us a warm greeting. His introductory overview demonstrated Fowlers to be a well-run worldwide manufacturing conglomerate with the seeds of supply chain improvement already in place. "In fact," he said proudly, "we are six months past our SAP® go-live and have closed the books on time each month." But more on that later.

The supply chain action plan had been developed at the division level by David Able, vice president of operations in the technology products group—one of the four operating units. He had pieced it together with just a little background in supply chain management

and a whole lot of operating pain at the global level. His efforts had
been encouraged by his boss, the division president, who had
brought the concept of more integrated global supply chain improvement to the attention of other executives in the company. His
last comment in most conversations on the subject went something
like, "Not all of the company is on an SAP platform and most of the
regions outside North America are *not* figuring out how to improve."

They had become a self-selected "gang" whose common feeling
was that although David's ideas would solve some short-term issues,
there had to be a way to solve the company's global supply chain
problems to move as one at a more strategic level. Figure 2-1 is
Fowlers' current organizational chart.

We began the formal meeting in the company's boardroom, with
several executives present and a few others in teleconference from
around the world. It didn't take much prodding to get this gang to
start sharing their thoughts.

"Our products are good for a week, maybe ten days, in the

Figure 2-1. Fowlers' executive-level organizational chart.

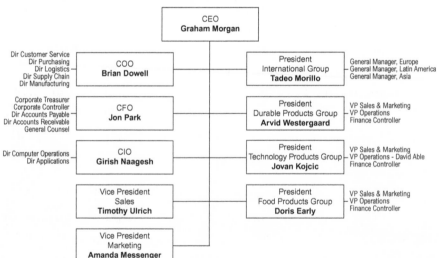

store," said Doris Early, president of the food products group. "We've got to move a lot of product around with a lot of speed. And if regulators were to bring in the label from something we processed six months ago, we need to be able to identify the plant, the line, the day, and the names of everyone on the shift who produced it."

"Our shelf life is short, but not that short," added Jovan Kojcic, David's boss and the president of the technology products group, from an office in Warsaw. "We also have some other things in common with the food group; we buy a lot of commodities. The prices we pay change daily, but our customers won't let us be so flexible. There's seasonality in our sales, and many new products that are harder to forecast—all of which makes it difficult to maintain consistent margins." He added, "We've been challenged to be more flexible in shorter time with less cost and minimal inventory. The experts are telling us that we need to think about how to respond to consumer demand—that is to say, point of sale—more effectively."

Arvid Westergaard, president of the durable products group, spoke up from Sweden: "Our issues are about the rate of improvement. We have tried to address the performance issues in our group through our continuous improvement program. Four years ago, we invested in a Lean Six Sigma program that has trained hundreds of black, green, and yellow belts. We have been disciplined as an executive team managing the project list. We started out quickly with most of the work directed at our manufacturing plants. In the past year, it seems we started to run out of steam; most of our projects now seem to be smaller and smaller in scope. They are smaller in payback too. But we still believe there are big issues to address. So how do we identify a more strategic list? How do we integrate supply chain improvement with Lean Six Sigma?"

Last, Graham Morgan, the chief executive officer, added, "In our strategic planning session cycle in January we—the business presidents and I—asked ourselves, 'How good is our supply chain strategy? What do we need to address as an executive team and what should we delegate to the business units? It seems that our corporate supply chain–related roles are always complaining about the business and vice versa.' It raised the question: How should we organize ourselves for the future and prepare a clear strategic roadmap for supply chain improvement?"

The last conversation was about the SAP implementation. Girish Naagesh, the chief information officer, started off by saying that Fowlers' initial SAP scope was North America. This was to be followed by regional implementations in Europe, Asia Pacific, and everywhere else. He also stated that he and his consulting partners followed the basic AcceleratedSAP (ASAP) Roadmap for implementation (Figure 2-2).

This was the longest discussion of the day; it generally filtered into three streams of dialogue. The first had to do with *getting information* out of the system. Admittedly, there was a gross underinvestment in reporting capability. That, in combination with leadership's stubborn demands about wanting to see the SAP report "exactly like

Figure 2-2. AcceleratedSAP Roadmap for implementation.

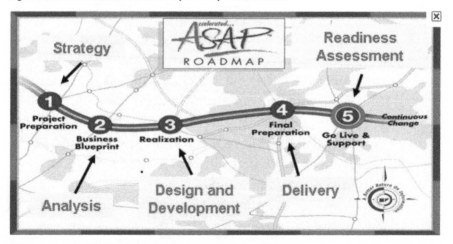

their current legacy reports," left data analysts creating custom Z reports as opposed to developing data warehouse capability. The second stream was the frustration that some of the plants were having around *capacity planning*. The unverified feedback was that the SAP system was adding days of work on the backs of an already stressed team. Lines were either too loaded or not loaded enough, or material was not showing up at the right time to run the schedule, causing unnecessary changeovers. In fact, manufacturing variances were going up. The third stream was concern for a general *increase in inventory* and *decline in customer service*. The embarrassing fact was customers were calling to tell their reps about the late orders, as opposed to the reps calling them.

It all came together as they spoke: products that have short shelf life and short life cycles; disconnected supply chain and product development; price-sensitive customers sold through varied and sophisticated channels with volatility on both ends—demand and supply; a continuous improvement program that needed to be rejuvenated; poor assimilation to SAP processes; and an organization that needed the right focus and alignment.

The executives described how a chosen leader, David Able, had outlined an improvement plan and its main components. They then assigned the plan to their direct reports in other divisions to execute.

Brian wasn't quite ready to admit this at our first meeting, but it was clear what happened: The business-unit leaders at the next level down thought they'd just been briefed on the latest program-of-the-month and, still frustrated with the new system, did very little with the strategy. To placate the executives, they did take some small steps: they identified a few projects, assigned some green belts, and improved a metric here or there—generally at the expense of others. But after three months, Brian pushed Arvid, Jovan, and Doris to join him in looking for an outside perspective. "We can't be the only ones with this dilemma," he said.

Without realizing it, Brian had already taken a few important steps to ensure a successful approach. Selling supply chain management to an organization is tough. It's an educational sell to everyone involved. Not only is the reality of an integrated supply chain complex; everyone has his or her own preexisting ideas of what supply chains are all about, how they fit in with operational strategy, and what to do to fix them.

SCOR, as an industry standard, makes the sell easier because it has gained credibility from a long list of successful case studies, but the model can't sell itself, and it can't teach people who aren't ready to learn. That's why any SCOR project will depend on four key roles in the education process. These are the evangelist, an active executive sponsor, the core members of an executive steering team, and the analytical design team. Without these, you can't hope for a project's success.

The Evangelist

As is the case with any successful SCOR application, the people who brought SCOR to Fowlers started by educating the organization to support the effort. Their first step was to develop an evangelist. This is the person who is best able to learn the SCOR model; who can sell it to upper management; who has the experience to pilot a project and gain early results; and who can become the executive-level project manager, charged with spreading the model throughout the business. If nobody steps up to this role, then a SCOR-based project probably cannot succeed.

The evangelist, who may be self-selected or appointed from above, typically acts as project manager of the first SCOR project.

At Fowlers, David Able, vice president of operations in the technology products group, placed himself into the role of evangelist based on his interest in supply chain integration, his diverse background, and his reputation as an effective, influential leader. He was readily confirmed by Brian Dowell, the company's chief operating officer and the man who would quickly assume the important role of executive sponsor.

The Evangelist's Resume

As the appointed evangelist, David Able had a portfolio of experiences that would help create general understanding of the relationship between financial performance and the central factors of organization, process, people, and technology. Over the course of 15 years at the company, he had demonstrated knowledge of "how things work" and had built a strong foundation of leadership roles. He had participated in a large-scale reengineering effort a few years before, and so had seen the way an enterprise project works. Those who worked for him also confirmed such important qualities as the ability to teach, communicate, resolve conflict, and add humor at just the right time.

Experience

The right evangelist candidate will have the following experience on his or her resume:

Financial Responsibility and Accountability. The former means understanding the details of how cost, revenue, and assets are assembled on a profit and loss statement and balance sheet—and all the financial impacts in real time. The latter means being able to tell the business story behind the numbers. Accountability also means defending executive critique, explaining bad news with confidence, preparing for operations reviews, and having the ability to focus and effectively motivate an entire organization to "hit" a common set of financial goals and objectives.

Aligning Business Goals with Appropriate Strategy. Cascading goals is the art of organizing objectives in such a way that every employee understands the higher levels of success and how day-to-day goals support that success.

Setting the Organizational Learning Pace. This means developing an atmosphere that supports team learning and fosters dialogue among individuals, teams, and departments. In managing the performance of individuals and departments, evangelists understand the day-to-day effort that is required to achieve success.

Multiple Worker Roles. The evangelist will have firsthand experience in a variety of business functions that map to the SCOR Level 1 elements of PLAN, SOURCE, MAKE, DELIVER, and RETURN. Leading practices in PLAN—such as sales and operations planning, materials requirements planning, and promotional event forecasting—can come from experiences as a demand planner, forecast analyst, supply planner, and inventory analyst. Leading practices in SOURCE and MAKE—such as Kanban, vendor-managed inventory, rapid replenishment, cellular manufacturing, Six Sigma, total quality management, ISO 9002, to name a few—can come from experiences as a buyer, production superintendent, master production scheduler, and engineer. Leading practices in DELIVER and RETURN—such as available-to-promise, cross-docking, cellular kitting and packaging, and so on—can come from experiences as a customer service representative, transportation analyst, and supervisor for shipping and receiving.

As vice president of operations for one of the operating divisions at Fowlers, David Able had experience with a number of these areas. In addition, his previous participation in a well-run reengineering effort had exposed him to disciplines in four important areas necessary to a supply chain improvement: process mapping, recommendations, justification, and project management.

Natural Talent. The right evangelist candidate will demonstrate the following five talents in his or her daily work:

1. *A Talent for Teaching.* This is part skill and part art. The skill is showing employees how to perform a task, modeling the appropriate skill, guiding them to understanding, and finally letting them try it on their own. The art is a sixth sense that seems to monitor everyone's level of understanding and automatically adjusts the lesson for each individual involved in a project. The ability to generate examples or anecdotes in the context of each individual's understanding can separate the great teachers from the average ones. Good evangelists are effective storytellers.

2. *A Talent for Listening.* It's important to know when to ask clarifying questions and when not to interrupt, further building an understanding of the speaker's point of view. For a successful evangelist, listening and clarifying are more valuable than preaching.

3. *A Talent for Communicating with Executives and Peers.* There are four prerequisites for effective executive communication. The evangelist must:

   ◆ Have earned personal and professional credibility with members of the executive team.

   ◆ Be a subject matter expert.

   ◆ Be able to assemble effective executive presentations.

   ◆ Balance formal group communications (presentations, proposals, meetings) with informal one-on-one communications (lunch, golf, hallway, in private).

4. *A Talent for Using Humor Appropriately.* Every good evangelist has a great sense of humor and can introduce comic relief at just the right moment—whether planned or unplanned. The evangelist doesn't have to be the funniest person in the room;

on a team of 15 people, there will be at least two or three
others who can be counted on to help at any time.

5. *A Talent for Conflict Management Among Groups and Peers.* The
   constraint to successful supply chain projects does not always
   lie in the technical challenges of material flow and application
   architecture; it's often in the conflicts that occur between
   people. Successful evangelists can handle large-group conflicts
   and individual conflicts—not by quashing them, but by constructively helping one side or both to move toward common
   ground.

The Active Executive Sponsor

The active executive sponsor represents the leaders in the organization who will sign off on resources needed to make the changes
happen. This person has the most to gain or lose based on the success
of the project and therefore takes on responsibility to review and
approve recommended changes as proposed by the project design
team. Behind the scenes, the executive sponsor needs to sell the
changes up to the chiefs and down to their managers, eliminate barriers to progress, take ownership of the financial opportunity that
comes through improvement, and prepare the organization for implementation.

As with the evangelist, picking the right person is critical. At
Fowlers, the obvious choice was Brian Dowell, the chief operating
officer and the executive with supervisory responsibility over the
directors of planning (PLAN), purchasing (SOURCE), manufacturing (MAKE), logistics (DELIVER and RETURN), and customer
service. Organizational role is just one factor.

One gauge of the right executive sponsor uses the scale of "more
savings faster" (MF) versus "less savings later" (LL). The choice of
MF sounds intuitive, but there are a lot of LL executives in the
world; they behave in a manner that slows the rate of improvement

and lengthens timeframes. The nature of a project life cycle demands different behaviors at different times from the active executive sponsor. In all cases, the sponsor will be better served by MF behaviors.

Educate-for-Support Behaviors of the Active Executive Sponsor

MF executives can look at their organizations from a process perspective as opposed to seeing them as a collection of individuals grouped by a functional silo. They have experienced the power of process improvement and understand key roles in process management. MF executives have invested personal time learning about the strategic value of supply chain in their respective marketplace. That's why they are comfortable learning new things in a public forum regardless of rank—sometimes setting the capacity for change of the entire organization.

MF executives accelerate the educate-for-support step of a project (often from six months to one year) by encouraging the progress of the evangelist as a SCOR subject matter expert and by facilitating core team buy-in.

LL executives, when in public, seem to know everything—whether they do or not. They depend on individual heroics to make things better. Thus, LL executives need to be sold on the merits of supply chain improvement.

Planning and Organizing Behaviors of the Active Executive Sponsor

In this second step of the project life cycle, the focus is on three essential areas: an understanding of how organizational change occurs, a respect for supply chain complexity, and an effective integration of business resources. The critical output of this step is a project charter that defines project scope, objectives, organization, benefits, and approach. MF executives understand their sponsor role and can

articulate a burning platform for change. They learn to look at supply chain performance needs from various perspectives such as organization, process, people, technology, and strategy. MF executives
can accelerate the discovery stage by effectively involving business
leaders and participating directly in early steps of the project design.

LL executives, on the other hand, short-circuit the discovery
work by directing efforts to focus on one or two prescribed metrics,
rather than actively engaging business teams to define scope and opportunity. LLs delegate learning about SCOR to subordinates rather
than understanding the basic steps of the SCOR Project Roadmap
and associated deliverables themselves.

Measures and Strategy Behaviors of the Active Executive Sponsor

At this stage of the project life cycle, important behaviors are respect
for the schedule and fueling the fire on the platform for change.

MF executives commit themselves, their evangelists, and their
design teams to the detailed, 17-week analyze-and-design process.
This process involves two days per week for 17 weeks plus homework for design team members and half a day two times per month
plus homework for executive members of the steering team. The
project manager will work on the effort full time, and the MF executive sponsor will spend part of each week in oversight and review.

MF executives spend time understanding how actual, benchmark, and other comparative data were gathered, and they accept
the completed analysis at face value as a defined opportunity. MF
executives begin laying the groundwork for organizational change
by initiating regular communication regarding the relative opportunity, the expected changes, and the approximate timing of the
project.

LLs skip design team sessions, miss some executive sponsor reviews, and don't put in any personal time. They discount the validity

of the data because they don't understand how they were gathered, and they view the analysis as the end of the project—not the beginning.

Design Solutions Behaviors of the Active Executive Sponsor

At this stage of the project life cycle, the focus is on understanding the integrated nature of material, work, and information flow; sparring with the difficulties of designing improvement; and prioritizing change.

To this end, an MF executive sponsor will spend time each week with the design team learning about the basic steps of producing desired material, work, and information and then leverage this knowledge to educate his or her other C-level peers and prepare them for anticipated supply chain changes.

MF executives constructively challenge the design team on assumptions and results, and invest time to understand the scope and sequence of recommended changes. LL executives are only concerned with the "what," not with how key milestone deliverables were built. LLs use a shotgun approach to savings by initiating all projects at the same time and letting the strong survive.

Establishing Core Team Buy-In

Once Brian Dowell was established as the active executive sponsor, he recruited Jovan Kojcic as the business unit sponsor; together they affirmed David Able as the evangelist and project leader, and the three became solely responsible for picking the rest of the people for the steering team.

This group would bear responsibility to review and approve the project as it progressed. The challenge was to build the right mix of leaders who ultimately will determine the supply chain changes that happen.

It's a reality in any corporation that an executive steering team will contain some members who are not going to be helpful and forward thinking. That's why it was so important for Brian, David, and Jovan to hand-select the core of this team—an elite group who would actively power the steering team to provide constructive oversight and help keep the project moving. Leveraging momentum and knowledge gained in David's earlier supply chain strategy discussions, David, Jovan, and Brian picked the steering team to include Tadeo Morillo, president of the international group, and Amanda Messenger, vice president of marketing and a long-time proponent of organizational alignment. They also included Timothy Ulrich, vice president of sales; Girish Naagesh, CIO; Jon Park, CFO; and two executives from the technology products group, the vice president of sales and marketing and the finance controller.

There are four important criteria for the evangelist and executive sponsor(s) to consider as they begin assembling this core group: collective experience, attitude, effective communication skills, and ability to cope well in chaos.

Collective Experience

Experience is measured individually and as a team. In either case, important considerations when forming this group include the following:

Level of Authority. Effective steering teams have members at similar levels of authority within the organization who are willing to assign resources from their own teams to the project design effort and have earned confidence from the senior executive team.

Cross-Functional Relationships. An effective steering team member has built relationships over time instead of leaving a trail of "my way or the highway" casualties. The best contributors have a sense of how the whole business works and have developed cooperative relationships with other functional leaders.

Knowledge Contribution. Depth of historical perspective is important—not only of the business process evolution but also of the organizational response to change. This perspective can be both good and bad; the right steering team members can balance their application of knowledge with the occasionally unavoidable attitude of "we've tried that before."

Attitude

Steering team members don't have to go through a battery of psychological tests to determine whether they have the right attitude, but they should pass three simple ones. First, they should be immune to the "not invented here" syndrome. Second, they should have a controlled and adaptable style of communication. Third, they should be effective learners.

Effective Communication Skills

An effective steering team sets the learning pace of a SCOR project by dictating the effectiveness of the learning environment. It is deliberate about expectations and spells out exactly the type and frequency of feedback it needs to help keep the project moving. The most valued feedback can be categorized as critique, opinion, or clarifying dialogue (team learning). Effective critique assumes that the steering team members understand the material under review, have assembled a list of checking questions for the design team, and are comfortable exploring the logic to check the integrity of the work. Opinion is reserved for forks in the road at which decisions must be made to go forward with the project. Opinion is rendered only after initial dialogue and critique. Clarifying dialogue is as simple as asking questions and discussing work both spontaneously and at planned reviews. The objective is simply to understand the design team's point of view with an open mind.

Ability to Cope Well in Chaos

Many leaders in industry suggest that the closer an organization can get to the edge of chaos without going over, the more it will thrive in today's business environment. Let's not kid ourselves; moving toward the edge of chaos is stressful, so steering team members need an intuitive feel for how close is too close. Process thinking helps set the appropriate distance from the edge. Process thinkers look at performance as the result of the interaction of process steps. They look at an organization from a systems point of view. They can articulate the basic relationships between the supplier inputs (capital, human resources, raw materials), the organization (business processes and functions), the customer (who buys products and services), the competitors (who compete for supplies and customers), and other factors that touch the system. The alternative to a process thinker is a functional thinker who stakes out some territory, builds a big wall, and shuts out the rest of the world. This silo behavior is, at some level, an attempt to avoid chaos, and it is one of the first big changes to be addressed in a SCOR project.

The Fowlers core team rounded out the short list for an executive steering team to include Jon Park, chief financial officer; Tim Ulrich, vice president of sales; and Girish Naagesh, chief information officer.

Picking the Project Design Team

Once the steering team was in place, its first official duty was to pick the right project design team, the group of people who would ultimately spend time analyzing supply chain issues and assembling recommendations for change. As is the case with every other significant initiative, the obvious guideline was to pick "the best and brightest." Experience has proven that four additional factors equally contribute to the quality of project output: problem-solving experience, personality factors, dedication/discipline to task, and access to data.

Problem-Solving Experience

Design teams that have at least one black belt or green belt take the analysis deeper and faster at each project phase than do those without such training. Real experience with certain Lean Six Sigma disciplines will help the team pinpoint root causes of problems, identify effective solutions, and more accurately predict the value of and confidence in improvement recommendations. Particularly useful disciplines include value stream analysis and eliminating the eight areas of waste; Kano, voice of the customer, and force field analyses; calculating cost of poor quality; putting together data collection plans; calculating process sigma levels; using data analysis tools such as Pareto and run charts, histograms, and scatter plots; and using process analysis tools such as SIPOC (suppliers-inputs-process-outputs-customers), value stream, and cross-functional maps.

Personality Factors

There seem to be four personality factors to consider when picking individuals for the project design team. The first scale contrasts *facts* and *feelings*. The *facts* side of the scale describes people who prefer to look just at the numbers and let the data do the "talking," whereas the *feelings* side describes people who look only at the human factors of change. The second scale contrasts *details* and *vision*. The *details* side of the scale describes people who look at situations from the "ground up"; they come to conclusions by putting the pieces together. The *vision* people look at the whole, the big picture, and come to their conclusions by looking at the trends. The third scale contrasts *introvert* and *extrovert*. The *introvert* side of the scale describes people who "think inside" and stereotypically are the quiet ones in groups. The *extrovert* side of the scale describes people who "think

out loud" and, right or wrong, will refine their hypotheses in public
and can sway a group through verbal skills. *Introverts* gain energy
with individual down time, whereas *extroverts* gain energy in the
group. The fourth scale is focused on degree of *organization*. This
scale contrasts the unorganized on the one side with the highly organized on the other.

Although these personality factors may seem trivial, considering
the right mix of people on the team can help avoid two common
pitfalls. The first we'll call the Loud Lead. Characterized by *feelings*,
vision, *extroverts*, and low *organization*, this team talks a good game
but will likely not have the details to stand up to executive scrutiny
at the end. We'll call the second pitfall Analysis Paralysis. Characterized by *facts*, *details*, *introverts*, and high *organization*, this team always
needs more data and often freezes when confronted with executive
teams who want a recommendation or decision.

Dedication: Discipline to Tasks

There was a sign that hung in a colleague's office that read, "The
reward for good work is more work." As you will come to appreciate, each deliverable in a *Supply Chain Excellence* project helps make
a decision; each decision then becomes a part of the next deliverable
and so on until the end. It's like learning algebra (I can hear you
groaning): You need to understand multiplying and dividing frac-
tions before you can begin to simplify algebraic expressions; if you
don't do your homework, it's difficult to move ahead. Likewise, if
the team doesn't complete its project homework, it will be ill prepared to make the next decision.

Access to Data

The last thing to consider in selecting your team is access to data.
Although this one is fairly self-descriptive, there are several nuances
to consider. The first nuance is in regard to data. During each phase

of the project, different "cubes" or "tables" will be queried from your information system in an attempt to extract data. This may be in the form of extracts from the production system, a data warehouse, or standard reports. The second nuance is in regard to access. Team members who have access directly or indirectly to the data versus having to submit a data request generally progress faster and more reliably. The third nuance is in regard to analysis. Team members who have knowledge and skill with applications such as Microsoft Excel and Access and Minitab, which allow them to summarize, segment, and otherwise study data, progress faster and more effectively than team members who don't.

Considering each of the four factors, Fowlers assembled the project design team. It consisted of the following:

- Director, Logistics
- Director, Customer Service
- Director, Manufacturing
- Director, Purchasing
- Director, Planning
- Vice President of Sales and Marketing—Food Products Group
- Corporate Controller
- Director, Applications
- David Able—Project Manager
- SCOR Coach

CHAPTER 3

Phase 1: Define Project Scope

▶ **Planning and Organizing a Supply Chain Excellence Initiative**

Understanding the business reasons for a project and then properly defining its scope are critical steps to a successful launch. The Fowlers executive team had already provided the "go" decision during an on-site briefing on March 11; now the members wanted to know who, what, when, how, and, of course, how much. During the on-site visit the SCOR coach, Brian, Jovan, and David organized web-based conference calls for the week of April 18, which would be used to review Phase 1 deliverables in preparation for the targeted April 25 project kickoff. There are three primary deliverables for Phase 1: (1) the business context summary, (2) a supply chain definition matrix, and (3) an approved project charter. A fourth deliverable in the first week of active project planning is to assemble a complete presentation of information to be used in the project kickoff meeting.

The Business Context Summary

This deliverable is not raw research. It merely collates existing information into a simple reference source for the duration of the project. Most often, the project leader can assemble this in a few hours. To make it easy, start with a checklist of information that needs to be reviewed and summarized to gain a full understanding of (and appreciation for) the business context for supply chain improvement. This information sets the strategic backdrop for supply chain focus and ultimate project scope.

Just as important, though, are the soft benefits of working through the checklist. Involving the business leaders in this process allows them to help set the agenda for the company's supply chain. Getting these important people engaged in the earliest stages of a project has untold value in the change management challenge that all companies face. Understanding their problems, asking for their point of view, and acknowledging their good work goes a long way toward positioning the supply chain as "our thing" versus "a corporate thing."

Assembling the business context summary involves several techniques, including interviewing key stakeholders; scouring the company's Web site and 10K earnings reports; reviewing existing business plans as found in the annual report or any other big-picture document; locating and reviewing competitive analyses that have been conducted internally or by any external entity; and checking out the reviews of financial analysts readily available on such Web sites as hoovers.com, forbes.com, marketguide.com, and reuters.com.

Why all the emphasis on public documents and financial statements? Because the important step you're taking is to create the often-overlooked connection between the company's operations and the real-world business goals as defined by the people who hold the purse strings. There's always a temptation to dismiss investors and bean counters as being out of touch and unrealistic in their demands, but by understanding their goals and creating a bridge to operations, you can establish the basis for high performance at all levels over the long term.

There are four categories of information that make up a business context summary: (1) strategic background, (2) financial performance, (3) internal profile, and (4) external profile.

Strategic Background

Strategic background summarizes the business and its supply chain performance status in a competitive environment relative to competitors.

A *business description* is the first component of the strategic background. It describes the enterprise, its businesses, and a high-level view of the competitive landscape. It's the kind of information that managers should be able to develop off the top of their heads, or by drawing from the dozens of such descriptions that probably reside in brochures, memos, and written documents throughout the organization.

A strengths/weaknesses/opportunities/threats (SWOT) analysis is another source of information that describes the relationship between the enterprise and its marketplace. First, it outlines where the company surpasses direct competitors and where it falls short. Then it projects ways in which it might grow and ways in which it is most likely to be overtaken by competition. On its surface, the SWOT analysis is a simple, four-point document, but for large or diversified organizations, this can become an intricate document with information on each major product or served market.

Another piece of the strategic background is a *value proposition statement*, which describes the competitive value of a business from the customer's point of view. Inherent in a good value proposition is an intimate understanding of the business requirements of each major customer or customer segment.

For example, a company such as Procter & Gamble—with a broad range of consumer products sold primarily through large retailers—might view its relationship with Wal-Mart as deserving its own value proposition, owing to Wal-Mart's particular requirements of suppliers. At another level, it might include Wal-Mart in a "large retailer" value proposition while developing a separate value proposition for its network of distributors that serve grocery chains and small retailers.

Common requirements in a value proposition statement are price, product quality, technical innovation, customized packaging, delivery reliability, order lead time, strategic relationship, and value-added services such as inventory management. Customer value propositions are commonly found directly or indirectly in contracts or service-level agreements.

The last important components of the strategic background document are critical success factors and critical business issues.

Critical success factors describe three to five variables most central to an organization's success. Success is defined as thriving—not merely surviving.

Supply Chain Operations Reference defines the following as critical success factors in supply chain performance: delivery reliability, flexibility and responsiveness, supply chain cost, and effective asset management.

Critical business issues describe how well an organization stacks up against the competition for each of these factors. In each category, the comparative performance level will be rated as disadvantage, parity, advantage, or superior. Sources for these perspectives are not standardized. Good places to look for ratings include annual business plans, quarterly business reviews, annual reports, analyst web casts, 10K reports, and regular company communications.

Fowlers Inc. Strategic Background

Here are highlights of the strategic background for Fowlers from the business context summary developed by the core team.

Business Description

Fowlers Inc. is a billion-dollar conglomerate with worldwide leadership in three businesses: food processing (food products group), optical technology products (technology products group), and business services (durable products group).

Fowlers' food products group is a leading North American supplier of premium fresh and frozen meat products and management services to the food service, retail, online retail, and government sectors. Customers include SuperValu, Wal-Mart, Aramark, Simon Delivers, and thousands of independent grocers and specialty restaurants.

Fowlers' technology products group is one of the world's largest independent suppliers of optical storage products and services such as CD-ROM replication, CD-read and CD-write media, title fulfillment and distribution services, and optical drives. Customers include retail leaders such as Wal-Mart and Target, and category leaders such as Best Buy and Office Depot. Fowlers is also a major supplier to original equipment manufacturers (OEMs) for the personal computer market. Customers include HP, Dell, and Apple.

Fowlers' durable products group was formed by acquiring one of the fastest-growing suppliers of business services, providing personalized apparel, office supplies, and promotional products to more than 14,000 companies and a million individual wearers. By using a dealer franchise as the route delivery mechanism, Fowlers' durable products group has gained a competitive edge by being both knowledgeable and responsive to individual customers in the markets it serves.

SWOT Analysis

Strengths

◆ Superior product quality in the food products group and technology products group.

◆ Low-cost manufacturer status in the technology products group existed before outsourcing several key items in the product line.

◆ The durable products group is perceived as the most responsive in its chosen geographic markets, often delivering products and services on the same day as ordered.

◆ The food products group has a reputation for superior delivery performance, mitigating criticism of its premium prices in a commodity marketplace.

◆ The company's growth in durable goods exceeded expectations.

Weaknesses

◆ Lack of organization-wide assimilation of SAP functionalities.

◆ Delivery performance is inconsistent, especially in the technology products group. Customer complaints in this market are especially high. Because the market visibility is so high, Fowlers is developing a reputation in customers' eyes as being tough to do business with (hard to place an order with, incomplete and incorrect product shipments, inaccurate pricing, poor order status capability, and so on). This is negatively affecting overall satisfaction ratings.

◆ Operating income of the food and technical product groups is eroding because of price pressure and a too-flat cost-reduction slope.

◆ High indirect purchasing costs, despite lower cost of sales.

♦ The rate of cost increase for customer service is significantly higher than the rate of sales growth.

♦ Despite sales growth, Fowlers' stock price has taken a hit because of five quarters of poor profit-after-taxes and a bloating cash-to-cash cycle. Analyst criticism focuses on the inability to effectively manage return on assets and integrate profit potential of the business services acquisition.

Opportunities

♦ Leverage commodity buys across all product groups to improve gross profit.

♦ Increase effectiveness and efficiency of order fulfillment to improve customer satisfaction and reduce rate of spending on indirect goods and services (those that don't add value to the product being produced).

♦ Develop more advanced knowledge management capability to add financial value to customers beyond simple price cutting.

♦ Accelerate market share in the durable products group by introducing an online catalogue for its end customers.

♦ Leverage cost-to-manufacture leadership in the technology products group to increase profits.

♦ Improve the efficiency and effectiveness of SAP utilization.

Threats

♦ Key competitors in the food products group are buying their way into the marketplace with a "lowest list price" strategy.

♦ Although the overall market for the technology products group has been in a period of decline, the group's market share is declining even faster; customer satisfaction scores put this group in the lowest quartile of performance.

♦ Price point in the technology products group is getting too low to meet profit targets with the current cost structure.

♦ Established catalogue apparel companies are potential competitors to the online sales channel being introduced this quarter.

Value Proposition

♦ The Fowlers Inc. corporate value proposition is summarized by profitable growth as the preferred supplier of customers in targeted markets, driven by exceeding customer requirements.

Critical Success Factors

♦ Maintaining revenue contribution by increasing the share of the food products group in existing markets.

♦ Driving revenue growth by introducing durable products in the direct-to-consumer market and capturing targeted share.

♦ Achieving overall revenue growth for current year, targeted at 10 percent, and achieving targeted after-tax profit of 7 percent.

♦ Maintaining an image as technical leader in the technology products and food products groups, while improving overall return on assets and aggressively driving cost out of operations.

♦ Improving overall cash-to-cash position.

♦ Optimizing the utilization of SAP modules.

♦ Effectively integrating assets of the new durable products acquisition.

Critical Business Issues

♦ Customer satisfaction from all channels in the technology products group is negatively affecting sales.

♦ Profits are disappearing from the technology and food products groups because of higher direct and indirect costs.

♦ Revenue is targeted to grow to $1.02 billion, but actual projection after nine months is $1 billion.

♦ The durable products group integration of online capability is behind schedule.

♦ Inventory and receivables are expanding, seemingly uncontrollably.

♦ Key customers in the food products group are leaving on the basis of price-only criteria.

Financial Performance

Finding information about a publicly traded company's financial health is as easy as knowing the stock symbol and logging on to hoovers.com. There you can find all the ratio statistics, share price analyses, profit reports, and cash flow data necessary to paint the relative financial picture of a company.

To complete a current-state summary, you'll need information about income and cash position. The income statement contains revenue, cost, and profit data. The balance sheet looks at the right-now cash position by documenting assets and liabilities, including inventory.

In the *business context document*, profit is considered three ways, and each will eventually have its place in planning a supply chain project.

1. *Gross Margin*. Revenue less the cost of goods sold. This picture of profit is usually stated as a percent of total revenue.

2. *Operating Margin* (also referred to as operating income). Gross margin less the costs of sales and administration. In effect, it's the gross margin with all indirect costs removed. It, too, is usually represented as a percent of total revenue.

3. *Economic Profit*. Operating margin less taxes and interest expense. The interest expense is affected by the amount of cash tied up in the business through inventory, receivables, and payables.

By using these industry standards for developing your profit picture, you'll gain a better understanding of how your business fits into its competitive environment—an important piece of the business context summary.

Internal Profile

The internal profile summarizes the physical aspects of the company as well as other performance measures that influence results. The first physical aspect is the *organization chart*. In a publicly held company, you can find this at the top level—usually down to the management of operating units or divisions—in the executive profile section of a corporate-reporting Web site such as hoovers.com. Many companies also share this information, including names, titles, and brief biographies, on their own Web sites. Good starting places for this hunt are the "investor relations" or "about the company" sections of the Web site.

The second physical aspect of the internal profile is *identification of all locations* where the company has operations, including manufacturing sites, warehouses, call centers, technical service centers, return locations, headquarters, and all contract locations, in cases in which these functions are outsourced. This usually takes some work to collect; good sources for this information are the human resources department, the information technology department, the purchasing department, and accounting.

The third physical aspect of the internal business context is a *picture of how the organization is set up* to plan, manage, and execute key performance measures or indicators. For example, Fowlers' organization chart in Chapter 2 (Figure 2-1) reflects that sales, operations, and finance are controlled at both the corporate level and the business unit level. Note that the chief operating officer is at the same hierarchical level as the product group presidents, and that corporate directors have potential for conflict with the vice presidents of operations in each product group.

Most companies have such intricacies built into their reporting structures, and it can lead to overly complicated supply chains and delays in making improvements, as politics of control get in the way.

Fowlers' physical locations contain similar quirks. Each product group manages its own manufacturing locations, but the distribution locations are a mix—some are managed by a product group, and others are managed at the corporate level, demonstrating previous efforts to manage efficiency.

A final element of the internal profile is *how success is measured*. At Fowlers, the project team discovered five key performance indicators that were on the business team's dashboard:

1. Unit Cost
2. Line Item Fill Rate
3. Operating Income
4. Revenue
5. Backorders

External Profile

The external profile lists customers and suppliers in the context of groups that have significant impact on your supply chain. To keep it simple, a customer group is most easily defined by revenue reporting groups. Often these revenue categories are established by business model (i.e., direct-to-consumer, retail, distributor, and OEM).

Likewise, a supplier group is often defined by a major commodity type, such as packaging; tooling; process materials; maintenance, repair, and operations; value-added service; and so on. In both cases, use the 80/20 rule to list the largest customers and suppliers within each group—the 20 percent who get 80 percent of your revenue and material spend.

In Fowlers' case, the customer profile summary yielded seven market/customer channels across all of the product groups:

1. Retail markets, including mass merchant and category killer
2. Distributor/wholesaler markets
3. Direct-to-consumer markets
4. OEM/key account customers
5. U.S. government
6. Home delivery/route sales markets
7. International markets

Fowlers' key supplier profile included raw material commodity types of resins, packaging, electronic components, live produce, hard goods, and apparel. In addition, the supply base included several contract manufacturers that supply apparel, optical media, precooked food, and computer hardware.

The Supply Chain Definition Matrix

Up to this point in the discovery process, the emphasis has been on gathering background pieces of contextual information. Now is the time when the team needs to develop a consensus on how the company's supply chains are defined—a key to defining the project's scope.

In most cases, a supply chain is defined by a combination of product, customer, and geography. It can also include financial reporting and other factors. To create its definition, the team must take into account all points of view and prioritize the importance of each.

Using a supply chain definition matrix can help. (See Table 3-1 for an example of Fowlers' supply chain definition matrix.) The *financial reporting hierarchy* can help identify "major" geographies of the world. For example, if a company has profit-and-loss reports for Europe, Latin America, the Far East, North America, and Japan, then start with five matrices. To start, choose the geography that either has the most sales or serves as the location of the corporate headquarters.

The columns of each matrix represent demand including markets, customers, and/or channels. To build the columns on your first matrix, look at how sales regions are tracked, market channels are organized, and/or customers are segmented. Adding the revenue in each column should yield total revenue for geography represented

Table 3-1. Fowlers' supply chain definition matrix.

Fowlers North America	Customer/Market Channels						
	Retail Markets	Distributor Markets	Direct-to-Consumer Markets	OEM and Key Accounts	Government	Home Delivery	International
Food Products	X	X			X		
Technology Products	X	X	Developing	X	X		X
Durable Products			X			X	X

in the matrix. The lowest level of detail in a column can be an
"invoiceable" customer ship-to address.

The rows in the matrix focus on supply, including business lines
or products; indirectly the rows address locations (manufacturing and
distribution) and suppliers. To build the rows, start with the highest
level of business lines or product families or groups. The lowest level
of detail in a row is a stock keeping unit (SKU); the rows should
total your costs. There may be disconnects between how financial
costs are aggregated versus how product families are aggregated. This
has been a challenge in nearly every project; the use of more sophisticated data warehouse applications has started to make data more
accessible.

Most companies are in the habit of defining their supply chains
from a product cost perspective—solely by product and financial
definitions, regardless of the customer. They worry about how the
product is made, what suppliers are involved, and where the reve-
nues and earnings are credited, but they often don't view a supply
chain from the customer point of view. This can potentially derail a
project's success. First, customer requirements are key factors that
drive supply chain performance; although the gross margin may look
good, the net profit might suffer because of high indirect costs to
serve. Second, manufacturers are often indiscriminate about what
items of the total product line should be available to a particular
customer segment. Third, with a product-only view, supply chain
costs can evolve to support the delivery requirements of the most
aggressive customers—meaning the manufacturer provides superior
delivery performance even where it is not needed or valued.

At Fowlers, the number of supply chains could be viewed in
more than one way. If defined by product, the company would
have three supply chains: food, technology, and durable products.
If defined by market or customer channel, there would be seven
supply chains: retail/mass merchant, distributor/wholesaler, direct-
to-consumer, OEM, U.S. government, home delivery/route sales,

and international. Fowlers could also define supply chain by geography, in which case there would be two: international and North America. Last, and the preferred view, Fowlers could say there are eleven mature supply chains as defined by customer and product (count the X's in Table 3-1) with one developing supply chain.

The next step is to collect data for each supply chain in order to help the team determine a project scope. The mantra *Think big, act small, and scale fast* works here. The idea is to pick supply chains for the analytical scope that would be representative of the rest. It is important to understand supply chain performance at a detailed level; knowing more about less and then applying knowledge to the broad implementation scenarios is a good rule of thumb.

Common data elements include revenue (units and $), profit ($ and % margin), inventory (units and $), number of SKUs, and strategic importance. Between the business context document, critical success factors, critical business issues, the definition matrix, and the data, a project scope generally is readily apparent. If not, the project sponsor and steering team become the ultimate decision-makers on scope. By using its data and some good sparring, the Fowlers core team narrowed the scope for its supply chain project to six supply chains as defined by the U.S. sales of technology products and food products:

Food Products

 ♦ U.S. Retail Markets

 ♦ U.S. Distributor Markets

 ♦ U.S. Direct-to-Consumer Markets

 ♦ U.S. Government

Technology Products

 ♦ U.S. Retail Markets

 ♦ U.S. OEM—Key Accounts

Now, with the four basic components of a business context summary complete—strategic background, financial performance, internal profile, and external profile—the team was able to move ahead to the project charter.

The Project Charter

The project charter is created during this phase to establish a complete understanding of the project's scope and objectives. The document helps to align assumptions and expectations among executive sponsors, stakeholders, and team members. The page most project members jump to first is the *schedule*.

On the schedule, there are three project delivery formats.

Format 1. Two days of classroom each week, focused on specific deliverables to be completed as "homework" before the next session.

Format 2. This completes the same deliverables in the same elapsed time, but the classroom sessions are organized by phase rather than week. Figure 3-1 illustrates an alternative Fowlers schedule using the "by phase" approach. This utilizes three days of classroom work followed by two weeks of time to complete the deliverables. This approach makes more productive use of teams with members who must travel (domestically) as part of the project. Until 2009, this was the most frequently used schedule and still is the one recommended for larger and more complex companies.

Format 3 (which was used to outline this third edition of *Supply Chain Excellence*). This is for global business units in smaller regions and for small businesses. It utilizes a remote meeting schedule—with such teleconferencing platforms as GoToMeeting, Cisco, or Microsoft Office Communicator or Lync—to collect data, followed by a week on-site to develop the project portfolio, with implementation to proceed as normal (Figure 3-2). This option reduces the resource

Figure 3-1. Project schedule by phase.

Schedule by Phase	Deliverable	Classroom Dates
	February 1 to May 1, 2011	
Phase 0 **Build Organizational Support**	Supply Chain Excellence Overview with wide audience	February 7, 2011
	SCOR Framework Workshop	February 21, 2011
	SCOR Implementation Workshop	March 21, 2011
	Organizational Briefings	As Needed
	Executive Briefing - GO/NO GO	April 11, 2011
	May 1 to June 7, 2011	
Phase 1 **Define Project Scope**	Business Context Summary	
	Supply Chain Definition Matrix (with data)	
	Project Charter	
	Metric Definitions and Data Collection Plan	
Phase 2 **Analyze Performance**	Defect Data Collection Plan	May 2, 3, and 4, 2011 May 23, 24, 25, 2011
	Defect Analysis	
	Industry Comparison	
	Competitive Requirements	
	Benchmark Data	
	Preliminary Scorecard	
	Scorecard Gap Analysis	
	June 7 to July 22, 2011	
Phase 3 **Develop Project Portfolio**	Staple Yourself to an Order Interviews	June 13, 14, and 15, 2011 July 5, 6, and 7, 2011
	AS IS Process Diagram	
	Defect Analysis Part 2	
	Brainstorm Event and Documentation	
	Preliminary Project Portfolio	
	Opportunity Analysis	
	Assemble and Approve Implementation Project Charters	
	September 1, 2011, to August 31, 2012	
Phase 4 **Implement Projects**	Kickoff Projects	August 15, 16, and 17, 2011
	Develop Performance Baselines for Metrics	
	Conduct Level 3 and 4 Process Gap Analysis	September 1, 2011, to August 31, 2012
	Conduct Leading Practice Assessment	
	Develop TO BE Process Blueprint	
	Assemble Solution Storyboard	
	Approve Solution Design	
	Build and Test Solution	
	Pilot and Verify Solution - Twice	
	Define Process Control Measures	
	Rollout to Project Scope	
	Rollout to Enterprise	

Figure 3-2. Project schedule for global, remote, and/or small business units.

Schedule for Global and Small Business Applications	Deliverable	Classroom Dates
	February 1 to May 1, 2011	
Phase 0 **Build Organizational Support**	Supply Chain Excellence Overview with wide audience	February 7, 2011
	SCOR Framework Workshop	Opportunity
	SCOR Implementation Workshop	Opportunity
	Organizational Briefings	As needed
	Executive Briefing--GO/NO GO	March 11, 2011
	May 1 to July 1, 2011	
Phase 1 **Define Project Scope**	Business Context Summary	Remote Web-Based Meetings
	Supply Chain Definition Matrix (with data)	
	Project Charter	
Phase 2 **Analyze Performance**	Kickoff	April 18 April 25 May 2 May 9 May 16 May 23 May 30 June 6
	Metric Definitions and Data Collection Plan	
	Defect Data Collection Plan	
	Defect Analysis	
	Industry Comparison	
	Competitive Requirements	
	Benchmark Data	
	Preliminary Scorecard	
	Scorecard Gap Analysis	
	IDEALLY DEDICATED ON-SITE Staple Yourself to an Order Interviews	On-Site
	IDEALLY DEDICATED ON-SITE AS IS Process Diagram	June 13 to 17, 2011
	July 11 to August 1, 2011	
Phase 3 **Develop Project Portfolio**	OPTIONAL AS IS Process Diagram	On-Site July 11 to 15, 2011
	Defect Analysis Part 2	
	Brainstorm Event and Documentation	
	Preliminary Project Portfolio	
	Opportunity Analysis	
	Assemble and Approve Implementation Project Charters	
	Prioritize Implementation Projects	
	August 1, 2011, to July 31, 2012	
Phase 4 **Implement Projects**	Kickoff Projects	Combination On-Site and Remote Management August 1, 2011, to July 31, 2012
	Develop Performance Baselines for Metrics	
	Conduct Level 3 and 4 Process Gap Analysis	
	Conduct Leading Practice Assessment	
	Develop TO BE Process Blueprint	
	Assemble Solution Storyboard	
	Approve Solution Design	
	Build and Test Solution	
	Pilot and Verify Solution--Twice	
	Define Process Control Measures	
	Rollout to Project Scope	
	Rollout to Enterprise	

requirements by about 50 percent through to portfolio development, but increases difficulty building broad awareness and support for the initiative. In both formats 2 and 3, the majority of material, work, and information flow analyses have moved to implementation so that only those processes scoped in the projects are analyzed. The exception is the staple-yourself interviews needed to assemble the SCOR AS IS process diagram. In Format 3, there are two options to document the AS IS. The first dedicates a week in advance of the brainstorm event; this allows for more thorough understanding of the process and truly walks the path of the transaction. The second option is to spend a day going through the build of the SCOR AS IS process diagram during the brainstorm week. Essentially, all parties are brought into a conference room and the diagram is created interactively.

The second-most popular page that people turn to in the charter is the one defining *roles and responsibilities*. Other important components of the project charter are scope; business and project objectives; methodology; deliverables; risks and dependencies; budget; organization chart; stakeholder expectations; benchmarks; benefit analysis; critical success factors; and communication plan. Fowlers' entire project charter is included as the Appendix.

CHAPTER 4

Phase 2: Analyze Performance

➤ **April 18 and 25: Project Kickoff and SCOR Metrics**

The theme for this phase is *analysis*. The candidate list includes the SCOR metrics, performance defects, benchmarks, and "staple yourself to an order" interviews. The key outputs are a scorecard, a set of competitive requirements prioritized by market, and the AS IS SCOR Level 3 process diagram. To kick things off, we start with a kickoff! For the Fowlers team, the kickoff would be a combination of an on-site at the world headquarters in North America and a video conference for international team members congregating at their regional offices. The time zone was the biggest challenge, as team members included Europe, Asia, and North America. The team decided that two kickoff meetings were necessary because Europe was seven hours ahead of central standard time and China was fourteen hours ahead.

The Project Kickoff

There are two ingredients for a great kickoff. First, all the right people have to be a part of it. The audience should include all resources participating on the project, including the steering team, active executive sponsor, project manager, design team, and extended team. If in doubt about a particular person or group, extend the invitation. Providing the big picture to anyone who might participate in the project makes his or her support in gathering details more productive.

At Fowlers Inc., executive sponsors Brian Dowell and Jovan Kojcic invited the seven-member steering team and ten-member design team as identified on the project charter. They also invited extended team resources from information technology, finance, and site operations. In all, 36 people were on the list.

The second ingredient to a great kickoff is having the right materials presented by the right people. The most popular and effective agenda organizes the content into three basic chunks:

1. Setting the strategic context for supply chain improvement, delivered by the executive sponsor(s);

2. Providing a high-level overview of how Supply Chain Operations Reference (SCOR) works, delivered by the coach;

3. Summarizing critical elements of the project charter, delivered by the project manager.

To prepare for the kickoff, Brian Dowell and Jovan Kojcic prepared "state of the business" summaries highlighting the issues related to both Fowlers' and its technology products group's supply chain improvement. Their presentations summarized business plans, strategy, critical success factors, critical business issues, and expectations with regard to supply chain improvement.

The coach prepared the SCOR overview presentation. It provided the big picture of the SCOR Framework, highlighted the *Supply Chain Excellence* project roadmap, and gave examples of the deliverables that individuals across the design and extended teams would be asked to produce in the coming weeks.

Finally, David Able prepared key points from the approved project charter, emphasizing the thing most people were interested in—the schedule. He allowed time for everyone to synchronize their own calendars to the rhythm of the project as outlined in the project charter. There was a big sigh of relief that not all weeks were travel weeks and that the meetings would be rotated among geographic locations. A side benefit of this approach would be to help the team understand regional supply chain challenges and develop more effective relationships. In addition to the schedule, the kickoff provided the opportunity to set remaining stakeholder interviews left over from Phase 1. These would be incorporated into a revised project charter, in the stakeholder expectations section.

Mixing the three ingredients—the business context for supply chain improvement, the SCOR education, and key points of the project charter—built a powerful shared vision of the pace of the project. It aligned expectations for deliverables and outlined the effort required for the various project roles.

Picking a Balanced Set of Supply Chain Metrics

With the kickoff meetings complete during the week of April 18, the real work begins. Typically, the only people online or in the room for the next session are the project manager, coach, and design team; 10 p.m. central standard time seemed to be the best slot for this first design team meeting. The team agreed that one of the three geographies would be inconvenienced each week and that the burden would be rotated. The team selected an online web-conference platform for remote meetings, allowing all to share content from the computer, see a presenter's material, and use Voice over IP (VoIP) to minimize phone bills. The primary order of business is to select the appropriate metrics from the SCOR 10.0 Level 1 Strategic Metric list (Figure 4-1).

Figure 4-1. SCOR Level 1 Strategic Metrics.

Performance Attribute	Performance Attribute Definition	Level 1 Strategic Metric
Supply Chain Reliability	The performance of the supply chain in delivering: the correct product, to the correct place, at the correct time, in the correct condition and packaging, in the correct quantity, with the correct documentation, to the correct customer.	Perfect Order Fulfillment (RL.1.1)
Supply Chain Responsiveness	The speed at which a supply chain provides products to the customer.	Order Fulfillment Cycle Time (RS.1.1)
Supply Chain Agility	The agility of a supply chain in responding to marketplace changes to gain or maintain competitive advantage.	Upside Supply Chain Flexibility (AG.1.1)
		Upside Supply Chain Adaptability (AG.1.2)
		Downside Supply Chain Adaptability (AG.1.3)
		Overall Value At Risk (AG.1.4)
Supply Chain Costs	The costs associated with operating the supply chain.	Supply Chain Management Cost (CO.1.1)
		Cost of Goods Sold (CO.1.2)
Supply Chain Asset Management	The effectiveness of an organization in managing assets to support demand satisfaction. This includes the management of all assets: fixed and working capital.	Cash-to-Cash Cycle Time (AM.1.1)
		Return on Supply Chain Fixed Assets (AM.1.2)
		Return on Working Capital (AM.1.3)

There are three common approaches to selecting the right mix of metrics. The first is to educate the team on the pure SCOR definition, calculation, and collection requirements using Section 2 of the SCOR 10.0 manual. The team can then contrast the SCOR ideal with its current metrics and ultimately achieve consensus on inclusion, exclusion, or modification.

A second approach is to use the generic (non–Fowlers) guides provided by Tables 4-1 through 4-9, where the SCOR 10.0 definitions are compared to practical calculation components built from multiple project experiences.

Table 4-1. Perfect Line Fulfillment. Also called Line Item On Time and In Full.

Perfect Line Fulfillment	Perfect Line Fulfillment is not an official SCOR 10.0 metric. In practice this measure mimics the definition of Perfect Order Fulfillment but judges good or bad at the line level. In a 10-line order where 5 are delivered perfectly and 5 are not, the Perfect Order Fulfillment would be 0% and the Perfect Line Fulfillment would be 50%. This metric has evolved on mixed orders for which products have different commit dates and lead times. Most ERP packages operate at the line level.			
Measurement Component	**Score**	**Data**	**Calculation Component**	**Query Assumptions**
Line On Time and In Full to Customer Request	**68.4%**	10000	Total Number of Customer Lines	Self-explanatory. This is the base for Request, Commit, and Perfect Order. In this case the 100 orders averaged 100 line items.
		7100	Total Number of Lines Delivered On Time to Customer Request Date	Request date is the first request date from the customer at the line level. This includes agreed-to lead times by SKU that may ultimately be part of the customer's master data settings. This also helps differentiate MTO and MTS items that are on the same order.
		6900	Total Number of Lines Delivered In Full	Request quantity is the first request quantity prior to application of Available To Promise (ATP) checks at the line level.
		6840	Total Number of Lines Delivered On Time and In Full to Customer Request Date	Many applications have a difficult time with both on-time and in-full, even by line. Each line needs to be evaluated and considered good if quantity and date are met. As with the order, many companies do not store original request data and, hence, do not calculate this component.
Line On Time and In Full to Customer Commit	**72.0%**	7456	Total Number of Lines Delivered On Time to Customer Commit Date	Commit date is the original confirmation date first given the customer after the first ATP check at the line level. Ideally this is a committed delivery date to the customer. Many companies are not getting receipt data from their carriers and measure to the committed ship date.
		7209	Total Number of Lines Delivered In Full	Commit quantity is the first confirmation quantity after the application of ATP checks at the line level.

(continues)

Table 4-1. (Continued)

Measurement Component	Score	Data	Calculation Component	Query Assumptions
		7199	Total Number of Lines Delivered On Time and In Full to Customer Commit Date	Many applications have a difficult time with both on-time and in-full even by line. Each line needs to be evaluated against original commit and is considered good if quantity and date are met. Many companies do not store original commit data and, hence, always measure against the latest commit, making the metric look like 100%.
Perfect Line Fulfillment	49.0%	4899	Total Number of Lines On Time and Complete Meeting 3-Way Match Criteria	This is the most difficult measure to get. The best method is to evaluate your three-way match percentage at the line level via your customers' purchasing or payables systems. Many companies try to measure this metric using the On-Time and In-Full to Commit as a base and then subtract order invoices that have some deduction associated with it.

A third approach is to rely on the SCORmark benchmark that is offered with membership in the Supply Chain Council. It has calculation components, is based on SCOR definitions, and helps assemble necessary benchmark data.

Whether you use the SCOR manual, SCORmark, and/or the reference tables, a good general rule is to *pick at least one metric from each performance attribute.* By day's end, the Fowlers design team had identified metrics for its balanced supply chain scorecard, created a blank scorecard template (Table 4-10 on page 71), and downloaded a SCORmark survey.

Here are the metrics the Fowlers design team identified, which happen to be the most frequently used metrics:

 ◆ Perfect Order Fulfillment

 ◆ Order Fulfillment Cycle Time

 ◆ Upside Supply Chain Flexibility

(*Text continues on page 63*)

Table 4-2. Perfect order fulfillment.

Perfect Order Fulfillment			The percentage of orders meeting delivery performance with complete and accurate documentation and no delivery damage. Components include all items and quantities on-time (using the customer's definition of on-time), and documentation—packing slips, bills of lading, invoices, etc., SCOR 10.0, page 2.1.1. While this definition comes straight out of the book, the calculations below have been adapted through the course of experience.	
Measurement Component	**Score**	**Data**	**Calculation Component**	**Query Assumptions**
Order On Time and In Full to Customer Request	38.0%	100	Total Number of Customer Orders	Self-explanatory. This is the base for Request, Commit, and Perfect Order.
		47	Total Number of Orders Delivered On Time to Customer Request Date	Request date is the first request date from the customer. This includes agreed-to lead times by SKU that may ultimately be part of the customer's master data settings.
		50	Total Number of Orders Delivered In Full	Request quantity is the first request quantity prior to application of Available To Promise (ATP) checks.
		38	Total Number of Orders Delivered On Time and In Full to Customer Request Date	Many applications have a difficult time with both on-time and in-full by order. Each line needs to be evaluated; if all of the lines are on-time and in-full to original request, then the order is considered good. Many companies do not store original request data and, hence, do not calculate this component.
Order On Time and In Full to Customer Commit	40.0%	47	Total Number of Orders Delivered On Time to Customer Commit Date	Commit date is the original confirmation date first given the customer after the first ATP check. Ideally this is a committed delivery date to the customer. Many companies are not getting receipt data from their carriers and measure to the committed ship date.
		50	Total Number of Orders Delivered In Full	Commit quantity is the first confirmation quantity after the application of ATP checks.
		40	Total Number of Orders Delivered On Time and In Full to Customer Commit Date	Many applications have a difficult time with both on-time and in-full by order. Each line needs to be evaluated; if all of the lines are on-time and in-full to original commit, then the order is considered good. Many companies do not store original commit data and, hence, always measure against the latest commit, making the metric look like 100%.

(continues)

Table 4-2. (Continued)

Measurement Component	Score	Data	Calculation Component	Query Assumptions
Perfect Order Fulfillment	24.0%	24	Total Number of Orders On Time and Complete Meeting 3-Way Match Criteria	This is the most difficult measure to get. The best method is to evaluate your three-way match percentage at the order level via your customers' purchasing or payables systems. Many companies attempt to measure this metric using the On Time and In Full to Commit as a base and then subtract order invoices that have some deduction associated with it.

Table 4-3. Order fulfillment cycle time for make-to-stock (MTS).

Order Fulfillment Cycle Time (MTS)	The average actual cycle time consistently achieved to fulfill customer orders. For each individual order, this cycle time starts from the order receipt and ends with customer acceptance of the order, SCOR 10.0, page 2.2.1. The calculations below are adapted for MTS.		
Score	**Data**	**Calculation Component**	**Query Assumptions**
12.0	4	Customer Authorization to Order Entry Complete	In practice, this is the time from initial receipt of the customer order Purchase Order (PO) until the order entry is complete. For EDI transmissions, the clock starts with the system receipt day and time.
	5	Order Entry Complete to Order Received at Warehouse	This is normally from the time of order-entry-complete until the order delivery is created at the warehouse. This is also where future dated orders sit (dwell time).
	1	Order Received at Warehouse to Order Shipped to Customer	This is the time from delivery creation in the warehouse until the order is shipped to the customer.
	1	Order Shipped to Customer to Customer Receipt of Order	This is often referred to as "in transit" time.
	1	Order Received at Customer to Installation Complete	This category is reserved for those having an installation component, and is calculated from receipt of first good until installation complete.

Table 4-4. Order fulfillment cycle time for make-to-order (MTO) and engineer-to-order (ETO).

Order Fulfillment Cycle Time (MTO ETO)	SCOR 10.0 does not have distinct calculations for MTS, MTO, and ETO. This spreadsheet adds two segments to account for manufacturing time. The calculations below are adapted based on project experience.		
Score	**Data**	**Calculation Component**	**Query Assumptions**
39.0	1	Customer Authorization to Order Entry Complete	In practice, this is the time from initial receipt of the customer order Purchase Order (PO) until the order entry is complete. For EDI transmissions, the clock starts with the system receipt day and time.
	5	Order Entry Complete to Start Manufacture	This is normally from the time of order-entry-complete until the production order is created in manufacturing. This is also where future dated orders sit (dwell time).
	21	Start Manufacture to Manufacturing Ship	This is the time from production-order-create to ship to the warehouse or customer.
	2	Manufacturing Ship to Order Received at Warehouse	This is often referred to as "in transit" time.
	1	Order Received at Warehouse to Order Shipped to Customer	This is the time from delivery creation in the warehouse until the order is shipped to the customer.
	4	Order Shipped to Customer to Customer Receipt of Order	This is often referred to as "in transit" time.
	5	Order Received at Customer to Installation Complete	This category is reserved for those having an installation component and is calculated from receipt of first good until installation complete.

+ Cost of Goods

+ Supply Chain Management Cost

+ Inventory Days of Supply—a subset of Cash-to-Cash Cycle Time

Building on the momentum of the kickoff, and knowing that relationships were critical to executing the schedule, Brian and Jovan sponsored a social event to finish up a day that all agreed was one of the best project launches anyone at the company could recall.

Table 4-5. Upside supply chain flexibility.

Upside Supply Chain Flexibility	The number of days required to achieve an unplanned sustainable 20% increase in quantities delivered. Note: 20% is a number provided for benchmarking purposes. For some industries and organizations a different percentage may be appropriate. The new operating level needs to be achieved without a significant increase of cost per unit, SCOR 10.0, page 2.3.1. The calculation below is a practical adaptation using master data. Essentially, it is the stacked lead time of MRP refresh period plus longest sourced component, plus manufacturing schedule wheel plus delivery lead time.		
Score	**Data**	**Calculation Component**	**Query Assumptions**
113.0	30	Re-Plan Planned Lead Time	Often associated with frequency of MRP update.
	33	Source Planned Lead Time	This is the longest component planned lead time for a SKU's bill of materials.
	45	Make Planned Lead Time	This is frequently associated with a SKU's manufacturing scheduling cycle, i.e., weekly, monthly, quarterly, etc., or it can be part of the "replenishment lead time" found in item setup screens for ATP.
	5	Deliver Planned Lead Time	This is also associated with the "replenishment lead time" and refers to the planned time from order entry to ship.

Data Collection and Benchmarks

The next step is the process of assembling a data collection plan. There are generally five important elements to a data collection plan. First and most important is a *definition of the metric*; as stated previously, we recommend using the SCOR definitions as a baseline.

Second, it's necessary to assemble a *segmentation strategy* that will allow for aggregation and desegregation. Examples of segmentation options are by location, customer, item, country, forecast planning family, or commodity. The third requirement is a *data extract query* (taking into account the segmentation strategy) that includes specific data tables and fields from either the live system or data warehouse. The fourth consideration is the *sample size* of the data. Collecting customer order data for perfect order fulfillment and order fulfillment cycle time may use a sample size of the last three months, whereas total supply chain management cost may use a sample size

Table 4-6. Supply chain management cost.

Supply Chain Management Cost	The sum of the costs associated with the SCOR Level 2 processes to Plan, Source, Deliver, and Return, SCOR 10.0, page 2.4.1. This metric was redefined in the 7.0 release. Aside from SCORmark, much of the benchmark data is based on the definition in version 6.1. This worksheet still uses the 6.1 calculation components but is easily mapped to SCOR 10.0.		
Score	**% of Revenue**	**Raw Data (000s)**	**Calculation Component**	**Query Assumptions**
		$1,000,000	Revenue	
	9.8%	$98,011	**Order Management Cost**	
	3.5%	$35,098	Customer Service Cost	Cost centers that have to do with entering customer orders, reserving inventory, performing credit checks, consolidating orders, processing inquiries and quotes.
	2.4%	$23,908	Finished Goods Warehouse Cost	Cost centers that have to do with the storage, receiving, picking, and shipment of finished goods products.
	2.1%	$21,098	Outbound Transportation Cost	Cost centers that have to do with the transportation (all modes, including export) of finished goods products.
21.9%	0.9%	$9,000	Contract and Program Management Cost	Cost centers that have to do with the initiation and ongoing management of customer contracts, including master agreements, compliance to volume-based incentives, and other special incentives.
	0.0%	$0	Installation Planning and Execution Costs	Cost centers that have to do with the planning and execution of product installation at customer-designated locations.
	0.9%	$8,907	Accounts Receivable Cost	Cost centers that have to do with the processing and closure of customer invoices, including collection.
	6.2%	$61,638	**Material (Product) Acquisition Cost**	
	1.9%	$18,997	Purchasing Cost	Cost centers associated with the strategic as well as the tactical parts of the purchasing process.
	0.6%	$5,987	Raw Material Warehouse Cost	Cost centers associated with receiving, storage, and transfer of raw material product.
	0.1%	$1,099	Supplier Quality Cost	Cost centers associated with supplier qualification, product verification, and ongoing quality systems for raw materials.

(continues)

Table 4-6. (Continued)

Score	% of Revenue	Raw Data (000s)	Calculation Component	Query Assumptions
	0.3%	$2,987	Component Engineering and Tooling Cost	Cost centers associated with engineering (design and specification) and tooling costs for raw materials, i.e., packaging.
	2.5%	$24,678	Inbound Transportation Cost	Cost centers that have to do with transportation (all modes including import) of raw material and/or purchased finished goods products.
	0.8%	$7,890	Accounts Payable Cost	Cost centers that have to do with processing and closure of supplier invoices, including credit and disputes.
	0.8%	**$8,092**	**Planning and Finance Cost**	
	0.2%	$2,349	Demand Planning Cost	Cost centers allocated to unit forecasting and overall demand management.
	0.5%	$4,509	Supply Planning Cost	Cost centers allocated to supply planning, including overall supply planning, distribution requirements planning, master production planning, and production scheduling.
	0.1%	$1,234	Supply Chain Finance Control Cost	Cost centers in finance allocated to reconcile unit plans with financial plans, account for and control supply chain cost centers, and report financial performance of the supply chain Scorecard.
	3.1%	**$30,806**	**Inventory Carrying Cost**	
	2.6%	$25,609	Opportunity Cost	The value of inventory multiplied by the cost of money for your company.
	0.3%	$3,452	Obsolescence Cost	Additional cost of obsolescence in the form of accruals and/or write-offs.
	0.1%	$1,245	Shrinkage Cost	Additional cost of shrinkage in the form of accruals and/or write-offs.
	0.1%	$500	Taxes and Insurance Cost	Cost centers allocated to the payment of taxes and insurance for inventory assets.
	2.0%	**$20,000**	**IT Cost for Supply Chain**	

(continues)

Table 4-6. (Continued)

Score	% of Revenue	Raw Data (000s)	Calculation Component	Query Assumptions
	1.0%	$10,000	Supply Chain Application Cost	Cost centers summarizing the fixed costs associated with supply IT application costs to PLAN, SOURCE, MAKE, DELIVER, and RETURN.
	1.0%	$10,000	IT Operational Cost for Supply Chain	Cost centers summarizing the ongoing expenses associated with maintenance, upgrade, and development of IT costs to support PLAN, SOURCE, MAKE, DELIVER, and RETURN.

of the last fiscal year. The fifth element in the data collection plan is to identify a *data collection team*. This team will follow the collection all the way through defect analysis.

As part of the effort to benchmark performance, it's important to consider the level of detail necessary, comfort level of divulging company data, and effort required to get the data back. With this in mind, there are two types of sources for benchmark data. First, there are subscription sources, which generally require a fee to access the data. Subscription data are evolving in the level of detail, require no company data, and can be acquired with little or no effort. Second, there are survey sources, which require a company to complete a survey of supply chain metrics and submit them as contribution to a larger sample. Although the effort is greater (up to 40 hours), this type of resource provides a higher level of detail. The appendix provides some frequently used benchmark sources. In any case, the goal is to get multiple sources of benchmark data for each selected metric.

With the data collection plans in place, the second part of the day focuses on planning how to assemble an industry comparison spreadsheet using information available at www.hoovers.com (Table 4-11 on page 72). This spreadsheet template illustrates actual and benchmark data for profitability, returns, and share performance. The industry comparison list should contain at least 25 companies for statistical reasons; using fewer is considered more of a point-to-point comparison.

Table 4-7. Returns management–warranty costs.

	Cost to Return Defective Product—the sum of the costs associated with returning a defective product to the supplier. (Processes: sSR1, sDR1.) Cost to Return Excess Product—the sum of the costs associated with returning excess product to the supplier, SCOR 10.0, page 2.4.8.
Returns Management– Warranty Costs	This metric was redefined in the 7.0 release and was no longer considered a stand-alone metric. Aside from SCORmark, much of the benchmark data is based on 6.1. This worksheet still uses the 6.1 calculation components. Returns Management–Warranty Costs is a discrete measure that attempts to segment the cost centers associated with defective product returns, planned and unplanned returns of maintenance, repair and overhaul products (MRO), and returns associated with excess customer inventory. Total Returns Management–Warranty Cost is additive to Supply Chain Management Cost.

Score	% of Revenue	Raw Data (000s)	Calculation Component	Query Assumptions
		$1,000,000	Revenue	
	0.01%	$134	Returns Authorization Processing Costs	Cost centers that have to do with entering return authorizations, scheduling receipts, and processing replacements or credit.
	0.22%	$2,222	Returned Product Facility Cost	Cost centers that have to do with labor and space for receipt and storage of returned products.
0.5%	0.02%	$222	Returned Product Transportation Costs	Cost centers that have to do with the transportation cost of returned products.
	0.10%	$1,000	Repair Costs	Cost centers that have to do with the material, labor, and repair of damaged products.
	0.10%	$1,000	Warranty Costs	Cost centers that have to do with the material, labor, and problem diagnosis for verification and disposition of returned products.

At Fowlers, the finance controller from technology products group, the corporate directors of logistics, and customer service divided up the metric data collection because those people had the easiest access to the financial and customer order information and also had extended team resources who could help collect the data. The vice president of sales and marketing in the technology products group and David Able—in his capacity as vice president of operations for the technology products group—took responsibility for assembling their industry comparison spreadsheet. Because the team

Table 4-8. Cost of goods sold.

Cost of Goods		The cost associated with buying raw materials and producing finished goods. This cost includes direct costs (labor, materials) and indirect costs (overhead). This is not intended to be additive to Total Supply Chain Management Cost, SCOR 10.0, page 2.4.2.		
Score	% of Revenue	Raw Data (000s)	Calculation Component	Query Assumptions
		$1,000,000	Revenue	
76.5%	55.6%	$556,000	Material Cost	Cost centers that include all materials directly incorporated into the cost of the finished good product.
	13.4%	$134,000	Direct Labor	Cost centers that include all labor that directly impacts the manufacturing–assembly of the finished good product.
	7.5%	$75,000	Indirect Labor	Cost centers that include indirect labor and overhead supporting the manufacturing–assembly of the finished good product.

members knew that Fowlers' own data were listed in its industry profile on Hoovers.com, they requested that food and computer industries be added to the list for more specific comparisons with the operating groups. Meanwhile, the director of applications was putting together a short list of analysts for the extended team who could help with data queries and segmentation capability.

Table 4-9. Cash-to-cash cycle time.

Cash to Cash Cycle Time	The time it takes for an investment to flow back into a company after it has been spent for raw materials. For services, this represents the time from the point at which a company pays for the resources consumed in the performance of a service to the time that the company receives payment from the customer for those services, SCOR 10.0 page 2.5.1. The calculation components below are based on project experience. Inventory Days of Supply is the most utilized sub-measure for this performance attribute.

Score	Raw Data (000s)	Calculation Component	Query Assumptions
117.4	$556,000	**Material Cost**	
	$765,000	**COGS**	
	$1,000,000	**Revenue**	
	95.4	**Inventory Days of Supply**	Total Inventory $ / (COGS / 365); Inventory Turns is calculated by COGS / Total Inventory $
	$200,000	Total Inventory	As defined on your balance sheet.
	$100,000	Finished Goods Inventory	Includes manufactured and purchased FG.
	$25,000	Work In Process Inventory	
	$75,000	Raw Material Inventory	
	54.8	**Days Sales Outstanding**	Total Receivables $ / (Revenue / 365)
	$150,000	Total Receivables	As defined on your balance sheet.
	32.8	**Days Payables Outstanding**	Total Payables $ / (Material Cost / 365)
	$50,000	Total Payables	As defined on your balance sheet.

Table 4-10. Fowlers' scorecard template.

Fowlers, Inc.				Benchmark Data				
7-Feb-11	Performance Attribute or Category	Level 1 Performance Metrics	2010 Act	Parity 50th Percentile	Advantage 70th Percentile	Superior 90th Percentile	Gap	Source
External	Supply Chain Delivery Reliability	Perfect Order Fulfillment						
	Supply Chain Responsiveness	Order Fulfillment Cycle Time						
	Supply Chain Flexibility	Upside Supply Chain Flexibility						
	Supply Chain Cost	Cost of Goods						
		Supply Chain Management Cost						
Internal	Supply Chain Asset Management Efficiency	Inventory Days of Supply						

Table 4-11. Summary of actual and benchmark data for profitability, returns, and share performance at the enterprise level.

Industry Comparison—Computer Network Industry—Hoovers.com	Revenue MM	SG&A	Cost of Goods	Cash-to-Cash Cycle Time	Inventory Days of Supply	Asset Turns	Gross Margin	Operating Income	Net Operating Income	Return on Assets
YOUR COMPANY	$176.1	40.9%	47.2%	158.6	98.3	0.7	52.8%	11.9%	6.8%	7.8%
Network Appliance, Inc.	$1,006.0	29.0%	40.0%	58.28	20.4	1.6	60.0%	31.0%	7.5%	49.1%
Dassault Systemes S.A.	$546.0	57.4%	14.3%	91.00	0	1.2	85.7%	28.2%	16.5%	33.0%
The Titan Corporation	$1,033.0	25.2%	73.3%	104.9	12.2	2.2	26.7%	1.5%	-1.8%	3.3%
RadiSys Corporation	$340.7	24.3%	65.7%	129.8	86.8	1.3	34.3%	10.0%	9.6%	12.9%
Convergys Corporation	$2,320.6	29.5%	54.7%	34.96	0	6.0	45.3%	15.8%	9.3%	70.0%
3COM	$2,820.9	64.3%	81.1%	39.04	32	1.6	18.9%	-45.4%	-34.2%	-54.9%
Enterasys Networks, Inc	$1,071.5	66.4%	52.1%	106.0	64.2	1.1	47.9%	-18.5%	-56.6%	-15.0%
Jack Henry and Associates	$345.5	19.1%	56.1%	93.71	0	2.7	43.9%	24.8%	16.1%	49.8%
Novell, Inc.	$1,040.1	80.1%	31.5%	50.66	1.00	1.3	68.5%	-11.6%	-26.2%	-11.8%
Reynolds and Reynolds	$1,004.0	38.8%	44.1%	24.34	8.90	4.7	55.9%	17.1%	9.9%	60.0%
Cerner Corporation	$404.5	71.4%	22.3%	148.6	8.91	1.9	77.7%	6.3%	26.0%	8.9%
The Black Box Corporation	$827.0	26.1%	59.7%	78.78	37.8	4.1	40.3%	14.1%	7.8%	43.7%
Integraph Corporation	$690.5	40.0%	63.5%	85.64	21.1	2.4	36.5%	-3.4%	1.5%	-6.3%
Entrada Networks, Inc.	$25.7	66.1%	66.9%	130.1	97.6	1.6	33.1%	-33.1%	-82.5%	-38.6%
Inrange Technologies Corp	$233.6	34.9%	44.9%	196.9	102	1.0	55.1%	20.2%	6.1%	15.6%
Computer Networks Industry	$100.0	35%	52%	58.27	19.7	1.2	48.0%	13.0%	2.4%	12.0%
Networking Solutions Q3	$38.9	50.1%	47.0%	NA	NA	NA	53.0%	2.8%	NA	NA
Storage Solutions Q3	$16.5	17.0%	90.9%	NA	NA	NA	9.1%	-7.9%	NA	NA
50th Percentile	$758.8	39.4%	53.4%	92.35	20.8	1.6	46.6%	10.9%	7.1%	10.9%
70th Percentile	$1,164.9	32.1%	40.6%	64.88	10.4	3.0	59.4%	18.6%	11.7%	32.4%
90th Percentile	$1,571.1	24.9%	27.8%	37.41	0	4.3	72.2%	26.2%	16.2%	53.9%

CHAPTER 5

Phase 2: Data, Benchmarks, and Competitive Requirements

▶ **May 2 and 9: Putting Performance in Perspective**

The objectives for these sessions are to review the work in progress from the data collection for each metric, review the industry comparison, prepare the SCORmark submission, set competitive requirements, and begin to think about the defect analysis. In terms of file mechanics, the project leader organized a simple file-management plan. First, he set up a global storage folder named "SCEProject." Inside the folder were four subfolders: Presentations (from the coach), Templates (also from the coach), Deliverables, and Reference (SCOR 10.0 from the Supply Chain Council). Inside of the deliverables folder, the coach recommended the following file-naming convention: phase number.deliverable name.date. For example, the supply chain definition matrix was labeled *1.supplychaindefinitionmatrix.022411*. Each time a team member needed to revise the file, he or she would change the date. Inside the deliverables folder, the project leader had set up another called *archive* to store older versions.

For the web conference, each file owner downloaded a copy of the deliverable to his or her desktop. The meeting leader was then able to display each presenter's files at the click of a button.

Initial Data Review

The first file to review was the industry comparison. The second set of files to review were the spreadsheet results of the metric data collection efforts. The last thing to do was fill out the SCORmark survey.

David Able presented the industry comparison findings of the computer network industry (Table 5-1) and conglomerates (Table 5-2). Even on first examination of the data, several things jumped out.

First, the wide range of figures for cost of goods as well as selling, general & administrative (SG&A) costs made it clear that there is no standard for reporting these numbers from one company to another. Operating income seemed to be a good comparison point for expenses. "But there's still no way to compare supply chain costs using the data we have so far," the coach pointed out. "You can't add cost of goods and SG&A and supply chain costs to create a working scorecard metric. Total supply chain management costs are more activity based, and they can borrow from the other two categories, so you'd be double-counting certain costs if you just added them." The SCORmark survey would help with that comparison.

Second, the metrics on the conglomerates comparison for cash-to-cash cycle (197 days) and asset turns (1.5) for Fowlers confirmed what many in the finance community seemed to think about the company: It used physical assets well and cash assets poorly.

Third, as the team members looked at the "parity opportunity" portion of the table, their eyes got wide. As a conglomerate with $1 billion in revenue, Fowlers' 7 percent operating income ($70 million) was only half the level of the conglomerate industry benchmark. To achieve parity in operating income, the company would need to find another $70 million of benefit through supply chain performance.

Table 5-1. Fowlers' comparison data for computer network industry.

Industry Comparison—Computer Network Industry—Hoovers.com	Revenue MM	SG&A	Cost of Goods	Cash-to-Cash Cycle Time	Inventory Days of Supply	Asset Turns	Gross Margin	Operating Income	Net Operating Income	Return on Assets
Network Appliance, Inc.	$1,006.0	29.0%	40.0%	58.28	20.4	1.6	60.0%	31.0%	7.5%	49.1%
Dassault Systemes S.A.	$546.0	57.4%	14.3%	91.00	0	1.2	85.7%	28.2%	16.5%	33.0%
The Titan Corporation	$1,033.0	25.2%	73.3%	104.9	12.2	2.2	26.7%	1.5%	-1.8%	3.3%
RadiSys Corporation	$340.7	24.3%	65.7%	129.8	86.8	1.3	34.3%	10.0%	9.6%	12.9%
Convergys Corporation	$2,320.6	29.5%	54.7%	34.96	0	6	45.3%	15.8%	9.3%	70.0%
3COM	$2,820.9	64.3%	81.1%	39.04	32	1.6	18.9%	-45.4%	-34.2%	-54.9%
Enterasys Networks, Inc	$1,071.5	66.4%	52.1%	106.0	64.2	1.1	47.9%	-18.5%	-56.6%	-15.0%
Jack Henry and Associates	$345.5	19.1%	56.1%	93.71	0	2.7	43.9%	24.8%	16.1%	49.8%
Novell, Inc.	$1,040.1	80.1%	31.5%	50.66	1.00	1.3	68.5%	-11.6%	-26.2%	-11.8%
Reynolds and Reynolds	$1,004.0	38.8%	44.1%	24.34	8.90	4.7	55.9%	17.1%	9.9%	60.0%
Cerner Corporation	$404.5	71.4%	22.3%	148.6	8.91	1.9	77.7%	6.3%	26.0%	8.9%
The Black Box Corporation	$827.0	26.1%	59.7%	78.78	37.8	4.1	40.3%	14.1%	7.8%	43.7%
Integraph Corporation	$690.5	40.0%	63.5%	85.64	21.1	2.4	36.5%	-3.4%	1.5%	-6.3%
Entrada Networks, Inc.	$25.7	66.1%	66.9%	130.1	97.6	1.6	33.1%	-33.1%	-82.5%	-38.6%
Inrange Technologies Corp	$233.6	34.9%	44.9%	196.9	102	1.0	55.1%	20.2%	6.1%	15.6%
Computer Networks Industry	$100.0	35.0%	52.0%	58.27	19.7	1.2	48.0%	13.0%	2.4%	12.0%
Networking Solutions Q3	$38.9	50.1%	47.0%	NA	NA	NA	53.0%	2.8%	NA	NA
Storage Solutions Q3	$16.5	17.0%	90.9%	NA	NA	NA	9.1%	-7.9%	NA	NA
50th Percentile	$827.0	38.8%	54.7%	91.0	20.4	1.6	45.3%	10.0%	7.5%	12.9%
70th Percentile	$1,027.6	29.1%	44.3%	62.4	8.9	2.4	55.7%	16.8%	9.5%	41.6%
90th Percentile	$1,821.0	24.7%	26.0%	36.6	0.0	4.5	74.0%	26.9%	16.3%	55.9%

Table 5-2. Fowlers' comparison data for conglomerates.

Industry Comparison—Conglomerate Industry—Hoovers.com	Revenue	SG&A	Cost of Goods	Cash-to-Cash Cycle Time	Inventory Days of Supply	Asset Turns	Gross Margin	Operating Income	Net Operating Income	Return on Assets
Fowlers	$1,000	7.0%	86.0%	196.7	91.3	1.5	14.0%	7.0%	3.5%	10.7%
National Service Industries	$563	32.3%	62.3%	47.6	20.0	0.6	37.7%	5.3%	4.8%	3.4%
Maxxam Inc	$2,448	6.9%	81.7%	120.1	82.4	0.5	18.3%	11.4%	1.4%	6.2%
US Industries	$3,088	23.3%	66.1%	119.5	88.4	1.2	33.9%	10.6%	1.2%	13.1%
Pacific Dunlop Limited	$2,120	29.7%	66.3%	131.8	105.2	1.6	33.7%	4.0%	–3.4%	4.8%
Sequa Corporation	$1,773	13.9%	75.3%	127.1	102.2	1.4	24.7%	10.8%	1.4%	11.1%
GenCorp Inc	$1,047	3.8%	81.7%	94.8	77.7	1.1	18.3%	14.5%	12.3%	11.5%
Olin Corporation	$1,549	8.5%	77.2%	82.3	65.9	1.8	22.8%	14.3%	5.2%	19.7%
Federal Signal Corporation	$1,106	20.0%	66.9%	103.2	77.8	1.5	33.1%	13.2%	5.2%	14.7%
Kawasaki Heavy Industries Ltd	$8,395	12.4%	87.2%	253.4	136.8	1.1	12.8%	0.4%	–1.0%	0.4%
Valhi Inc	$1,192	16.9%	63.2%	144.1	117.7	0.7	36.8%	19.9%	6.4%	10.5%
Pentair Inc	$2,748	17.1%	71.1%	105.5	73.4	1.4	28.9%	11.9%	2.0%	12.3%
Tomkins PLC	$5,875	7.0%	81.4%	87.6	51.7	2.0	18.6%	11.6%	1.6%	17.5%
ITT Industries Inc	$4,829	23.6%	62.0%	96.4	64.8	1.4	38.0%	14.4%	5.5%	15.1%
Six Continents PLC	$5,939	27.2%	48.7%	39.0	16.8	0.6	51.3%	24.0%	11.4%	10.7%
TRW Inc	$17,231	9.0%	80.5%	42.4	22.9	1.4	19.5%	10.5%	2.5%	11.0%
Textron	$13,090	11.3%	72.8%	231.0	71.6	1.1	27.2%	15.8%	1.7%	12.7%
Johnson Controls Inc	$18,427	8.9%	83.1%	41.8	13.8	2.5	16.9%	8.0%	2.6%	14.9%
Dover Corporation	$5,401	20.8%	59.8%	119.5	88.5	1.5	40.2%	19.4%	9.6%	21.4%

Ratheon Company	$16,895	10.3%	76.0%	122.9	54.3	0.8	24.0%	13.7%	0.8%	8.7%
ABB Ltd	$22,967	19.0%	75.0%	170.0	67.7	1.0	25.0%	6.0%	6.3%	4.5%
RWE AG	$48,182	26.6%	67.8%	95.1	30.4	0.9	32.2%	5.6%	2.2%	3.6%
Emerson Electric	$15,480	19.9%	60.8%	103.7	73.6	1.4	39.2%	19.3%	6.7%	19.9%
Honeywell International	$25,652	12.2%	70.5%	111.1	75.3	1.4	29.5%	17.2%	6.5%	17.6%
United Technologies	$26,206	17.1%	69.1%	107.6	75.7	1.4	30.9%	13.8%	6.9%	14.3%
Koninklijke Philips Electronics	$35,658	15.5%	69.7%	105.7	73.1	1.3	30.3%	13.8%	25.4%	13.6%
3M	$16,724	30.3%	46.4%	141.8	108.7	1.5	53.6%	23.3%	10.7%	26.8%
Vivendi Universal SA	$40,138	22.3%	61.8%	212.9	44.6	0.4	38.2%	15.9%	5.4%	4.5%
Siemens AG	$86,208	26.9%	66.2%	134.3	84.9	1.3	33.8%	6.8%	2.4%	6.6%
Tyco International Ltd	$34,037	21.5%	53.4%	488.1	102.4	0.4	46.6%	25.1%	11.7%	7.7%
General Electric Company	$129,417	36.7%	34.1%	565.8	64.7	0.4	65.9%	29.3%	9.8%	8.7%
Conglomerate Industry	$100	30.0%	54.3%	291.0	77.7	0.7	45.7%	15.7%	11.2%	8.7%
Food—Meat Products Industry	$100	13.1%	82.7%	49.4	52.1	2.1	17.3%	4.2%	2.9%	6.7%
Media—Movie, Television, & Music Production Services and Products	$100	54.6%	45.6%	82.8	19.2	0.7	54.5%	-0.2%	-4.2%	-0.1%
Diversified Services—Miscellaneous Business Services	$100	35.1%	61.0%	47.6	16.7	1.3	39.0%	3.8%	-0.4%	3.8%
50th Percentile	$10,742	18.0%	68.5%	115.3	73.5	1.3	31.5%	13.8%	5.2%	11.3%
70th Percentile	$19,789	12.3%	62.9%	101.2	64.8	1.4	37.1%	15.9%	6.5%	14.4%
90th Percentile	$40,943	8.4%	52.9%	47.1	22.6	1.6	47.1%	23.4%	11.4%	19.7%

David and the team were trying to figure out how much Technology Products would have to contribute toward the $70 million.

As the review turned to the scorecard, the corporate controller, director of logistics, and director of customer service shared their *data collection experience*. First, they said they had been able to segment the Perfect Order Fulfillment and Order Fulfillment Cycle Time by SKU make-to-stock (MTS) or make-to-order (MTO), by customer, by plant, by customer order and line number, and by sales hierarchy.

The toughest part, as anticipated, was assembling the *Perfect Order Fulfillment*. For each line they were able to identify the expected quantity, requested and committed date, actual ship date, customer receipt date, and orders that were paid on time. While this is not exactly like the SCOR metric definition, it was close enough to understand overall customer reliability. They used both the template noted in Chapter 4 as well as the SCORmark questionnaire. *Order Fulfillment Cycle Time* was a blended number between MTS and MTO items; for this metric they also used the combination of the Chapter 4 template and SCORmark. *Supply Chain Management Cost* used the calculations as defined in the SCORmark survey. Figure 5-1 illustrates the enterprise scorecard performance for each of their targeted metrics.

There was a collective gasp in the room as the scorecard made its way to the screen. Each measure in the customer-facing section was new to Fowlers; as bad as it looked, it was the first time the team had really considered overall delivery reliability through customers' eyes.

The ensuing discussion sounded a bit like a session with a grief counselor; there was denial, bargaining, anger, and eventually acceptance of the data. Every member of the team wanted to bolt from the room and jump right into firefighting the problem—as they had all done so many times before. Fortunately, it was the end of the day. Tomorrow's agenda would focus the team on something else, and a good night's sleep would put this information in perspective:

Figure 5-1. Fowlers' enterprise scorecard.

Fowlers Inc.—Enterprise Scorecard				Benchmark Data				
25-Apr-11	Performance Attribute or Category	Level 1 Performance Metrics	2010 Act	Parity 50th Percentile	Advantage 70th Percentile	Superior 90th Percentile	Gap	Source
External	Supply Chain Delivery Reliability	Perfect Order Fulfillment	50.5%					SCORmark
	Supply Chain Responsiveness	Order Fulfillment Cycle Time (Days)	15.0					SCORmark
	Supply Chain Flexibility	Upside Supply Chain Flexibility (Days)	91.5					SCORmark
Internal	Supply Chain Cost	Cost of Goods	86.0%	68.5%	62.9%	52.9%		Hoovers
		Supply Chain Management Cost	15.5%					SCORmark
	Supply Chain Asset Management Efficiency	Inventory Days of Supply	91.3	73.5	64.8	22.6		Hoovers

The team had found an opportunity for the kind of improvement it needed to make. The team agreed to submit the SCORmark "as is" rather than waste any more time justifying something the customers had been saying for years.

The SCORmark Survey

The SCORmark™ survey is a service provided to Supply Chain Council members that utilizes a subset of the APQC database to create a scorecard using SCOR metric definitions. The last time I used the survey, it was 57 questions covering 157 Excel rows. Figure 5-2 illustrates a sample output for supply chain management cost.

Competitive Requirements Analysis

The next step is composed of three tasks: conducting competitive requirements (prioritizing performance targets relative to competitors), assembling a plan to complete a defect analysis for each metric, and preparing for steering team review number one.

Rules for Prioritization

As illustrated in Figure 4-1, there are five attributes of supply chain performance:

1. Delivery reliability
2. Responsiveness
3. Flexibility
4. Supply chain cost
5. Asset management efficiency

The objective of the *competitive requirements exercise* is to prioritize your company against competitors with respect to the five attributes for each customer or market channel—determining whether you

Figure 5-2. Sample output of SCORmark supply chain management cost.

Supply Chain Management Cost	Your Score $7.18
Description of supply chain management costs (5.023) with references to the question number in the survey (5.027)	

You chose the advantage target for this metric. While you have scored above parity by –$1.72, your target gap is $2.08.

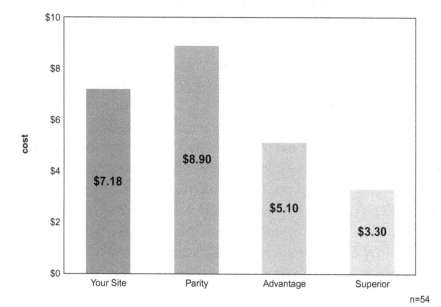

n=54

need to perform at a superior level (90th percentile), at a level of advantage (70th percentile), or at parity (50th percentile).

There is a catch: For each customer or market channel, the team is allowed to set only one performance attribute at the superior level and two at the level of advantage. The other two attributes must be set at parity.

One last note: the requirements are established from the company's point of view as they relate to the competitive landscape of

the future. This is not a firefighting exercise aimed at trying to identify where to improve the most; it's a strategic exercise, focused on
how to differentiate against stiff competition in the future.

Many companies are using the strategic categories discussed in
The Discipline of Market Leaders (written by Michael Treacy and Fred
Wiersema, Basic Books, 1997), which define operational excellence,
customer intimacy, or product innovation as the strategy driver. The
results of the competitive requirements exercise should reflect and
support the SWOT analysis and critical success factors as reviewed
in the business context summary. At the end of the exercise, the
team must reach consensus on the requirements for each market.
Empirically, it might help to assign numeric values to each chip:
three for superior, two for advantage, and one for parity.

The competitive requirements exercise is performed first by the
design team, then the steering team, and a third time by each relevant business team as part of a separate data-gathering task. In each
case, the coach should review the metric categories and definitions
with the players along with available benchmarks, but actual data
should not be revealed. That's because people tend to put the "superior" chip where they see the need for the most improvement, not
necessarily where the strategic advantage lies. At the end of the day,
leadership needs to make the decision based on its business strategy.

During the Fowlers web conference, the coach facilitated the
design team through the exercise, the results of which are seen in
Figure 5-3.

The team scored five channels and learned that there were two
basic supply chain design configurations, plus one with a twist. The
U.S. *retail markets* was typical for the store- and consumer-oriented
retail sector: superior service (meaning perfect order fulfillment),
better-than-average order cycle times, and better-than-average flexibility to respond to demand fluctuation within the quarter. Promo-
tions, short product life cycles, and order policy are examples
affecting demand variability.

Figure 5-3. Fowlers Technology Products Group competitive requirements summary.

SCOR 10.0 Strategic Metric Performance Attribute	Technology Products Group Competitive Requirements				
	U.S. Retail Markets	U.S. Distributor Markets	U.S. Direct-to-Consumer Markets	U.S. OEM and Key Accounts	U.S. Government
Supply Chain Delivery Reliability	Superior	Parity	Superior	Superior	Superior
Supply Chain Responsiveness	Advantage	Parity	Advantage	Advantage	Advantage
Supply Chain Flexibility	Advantage	Parity	Parity	Advantage	Advantage
Supply Chain Cost	Parity	Advantage	Parity	Parity	Parity
Supply Chain Asset Management Efficiency	Parity	Superior	Advantage	Parity	Parity

The U.S. *OEM and key accounts*, as well as the U.S. *government market,* shared similar requirements.

The U.S. *distributor market* is characterized by regular weekly shipments of goods in truckload quantity; effective inventory management practices would both support high turns for Fowlers and increase the gross margin return-on-investment for the distributor.

Last, the U.S. *direct-to-consumer markets*—though similar to retail—needed to give Fowlers the opportunity to shape demand patterns in order to mitigate inventory risk.

The team made plans to validate these preliminary results with the durables, food, and technology business teams and refine the input prior to the next weekly session.

Metric Defect Analysis

Metric defect analysis is borrowed from the Six Sigma and Total Quality Management disciplines. The basic idea is that for each metric identified in the scorecard, the data teams define and analyze the failures or defects.

This is not root-cause analysis. Many experienced master black belts would suggest that root cause is approached after the fifth or sixth "why" question. The objective here is to use the system (in this case SAP software) and simple analytical tools such as Pareto charts, run charts, histograms, control charts, and so forth, to help answer the first and second "why did this fail" question, as well as the "which question" relating to SKU, customer, location, etc.

Why use the system? Many companies resort to manual research right away. Although it is sometimes unavoidable, starting with manual research generally reduces the frequency of analysis, further reinforces "not using the system," and limits the sample size for analysis. Most important, the objective is to refresh the defect analysis each time the metric is refreshed—be it daily, weekly, monthly, quarterly, or semiannually.

The Fowlers data teams caught on quickly and started to think about what they would call a defect for each metric, and to brainstorm the data that would be required to get to the desired conclusion. The expectation would be to present the actual metric performance, the definition of what was deemed a failure or "defective" for the metric, the various ways the data could be segmented, the first sort (sortation) of failures (largest to smallest), a second sort of failures at the next level (largest to smallest), and an estimate of the level of effort required to get to the final root cause (often considered the fifth sort of failures).

Sponsor Update Considerations

In advance of the review of content with the sponsors and steering team members, the Fowlers design team considered the following points:

- The project manager, David, should be the principal person consolidating and preparing the presentation.

- Prior to the review, the team would conduct informal one-on-one discussions with sponsors and steering team members who may be surprised by the content.

- Any rumors, objections, and other cultural issues that arise during the one-on-one meetings would be addressed in a design team meeting and should be discussed candidly.

- Speaking roles for design team members would be determined for the steering team review. In addition to David, design team members who did a lot of homework would be given a chance for exposure.

Overall, the objectives of this update are to review supply chain metric definitions and preliminary query data, conduct the competi-

tive requirements exercise with the entire steering team, review preliminary industry comparison sample and benchmark data, and
establish expectations for the steering team review on May 16.

The corporate controller, the vice president of sales and marketing of the food products group, the director of logistics, and the
director of customer service worked with David to prepare the first
update. The topics included:

- Conduct competitive priority exercise with the steering
  team—review design team results.
- Review preliminary supply chain metric data.
- Review preliminary benchmark data.
- Set expectations for the steering team review.

CHAPTER 6

Phase 2: Scorecards and Gap Analysis

▶ **May 16 and 23: Estimating the Size of the Opportunity**

After a proper debrief of highlights from the sponsor and steering team updates, the design team starts to work on the objectives for the next set of deliverables: review data on the scorecard and begin the process of calculating and assigning financial value to gaps.

The Scorecard Review

For a scorecard to be complete, it must include actual data for each metric, appropriate industry benchmarks, competitive requirements, and gap calculations. In a perfect world, scorecards would cascade neatly from the enterprise level to each business or from the enterprise level to each market segment. But that rarely happens, as the Fowlers design team learned.

As the review process took shape, the team discovered that courageous conversations were necessary to make sense of the data and focus the design effort. The first part of the meeting centered on the actual and benchmark columns.

Discussion of the enterprise scorecard (Table 6-1), led by

Table 6-1. Fowlers' enterprise scorecard.

Fowlers Inc.				Benchmark Data				
2-May-11	Performance Attribute or Category	Level 1 Performance Metrics	2010 Act	Parity 50th Percentile	Advantage 70th Percentile	Superior 90th Percentile	Parity Gap	Source
	Supply Chain Delivery Reliability	Perfect Order Fulfillment	50.5%	74.0%	81.0%	88.0%	–23.5%	SCORmark
External	Supply Chain Responsiveness	Order Fulfillment Cycle Time	15.0	10.0	6.50	3.0	–5.0	SCORmark
	Supply Chain Flexibility	Upside Supply Chain Flexibility	91.5	60	45.0	29	–31.5	SCORmark
	Supply Chain Cost	Cost of Goods	86.0%	68.5%	62.9%	52.9%	–17.5%	Hoovers
Internal		Supply Chain Management Cost	15.5%	9.5%	6.8%	3.9%	–6.0%	SCORmark
	Supply Chain Asset Management Efficiency	Inventory Days of Supply	91.3	73.5	64.8	22.6	–17.8	Hoovers

the corporate controller and director of logistics, considered three issues. First, although enterprise-wide customer-facing data indicated "below parity" performance, the aggregate data were not helpful in pinpointing the severity of some of the issues. The team agreed that, in order to understand the issues and the potential opportunity, it was necessary to *segment the reliability, responsiveness, and flexibility metrics* by (1) business group, (2) stock-keeping unit (SKU), and (3) customer.

A second issue had to do with the fact that balance-sheet data were available only at the corporate level; trying to precisely allocate that information back to the supply chains (as defined by the definition matrix) would have taken a major balance-sheet restructuring and countless hours of allocating. As a result, the team simply used *percent of sales to total* as a means to allocate inventory on the product group scorecards.

Third, and most important, the scorecard wasn't organized in the same way as were the supply chain competitive performance requirements. The scorecard was organized by business—because that's how the data existed. The supply chain requirements were determined by market/customer channel—because that represented the ideal situation the team wanted to create. Translating from the competitive requirements to the scorecard would be a challenge.

"You'll come up against more than one roadblock like this," the SCOR coach said. "We're not always going to have complete data or perfect alignment. What is your preference? Go back and do some more homework, or pick a direction to go forward?" The team was impatient, and a few minutes of conversation made it clear that there probably was no perfect solution. In the interest of moving forward, the team agreed to apply the priorities of the retail channel because it represented the operating unit's largest share of revenue.

Discussion led by David Able about the technology products group (Table 6-2), summarized three unique learning points and considered two compromises.

Table 6-2. Fowlers' technology products scorecard with competitive requirements.

Technology Products Group				Benchmark Data						
2-May-11	Performance Attribute or Category	Level 1 Performance Metrics	2010 Act	Parity 50th Percentile	Advantage 70th Percentile	Superior 90th Percentile	Parity Gap	Competitive Gap	Competitive Gap Analysis	Source
External	Supply Chain Delivery Reliability	Perfect Order Fulfillment	30.2%	74.0%	81.0%	88.0%	−43.8%	−57.8%		SCORmark
	Supply Chain Responsiveness	Order Fulfillment Cycle Time	11.0	10.0	6.50	3.0	−1.0	−4.5	$6,750,000	SCORmark
	Supply Chain Flexibility	Upside Supply Chain Flexibility	91.5	60	45.0	29	−31.5	−46.5		SCORmark
	Supply Chain Cost	Cost of Goods	63.6%	54.7%	44.3%	26.0%	−8.9%	NA	$40,050,000	Hoovers
		Supply Chain Management Cost	12.8%	9.5%	6.8%	3.9%	−3.3%	−3.3%	$14,850,000	SCORmark
Internal	Supply Chain Asset Management Efficiency	Inventory Days of Supply	60.5	20.4	8.9	0.0	−40.1	−40.1	$31,442,000	Hoovers

The first learning point was this: Although the decision to outsource manufacture of several products succeeded at achieving lowest unit cost, it drastically reduced the flexibility metric, which in turn affected inventory levels. The second learning point was that the new metrics on service reliability provided empirical evidence in support of complaints by customers that the company was "hard to do business with." The third learning point was that by assembling supply chain costs through the SCORmark, it became clear that material acquisition expenses outpaced all other cost increases. Inbound transportation, normally calculated as a cost of material, was isolated for all to see. The last learning point was similar in all business units: There was considerable opportunity to improve operating income by attacking supply chain costs, improving use of working capital, and better leveraging SAP functionality.

The technology products group's first necessary compromise focused on how to distribute the market/customer channel performance requirements onto the technology products scorecard. Like corporate, the technology products business team agreed to adopt the retail superior/advantage/advantage/parity/parity (SAAPP) priorities for its scorecard gap baseline.

The Scorecard Gap Analysis

The next item on the agenda is focused on completing the competitive gap analysis. The gap analysis occurs from both top down (this section) and bottom up, using our defect analysis (Chapter 7). The first step in the *top-down process* is to calculate the mathematical opportunity for each metric. This is done by calculating the parity gap and/or the competitive gap, and then subtracting actual performance for each metric from the benchmark number determined by the competitive requirement for the category.

If the gap analysis results in a negative number (bad), it means actual performance is less than the benchmark (e.g., the gap between an actual delivery performance of 78 percent and competitive requirements of 92 percent is -14). The next step is to translate each gap number into a profit potential; the most frequently used measure is operating income.

The calculations are straightforward for the internal metrics but can be subjective for customer-facing metrics. The basic calculation that the design team, and ultimately the business team, must agree on is the anticipated effect on revenue through improvements to delivery reliability, responsiveness, and flexibility. This is often more art than science, but there are some accepted approaches:

- *The Lost Opportunity Measure.* This calculates the revenue lost before order entry because of lack of availability of a product.
- *The Canceled Order Measure.* This measure calculates revenue lost after order entry because of canceled orders that result from poor delivery performance.
- *The Market Share Measure.* This measure attempts to project a revenue increase based on achieving competitive advantage in the customer-facing metric categories.

Because any approach will have its tradeoffs, just make sure to document the assumptions and details for the financial analysis and identify some of the steering team or business team members to help validate preliminary numbers.

In Fowlers' case, the design team agreed on the organization of the gap analysis itself, agreeing with the norm that all the opportunity dollars should be calculated using an operating income; this would allow the team to add up the numbers for the "opportunity" of the scorecard. Here are some other conclusions reached by the team based on the information in Table 6-2:

- All customer-facing metrics must be grouped, and "lost opportunity" and "canceled order" calculation methods must be used. The technology products group's 2010 revenue was $450,000,000; the design team's analysis showed that 1.5 percent of the group's sales were either not entered, cut from the order due to availability, or canceled due to poor response to unanticipated demand. The $6,750,000 was calculated by multiplying revenue times 1.5 percent.

♦ Cost of goods for 2010 was $286,200,000. An 8.9 percent gain was valued at $40,050,000.

♦ Ending inventory for 2010 was $47,437,000, representing about $784,100 per day. A 40.1–day improvement is equivalent to a $31,442,000 inventory reduction.

♦ Supply chain management cost for 2010 was $57,601,000. A reduction of 3.3 points is the equivalent of a $14,850,000 reduction in expenses.

CHAPTER 7

Phase 2: Defect Analysis

▶ **May 30 and June 6: Answering the Questions of Who, What, Where, When, and How Much and Then Telling the Steering Team**

The concept of defect analysis now becomes the central focus for the design team, along with preparing the first performance review of the supply chain for the steering team. Specifically, the team will define data points for each metric considered to be a failure; segment the data by product, location, customer, supplier, etc.; and then answer with system-generated data at as many levels of "why" questions as possible.

Defect Analysis

Initiated on April 25, the preliminary results of the defect analysis for each metric are now ready for review. As noted in the web-based meeting agenda, the stated expectation was for each team to present the actual metric performance; review the definition of what was deemed a failure or "defective," the various ways the data could be segmented, the first sort of failures (largest to smallest), and a second sort of failures at the next level (largest to smallest); and build an estimate of the level of effort to get to the final root cause—(often considered the fifth sort of failures).

Whereas the benchmark and competitive requirements (Chapter 6) provide a top-down means of estimating the performance improvement opportunity, the defect analysis is a more precise bottom-up method. In fact, if a decision needed to be made as to how much time is allocated to benchmarking versus thorough defect analysis, I would allocate one hour to benchmarking for every ten hours of defect analysis. It is the ultimate source for prioritizing projects and estimating benefits, as illustrated in the next phase.

The entire design team agreed that the hardest task was to use the system alone to generate the first- and second-level sorts. Most of the team was accustomed to using the manual research method on the most recent issue of the day. They all agreed that while the system's sorts may not be perfect, they were repeatable each time the metric performance was reported. The following were their findings.

Perfect Order Fulfillment

As documented on the technology products group scorecard (Table 6-2), the actual perfect order fulfillment is 30.2 percent, which means that 69.8 percent of Fowlers' orders failed to be perfect for some reason. The customer-facing metric team defined failures for perfect order fulfillment as sales orders not meeting the quantity, commit date, delivery quality, pricing, and documentation expectations of the customer, as documented in Fowlers' sales order, invoice, and shipment documents. The team was able to segment sales orders by customer number, ship-to location, Fowlers shipping location, manufacturing plant, supplier ship-from location, SKU line number, shipping lane, and freight provider.

The first and second sorts (Figure 7-1) of the failures included three primary categories and twelve subcategories:

1. Sales Order Shipped Not Complete
- Product Not Available at Initial Available-to-Promise Check
- Manufacturing Late

Figure 7-1. Perfect order fulfillment defect analysis, first and second sorts.

Perfect Order Fulfillment Defect Analysis	41.0%	15.0%	13.8%
First Sort Categories (Columns)	**Sales Order Shipped Not Complete**	**Sales Order Delivered Late**	**Sales Order in Late-Pay Status**
Second Sort Categories (Rows)			
Product Not Available at Initial Available-to-Promise Check	11.0%		
Manufacturing Late	5.0%		
Inventory Reallocated to Another Customer	5.0%		
Actual Demand Exceeded Forecast	20.0%		
Warehouse Shipped Late		2.5%	
Credit Hold		5.0%	
Order Released to Warehouse Too Late		2.0%	
Freight Provider Delivered Late		0.5%	
Customer Picked Up Late			4.0%
Price Discrepancy		5.0%	5.0%
Delivery Issue Including Quality			4.8%

- Inventory Reallocated to Another Customer
- Actual Demand Exceeded Forecast

2. Sales Order Delivered Late

- Warehouse Shipped Late
- Credit Hold
- Order Released to Warehouse Too Late
- Freight Provider Delivered Late
- Customer Picked Up Late

3. Sales Order in Late–Pay Status

- Customer Picked Up Late
- Price Discrepancy
- Delivery Issue Including Quality

Order Fulfillment Cycle Time

As documented in the technology products group scorecard, the actual order fulfillment cycle time (blended MTO and MTS) is 11. Failure definition for this metric was tricky. First, the team assembled a histogram of a sample of 224 orders (Figure 7-2). Second, the team needed to *define a failure*. Their competitive target was 6.5 days; if they chose that number, all but 48 orders failed. The team settled on nine days, better than parity and on the way to their competitive target. So, if the actual days were greater than nine, the sales order was deemed a failure. There were 97 failed orders in the sample. For each failed sales order, the team also looked at time subsegments as defined in the SCOR metric definition and compared the actual subsegment time to what was defined in the master data for expected lead time. They used this data as the second sort of failures (Figure 7-3). The team was able to use the same segmentation strategies as defined in perfect order fulfillment.

Upside Supply Chain Flexibility

As documented in the scorecard, the actual upside supply chain flexibility (averaged across all SKUs in the project scope) is 91.5

Figure 7-2. Order fulfillment cycle time histogram.

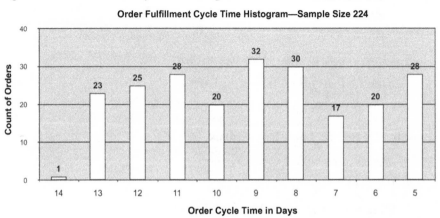

Figure 7-3. Order fulfillment cycle time defect analysis.

Order Fulfillment Cycle Time Defect Analysis	Defect Rate	Failed Orders	Target Days
Order Receipt to Order Confirmed	18.3%	41	1
Order Confirmed to Shipment Created	12.1%	27	2
Shipment Created to Order Picked	4.9%	11	1
Order Picked to Order Shipped	3.6%	8	1
Order Shipped to Order Delivered	4.5%	10	4

days. Failure definition for this metric included two parts: comparing actual to master data, and comparing master data to strategic requirement. First the team compared the overall actual stacked lead times of each SKU to the expected lead time as noted in the SKU master data. If the total actual days were greater than expected, the SKU was deemed a failure.

A second sort of this data took the analysis one step further. For each failed SKU, the team looked at time subsegments as defined in SCOR (including PLAN, SOURCE, and MAKE lead times) and compared the actual subsegment time to what was defined in the master data for expected lead time.

To compare the strategic requirement, the team used the histogram (Figure 7-4) of SKU total lead times; defined a targeted lead time–based competitive requirement; and defined as failures all SKUs above the target. They sorted the failures from highest to lowest in annual volume; this view of failures initiated a number of questions as to how to develop supply chain strategies that would make the macro supply chain more flexible to marketplace demand fluctuations. The team was able to segment upside supply chain flexibility data using the product hierarchy, bill of material, plant, DC location, volume, and sales and operations planning (S&OP) family groupings.

Figure 7-5 illustrates four part numbers that were strategic-

Figure 7-4. Upside supply chain flexibility histogram.

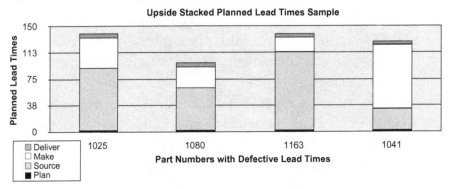

Figure 7-5. Strategic requirement failures by part number.

requirement failures. They were high-volume SKUs with lead times greater than 60 days (the parity requirement for U.S. Distributor Markets and U.S. Direct-to-Consumer Markets determined in the competitive requirements exercise).

Supply Chain Management Cost

As documented in the technology products group scorecard, the actual supply chain management cost is 12.8 percent cost-to-sales.

The defect analysis for this metric was a little more arbitrary than the previous three. The team members first developed a Pareto chart of supply chain costs (Table 7-1). They then defined failure modes for each category. As an example, failure modes for outbound transportation cost were defined as expedited freight, cost centers over budget, and routes that exceeded the expected cost per pound. The results gave the team a good indication of which process areas most affected cost-to-serve, and helped it visualize which failure modes

Table 7-1. Pareto chart of supply chain costs.

		2010 Supply Chain Management Cost	
Cum		57,601	
34.8%	34.8%	$20,033	Outbound Transportation Cost
57.2%	22.4%	$12,929	Finished Goods Warehouse Cost
70.9%	13.7%	$7,896	Inbound Transportation Cost
77.3%	6.4%	$3,694	Opportunity Cost
81.5%	4.2%	$2,401	Obsolescence Cost
84.6%	3.1%	$1,781	Supply Chain Finance Control Cost
87.5%	2.9%	$1,672	Purchasing Cost
89.8%	2.3%	$1,345	Customer Service Cost
91.5%	1.7%	$981	Supply Chain Application Cost
93.1%	1.6%	$946	Supply Planning Cost
94.6%	1.5%	$850	Supplier Quality Cost
95.7%	1.1%	$646	Shrinkage Cost
96.7%	1.0%	$562	Component Engineering and Tooling Cost
97.6%	0.9%	$504	Demand Planning Cost
98.4%	0.7%	$432	Raw Material Warehouse Cost
99.1%	0.7%	$403	IT Operational Cost for Supply Chain
99.6%	0.5%	$284	Accounts Receivable Cost
100.0%	0.4%	$242	Accounts Payable Cost

were making the biggest dent in gross profit. The team was able to segment metric data using the cost center hierarchy and S&OP defined business unit.

Inventory Days of Supply

As documented in the scorecard, the actual inventory days of supply (DOS) is 60.5 days. The defect analysis for this metric utilized both the classification (i.e., finished goods, work in progress, purchased finished goods, raw materials, packaging, etc.) and activity level as defined by customer, finance, and annual volume (i.e., A, B, C, D, Customer Liable, Excess, Shrink, and Obsolete). The team also determined that it needed to illustrate the defects using both inventory dollars ($) and days of supply. Defects were defined as:

All: Excess, Shrink, and Obsolete

  A: High-volume SKUs with DOS greater than 15

  B: Mid-volume SKUs with DOS greater than 30

  C: Lower-volume SKUs with DOS greater than 60

  D: Lowest-volume SKUs with DOS greater than 90

The results summarized where the most inventory dollars were invested and which SKUs were the poorest performing. The team was able to segment metric data using the product hierarchy, inventory classification, and S&OP defined business unit.

Planning for the First Team On-Site

The metric defect analysis sets the stage for the first on-site visit. As discussed in the project scheduling options, the first on-site with the team can focus on assembling the AS IS SCOR Level 3 processes diagram using the "staple yourself to an order" interview process. Alternatively, the first on-site may be the process diagram and brainstorm event initiating the next phase of the project: project portfolio development. Chapter 14 illustrates the techniques, instructions, and examples of the process analyses for either case.

The Steering Team Review

The initial focus on the agenda is for each assigned subteam to review its scorecard gap analysis, including revised assumptions, calculations, and feedback from validation resources. The goal is for the entire design team to achieve consensus for each metric on the total opportunity calculated on the scorecard. This review doubles as a dry run for a portion of the steering team review. As part of this review, each metric team must identify the design team member who will make the presentation. Do not underestimate the impact of a crisp, clear, and concise presentation delivered by the people who did the work. This review will be the first in which data that are presented may be contentious.

The agenda for this steering team *review* includes the following:

+ Competitive requirements
+ Scorecards
+ Gap analysis
+ Defect analysis
+ On-site plans for process analyses and brainstorm event

For Fowlers, the validation effort ultimately did not change the numbers or assumptions, but the process did reveal some change-management stages that would have to occur. The careful organization of the subteams for each metric and the choice of influential validation resources helped to manage the length of these stages as the wider Fowlers audience was introduced to "the numbers."

Change Management: Dealing with Denial

In the first stage, reactions are predictable as the design team's work spreads through the organization: The numbers are wrong; we aren't that bad.

The technology products business team members, when presented with the scorecard gap analysis, reacted predictably: They challenged the numbers. This happens in almost all projects. That's why it's important to have the right design team members from each of the product groups present to explain the data and have their validation resources sitting right next to them (as opposed to having a consultant). For people seeing the data for the first time, this builds confidence that the numbers are, in fact, reliable and quickly puts the focus on the issues.

Change Management: Placing Blame

The second reaction is to allocate blame, which is easier than taking responsibility for the results. Positioning design team members to share their personal perspectives on the gap analysis, and to review competitive performance facts, helps accelerate business unit leaders through this stage and moves them beyond the convenient catchall phrase: "But we're unique."

Change Management: Book the Numbers

The third reaction is to confuse acceptance of the analysis with actually having solved the problem. Agreeing on the opportunity does not improve anything. At this point, the business team is excited at the value of improving supply chain performance; based on benchmarks and competitive requirements, the numbers can add up fast. But it's too soon to start booking the savings in corporate forecasts and memos to the board. The real value of change will show up as part of the next phase.

In closing out the scorecard deliverable, the Fowlers project team members learned an important lesson—one that would be repeated again and again. They learned that the main goal of the analysis and validation effort is to manage change, not just to complete a deliverable. Their ability to quickly learn the *Supply Chain Excellence* process, understand the main idea of the deliverables, and then carefully transfer that knowledge to the wider Fowlers audience was critical. With advanced apologies to *Dilbert*, they realized the essential change management value of "greasing the skids," "getting others up to speed," and "touching base."

CHAPTER 8

Phase 3: Develop the Project Portfolio

▶ **June 16 and July 11–15: Building Shared Vision and the Project List**

What do the numbers 50, 20, 1,000, 15, and 3 have in common? They're the typical results of a successful project portfolio phase that is founded in data (defect analysis), experience (through the brainstorm event), and process (using SCOR).

Fifty can be the number of people who participate in a daylong brainstorm event. Twenty is how many disconnects or issues a typical person can come up with in an hour. A thousand is the number of disconnects or issues the whole team can generate in the same amount of time. Fifteen is a common number of projects that will be identified to eliminate the issues. Three is the percent of savings (relative to sales) that an average performing company will achieve by implementing these projects. In other words, a supply chain supporting $100 million in revenue can yield $3 million in gross opportunity savings split between revenue growth, productivity improvement, cost reduction, and asset turnover.

The objectives for the June 16 session are to plan and set the date for the brainstorm event (the week of July 11–15), conduct and document the on-site event, assemble the preliminary project portfolio, and begin to validate the metric impact.

Planning the Brainstorm Event

A well-planned brainstorm event takes the information collected and analyzed through the metric defect analysis and integrates it with employee experience and SCOR processes. The combination creates a positive feeling of teamwork, shared vision of the real issues, and confidence in the size of potential benefit. It also provides for greater stakeholder involvement in the project, giving extended team members and other invited participants a feeling of contribution, common understanding, and, ultimately, ownership of the changes.

There are six ingredients to a good brainstorming event:

1. An appropriate invitee list
2. Effective communication, including advance invitation, project overview, and instructions for event preparation
3. Organized brainstorm categories using the metric defect analysis and scorecard data
4. An appropriate venue
5. Predefined leadership roles for the design team that carry through from defect analysis to opportunity analysis
6. Documentation that captures the individual disconnects, problem groups, preliminary projects, and benefits estimate

Invitees

Select participants from among those people who are close to the day-to-day and week-to-week details of all facets of the movement of materials. Attempt to represent expertise from planning, sourcing, manufacturing, marketing and sales, warehouse, transportation, finance, and customer service. For the brainstorm event, the quantity of issues, with examples, is a critical factor. Don't reach too high in the organization; participants at higher levels of management have more trouble generating a detailed list and often cannot point to specific examples. The examples help drive the root cause analysis. Invitees can be considered part of the extended team listed in the project charter or invited guests. In either case, proper communication makes a big difference in the quality of the output.

Effective Communication

The invitation letter needs to clearly convey the purpose of the event, preparation instructions, and the basics of where, when, and so on. The invitation needs to be in participants' hands one to two weeks in advance; anything less gives the impression that the project is poorly planned and limits the quality of individual preparation. A project overview session conducted before the event provides participants with a wide-angle view of the project, including a status report on the key deliverables of the scorecard gap analysis and metric defect analysis. Further, it gives them a short tutorial on their homework assignment: understanding the defect analysis for their metric and coming up with 20 or so potential causes of the second sort of defects.

Many companies have automated collection of the disconnects using an Excel spreadsheet. The entire workbook might be labeled as *Disconnect Detail*. Each subsequent worksheet can be labeled with the participant's name. Filling out the worksheet (Figure 8-1) can be accomplished by using one file, with each person taking a turn, or by sending a copy of the file to each participant, with the files to be returned and consolidated prior to the event. The benefits of an electronic template are threefold. First, the disconnect IDs are easily referenced for future use using the "find" function in Excel. Second,

Figure 8-1. Sample disconnect detail worksheet.

Description for Disconnect or Issue—Example	Initials	ID	SCOR Process
Item master data-setup errors cause poor planning data to pass to plants and suppliers, resulting in poorer forecasts—item 093232	PB	1	EP.3
No visibility to customer demand—consumption rate leads to unpredicted spikes in demand, resulting in customer shortages—order 0930211	PB	2	P1.1
		3	
		4	
		5	
		6	
		7	
		8	
		9	
		10	
		11	
		12	
		13	
		14	
		15	
		16	
		17	
		18	
		19	
		20	

and more important, labels can be generated and applied to electronic sticky notes prior to the session, speeding up the process and making the output more legible. Third, the Excel worksheets are easy to share and review using a web-based meeting platform that allows you to share a desktop and provides file-sharing commands.

Organized Brainstorm Categories

Setting up brainstorm categories and teams in advance helps the participants stay focused, leverages their knowledge and experience, and ultimately provides better ideas about the causes of defects. Using the SCOR metrics from the scorecard as the brainstorm categories has proven to be the most effective way of organizing the teams and relating projects to benefit estimates.

The Appropriate Venue

The ideal venue is a large rectangular room with enough seating for all attendees. Tape the category titles (typed in large print on 8.5" × 11" paper), defect analysis (also in handout form), and scorecard data on the walls, spacing them evenly around the room. Many teams have used sticky notes, flip-chart paper, or butcher-block paper to capture the participants' ideas on causes for defects. Most of the time will be spent in small groups, frequently standing next to the collected items in a brainstorm category; therefore the activity does not work as well in a small conference room.

Predefined Leadership Roles

For the brainstorm event, design team members formalize their role in the knowledge-transfer process, transitioning from student to teacher. The project manager (or coach) serves as the master of ceremonies, reviewing the agenda and instructions for each step. He or she also serves as pace keeper, moderator of conflict, and general role model for everyone. Each design team member is assigned to lead (co-lead) a brainstorm category and facilitate the brainstorm steps. As will be discussed, this includes grouping similar issues by SCOR process, defining problem statements, estimating the weight of each problem, and assembling the preliminary project portfolio benefits. Be sure to keep those involved in each metric defect analysis together on the same team.

Documentation Approach

The project portfolio worksheet is the primary documentation tool for the next few chapters. It is prepared in advance with some of the fields being filled out in real time during the brainstorm event. Figure 8-2 illustrates the template and offers instructions defining the type of data required for each problem identified.

Based on our experience of facilitating more than 90 of these events, two lessons stand out. The first is that *preparation pays*. The more the participants understand about the metric and the first and second sorts of the defect analysis, the more effective they will be in identifying potential causes (answers to third-, fourth-, and fifth-level "why" questions).

The second lesson has to do with the process of *identifying the issues*; it can either be individual or group. The method that has been discussed so far has each participant identifying issues from his or her point of view, based on knowledge of the defect analysis and direct experience with issues. During the event, the team then groups individual ideas into a problem. The group method focuses on generating the problems through discussion and consensus, rather than generating individual issues.

Both methods have pluses and minuses. The first method has detail, and builds shared understanding and vision; the second builds consensus quickly. The risk with the first method is that it can take longer to eliminate redundancies. The risk with the second method is that it aggregates too quickly and misses some things. In addition, outspoken individuals can influence the output.

Conducting the Brainstorm Session

The day of the event, July 13, had finally arrived. The Fowlers brainstorm team included the entire design team; Chief Operating Officer Brian Dowell; product development managers; buyer/planners; customer service representatives; cost accountants; marketing

Figure 8-2. Sample project portfolio worksheet data definitions.

Metric	Level 1 Defect	Problem Statement Number	Problem Statement Phrase	Problem Statement Description	Individual Disconnect IDs	Level 2 Defect	Defect Rate	Problem Weight	Problem Impact	SCOR Process
Title of the brainstorm category is listed here; e.g., Perfect Order Fulfillment.	Label of the first sort of the Defect Analysis.	After the disconnects have been aggregated to problems, a number is assigned; e.g., 1.01, 1.02, etc.	Brief description of the problem using a noun, adjective, and verb.	A sentence or two that describes the problem. It must be relevant to all of the individual disconnects and include an example; e.g., part number, supplier, or customer.	The individual disconnect IDs are recorded here.	The label of the second sort of the Defect Analysis.	This is the overall defect rate for the Level 2 defect and is taken directly off the Defect Analysis Pareto chart.	This is the weight the team assigns to the problem. The sum of the problem weights within a Level 2 defect category can be no more than 100% and oftentimes less if not all the problems are known.	This is a calculated field multiplying the defect rate times the problem weight. This is the estimated impact to the SCOR Level 1 metric. For sure, this is the most difficult number to estimate.	Ideally, the team would have already attended a SCOR Framework class. Two or three team members will identify the SCOR element(s) where the problem occurs. SCOR Level 1, 2, or 3 can apply here.

analysts; material planners; focus factory managers; sales managers; product line managers from both the technology and food products groups (the latter was the next SCOR project candidate); functional experts for purchasing, order management, planning, distribution, and manufacturing from the corporate applications group; a transportation manager; an import/export manager; a warehouse manager from corporate logistics; a market research analyst; forecast analysts for each of the product families; and a business development manager from the corporate marketing group. In all, there were forty people on the list. As mentioned earlier, the design team agreed to use its six SCOR Level 1 metrics as the brainstorm categories. The rationale was to get the extended team thinking about the relationship of each issue to the defect data and why things failed.

The team took the coach's advice and stayed with the metric and defect analysis teams. Design team leaders were assigned. The planning director was assigned to be team leader for the perfect order fulfillment category. Order fulfillment cycle time was led by the purchasing director; the director of manufacturing oversaw discussion of upside supply chain flexibility; supply chain management cost was handled by the director of logistics/customer service; the corporate controller led the cost of goods discussion; and the vice president of sales and marketing for the food products group led inventory days of supply with help from the director of applications. David Able served as the master of ceremonies, and the coach was used as a floater among teams, helping them as needed.

The Fowlers Brainstorm Event

The agenda for the brainstorm event at Fowlers had five line items and looked like this:

1. *Introduction.* David reviewed the agenda, room layout, brainstorm categories (perfect order fulfillment, order fulfillment cycle time, upside supply chain flexibility, supply

chain management cost, cost of goods, and inventory days of supply), and associated defect analysis, and introduced the category leaders.

2. *Initial Brainstorm: 60 Minutes.* David facilitated the brainstorming activity, getting all those involved to place their 20 individual causes of Level 2 defects onto the appropriate metric charts. Brian insisted on the electronic method, through which participants had entered their data the previous week and labels were put on sticky notes prior to the session.

3. *Affinity Diagrams: 120 Minutes.* By using the predetermined team lists, David moved people to their appropriate metrics with their team leaders. They spent two hours reading through the ideas, grouping them into similar problems within each Level 2 defect category.

4. *Documentation: 120 Minutes.* The team was tasked with completing the project portfolio worksheet. The team leader had assigned a documentation role and had prepared the worksheet template ahead of time. This was the most difficult part of the day; gaining agreement on the problem definition and the metric impact of eliminating the issue spawned many passionate discussions.

5. *Question-and-Answer Review: 60 Minutes.* Fowlers' disconnect analysis session yielded 838 individual disconnects in six brainstorm categories, and an initial 62 problem groups with their own statements. David then facilitated a public question-and-answer review of each team's problem statements to conclude the event.

Figures 8–3A and 8–3B illustrate a portion of the perfect order fulfillment team's project portfolio worksheet. In Figure 8–3A, the planning director had already filtered the defect Level 1 column to isolate "sales order shipped not complete" and the Level 2 column to isolate "actual demand exceeded forecast." Twenty-seven individual disconnects for the defect were grouped into three problems: "Poor Visibility to External Customer Sales Plan," "Poor Forecast Management," and "New Product-Manufacturing Lead Time & Planning Not Aligned."

Figure 8–3B illustrates that if all three of these problems were eliminated, the *impact* to perfect order fulfillment would be 20 percent (7.4 plus 7.4 plus 5.2). The formula takes the defect rate times the problem weight for each problem. Problem weights are the most difficult part of the exercise. Everyone is uncomfortable. This is the moment of truth at which experience has to help the data arrive at

Figure 8-3A. Fowlers' perfect order fulfillment team project portfolio worksheet, filtered.

Metric	Level 1 Defect	Problem Statement Number	Problem Statement Phrase	Problem Statement Description	Disconnect IDs	Level 2 Defect	Defect Rate
Perfect Order Fulfillment	Sales Order Shipped Not Complete	7.01	Poor Visibility to External Customer Sales Plan	For 70% of our planning, we have a lack of visibility to the customer's demand or promotions resulting in no forecast and a 36% sales plan error.	321, 255, 193, 157, 142, 689, 703, 567, 234, 6, 59, 43	Actual Demand Exceeded Forecast	20.0%
Perfect Order Fulfillment	Sales Order Shipped Not Complete	7.02	Poor Forecast Management	SKU level forecasts are inaccurate due to minimal analysis, poor input from known sales and marketing input, and a lack of corporate discipline to support one forecast.	217, 26, 267, 469, 551, 242, 431, 181, 236, 308	Actual Demand Exceeded Forecast	20.0%
Perfect Order Fulfillment	Sales Order Shipped Not Complete	7.03	New Product-Manufacturing Lead Time & Planning Not Aligned	New Product Development items are not planned and released to production with enough lead time for production to meet customer orders/demand in units and timetable.	385, 142, 203, 257, 418	Actual Demand Exceeded Forecast	20.0%

Figure 8-3B. Fowlers' perfect order fulfillment team project portfolio worksheet, with demonstration of impact.

Problem Statement Phrase	Problem Statement Description	Level 2 Defect	Defect Rate	Problem Weight	Impact
Poor Visibility to External Customer Sales Plan	For 70% of our planning, we have a lack of visibility to the customer's demand or promotions resulting in no forecast and a 36% sales plan error.	Actual Demand Exceeded Forecast	20.0%	37.0%	7.4%
Poor Forecast Management	SKU level forecasts are inaccurate due to minimal analysis, poor input from known sales and marketing input, and a lack of corporate discipline to support one forecast.	Actual Demand Exceeded Forecast	20.0%	37.0%	7.4%
New Product-Manufacturing Lead Time & Planning Not Aligned	New Product Development items are not planned and released to production with enough lead time for production to meet customer orders/demand in units and timetable.	Actual Demand Exceeded Forecast	20.0%	26.0%	5.2%

a realistic number. Conservative realism is ideal; gross sandbagging is not helpful. As the weight is assigned, participants are usually already thinking about how to validate the numbers and document their assumptions. An important note: The sum of the problem weights within a Level 2 defect category can never be more than 100 percent. Less than 100 percent means that not all of the problems have been identified; more than 100 percent means the team is being overly optimistic.

Phase 3: Refine the Project Portfolio

▶ **July 11–15: Validating the Project Benefits and SCOR Processes**

There is no easy way to take the impacts and process areas documented in the brainstorm session and validate them at the level of confidence "to simply book the numbers" with leadership. But that's the challenge for this session: consolidating the 62 problems across six metrics into a concise set of SCOR process–based projects and finalizing impacts for each of them.

Consolidating Problems to Projects Using SCOR

Consolidating problems into projects is an easier task when someone is experienced with the filter and sort functions of Excel spreadsheets. The ability to organize a pivot table is even more useful.

In preparation for the first day's meeting, the project manager consolidates the problems from all of the metric worksheets by copying and pasting them onto a single worksheet called *Project Portfolio*. With the Auto Filter on, the consolidation process begins.

The first step in the process is to filter the heading "SCOR Process" by SCOR Level 3 process ID. At this point, some problems may have more than one SCOR Level 3 ID, such as P1.1, D1.3, and P1.3; and some may have Level 2 IDs, such as P1. In the case of multiple Level 3 IDs, gain consensus on which process area is the most influential relating to the problem. In the case of Level 2 IDs, try to pick the most influential Level 3 process relating to the problem.

The second step in the process is to assign an arbitrary project number to all the problems resulting from the SCOR Level 3 filter; for example, all problems containing the SCOR Level 3 ID D1.3 get assigned the same project number. This routine is repeated for each SCOR Level 3 ID until all problems have a project number assigned.

To be clear, after the filtering, all problem statements should have a project number. It is conceivable (though not probable) that there could be 184 projects—one for each SCOR Level 3 element: 20 for PLAN, 17 for SOURCE, 22 for MAKE, 52 for DELIVER, 26 for RETURN, and 47 for ENABLE.

The focus for the next level of filtering, called *Process Similarity*, again uses the field called SCOR Process. This time the team uses a custom filter containing a SCOR Level 2 ID (i.e., S1, M2, P1, or D3). For this filter, the team attempts to consolidate projects based on process scope. For example, a filter using S1 may yield five projects—one each for S1.1, S1.2, S1.3, S1.4, and S1.5. There are at least *four factors* that influence project consolidation within a SCOR Level 2 process. The *first* is the physical location of where the process occurs. For example, S1.2, S1.3, and S1.4 (receiving, quality assurance, and "put-away") are typically carried out in the raw material warehouse and therefore are candidates for consolidation.

The *second* factor is the function or functions performing the process. For example, if your suppliers drop-ship their products to your customer's warehouse, purchasing may not only have to schedule the product but also enter the receipt transaction in the system when the shipment is physically received by the customer warehouse. In that case, S1.1 and S1.2 would be candidates for consolidation. The *third* factor is the degree of impact. If improving the scheduling process with suppliers accounts for 50 percent of the inventory benefit in the portfolio, the degree of effort and focus may warrant isolating the process with only one project. Likewise, consolidation is good if the benefit for each process is small but when added together they create a significant impact.

A *fourth* factor, consolidating plan projects, requires one more decision: horizontal vs. vertical grouping. For example, a frequent horizontal consolidation involves grouping P4.1, P4.2, P4.3, and P4.4 into a project called *distribution requirements planning*; or grouping P3.1, P3.2, P3.3, and P3.4 into a project called *master production scheduling*. Another horizontal grouping could involve grouping all P4, P3, and P2 processes into a project called *tactical planning*.

A common vertical grouping that focuses on improving capacity planning (both long term and near term) and scheduling and might include P1.2, all P3 processes, and M1.1. The decision for vertical vs. horizontal grouping sometimes can be as much art as science. Factors that influence a vertical grouping include linking rough-cut planning to scheduling, forecasts to available inventory at distribution centers, and annual volume commitments of suppliers to near-term purchase order releases. The main factors that influence a horizontal grouping are synchronizing customer orders, manufacturing schedules, and planned supplier receipts.

The focus of the next filtering step is called *strategic similarity*, which attempts to consolidate projects across the strategies of *make-to-stock, make-to-order, and engineer-to-order*. This custom filter uses an "or" statement in an effort to identify projects within the same process but in another strategy. For example, using the custom filter "contains P2, S1 or S2 or S3" will yield projects containing any of the SOURCE-related projects. The team would use the same four grouping strategies discussed in the preceding paragraphs.

The last filtering step, called *ENABLE*, again uses the SCOR Process field. This time the team uses the custom auto filter containing "E." This leaves all problem statements that are connected to some form of enabling process.

ENABLE filters can go three directions. First, often they are *grouped across the Enable process categories* EP.3, ES.3, EM.3, and ED.3 and may be consolidated into a project focused only on master data accuracy—including planning item data, source list, routings and recipes, and customer list. Second, they are often *grouped vertically with their associated planning and execution processes*. For example, a project focused on P1 (sales and operations planning) may also include EP.1, EP.3, EP.4, and EP.10. Third, if the scope is big enough, ENABLE elements *can be left as individual projects*. For example, EP.7 may be the process that includes an overall physical network evaluation using a sophisticated logistics engineering tool.

Figure 9-1 is the result of the Fowlers P1.1 filter. The team discussed each of the three problems and agreed to consolidate 7.01 and 7.02 into Project 1, and put 7.03 into another—Project 6—already identified and associated with ED.7, manage product life cycle.

Validating the Problem Weight

As already stated at least once, the hardest task to date is validating the problem weights, which were estimates based on team experience during the brainstorm event. These problem weights have the largest influence on the projected size of the benefit pool—and therefore are of the highest interest to the steering team.

Validating the problem weight follows a four-step process:

1. Collect a small random sample of data focusing on instances of the Level 2 Defect;

Figure 9-1. Fowlers' problem validation P1.1 filter.

Metric	Level 1 Defect	Problem Statement Number	Problem Statement Phrase	Problem Statement Description	Level 2 Defect	Impact	SCOR Process	Project Number
Perfect Order Fulfillment	Sales Order Shipped Not Complete	7.01	Poor Visibility to External Customer Sales Plan	For 70% of our planning, we have a lack of visibility to the customer's demand or promotions resulting in no forecast and a 36% sales plan error.	Actual Demand Exceeded Forecast	7.4%	P1.1 EP.3	1
Perfect Order Fulfillment	Sales Order Shipped Not Complete	7.02	Poor Forecast Management	SKU level forecasts are inaccurate due to minimal analysis, poor input from known sales and marketing input, and a lack of corporate discipline to support one forecast.	Actual Demand Exceeded Forecast	7.4%	P1.1	1
Perfect Order Fulfillment	Sales Order Shipped Not Complete	7.03	New Product-Manufacturing Lead Time & Planning Not Aligned	New Product Development items are not planned and released to production with enough lead time for production to meet customer orders/demand in units and timetable.	Actual Demand Exceeded Forecast	5.2%	P1.1 ED.7	6

2. Conduct root cause analysis for each instance;

3. Compare results to initial problem weight estimates;

4. Adjust accordingly.

The Fowlers perfect order fulfillment team started its validation effort by defining a query to extract sales-order data for the last forecasted month. For each item on these sales orders, members compared the forecast to the actual order volume and filtered for those items that were a part of Level 2 Defect, *actual demand exceeded forecast*. The good news is that the 20 percent overall rate used for the brainstorm event was validated.

To validate the 37 percent estimate surrounding *Poor Visibility to External Customer Sales Plan*, the team sorted the items by customer where order volume exceeded forecast. They found that 32 customers were involved. Of those, only five were providing some kind of forecast, planogram, sales plan, and/or point-of-sale data. For an additional seven customers, there had been a desire to gather demand data but none was being provided. This group of 12 customers represented 25 percent of the sample size. The team recommended changing the problem weight from 37 percent to 25 percent, changing the overall impact from 7.4 percent to 5 percent.

To validate the 26 percent estimate surrounding *New Product-Manufacturing Lead Time & Planning Not Aligned*, the team focused on items for the twenty non-strategic customers. New products were defined as any part number introduced in the previous six months. This filter isolated 20 percent of all orders in which demand for new items exceeded forecast. The team recommended changing the problem weight from 26 percent to 20 percent, changing the overall impact from 5.2 percent to 4 percent.

To validate the 37 percent estimate surrounding *Poor Forecast Management*, the team analyzed the remaining items (55 percent of the total) that were not new and were not part of the strategic customers' order count. The team refined the criteria to identify items where the best statistical model, for some reason, had not been used. This filter isolated 15 percent of the orders that were characterized by low-volume items. The team recommended changing the problem weight from 37 percent to 15 percent, changing the overall impact from 7.4 percent to 3 percent. Figure 9-2 illustrates the results of the validation for this single Level 2 Defect category.

As illustrated, the team changed the problem statement for Poor Forecast Management to *Poor Forecast Model*. It also changed the weights as specified in this section. The overall impact now totaled 12 percent. The team also acknowledged that the remaining 40 percent of the instances in which an item's order volume exceeded forecast was in a category of "other"—which it did not have time to analyze. The team proceeded in the next week with this validation method for every Level 2 Defect for each of the six metrics considered in the brainstorm. The result of the effort was a first view of the technology products group project portfolio summary (Figure 9-3)—which would be the first subject on the agenda for the next session.

Figure 9-2. Fowlers' poor forecast management Level 2 validation.

Problem Statement Phrase	Problem Statement Description	Level 2 Defect	Defect Rate	Problem Weight	Impact	SCOR Process	Project Number
Poor Visibility to External Customer Sales Plan	For 70% of our planning, we have a lack of visibility to the customer's demand or promotions resulting in no forecast and a 36% sales plan error.	Actual Demand Exceeded Forecast	20.0%	25.0%	5.0%	P1.1 EP.3	1
Poor Forecast Model	Poor SKU level statistical models were used to generate demand plans.	Actual Demand Exceeded Forecast	20.0%	15.0%	3.0%	P1.1	1
New Product-Manufacturing Lead Time & Planning Not Aligned	New Product Development items are not planned and released to production with enough lead time for production to meet customer orders/demand in units and timetable.	Actual Demand Exceeded Forecast	20.0%	20.0%	4.0%	P1.1 ED.7	6

Figure 9-3. Fowlers' technology products group project portfolio summary, first draft.

Project Number	Project Phrase	Project Description	Revenue ($)	Perfect Order Fulfillment (%)	Order Fulfillment Cycle Time (days)	Upside Supply Chain Flexibility (days)	Total Supply Chain Management Cost ($)	COGS ($)	Inventory ($)
		Baseline	$450,000,000	30.2%	11.0	91.5	$57,601,000	$286,200,000	$47,437,000
1	Improve Demand Management and Forecasting	This project will improve poorly defined practices, underutilized modeling techniques, and untrained personnel.		8.0%					$1,660,000
2	Optimize Supply Management Practices	This project will focus on enabling and execution of tactical processes with targeted suppliers.				5.0		$5,000,000	$1,550,000
3	Improve SAP Utilization	This project will focus on scaling up more effective and efficient data warehouse capability, and improve the business units' utilization of the PP and MM reporting.					$1,350,000		
4	Improve Data Integrity	This project will define a master data management process and correct errors in supplier, item, and customer master data.		5.0%	2.0	7.5			
5	Improve Supplier Flexibility	This project will focus on developing vendors' capability to respond to near-term demand fluctuations for source-to-stock and source-to-order items.				15.0	$1,350,000	$2,500,000	$1,320,000
6	Implement Formal Product Life Cycle Management Process	This project will design, develop, and implement an integrated management process for all phases of a product's life cycle, from introduction through commercialization to retirement.		4.0%		7.5		$5,000,000	$2,500,000

(continues)

Figure 9-3. (continued)

#	Project	Description							
7	Engineer an Integrated Tactical Planning Process	This project will design, develop, and implement effective and efficient tactical planning processes to help manage the short-term horizon balancing customer orders, stocking levels, replenishment orders to factories, and purchase orders to suppliers.		5.0%	1.0		$1,350,000	$2,500,000	$1,000,000
8	Implement Sales and Operations Planning	This project will implement a Sales and Operations Planning process integrating demand and supply planning with business plans and reconciliation to financial objectives.	$4,500,000	25.0%			$3,375,540	$1,182,000	$4,400,000
9	Improve the Efficiency and Effectiveness of the Physical Supply Chain Network	This project will focus on short- and long-term physical network strategy improving cycle time, transportation and warehouse spend, and align long-term capacity requirements.			-4.0		$5,400,000		$1,650,000
10	Tighten Up Order Management Discipline	This project will cover entry errors, EDI errors, and business rules from inquiry and quote through order entry and inventory allocation.		15.0%	2.0		$540,000		$500,000
11	Establish Formal Return Management	This project will define and implement a reverse logistics processes from goods movement to policy to the authorization process.					$1,350,000		$660,000
12	Eliminate Poor Inventory Control Practices	This project will focus on defects that relate to inventory record accuracy, shrinkage, and cycle counting.		2.5%					$1,660,000
		Benefit	$4,500,000	64.5%	1.0	35.0	$14,715,540	$16,182,000	$16,900,000
		Projected Performance Level	$454,500,000	94.7%	10.0	56.5	$42,885,460	$270,018,000	$30,537,000

Phase 3: Opportunity Analysis

► **July 11–15: Due Diligence for the Project List**

Three percent profit improvement to the sales value of the supply chain: As described in Chapter 1, that's the rule-of-thumb opportunity before the data are prepared (read: sanitized) for presentation to executives and the board. For every $100 million in revenue, that means an opportunity for an extra $3 million in earnings. This gem is worth repeating.

Where any company comes in against this rule, however, depends on its distance from parity on six key metrics: revenue, perfect order fulfillment, order fulfillment cycle time, upside supply chain flexibility, cost of goods, and total supply chain management cost. The more of these metrics to which a company performs at or better than parity, the more likely it is that the discovery and analysis process will yield opportunity of approximately 1.5 percent. Companies that perform below parity with respect to these metrics typically will find opportunities in excess of that amount—up to 4.5 percent.

Depending on how experienced design team members are at the budgeting process, the opportunity assessment will range from simple to mind-bending. The objectives of this last session in the July 11 to 15 on-site are to create, refine, and prioritize the weights and

129

impact analyses for each of the projects in the portfolio (Figure 9-3), and prepare for the third formal steering team review.

Summarizing the Opportunity

The objective for this portion of the session is to educate the team about the process of finalizing the project benefits through validating weights and impacts, documenting important assumptions, and beginning to think about implementation scope, sequence, and resources.

The final validation process follows six principles.

♦ *Principle One.* At a minimum, the subteams must, again, revisit the problem weights and the defect analysis with a critical view of the validation data, sample size, and relevancy.

♦ *Principle Two.* Factor out the effect of forecasted growth by assuming constant revenue for the financial period; usually savings are annualized. If the sponsor is willing, it's acceptable to include the profit improvement from revenue growth.

♦ *Principle Three.* Be realistic in the savings estimates; the steering team and ultimately the executive team should add the appropriate safety buffer to the numbers, observing the doctrine of "under-promise and over-deliver." As stated previously, conservative realism is normal; gross sandbagging is not helpful at this point.

♦ *Principle Four.* Document all assumptions behind the problem weight estimates and resulting impacts. This is the most important principle; any push-back by the steering team typically has more to do with the assumptions than the numbers.

♦ *Principle Five.* Identify finance and other resources that can objectively test or spar with the numbers and assumptions—before the estimates are shared with the steering team.

 ♦ *Principle Six.* Identify what type of savings this project will have: revenue growth, cost reduction, productivity improvement, or cost avoidance.

The Project Opportunity Worksheet

Each project requires some form of a spreadsheet (Table 10-1). The first section—*project phrase, project number, and project description*—is taken from the preliminary project portfolio. The first column is taken from the revenue, cost of goods sold, and supply chain management cost metrics. The columns under 2012, 2013, 2014, and 2015 are where the team needs to enter estimated savings recorded as a negative number for costs and a positive number for revenue. The bottom line—*operating income/economic value added impact*—simply adds the absolute value of *total cost of sales* benefits to *total supply chain management cost* benefits. The most frequent question from design teams at this point is how to portray project savings over multiple years. There is only one answer to this: It depends!

The finance and executive leadership teams will have the answer. The most common guideline is to count only new savings to be recorded in each year. To illustrate, let's use the inbound transportation example from Table 10-1 of cost savings over four years. Year one nets $110,100, or 10 percent of the total from savings in the western region; years two and three net another $275,300 or twenty-five percent each in savings in the central and eastern regions; and year four nets $440,400, or 40 percent in savings, by focusing on imports. By using the *new savings* guideline, the four-year total is $1,101,100.

The assumptions are the most important part of this exercise. There's no magic in assembling a good one. Each metric *category* (row) that shows benefit gets its own statement of assumption. It could include an item number or numbers by type (i.e., raw mate-

Table 10.1. Project Opportunity Analysis

	Project Phrase:	Implement Sales and Operations Planning				
	Project Number:	8				
	Project Description:	This project will implement a Sales and Operations Planning process integrating demand and supply planning with business plans and reconciliation to financial objectives.				
		YEAR OF IMPACT				
		2012	**2013**	**2014**	**2015**	
Revenue		$450.0	$1,125.0	$1,125.0	$1,800.0	**1**
Cost of Sales						
	Labor					
	Material	−$295.5	−$591.0	−$295.5	—	**2**
	Indirect					
Total Cost of Sales		−$295.5	−$591.0	−$295.5	$0.0	
Total Supply Chain Management Cost						
	Order Management Cost					
	Customer Service Cost					
	Finished Goods Warehouse Cost	−$79.0	−$79.0	−$79.0	−$79.0	**3**
	Outbound Transportation Cost					
	Material (Product) Acquisition Cost					
	Purchasing Cost					
	Raw Material Warehouse Cost					
	Supplier Quality Cost					
	Component Engineering and Tooling Cost					
	Inbound Transportation Cost	−$110.1	−$275.3	−$275.3	−$440.4	**4**
	Planning and Finance Cost					
	Demand Planning Cost					
	Supply Planning Cost					

	Supply Chain Finance Control Cost					
	Inventory Carrying Cost					
	Opportunity Cost	−$85.7	−$85.7	−$137.0	−$34.2	6
	Obsolescence Cost	−$240.0	−$240.0	−$240.0	−$240.0	5
	Shrinkage Cost					
	Taxes and Insurance Cost					
	IT Cost for Supply Chain					
	Supply Chain Application Cost					
	IT Operational Cost for Supply Chain					
Total Supply Chain Management Cost		−$514.8	−$680.0	−$731.3	−$793.6	
Operating Income/ EVA Impact		$1,260.3	$2,396.0	$2,151.8	$2,593.6	

rial, work in progress, finished goods, or returns); estimated volume, calculated using such data as market share, geographic segment, unit volume, or unit forecast; cost or revenue impact, calculated by cost per unit or margin per unit; and/or delivery reliability, lead time, and necessary business conditions.

There are different kinds of assumptions. One kind describes the impact of cost reduction or productivity improvement in direct or indirect categories. Another describes the revenue impact of delivery reliability through fewer lost opportunities or pure growth. Yet another type of assumption describes the working-capital impact of lead time and delivery performance, as measured in inventory, payables, and/or receivables.

As an example, in addition to the service and inventory improvements documented on the project portfolio, the Fowlers team validated assumptions for the major income statement opportunities that would result from Project 8 (Figure 9-3). The team aligned these opportunity assumptions with the numbers in the last column as summarized in the following:

1. By improving perfect order fulfillment by 25 percent, Fowlers would reduce lost opportunity orders, validated as 1.5 percent of total orders, or 18,000 orders missed on account of no immediate material availability or cancellations. At $250 average value per order, the four year revenue opportunity calculates to $4,500,000. *Metric: Revenue.*

2. Achieve a 1 percent decrease in price per part for the ability to provide accurate forecast data to all suppliers. At $1,182,000 material cost, that equates to a $1,182,000 cost decrease. *Metric: COGS.*

3. Have inventory immediately available. This will reduce 10 percent of the amount of time spent per order picking multiple times, expediting inventory transfer orders, and providing phone status to customer service representatives. At $4.40 warehouse cost per order with 71,818 orders per year, this equates to $316,000. *Metric: Total Supply Chain Management Cost.*

4. Reduce unplanned changes to purchase orders, decreasing the number of instances of expedited transportation within lead time. Sixty-five percent of purchase orders are currently expedited, incurring 35 percent higher inbound transportation costs than necessary. Inbound transportation totals $7,896,000; improvement would reduce cost by $1,101,100. *Metric: Total Supply Chain Management Cost.*

5. Reduce the annualized rate of accrual for obsolescence by $240,000. *Metric: Total Supply Chain Management Cost.*

6. Reduce working inventory for low-volume products equivalent to 9.2 percent decrease of overall inventory value. For the balance-sheet measure of inventory this is equivalent to $20,000,000; for the economic value add (EVA) measure of inventory this is equivalent to $2,000,000. *Metrics: Inventory, and Total Supply Chain Management Cost as illustrated in Table 10-1.*

Identify Further Validation Resources

As the team tweaks the assumptions, it also reviews the list of names of people involved in building them and considers additional validation resources.

There are two reasons to add more names. First, it may be necessary to add more content expertise about details to further refine assumptions. For example, one might include a marketing research analyst to help refine market share and volume numbers or a cost accountant to calculate the impact of accruals or balance sheet changes. Second, adding these subject matter experts gives them extra time to digest the information before deciding to stand behind the numbers and therefore widen support for the project. It is normal for the numbers from the preliminary project portfolio to change; as the team digs deeper into the numbers and assumptions behind them, confidence will grow. Now is the time when documentation discipline will start to pay off. The opportunity spreadsheets and the project metric summary are two of the most important items to keep accurate. For example, teams often need to add *Revenue Impact* to the project metric summary and adjust the benefit dollars as they are refined. The next session initiates implementation with time spent assembling implementation charters for each of the projects and putting them in an implementation plan. With the path to the next week clear, the team turns toward preparing for steering team review two.

Conducting Steering Team Review Number Three

Prepare and conduct steering team review number three with the following agenda items:

- Review project portfolio
- Review project benefits, assumptions, and validation logic
- Review brainstorm event highlights

Phase 4: Lay Groundwork to Implement Projects

▶ **Mapping Out the Details and Portfolio Implementation Plans**

Who, what, when, where, and how are the questions the team faces now that the "how much" question has been answered. The challenge in preparing to initiate this next phase is to complete implementation project charters and prioritize launch dates based on effort, impact, and dependencies, and then implement the projects. On the Fowlers technology products group schedule, the implementation timeframe officially starts August 1, 2011. The meeting format would be project dependent but includes periodic face-to-face meetings, remote web-based conferences, and site visits where necessary.

Implementation Project Charters

An implementation project charter is intended to be the one document that has all the answers. It begins with the project title and description. The *project title* is a short phrase describing the action and process targeted for change.

The *project description* attempts to identify known changes and best practices that will guide the project.

The *problem statement* summarizes the phrase from the brainstorm event and other relevant individual disconnects that accurately describe the issues at hand.

Project objectives include known outcomes that need to occur for the project to be considered successful and for benefits to be realized. These will include impact or changes regarding trading partners, the organization, processes, people, technology, goals, and metrics.

Scope potentially specifies the product, customer, supplier, process, metric, system (data), and organizational functions that will be used to identify the future solution. Scope may be equal to the one defined in Phase 1; it also is common to refine the scope yet again knowing that the implementation will scale as needed.

Potential issues and other assorted *barriers* are presented in a bulleted list in the implementation project charter that attempts to highlight known "show stoppers"—things that will prevent the project from successful implementation. For example, a project aimed at implementing a good forecasting process requires focus from a person who can manage the assembly of a forecast, and it requires a good tool that can provide a statistical model. Potential issues and barriers to this project could be the organization's unwillingness to assign or hire a forecaster and/or the investment probability of buying an adequate statistical forecasting tool. The concept is to list only the big issues rather than provide an exhaustive narrative of every potential barrier.

The benefit section simply copies and pastes, from the project portfolio, the summary of the project's impact from each metric. The detailed opportunity analysis, with assumptions, is attached as an appendix to the implementation project charter.

The action plan steps offer project milestones. There are 13 of these:

1. Identify and approve project resource plan
2. Establish project schedule, including informal kickoff date
3. Review project charter, background, and expectations with project team
4. Develop baseline for metrics selected as in-scope
5. Conduct AS IS Level 3 and Level 4 process gap analysis (synchronizing with any previous analysis)
6. Develop action plans to close "quick hit" gaps
7. Assemble TO BE Level 3 and Level 4 process based on leading practice
8. Develop and approve solution design storyboard
9. Build and test solution
10. Pilot and verify solution
11. Roll out solution to project scope and evaluate metric impact
12. Define process control measures
13. Scale implementation to targeted supply chains in the definition matrix

Implementation resources specify by name the project champion or sponsor from the steering team; the project leader, which is generally a priority time role; subject matter expert; and team members. The subject matter expert role can vary depending on the scope of the project. The role could be a software expert if the primary idea is to roll out system functionality. It could be a best-practice expert if process is the primary idea. It could be two roles if process and tools need to work together. The team-member role can be somewhat complicated. The analytical role may be straightforward, but the implementation may change the nature of the team members' jobs. For example, implementing sales and operations planning in an organization that doesn't yet have such a process will include the new roles of demand and supply planners on the project team—which will also define how these individuals do a significant part of their jobs in the pilot and beyond.

Schedule essentially puts dates against the milestones in the preceding list, and can be represented in a list form or a Gantt chart managed by the leader. The typical rhythm of an implementation project is six months, with the team meeting each week—even if the meeting's duration is short. The first month addresses milestones 1 through 4, and the second month completes milestones 5 through 7. The third month has two parallel activities, closing the actions in milestone 6 and completing milestones 8 through 10. The fourth, fifth, and sixth months focus on milestones 11 and 12 in a continuous improvement loop, and the sixth month completes milestone 13. Rollout speed is dependent on the complexity of the solution, but can range from one month to six months. In most cases, a well-run project takes no longer than twelve months to move through all thirteen milestones. The portfolio itself typically covers three to four waves over a three-year span (Figure 11-1).

Figure 11-1. Fowlers' high-level implementation time line.

Wave	2011			2012				2013				2014			
	Q2	Q3	Q4	Q1	Q2	Q3	Q4	Q1	Q2	Q3	Q4	Q1	Q2	Q3	Q4
1															
2															
3															
4															

Develop

Pilot

Roll Out

Excerpts from the Fowlers Project 7 Implementation Charter—Engineer an Integrated Tactical Planning Process

Project Description

This project will design, develop, and implement effective and efficient tactical planning processes to help manage overall capacity, customer orders, stocking levels, replenishment orders to factories, and purchase orders to suppliers. Best-practice models suggest three tiers of planning including long-term capacity and inventory planning (4–18 months), master scheduling (3–13 weeks), and plant scheduling (1–14 days). The project would also develop master data maintenance policies and programs, and assess and recommend changes to the supply chain organization.

Problem Statement

The planning and scheduling processes are not integrated between the PLAN and MAKE and DELIVER processes, nor with SAP utilization of functionality, which creates a void between the sales forecast, inventory replenishment, sales order commitments to customers, and the plant scheduling processes. In addition, capacity management cannot be performed in the system due to inaccurate master data fields (i.e. routes, run rates, and yield). Last, the organizational structure does not facilitate productive analysis and response to issues and, more important, also does not facilitate effort and attention to proactive supply planning.

Project Objectives

1. Produce an achievable production schedule (M1.1)
2. Develop effective rough-cut capacity plans (P1.2 and P1.3)
3. Comprehend inventory and customer demand in the master schedule (P3)
4. Align the production schedule to the master production plan (M1.1)
5. Update and maintain production master data (EM3)
6. Develop policies to support an effective production plan (EM1)
7. Develop process measures to drive accountability (EP2 and EM2)
8. Measure and analyze production schedule adherence (M1.3)
9. Recommend organizational changes to support future-state process

Scope of the Project

- Product and Channel: Top SKUs that contribute 50% of sales in retail channel
- Process: P1.2, M1.1, P3
- System: PP, MM, and SD

- Metrics
  - Manufacturing schedule adherence: weekly
  - Master plan adherence: monthly
  - Rough-cut capacity: monthly
  - Master data accuracy: weekly (rotating)
  - Percent of target stock: weekly

Potential Issues & Barriers

1. Approval to hire additional resources into the supply chain organization.
2. Resistance from business to change the supply chain organizational structure.

Benefits Summary

- The project benefits are summarized in Figure 11-2.

Action Plan (Milestones)

1. Identify and approve project resource plan
2. Establish project schedule, including informal kickoff date
3. Review project charter, background, and expectations with project team
4. Develop baseline for metrics selected as in-scope
5. Conduct AS IS Level 4 process gap analysis
6. Develop action to close "quick hit" gaps
7. Assemble TO BE Level 3 and Level 4 process based on leading practice
8. Develop and approve solution design storyboard
9. Build and test solution
10. Pilot and verify solution
11. Roll out solution to project scope and evaluate metric effect
12. Define process control measures
13. Scale implementation to targeted supply chains in the definition matrix

Implementation Resources

Champion

Leader

Subject matter expert

Team members

Figure 11-2. Project 7 benefits.

Project #	Project Phrase	Project Description	Perfect Order Fulfillment (%)	Order Fulfillment Cycle Time (days)	Total Supply Chain Management Cost ($)	COGS ($)	Inventory ($)
		Baseline	30.2%	11.0	$57,600,000	$286,200,000	$47,437,000
7	Engineer an Integrated Tactical Planning Process	This project will design, develop, and implement effective and efficient tactical planning processes to help manage the short-term horizon, balancing customer orders, stocking levels, replenishment orders to factories, and purchase orders to suppliers.	5.0%	1.0	$1,350,000	$2,500,000	$1,000,000

Phase 4: From Portfolio Development to Implementation

▶ **Organizing Supply Chain Improvement as Part of Daily Life: Faster, Better, and Cheaper**

The finish line! Or is it? After one of the toughest graduate classes at the University of Minnesota, Prof. Richard Swanson said, as he handed out the final exam, "True learning is a painful experience . . . I can see that all of you have learned a great deal in this course."

As the last of the students left the room at the end of the hour, he offered one more piece of advice: "Remember," he said, "the road never ends. It's the journey that must be your home."

In the first and second editions, this chapter was at the end of the book. In the third edition it finds its way to the middle. For the benefit of those who have followed the *Supply Chain Excellence* method since it was introduced publicly in 2003, we offer the following five reasons for this significant change. *First*, as with all operational improvement initiatives, *faster, better, cheaper is a driver of change.* To compete in a worldwide marketplace, the rate of supply chain performance improvement needed to increase; 17 weeks is too much time just to arrive at a list. The "new and improved" timeline of *Supply Chain Excellence* gets the project team to a validated project portfolio 25 percent faster, and to initiating the first project 50 percent faster. *Second*, increasingly *global projects* necessitated a change in the schedule. It is hard to meet every week in a face-to-face environment when the team needs to travel from several locations around the world. There certainly are milestones at which team members need to look each other in the eye, but for many other meetings, using teleconferencing technology is appropriate. *Third*, companies that had used the method more than five times were desiring to make *Supply Chain Excellence* an *implementation method*, not simply portfolio identification. This is because they were trying to eliminate loss of momentum between final approval of the portfolio and the approval to begin the first project; in cases requiring system investments, this could be six months or more. They also sought to minimize knowledge loss between the design team and the implementation teams—which also cost time.

The *fourth* reason the timeline has changed is to enable centralized supply chain leaders to *send a stronger message* to the business units (their customers) that the job wouldn't be finished until the needle was moved on key supply chain metrics. In earlier efforts, *Supply Chain Excellence* was "sold" in two parts: identify the project list and then implement it. While portfolio development was effective, attention waned at times during the implementation. The nuance is that the "new and improved" *Supply Chain Excellence* is "sold" on moving the needle in one effort—and therefore the timeline needed to include both pieces: project identification and implementation. *Fifth*, the relationship between continuous improvement resources, infrastructure, and already-invested Lean and Six Sigma training needed to be *integrated throughout* the *Supply Chain Excellence* timeline—not simply taking a hand-off at the end or providing data analysis in the beginning.

Design teams end the portfolio-development phase weary, but

also transformed, enlightened, broadened, deepened . . . changed. In many respects, individuals knew the answers to the problems the first day. When asked why they still needed this much time, most would summarize it something like this: "Each of us had our own biases, ideas, and agendas. The analysis and reflection time helped us put data behind the ideas, replace individual agendas with a shared vision, document every assumption, educate our leaders on the real issues, and gain support for some tough changes. Our company is about to undergo massive transformation; the time was necessary to change us, the foundation, first."

Initiating Implementation

Chapter 11 listed 13 milestone steps that define "implementation" of a single project from the portfolio. The remaining sections of *Supply Chain Excellence* will discuss key concepts and Fowlers' progress through to step 13—scale of implementation. The Fowlers technology products team picked Project 7, Engineer an Integrated Tactical Planning Process, as the one to initiate first.

Chapter 13

- ◆ Identify and approve project resource plan
- ◆ Establish project schedule, including informal kickoff date
- ◆ Review project charter, background, and expectations with project team
- ◆ Develop baseline for metrics selected as in-scope

Chapter 14

- ◆ Conduct AS IS Level 3 and 4 process gap analysis
- ◆ Develop action to close "quick hit" gaps

Chapter 15

- ◆ Assemble TO BE Level 3 process based on leading practice

Chapter 16

- ◆ Assemble TO BE Level 4 process based on leading practice
- ◆ Develop and approve solution design storyboard
- ◆ Define process control measures

Chapter 17

- ◆ Build and test solution
- ◆ Pilot and verify solution
- ◆ Roll out solution to project scope and evaluate metric impact

CHAPTER 13

Phase 4: Initiate Implementation

▶ **Getting Organized, Getting People, Getting Data**

There are several points during a Supply Chain Operations Reference (SCOR) project that seem to draw people into reflecting on the significance of their work. The scorecard gap analysis is often such an occasion. Initiating the first implementation project is another.

At this point, members of the design team have reason to feel that they've produced something of great value to their company—measured in millions of dollars and improved customer satisfaction. Better still is the feeling of confidence instilled by a detailed understanding of the improvements—knowing that the selected projects will deliver results.

The momentum has reached something close to full speed, and other people throughout the organization are looking for ways to participate, knowing that this work is in the executive team's center of attention. The organization stands poised for a transition to something big and new. After twelve weeks of analysis on metrics and portfolio development, everyone is eager to get started with implementing something.

With these thoughts as background, the objectives for initiating an implementation project are to identify and approve the project resource plan; establish the project schedule, including an informal kickoff date; review the project charter, background, and expectations with the project team; and develop baseline for metrics selected as in-scope.

Identify and Approve Project Resource Plan

Picking the team for implementation of change is critical to the sustained improvement. There are four considerations:

1. RACI (Responsible, Accountable, Consulted, and Informed) analysis is the first guide: determining who is responsible for doing the work, identifying the one accountable owner for the process, and figuring out who needs to be consulted prior to taking action as well as who needs to be informed afterward. Ideally the project leader is the person primarily responsible for doing the work or guiding the process and the project champion (sponsor) is the one person accountable for the process.

2. Each team needs appropriate subject matter experts. Expertise could relate to a certain best practice, such as vendor managed inventory; collaborative planning, forecasting, and replenishment; or an analytical continuous-improvement practice like Lean or Six Sigma. On large-scale, complex projects it is not uncommon for there to be multiple subject matter experts.

3. On projects for which there will be new system requirements, it is ideal for systems functionality experts to be on the team to translate business needs into software requirements and teach the team members how the software is supposed to work. This accelerates the *detail design, configure, and test phases* in the software development part of the project.

4. The project team should also have at least one former design team member either on the team or assigned to it as a mentor to help avoid re-analyzing past work and to provide access and perspective on the defect analysis, benefit projections, and assumptions.

With the Project Seven kickoff date set for the Thursday of the following week, the team roster started clearing its calendars. The team members included:

- Champion (sponsor): VP operations in the technology products group (David Able)
- Leader: director of planning and production control
- Subject matter experts: SAP expert for materials management and production planning; leading practice expert in rough-cut capacity planning (RCCP) and master scheduling
- Team members: forecast analyst, plant scheduler, distribution requirements planner, supply planner, and order fulfillment supervisor

Establish the Project Schedule and Kickoff Date

Implementation project schedules follow a discipline similar to that of the *Supply Chain Excellence* roadmap: regular, weekly, and focused on deliverables. Though the nomenclature is a bit different, the schedule also follows a path similar to AcceleratedSAP implementation methodology, from project preparation through to business blueprint, realization, final preparation, go-live, and support.

The project schedule essentially puts dates around each of the 13 action steps highlighted in the implementation project charter. A regular team meeting was set for Thursday mornings from 9 a.m.

to noon, and it became the focal point for review and approval of deliverables. The project task summary and schedule is as follows:

1. Identify and approve project resource plan: week of August 1

2. Establish project schedule, including informal kickoff date: week of August 8, kickoff August 11

3. Review project charter, background, and expectations with project team: kickoff August 11

4. Develop baseline for metrics selected as in-scope: week of August 15

5. Conduct AS IS Level 3 and 4 process gap analysis: week of August 22

6. Develop action plans to close "quick hit" gaps: week of August 22

7. Assemble TO BE Level 3 and 4 process based on leading practice: weeks of August 29 and September 5

8. Develop and approve solution-design storyboard: weeks of September 12 and 19

9. Build and test solution: weeks of September 26 and October 3

10. Pilot and verify solution: weeks of October 10, 17, 24, and 31

11. Roll out solution to project scope and evaluate metric impact: month of November

12. Define process control measures: month of November

13. Scale implementation to targeted supply chains in the definition matrix: initiate in December

Steps 8, 9, and 12 are the most variable, driven mostly by the complexity of necessary system solutions. In Fowlers' case, SAP functionality for Materials Management and Production Planning was already installed but was not working at its fullest potential. In fact, people at the plant level were so frustrated that they stopped using some of the functionality. The team members did admit that they were not strict with setting up the resources in their plant. They also alluded to the fact that leading-practice master-scheduling concepts were secondary to correctly setting SAP master data elements to automate existing processes. Step 10 focuses on piloting the solution on a subset of the project scope. In Fowlers' case, the pilot focused on an important set of resources (production lines) in one plant. Step 11 would roll out the solution to the rest of the plant. Step 13 would roll out the solution to the rest of the division plants.

Review Project Background and Develop the Performance Baseline

The kickoff meeting included a candid discussion presented by David Able, the project sponsor. He set the strategic challenge as to why this project was critically important and why it was selected. He put the problem statement, project description, and project objectives into his own words and emphasized both the timing and the size of expected benefits (see Figure 11-1 and the sidebar that follows it).

The project leader then reviewed the scope, including the product and channels, process, SAP modules (PP and MM), plants (North America manufacturing and distribution centers), and the metrics. The product and channel scope includes the SKUs contributing 50 percent of sales in the retail channel. The process scope includes P1.2 Identify, Prioritize and Aggregate Supply-Chain Resources (RCCP), all the P3 PLAN MAKE elements (master scheduling), and M1.1 Schedule Manufacturing Activities (factory floor or finite scheduling).

The team suggested that the processes that touch these should also be added for contextual (not analytical) purposes. The rest of the P1.1 Identify, Prioritize and Aggregate Supply Chain Requirements (demand plan or forecast), P1.3 Balance Supply Chain Resources with SC Requirements (demand-supply imbalance), P2 Plan Source (resulting MRP by component), and P4 Plan Deliver (distribution requirements plan) were added. The metric scope included manufacturing schedule adherence on a weekly basis, master plan adherence each month, rough-cut capacity plan each month, master data accuracy on a weekly rotating basis, and in-stock percentage each week.

The next task was to assemble the data collection plan to establish the project's performance baseline. The data collection, like building the scorecard, required a consensus around the definition of each metric, a reasonable sample size, and the identification of the source for the data. The Fowlers leadership team members admitted that in their haste to "get the SAP system in," they grossly underestimated the requirements for data warehousing and extracting information out of system using the standard reports. This implementation project, then, would be considered an opportunity to learn relevant SAP standard reports, develop a more robust data warehouse strategy (see Data Warehouse Strategy sidebar), and figure out how to better utilize the ways in which SAP data can be exported to both Microsoft Excel and Access. The following is a summary of the Fowlers Project 7 data collection plan.

Manufacturing schedule adherence is defined using the principles of perfect order fulfillment. The three critical pieces are quantity, ship date, and product quality. A schedule is defined as a collection of process orders. If each process order meets the quantity, date, and quality requirement, it is considered good. If a process order misses one of the three criteria, it is considered bad. The method for defining schedule adherence is to divide good process orders by total process orders for the week. The team established a 26-week baseline using a run-chart format. At the moment, the team was sorting through the list of standard SAP reports, looking for the one that could help satisfy the data requirements to calculate the baseline. CO46, Order Progress Report, seemed to contain all the data necessary to judge schedule adherence.

Master schedule adherence looks at the plant's ability to achieve the overall volume and mix requirements, and the ability of the planner to resolve capacity constraints in the future. A master plan is a collection of resource (production lines) plans one week in the past and 13 weeks in the future. If a resource's volume commitment was met for the previous week within a tolerance of ± 5 percent and there are no over-capacity circumstances in the next 13 weeks, it is considered good. The definition of master schedule adherence is the number of resources achieving "good" volume and capacity commitments divided by the total number of resources. The team chose the same 26-week baseline and likewise needed to develop a report similar to that of the schedule attainment. CM01, capacity planning, would be the SAP data source for this metric; though not a report, it relates requirements to planned capacity in hours or units and highlights capacity concerns when requirements are greater than capacity. It can be viewed in weeks or months.

Rough-cut capacity planning is similar to master schedule adherence but looks at monthly volume commitments over 18 months as part of the sales and operations planning process. The definition of rough-cut capacity plan is the number of resources achieving "good" volume and capacity commitments divided by the total number of resources. In this case, the team selected the next month's rough-cut capacity performance as the baseline. CM01 would also be the data source for this measure.

Master data accuracy, while conceptually understood, lacked the systematic analytic discipline to make it a real performance metric. To make it more realistic, the team agreed the measure would be modeled after inventory record accuracy, which relied on cycle counting to publish its performance. Thus, the team identified four categories of SKUs: large volume, medium volume, low volume, and no usage. Each category was assigned a different frequency of review. The team then identified the SAP item master data transactions and settings that were the most critical to daily operation, and verified the accuracy of the data. Master data accuracy then was the aggregate accuracy of the SKUs reviewed for the week. For a SKU to be considered good, all fields needed to be valid. Since the team did not measure this, the baseline would be established by the initial week of data collection.

In-stock percentage was a measure for SKUs defined as make-to-stock. It simply measured whether or not a SKU had available stock in a given week. This measure was similar to a historical measure called *fill rate*. The team suggested using the fill rate by week for the previous 52 weeks as the baseline. This would help illustrate seasonality and manufacturing performance. There are a number of inventory reports in the standard SAP report list. The team was considering the following as options: MB52, Plant Stock Availability; MB5B, Stock On Posting Date; and MC44, Inventory Turnover.

With the metric data collection plans in place, the team members challenged themselves to have some data samples by the following Thursday. On your mark, get set, measure!

Data Warehouse Strategy

With the help of the business intelligence expert, the Fowlers project team reviewed two options, a vision, and more than a dozen goals in creating the data warehouse strategy.

Data warehouses (DW) are distinct from transactional systems. Transactional systems are designed to move information efficiently, and they generally have low data retention. DW are built for reporting and analysis and are good at retaining data. DW are also designed to integrate data from multiple sources.

There are *two* approaches to data warehousing that the Fowlers team discussed: conventional and holistic. The *conventional* approach, used since the 1990s, essentially utilizes *multiple single-purpose* data warehouse models (tables), each addressing a specific area of the business (purchasing fact table, production fact table, sales fact table, etc.) Each table has its own dimensions. For example, dimensions of the purchasing table include buyer, materials, and supplier (Figure 13-1).

Systems experts design ways to pull data from tables and associated dimensions and create reports for people to use. Anyone who has asked for a new report to be created within a conventional data warehouse model knows that this seemingly simple request can take a lot of time and money.

An alternative model, a *holistic* DW, is *one multi-purpose* data warehouse for all business intelligence needs (Figure 13-2). It can be implemented as a template, and is designed to adapt on the fly to additional requirements without modification (Figure 13-3).

The project team's *vision* was "one simple and easy system with minimal limitations, providing the one view over the whole business and its supply chain in which the user can use filtering techniques to select data that will appear on a report."

Data Warehouse Goals

◆ Minimize inconsistent reports and reconcile different views of the same data

◆ Improve quality of data

◆ Consolidate enterprise data from multiple sources and time periods

◆ Make the data easily accessible and provide transparency

◆ Enable common and flexible calendars

◆ Save time on report preparation and construction

◆ Address the weaknesses of current reporting systems

◆ Empower people with information

◆ Enable pre-emptive reporting of events that are expected to happen

◆ Develop and enable single cross-functional business reports (Figure 13-4)

◆ Offer all supply chain–related information (Figure 13-5)

◆ Effortlessly replace all "standard" reporting needs

◆ Address deficiencies in the operational systems

◆ Be capable of reporting "unlimited" measures

◆ Allow "unlimited" product hierarchies

◆ Utilize holistic data warehouse dedicated supply chain reporting capability (Figure 13-5).

Figure 13-1. Conventional data warehouse table dimensions for purchasing.

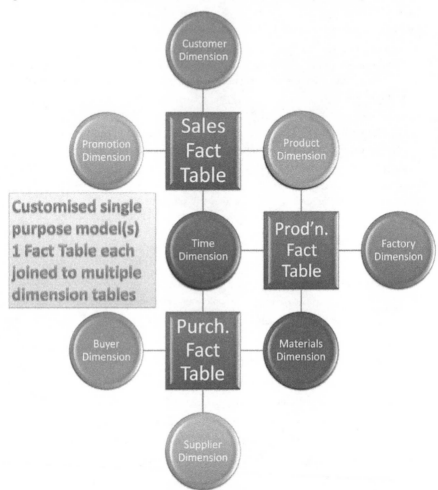

Figure 13-2. Structure of a holistic data warehouse.

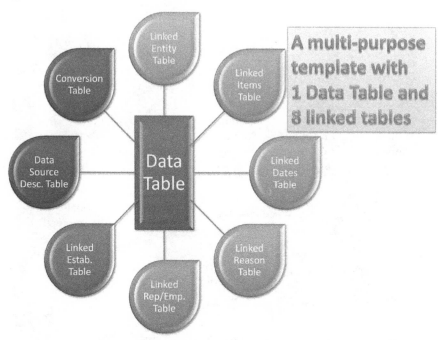

Copyright 2011. Reprinted from *Holistic Data Warehousing on Microsoft SQL Server 2008*, Gerry Phillips and Jane McCarthy; For-tee Too Sight Publishing, 2010. Used with permission.

Figure 13-3. Holistic data warehouse implemented as a template.

Customer Scan Data	Competitor Scan Data	Full Cost Breakdown History	Full Cost Breakdown Budgets	Full Cost Breakdown Latest
Customer Trading Terms Budget	Customer Marketing Co-op Actuals	Customer Marketing Co-op Estimate	Customer Marketing Co-op Budget	Consumer Complaints
Customer Special Deals Actuals	Customer Special Deals Estimates	Customer Special Deals Budgets	Customer Trading Terms Actuals	Customer Trading Terms Forecast
Purchases Actuals	Purchases on Order and Planned	Inventory Actuals	Inventory Projected	Sales Credit & Debit Notes
Labour Spend Actuals	Labour Recoveries Actuals & Planned	Overhead Recoveries Actuals & Planned	Production Out & In Actuals	Production Out & In Planned
Sales Actual/ Forecast	Customer Orders	Customer Shortages Actuals	Customer Shortages Projected	Today's Sales ½ hourly update
Sales Actuals	Sales Working Forecasts	Sales Live Forecast	Sales Budget	Sales & Operations Planning Forecast

Figure 13-4. Single cross-functional business report.

Frequency	Monthly						
ItemCategory	(All)		Sales and Operations Report				
ItemSubcategory	(All)						

Amt $'000			CMonth				
DataType	Cal Year	Version	Jan	Feb	Mar	Apr	May
Sales	2009	Actuals	$ 463,608	$ 848,663	$ 554,222	$ 570,051	$ 934,389
	2010	Act/Forecast	$ 490,342	$ 899,246	$ 521,655	$ 622,325	$ 905,926
	2010	Budget	$ 421,000	$ 936,000	$ 558,000	$ 566,000	$ 943,000
Cost of Sales	2009	Actuals	$ 214,860	$ 339,687	$ 225,302	$ 307,374	$ 386,347
	2010	Act/Forecast	$ 209,443	$ 363,285	$ 274,233	$ 251,283	$ 427,758
	2010	Budget	$ 209,831	$ 485,294	$ 262,074	$ 270,536	$ 442,397
Margin	2009	Actuals	$ 248,748	$ 508,976	$ 328,920	$ 262,677	$ 548,042
	2010	Act/Forecast	$ 280,899	$ 535,961	$ 247,422	$ 371,042	$ 478,168
	2010	Budget	$ 211,169	$ 450,706	$ 295,926	$ 295,464	$ 500,603
Margin%	2009	Actuals	53.7%	60.0%	59.3%	46.1%	58.7%
	2010	Act/Forecast	57.3%	59.6%	47.4%	59.6%	52.8%
	2010	Budget	50.2%	48.2%	53.0%	52.2%	53.1%
Purchases	2009	Actuals	$ 158,876	$ 242,787	$ 218,365	$ 203,310	$ 287,902
	2010	Act/Plan	$ 134,261	$ 232,693	$ 142,640	$ 137,367	$ 251,589
Prodn Out	2009	Actuals	$ 219,219	$ 341,146	$ 245,502	$ 299,191	$ 371,857
	2010	Act/Plan	$ 201,617	$ 344,089	$ 253,605	$ 242,706	$ 414,771
Prodn Scrap	2009	Actuals	$ 771	$ 2,733	$ 4,997	$ 8,945	$ 7,121
	2010	Act/Plan	$ 7,645	$ 10,703	$ 2,568	$ 2,500	$ 2,500
Prodn In	2009	Actuals	$ 146,817	$ 226,958	$ 205,909	$ 189,533	$ 277,862
	2010	Act/Plan	$ 134,194	$ 221,429	$ 138,425	$ 124,593	$ 230,544
Labour	2009	Actuals	$ 33,852	$ 53,728	$ 35,642	$ 46,160	$ 66,737
	2010	Act/Forecast	$ 33,569	$ 55,914	$ 44,903	$ 44,000	$ 72,000
	2010	Budget	$ 34,000	$ 79,000	$ 39,000	$ 42,000	$ 77,000
Inventory	2009	Actuals	$ 449,906	$ 467,195	$ 499,851	$ 505,445	$ 500,995
	2010	Act/Plan	$ 526,571	$ 518,638	$ 502,225	$ 506,421	$ 514,479
Inventory KPI	2009	Actuals	2.09	1.38	2.22	1.64	1.30
	2010	Act/Plan	2.51	1.43	1.83	2.02	1.20
Complaints	2009	Actuals	260	796	829	209	175
	2010	Actuals	133	558	336		

Figure 13-5. Holistic data warehouse dedicated supply chain reporting capability.

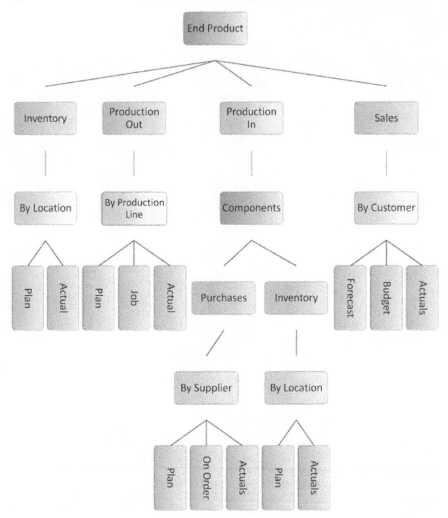

Phases 2–4: The Staple Yourself Interview and SCOR Level 3 Process Diagram

> ➤ **June 13 to 17*: How the Work Really Gets Done; a Tool for All Phases**

The tasks for this set of deliverables can be applied during any one of three points during the project as part of the analysis, portfolio development, and/or project implementation. In fact, these tasks integrate very well with the AcceleratedSAP implementation methodology in the business blueprint phase. Girish Naagesh, Fowlers' CIO, commented in hindsight that if the team had completed this comprehensive SCOR Level 3 analysis either in advance or as part of the AcceleratedSAP deployment process, the details related to the Question and Answer Database (QAdb) and Customer Input Templates would have been easier to manage because the entire supply chain process would have been put in the proper context.

The first opportunity to use the interview and diagramming process is during Phase 2. In this case, the design team chose the recommended option of conducting an on-site process analysis in

---

*May also take place July 11 or the week of August 22, depending on organizational schedule (see the appendix).

preparation for the brainstorm event. The scope would include all relevant SCOR Level 3 process elements. More important, this option gives the team members an opportunity to meet and build relationships with members of the regional team with whom they are working, adding to the global perspective of the project. This option is represented in the schedule that is part of the Appendix.

The second option consolidates the activity into the first day of the brainstorm week. This scenario skips the face-to-face "staple yourself to an order" interviews and focuses the team on developing the process diagram in a conference room meeting format. Some project teams have introduced the staple yourself to an order worksheet the week before arrival using a web-based conference, with the expectation that the interviewees will do their best to complete it. The process scope, like the first option, includes all of the SCOR Level 3 elements.

The third option falls into the implementation phase of a project. This scenario uses the staple yourself to an order worksheets and assembles a process diagram—but only for those processes named in the scope for the project. On the project schedule, this deliverable can be noted as Staple Yourself to an Order Interviews and AS IS Process Diagram in Phase 2, or AS IS Process Diagram in Phase 3 and Conduct Level 3 and 4 Process Gap Analysis in Phase 4, as seen in the Appendix. In complex projects, teams have included both the first option and a refinement of the third.

The staple yourself interview is fieldwork that attempts to learn how things are done in the real world. The notion of a guided tour is discussed in the classic *Harvard Business Review* article "Staple Yourself to an Order" (July 1, 1992; Benson P. Shapiro, V. Kasteri Rangan, and John J. Sviokla). Guided by an interview plan, members of the project team travel to the site(s) where the processes scoped for the project begin and follow them to their closure—literally cradle to grave. For example, a sales-order field trip may start at a salesperson's home office, where the quote is generated; then move back to headquarters to see how the order is received, validated, and entered; then go to the warehouse to watch how the inventory is allocated to the order, so the customer service representative can communicate a delivery date to the customer; and ultimately end in accounts receivables, where reconciled invoices are archived.

Preparing for the Staple Yourself Interview

The preparation and interview process is composed of four basic steps. First, the project team thoroughly reviews the master data appropriate for the processes under review. This is a follow-up activity to data collection efforts of the past week (see "Master Data in SAP Capacity Planning Modules" sidebar). Second, also before the site visit, the team prepares the process analysis worksheets; this essentially means populating sections such as the name of the interviewee(s), accountable function, primary input(s), SCOR process element, and primary output(s). The inputs and outputs (stated in terms of the current state rather than SCOR) are especially important because they give the interviewees perspective on the beginning and end of the process.

Third, the project leader—on arriving at the site—provides a quick briefing to the interviewees about the SCOR Level 3 processes under investigation. This is normally done in a small conference room. After reviewing the inputs and outputs from the process analysis worksheets, the interviewees can help determine the best locations and strategies for conducting the interviews.

Fourth, the team and interviewees should proceed to the planned locations and complete the interviews. A location could be a desk, workstation, production line, warehouse, or any other place deemed appropriate. If the processes are completed primarily on the computer system, then physically the interview may be accomplished at the desk; the real tour will be through the computer system screens. In other cases, the design team may perform the main interview in a conference room with a live computer log-on, tour the system path, and then add the finishing details with a physical walk-through of the appropriate area.

Understanding the Staple Yourself Interview Worksheet

On the worksheet (Figure 14-1), interviewee and SCOR element sections are self-explanatory. Accountable Function and Responsible borrow the "R" and the "A" from the RACI (Responsible, Accountable, Consulted, Informed) analysis process. As noted previously, *responsible* refers to the roles that perform the work for a given process. *Accountable* is reserved for the one role that ultimately owns the process performance.

Primary Input(s) and Output(s) refer to the primary trigger(s) to start the process and the primary output(s) of the process. Level 4 Step and Description refers to a maximum of 10 tasks to complete the SCOR Level 3 process element. Why 10? Some teams need more processes to describe how they do their work; the important idea is to use the same maximum number of process steps for each SCOR element to help normalize the level of detail.

System Module refers to the information tools, screens, and/or transactions used to complete the tasks identified in each Level 4 step. The tools can range from a system functionality or module (SAP SD, MM, PP, FI, etc.) to SAP transaction codes, like CM01, VA01, CO09, MD04, etc.; Internet signal to a fax; EDI; Excel spreadsheet; phone call; or simple sticky note. Event Time is the time spent from start to finish on the Level 4 step, assuming no lag time; the team tries to normalize this to time per step.

Business Rules are policies and informal guidelines that govern decisions and behavior. Processing all orders by 3 p.m. may be a policy, but onsite supervisors might enforce an unwritten practice of accepting an order an hour later—with the same delivery expectations—as part of a customer-focused culture. Both are business rules.

Disconnects causing rework and/or extended wait time are issues

Figure 14-1. Staple yourself interview worksheet.

Interviewees	Enter the interviewees from the interview planning worksheet.				
Accountable Function	Enter the title of the ultimate role accountable to the performance of this SCOR Level 3 process.				

Primary Input(s)		SCOR Element		Primary Output(s)	
Enter the primary transactional input(s) to this process		Enter the SCOR Level 3 Process element ID and description, i.e., M1.1 Schedule Production Activities		Enter the primary transactional output(s) to this process	

	Level 4 Step	Description	System Module	Responsible	Event Time
Process Steps (>4 and <11)	1	Enter the description of each of the process steps; often referred to as Level 4 process steps	Enter the System Module and/or Transaction	Enter the title(s) of those doing the work	This is an effort of the amount of time (often calculated in minutes) and is normalized to one of five transactions, i.e., purchase order, work order, sales order, return authorization, or forecast
	2				

Total Event Time for Process Steps					0

Business Rules	Enter the business rules, both formal and informal, that directly or indirectly influence process performance		

	Disconnect Description	Initials	Relative Weight
Disconnects causing rework and/or extended wait time	Describe major disconnects that cause process steps to be reworked and/or add to process wait time (delay)	Interviewee's Initials	This compares the relative impact to the rest of the disconnects in the list

that result in gaps between elapsed time and event time—too much waiting—and/or cause unnecessary rework. Figure 14-2 illustrates a process analysis example for the SCOR element D1.2 Receive, Enter, and Validate Order.

Figure 14-2. Process analysis example: SCOR Element D1.2 Receive, Enter, and Validate Order.

Interviewees	Susan, Terri, Julie, Jane, Dan, and Mike				
Accountable Function	Customer Service Director				
Primary Input(s)		**SCOR Element**		**Primary Output(s)**	
Customer call, fax, or email Web order Field sales contact Customer profile		**D1.2** Receive, Enter, and Validate the Order		Entered sales order	
	Level Four Step	**Description**	**SAP Module-- Transaction**	**Responsible**	**Event Time**
	1	Retrieve or enter new customer master record.	Sales & Distribution-- VA01	Customer Service Representative	1
	2	Verify ship to/bill to addresses. Overview screen.	Sales & Distribution-- VA01	Customer Service Representative	1
	3	Enter customer contact, payment terms, ship method and P.O. number. Overview screen.	Sales & Distribution-- VA01	Customer Service Representative	1
	4	Enter requested ship date. Overview screen--sales tab.	Sales & Distribution-- VA01	Customer Service Representative	1
Process Steps (>4 and <11)	5	Enter part number and quantity. Overview screen--sales tab.	Sales & Distribution-- VA01	Customer Service Representative	1
	6	Review part description and modify as necessary. Overview screen-- sales tab.	Sales & Distribution-- VA01	Customer Service Representative	1
	7	Input default price and unit of measure. Overview screen--sales tab.	Sales & Distribution-- VA01	Customer Service Representative	1
	8	Update or save order record. Overview screen--sales tab.	Sales & Distribution-- VA01	Customer Service Representative	1
	9	Call back customer when inventory allocation fails and re-date the order. Allocation is checked when saving the order for each item line entered.	Sales & Distribution-- VA01	Customer Service Representative	2
	Total Event Time for Process Steps				**10**
Business Rules	Formal--Orders can be held waiting for payment for a maximum of 30 days after stock is committed.				
	Formal--Credit reviews "holds" once daily.				
	Informal--Once an order is entered, each order line is manually reviewed for correct quantity, part number, and price.				
	Informal--If the ship-to address or bill-to address is modified or a new address is added, the order will go on a sales hold. Customer Service must review and approve the address change/addition before it becomes a permanent change/addition.				
	Disconnect Description			**Initials**	**Relative Weight**
	System pricing does not match spreadsheet version of the customer price.			JH	40
Disconnects causing rework and/or extended wait time	Manual entry to add new customer ship-to addresses for drop shipments from suppliers.			ST	20
	Customer requests different terms than contract.			MJ	20
	Customer order incorrect increments, i.e., unit of measure and order minimums.			DS	10
Copyright 2003 SCE Limited	Customer part number cross-reference is not correct.			JK	10

Fowlers Analysis of P3 Plan Make

The team members landed at the plant ready to go. They had followed all the rules. During the previous week, they and the plant manager had discussed the targeted interviewee list, which included the master scheduler, finite scheduler, and materials planner. They had memorized the SCOR element P3 Plan Make. Technically defined as "the development and establishment of courses of action over specified time periods that represent a projected appropriation of production resources to meet production requirements," it was synonymous with the leading practice of master scheduling. They entered the preliminary inputs and outputs and sorted out an interview approach to include all the Level 3 elements in one process analysis worksheet, thinking that the process would be smoother.

When they entered the conference room, there sat the plant manager and the scheduler, six months after their SAP go-live. The first lesson in these analyses is that the current state is not always as it seems. The second lesson is to not assume but simply observe; sometimes in supply chain your brain fills in the unknown with your conception of how you'd like it to work. The project leader introduced everyone and proceeded to review the process analysis worksheet. The first part of the discussion focused on the meaning of P3 Plan Make, which was a great learning opportunity that allowed all to get centered on the theory of master scheduling.

The next part of the interview attempted to dissect the inputs and outputs. After a rather animated philosophical discussion about master data, resource profiles, and smoothed eight-week schedules, the plant manager stated very plainly, "This is simple; I take the expected units for the month as committed to in the budget and divide by four. I then tell the scheduler what to run each week. There are three things that drive us crazy. The first is when we don't have parts to run something that is scheduled. The second is the customer orders that keep getting inserted in the schedule from corporate. Both cause more changeovers, unnecessary yield loss, and higher unit cost for me. The third is that the plan that spits out of the SAP scheduling module is not accurate; I can't trust it to hit my numbers."

When asked about his use of the SAP module, the scheduler said, "We tried it for a month but it didn't work. So we only use it to enter production orders, estimate material availability, report output and enter purchase orders for suppliers." Figure 14-3 summarizes the analysis.

Figure 14-3. Fowlers' P3 Plan Make staple yourself analysis.

Interviewee(s)	Barry and Jorge				
Accountable Function	Plant Manager				
Primary Input(s)		**SCOR Element**		**Primary Output(s)**	
Monthly Unit and Cost Objectives		**P3** Plan Make		4 Week Schedule	
	Level 4 Step	**Description**	**SAP Module-- Transaction**	**Responsible**	**Event Time**
	1	Calculate the monthly plan by week.	Excel	Plant Manager	60
	2	Check work order status from last week.	Paperwork from Morning Scheduling Meeting	Scheduler	60
Process Steps (>4 and <11)	3	Re-sequence orders not completed from past week.	Paperwork from Morning Scheduling Meeting	Scheduler	15
	4	Work with supervisor to create this week's schedule using monthly plan.	Excel	Scheduler	15
	5	Calculate materials availability for the new schedule.	Materials Management--MD04	Scheduler	60
	6	Work with customer service to slot new orders in the near-term weeks.	Excel	Scheduler	60
		Total Event Time for Process Steps			270
Business Rules	Formal: Achieve plant unit cost objectives.				
	Informal: Exceeding the volume plan helps the plant overachieve performance expectations.				
	Disconnect Description			**Initials**	**Relative Weight**
Disconnects causing rework and/or extended wait time	Customer orders are inserted, causing unnecessary changeovers.			JP	30%
	The plant does not hit its commitments each week by SKU.			JP	30%
	Packaging and raw materials not available to run schedule.			BM	20%
	The system plan (resource load) is wrong.			BM	20%

Assembling the AS IS Process and RACI Diagrams

Coming off an intense on-site visit (assuming use of the recommended option one as described at the beginning of this chapter), the design team is armed with a packet of interview summaries covering more than 40 SCOR Level 3 process elements. Team members have discovered unwritten rules, policy shortcuts, work-arounds, and a real-time validation of how silo mentality is destroying productivity; they may have even learned a few words from the host country. Now they're ready to start assembling the picture of how their supply chain processes function (or not) in the current state. Process mapping is not a new technique for analyzing operational efficiency. Its effectiveness rests in the ability to pictorially portray how seemingly disparate processes are connected, to illustrate the essential information needed to drive the work, and ultimately to illustrate how process flow relates to organizational roles and responsibilities.

The SCOR approach to process mapping considers the Level 3 elements as the "work" in "work and information flow." The input–output is the "information" or transaction. The process mapper stands at the whiteboard, draws a box representing one SCOR element, adds the inputs and outputs from the interview worksheet, and then moves on to the next SCOR element in the list.

Figure 14-4 is a sample case involving multiple SCOR processes in PLAN, SOURCE, MAKE, and DELIVER. The system's material requirements planning (P2.1 and P2.2) generated planned requisitions for a planner to (1) balance, (2) convert (P2.3) to firm requisitions, and (3) release to the buyer (P2.4). The released requisitions are converted to purchase orders (S1.1) by a buyer; the purchase order record on the system and the physical delivery of the material and packing slip trigger receipt of the product (S1.2). The

172

Figure 14-4. Sample SCOR Level 3 process map illustrating PLAN, SOURCE, MAKE, and DELIVER.

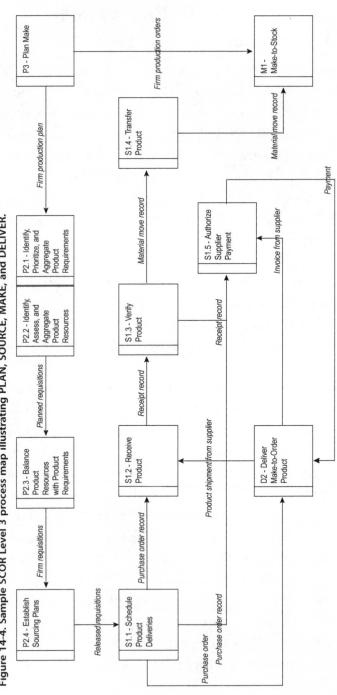

initial receipt record triggers appropriate quality checks (S1.3); then a material move record assigns the material to a warehouse location (S1.4). The purchase order record, receipt record, and invoice from the supplier (D2) trigger accounts payable to issue payment (S1.5). Meanwhile planning is transmitting the next firm production plan (P3), which triggers the manufacturing team to send a signal to issue stored raw material (M1) to a production line. The firm production plan also then begins the next cycle of material requirements planning (P3 to P2.1). Using an alternative mapping approach, the concept of a RACI diagram (Figure 14-5) can illustrate for each location the functions that participate in the performance of each SCOR process. Furthermore, it can also illustrate the role each function plays in each SCOR process (Figure 14-6).

The conclusion by the Fowlers team members around P3 Plan Make is that they really didn't have an AS IS Level 3 map; the processes discovered in the interviews were either scheduling or aligning to unit volume commitments.

Master Data in SAP Capacity Planning Modules

With the help of the SAP expert, the Fowlers project team reviewed five critical master data areas affecting the performance of the tactical planning process: plants, materials, work centers, bills of materials, and routings (or recipes). Following is a summary of the plant and materials discussion.

Plants within the SAP platform are used to define both factories and distribution centers, and are initially set up during the configuration part of *realization* (Figure 2-2). They typically are added only as a company grows and expands.

Materials in SAP are also commonly referred to as items, products, and SKUs; they are the hub of the information needed to run the supply chain. For Fowlers and other consumer products companies, this refers to materials that you SOURCE, MAKE, DELIVER, and RETURN. Basic material data include description, base unit of measure, weight, and size—all which are common to every plant in the Fowlers technology products group.

(*Text continues on page 176*)

174

Figure 14-5. Sample RACI diagram of functions by location in SCOR Level 3 processes.

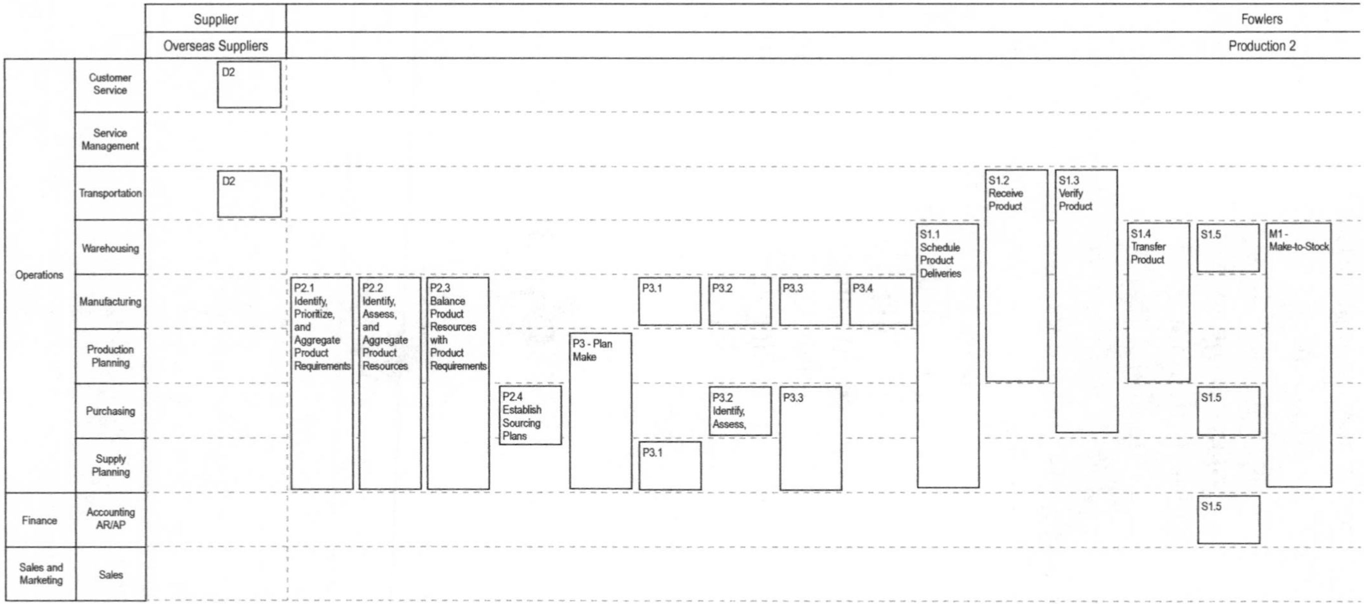

Figure 14-6. Sample RACI diagram of functions by SCOR Level 3 process.

	Customer Service	Transportation	Warehousing	Manufacturing	Production Planning	Purchasing	Supply Planning	Accounting AR/AP	Sales
P4 - Plan Deliver									
D2 - Deliver Make-to-Order Product									
P2.1									
P2.2				C	R		C		
P2.3						R, A			
P2.4 - Establish Sourcing Plans									
P3 - Plan Make					C	I	R, A		
S1.1 - Schedule Product Deliveries				C	R, A	C	I		
S1.2 - Receive Product		R	R, A	I					
S1.3 - Verify Product		C	R	R, A	I	I			
S1.4 - Transfer Product			R, A	C					
S1.5 - Authorize Supplier Payment			C			R, A		R	
M1 - Make-to-Stock				R, A	C				

© Copyright 2007 Xelocity. Used with permission.

Some material information is applicable to all plants and some can be different by plant. The SAP platform uses the term *transaction* to name a view of data within an SAP module of functionality. Using SAP transaction *MM03—Display Material*, the Fowlers team reviewed one of the materials in scope (Figure 14-7). Supply chain settings are found in the *MRP 1, MRP 2, MRP 3, and MRP 4* material master screens. The team reviewed critical parameters on the *MRP 1* tab including:

♦ *MRP type* influences the timing of receipts generated and firmed during a *Material Requirements Planning* (MRP) run.

♦ An *MRP controller* is the person or department that is typically the most familiar with the MRP data settings for the material, and also responsible for ensuring that sufficient stock of the material is available at the plant. For Fowlers, MRP controller "001" has been defined and assigned to the material reviewed. The MRP controller can be used to look at requirements exceptions for many materials at the same time, making the exception-management process more efficient.

♦ *Lot size* data governs the size of the receipts generated during the MRP planning run. At Fowlers, material F1000 has a lot size setting of WB, which causes all unfulfilled requirements within a week to be aggregated and served by one receipt.

♦ A *quantity rounding value* is used when generating new orders (receipts). For Fowlers, a value of 10 has been set. This adjusts the receipt quantity to a multiple that Fowlers believes is efficient when it is assembling the material.

On the *MRP 2* screen (Figure 14-8), Fowlers has maintained the following information:

♦ The *procurement type* "F" means that Fowlers will buy the material. This, combined with the *special procurement* setting of "40," which was defined when the system was configured, means that plant 2105 is "buying" the material from its sister plant 2106, where the product is assembled.

♦ The *scheduling* data, specifically the *planned deliv time* and the *GR processing time* (GR = goods receipt) controls the time the MRP planning run will use for determining when a product will become available to promise. For Fowlers, when running a standard availability check, any requirements outside of this lead time will be assumed to be fulfilled; the requirement will not be checked against actual stocks or future firmed receipts.

♦ The *scheduling margin key* is used to determine the types of order proposals—planned orders or purchase requisitions—that will be created. For Fowlers, a setting of "001" at plant 2105 generates purchase requisitions within the first 10 work days— the *opening period*—and planned orders further in the future. By using transactions ME55 or ME59N, this allows a buyer to collectively create purchase orders from purchase requisitions, while letting SAP MRP manage the generation or deletion of planned orders.

Figure 14-7. Fowlers' SAP display material MRP 1 tab.

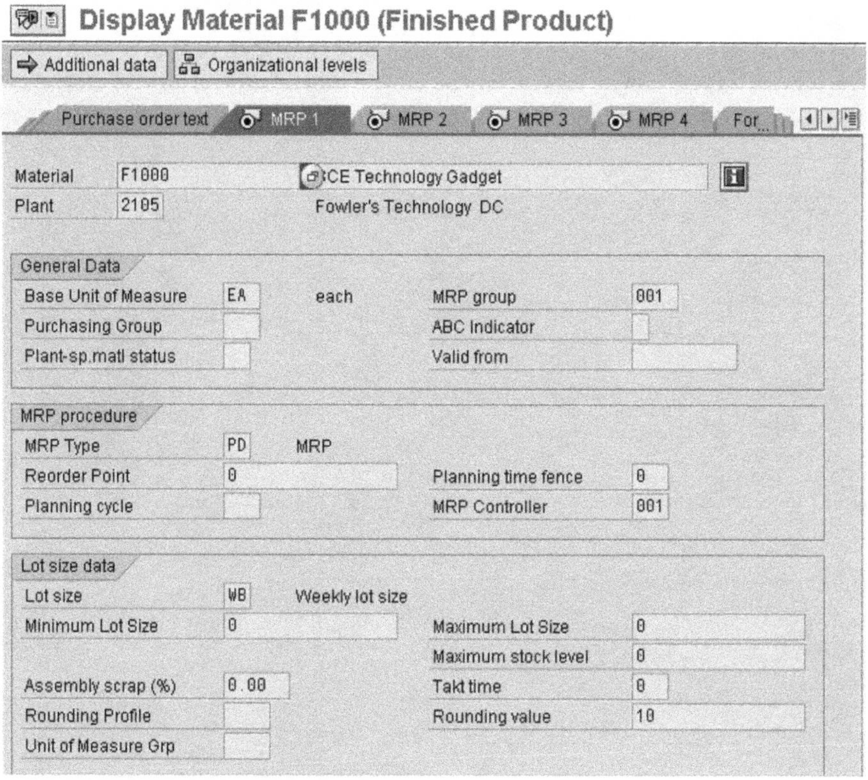

Display Material F1000 (Finished Product)

⇒ Additional data | 品 Organizational levels

Purchase order text | ⊙ MRP 1 | ⊙ MRP 2 | ⊙ MRP 3 | ⊙ MRP 4 | For... | ◀ ▶ 巪

| Material | F1000 | ⊡CE Technology Gadget | ℹ |
| Plant | 2105 | Fowler's Technology DC | |

General Data

Base Unit of Measure	EA	each	MRP group	001
Purchasing Group			ABC Indicator	
Plant-sp.matl status			Valid from	

MRP procedure

MRP Type	PD	MRP		
Reorder Point	0		Planning time fence	0
Planning cycle			MRP Controller	001

Lot size data

Lot size	WB	Weekly lot size		
Minimum Lot Size	0		Maximum Lot Size	0
			Maximum stock level	0
Assembly scrap (%)	0.00		Takt time	0
Rounding Profile			Rounding value	10
Unit of Measure Grp				

Figure 14-8. Fowlers' SAP display material MRP 2 tab.

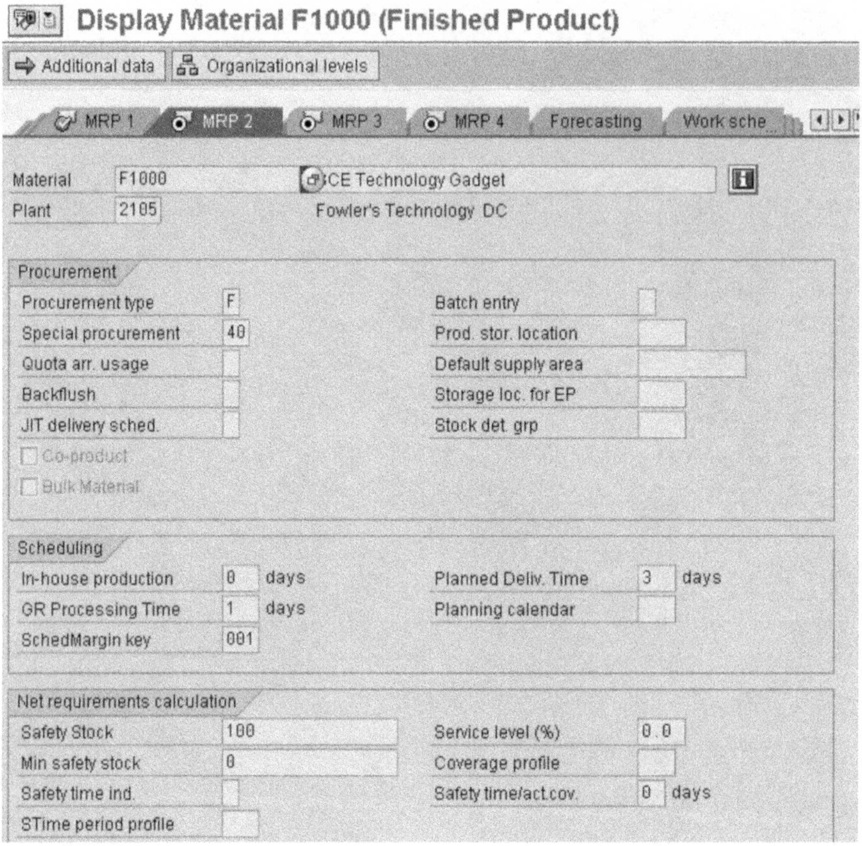

Display Material F1000 (Finished Product)

⇒ Additional data | 🔓 Organizational levels

| MRP 1 | MRP 2 | MRP 3 | MRP 4 | Forecasting | Work sche |

Material   F1000   CE Technology Gadget
Plant   2105   Fowler's Technology DC

Procurement

Procurement type	F		Batch entry	
Special procurement	40		Prod. stor. location	
Quota arr. usage			Default supply area	
Backflush			Storage loc. for EP	
JIT delivery sched.			Stock det. grp	

☐ Co-product
☐ Bulk Material

Scheduling

In-house production	0	days	Planned Deliv. Time	3	days
GR Processing Time	1	days	Planning calendar		
SchedMargin key	001				

Net requirements calculation

Safety Stock	100		Service level (%)	0.0	
Min safety stock	0		Coverage profile		
Safety time ind.			Safety time/act.cov.	0	days
STime period profile					

CHAPTER 15

Phase 4: Solution Design

▶ **Defining How the Process Should Work at SCOR Level 3**

The goal of many solution-development efforts is to "think outside the box." There was some kind of brain research from a college psychology class indicating that children who haven't yet started school will score an average of 95 percent on a creativity test, while third graders score 30 percent on the same test and adults in the workplace score 5 percent. So much for "outside the box."

Blend brain research with the fact that the relationships among supply chain processes are integrated and complex and you'll see that it's asking too much to expect a project team to start building TO BE processes from scratch. So the objectives for these steps of implementation are not fluid creativity; rather, they are to help define how the business should work using proven best practices, common sense, and native SAP functionality for organizations in that environment.

At Fowlers, as part of assembling the Project 7 solution design, the project team needed to understand the context of tactical planning within the rest of the SCOR Level 3 blueprint. The challenges were to understand how SAP capacity planning was supposed to work based on the original configuration, what other best practices would add to the process, and how to illustrate the TO BE blueprint with SCOR Level 3 elements (see the SAP Modules and Transactions sidebar).

The SCOR Level 3 Blueprint

The SCOR process blueprint (Figure 15-1) shows the integrated processes for five leading practices: sales and operations planning, distribution requirements planning, master production scheduling, material requirements planning, and available to promise. The blueprint also incorporates closed–loop execution processes for all SCOR Level 3 SOURCE, MAKE, DELIVER, and RETURN process elements.

The tour took the team sequentially from PLAN P1 to P4 to P3 to P2 to the SOURCE execution processes S1.1 through S1.5. Then it went on to the MAKE execution processes M1.1 to M1.7 and finally to DELIVER execution processes D1.1 to D1.14. Finally, the tour ended with the RETURN execution processes DR1.1 to DR1.4 and SR1.1 to SR1.5. The following section provides some of the words that go with the blueprint.

PLAN Supply Chain P1. This is the process of taking actual demand data and generating a supply plan for a given supply chain (defined in this case by customer, market channel, product, geography, or business entity). This process step is most closely associated with the discipline of sales and operations planning. The basic steps require a unit forecast that's adjusted for marketing and sales events; a supply plan that constrains the forecast based on resource availability (resources could be inventory, manufacturing capacity, or transportation); and a balance step in which demand/supply exceptions are resolved and updated in the system. The output between this process step and the next PLAN DELIVER (P4) is a constrained unit plan.

PLAN DELIVER P4. This is the process of comparing actual committed orders with the constrained forecast, and generating a

Figure 15-1. Typical SCOR Level 3 blueprint.

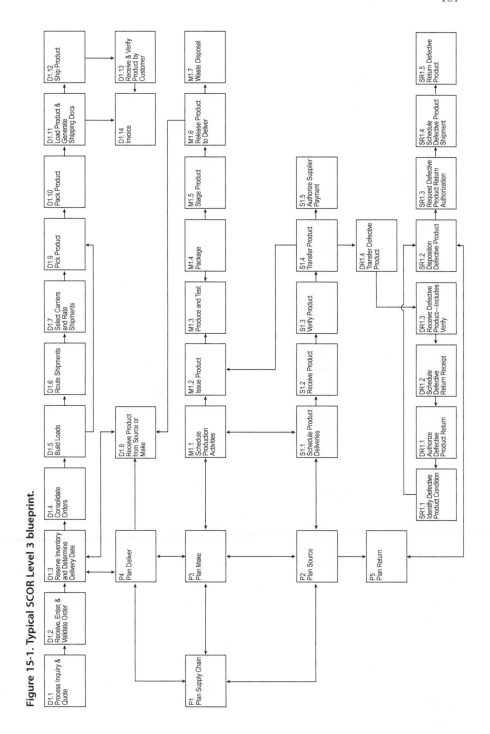

distribution resource plan to satisfy service, cost, and inventory goals. It is carried out for each warehouse stocking location and may be aggregated to region or another geography type. This process step is most closely associated with the discipline of distribution require-ments planning. The relationship between this process step and PLAN MAKE P3 are replenishment requirements, which tell the plant manager how much product to plan for. Reserve inventory and promise date (D1.3) is a distribution requirements plan, which lets customer service know how much inventory will be available to promise.

PLAN MAKE P3. This is the process of comparing actual pro-duction orders plus replenishment orders with the constrained fore-cast, and then generating a master production schedule resource plan to satisfy service, cost, and inventory goals. It is carried out for each plant location and may be aggregated to region or another geogra-phy type. This process step is most closely associated with the disci-pline of master production scheduling. The relationship between this process step and PLAN SOURCE P2 are replenishment re-quirements, which tell the purchasing manager how much product to plan for. It's all passed down to schedule production activities (M1.1), which lets the plant scheduler know how much total prod-uct must be made by the ship date.

PLAN SOURCE P2. This is the process of comparing total ma-terial requirements with the constrained forecast, and generating a material requirements resource plan to satisfy landed cost and inven-tory goals by commodity type. It is carried out for items on the bill of materials and may be aggregated by supplier or commodity type. This process step is most closely associated with the discipline of material requirements planning. The relationship between this proc-ess step and schedule product deliveries is the material requirements plan, which lets the buyer know how much product must be pur-chased on the basis of current orders, inventory, and future require-ments.

SOURCE Sx. The *x* in Sx is a wildcard-type indication that includes all of the SCOR Level 2 configurations. This set of execution processes involves the material acquisition process initiating and scheduling the purchase order, receiving and verifying product, transferring the product to available raw material, and authorizing supplier payment through. In the case of sourcing engineer-to-order products, there are accommodations to identify and select appropriate suppliers.

MAKE Mx. This set of execution processes encompasses the conversion process of raw materials to finished goods: scheduling production activities, issuing and staging the product, producing and testing, packaging, and releasing finished goods to customers or warehouses. In the case of making engineer-to-order products, there are accommodations to finalize engineering specifications before initiating a manufacturing work order.

DELIVER Dx. This set of execution processes involves the order fulfillment process: processing inquiries and quotes, entering orders, promising inventory, consolidating orders, planning and building loads, routing shipments, selecting carriers and rating shipments, receiving, picking, shipping, customer receipt, necessary installation, and final invoicing. In the case of delivering engineer-to-order products, there are accommodations to include the request for proposal or quote and negotiating contracts before order entry.

RETURN DRx and SR1x. This set of execution processes involves the return authorization process, return shipment and receipt, verification and disposition of product, and replacement or credit process for defective and excess inventory. In the third case of RETURN, more detailed scheduling, determination of product condition, and transfer of maintenance, repair, and overhaul items are modeled.

ENABLE Processes. Enable processes prepare, maintain, and manage information or relationships on which planning and execution processes rely. There is no decomposition of ENABLE elements. Think of them as necessary processes. There are eight management categories of ENABLE that are applied appropriately to PLAN, SOURCE, MAKE, DELIVER, and RETURN. They are business rules, performance improvement, data collection, inventory, capital assets, transportation, physical network configuration, and regulatory compliance. Another ENABLE process, unique to PLAN, manages alignment of the financial and unit plans; still another ENABLE process, unique to SOURCE, manages supplier agreements. Supply chains can have well-integrated planning and execution processes and still underperform if ENABLE processes are poorly managed. For example, a good sales and operations planning process cannot overcome a poor EP.9 align unit and financial plans.

Configuring the Level 3 Blueprint for Project 7

One of the first tasks in configuring the blueprint is to find a best-practices resource that can help define the proper ENABLE process elements. For Project 7, the project team picked the resource *Master Scheduling in the 21st Century: For Simplicity, Speed, and Success—Up and Down the Supply Chain* (by Thomas F. Wallace and Robert A. Stahl; T. F. Wallace & Co., 2003). Prior to configuring their blueprint the team members completed the master scheduling effectiveness checklist, assembled their first draft of a master scheduling policy, and outlined the basic responsibilities of a master scheduler, which the team considered part of the EP ENABLE PLAN processes.

The policy (EP.1) helped sort out some potentially contentious issues. First, the team defined the planning time zones: 0–14 days was considered fixed with no unauthorized changes; 3–8 weeks was considered firm with mix changes only by authorized roles; and 3–18 months was considered open, wherein volume decisions needed to reconcile with the rough-cut capacity plan as approved in the sales and operations planning process (P1).

Second, the decision-making authority for the fixed and firm zones were defined relative to the type of product, level of change, and date of impact. Third, the policy required use of the SAP order entry and available-to-promise (D1.2 and D1.3) in making customer commitments. Fourth, the forecasts (P1.1) were consumed properly using one of the SAP consumption algorithms.

Fifth, the master schedule could have no past-due production orders carried over into the new week. Sixth, production schedule attainment was defined and elevated to a critical metric with a target of 95 percent each week. Seventh, a weekly meeting with sales, marketing, and customer service would review the available capacity against customer orders to achieve consensus priority and resolution of issues.

Next, the team next constructed Level 3 process flow (Figure 15-2), adding appropriate SAP language as the inputs and outputs. The relationship between the supply planning step in sales and operations planning (P1.2) and the master scheduling process (P3) was labeled as rough-cut capacity plan. Essentially, it was a monthly view of the CM01 capacity from month 3 through month 12 that has netted the forecasted requirements (P1.1) against the resource capacities. The expectation, as part of the policy, is that there are no instances in which a resource (production line) is "red" (more requirements than capacity). The relationship between P4 and P3 is focused on the zero- to 8-week horizons, and is defined both by customer orders and replenishment orders called stock transport order (STO). An STO is a replenishment order that is generated when a product stock position in a warehouse has slipped below target, therefore putting product availability at risk. The relationship between D1.3 and P4 is where available-to-promise (ATP) functionality operates.

The point is that orders are now driving requirements in the master scheduling horizon. The other important factor in P4 is how the team has set forecast consumption logic in SAP master data settings. In the open-time horizon, forecasts define the requirements of capacity. As the time horizon approaches the current day, real orders

Figure 15-2. Fowlers' tactical planning SCOR process blueprint.

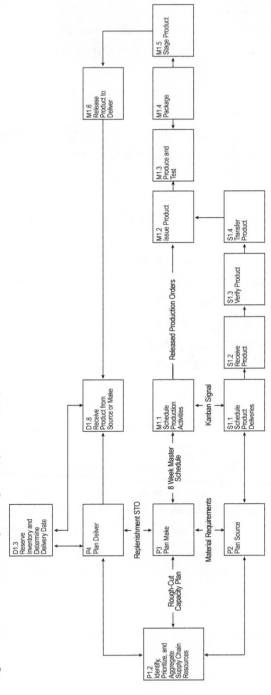

for needed stock replace (or consume) the forecasts. SAP functionality offers a number of ways that forecasts can be consumed.

The relationship of P3 to M1.1 is a two-week fixed plan that the scheduler can release for each product to each production line. If today is Thursday, then next week is considered fixed as Week 1 and the following week is considered fixed as Week 2. All materials should be available for Week 1, and the scheduler typically is working to confirm availability for Week 2. The relationship between P3 and P2 is called *material requirements*. It utilizes both the firm and the open capacity plans and converts them (using MRP) into material, packaging, and/or component requirements for suppliers. The important information includes date, quantity, and source. P2 then converts these requirements into requisitions that pass to S1.1, which then converts them to purchase orders.

Having finished the Level 3 process flow and the SAP module and transaction "should-be" education, the team is excited to dive into the detailed solution design, SCOR process Level 4 flows, and the SAP transaction storyboard.

SAP Modules and Transactions

Under the facilitative guidance of the SAP expert, the Fowlers project team reviewed all of the major *modules* that were part of the original configuration, along with their associated key *transaction codes*.

Modules for the SAP software are portions of functionality within an application *component* that are geared toward addressing specific business tasks. Figure 15-3 illustrates the modules that were a part of the original configuration using the SAP navigation screen for the Logistics component.

Transaction codes in the SAP software are alphanumeric codes (shortcuts) that are a subset of functionality (screens) under each module that help users complete necessary business tasks. For Fowlers, *CM01* capacity planning-work center load is a transaction that supports tasks to be completed in the SCOR processes of P3 PLAN MAKE. For most SAP transactions, the last number indicates the purpose of the transaction (1 to create, 2 to modify, 3 to display data). Figure 15-4 illustrates the SAP navigation screen the Fowlers team used to find the transaction CM01. Table 15-1 is a partial list of SCOR Level 3 elements, related SAP modules, common SAP transactions, and common SAP standard reports related to the Fowlers tactical planning solution.

Figure 15-3. SAP logistics modules.

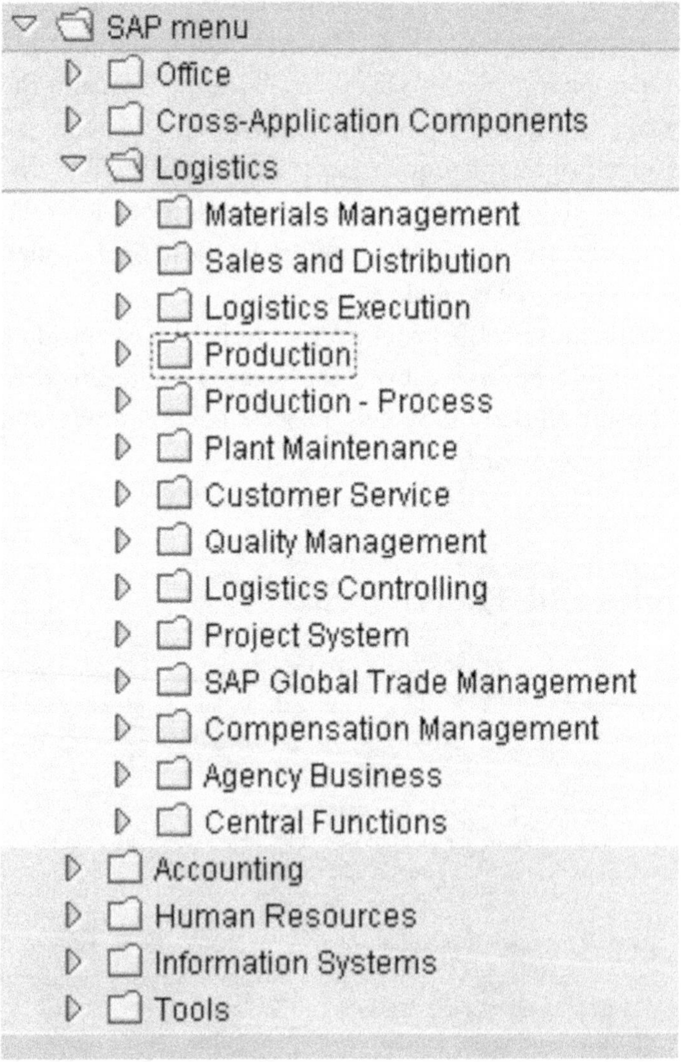

```
▽ 🗁 SAP menu
   ▷ 🗀 Office
   ▷ 🗀 Cross-Application Components
   ▽ 🗁 Logistics
      ▷ 🗀 Materials Management
      ▷ 🗀 Sales and Distribution
      ▷ 🗀 Logistics Execution
      ▷ 🗀 Production
      ▷ 🗀 Production - Process
      ▷ 🗀 Plant Maintenance
      ▷ 🗀 Customer Service
      ▷ 🗀 Quality Management
      ▷ 🗀 Logistics Controlling
      ▷ 🗀 Project System
      ▷ 🗀 SAP Global Trade Management
      ▷ 🗀 Compensation Management
      ▷ 🗀 Agency Business
      ▷ 🗀 Central Functions
   ▷ 🗀 Accounting
   ▷ 🗀 Human Resources
   ▷ 🗀 Information Systems
   ▷ 🗀 Tools
```

Figure 15-4. SAP menu drilldown to transaction CM01.

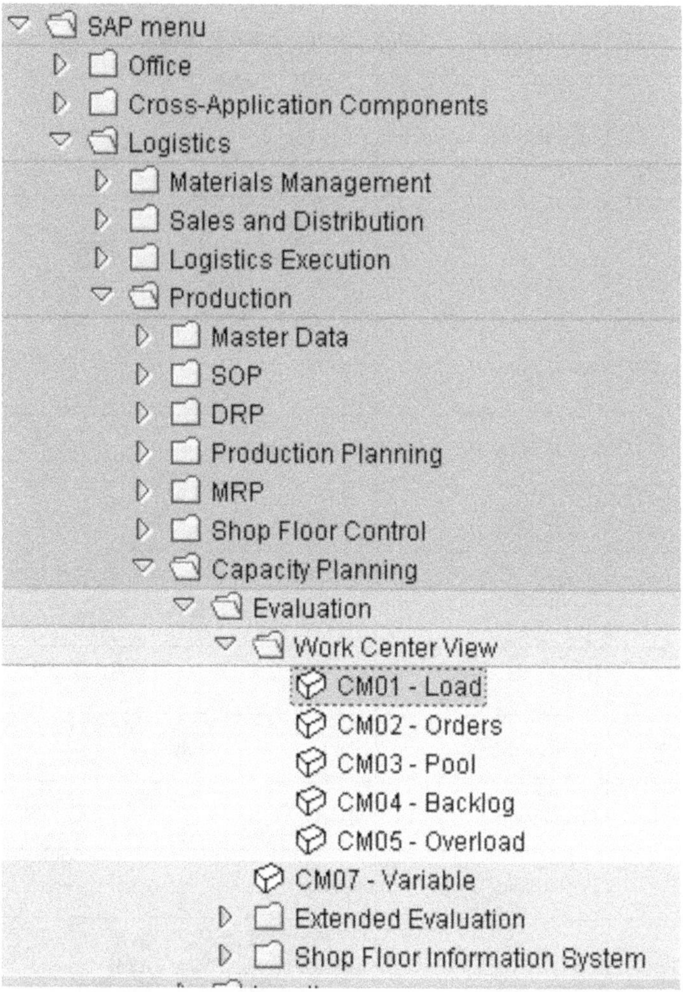

- ▽ 🗐 SAP menu
  - ▷ 🗀 Office
  - ▷ 🗀 Cross-Application Components
  - ▽ 🗐 Logistics
    - ▷ 🗀 Materials Management
    - ▷ 🗀 Sales and Distribution
    - ▷ 🗀 Logistics Execution
    - ▽ 🗐 Production
      - ▷ 🗀 Master Data
      - ▷ 🗀 SOP
      - ▷ 🗀 DRP
      - ▷ 🗀 Production Planning
      - ▷ 🗀 MRP
      - ▷ 🗀 Shop Floor Control
      - ▽ 🗐 Capacity Planning
        - ▽ 🗐 Evaluation
          - ▽ 🗐 Work Center View
            - 🔷 CM01 - Load
            - 🔷 CM02 - Orders
            - 🔷 CM03 - Pool
            - 🔷 CM04 - Backlog
            - 🔷 CM05 - Overload
            - 🔷 CM07 - Variable
          - ▷ 🗀 Extended Evaluation
          - ▷ 🗀 Shop Floor Information System

Table 15-1. SCOR Level 3 elements related to SAP modules and common transactions.

SCOR 10.0 Level 3 Element	SAP Module	Common SAP Transaction Codes
P1.3 Balance Supply Chain Resources with Supply Chain Requirements	Materials Management	CM01
P2.3 Balance Product Resources with Product Requirements	Production	CM01
S1.1 Schedule Product Deliveries	Production	CM29
S1.2 Receive Product	Production	MIGO, MB31
S1.4 Transfer Product	Production	MB1B
M1.1 Schedule Production Activities	Production	CM29
M1.2 Issue Product	Production	MIGO
M1.3 Produce and Test	Production	MB1C—receipt only
M1.4 Package	Production	MB1C
M1.5 Stage Product	Production	MB1B
D1.1 Process Inquiry & Quote	Sales and Distribution	Inquiry: VA11, VA12, VA13 Quote: VA21, VA22, VA23
D1.2 Receive, Enter, & Validate Order	Sales and Distribution	VA01, VA02
D1.3 Reserve Inventory and Determine Delivery Date	Sales and Distribution	Within sales order processing VA01 or VA02 or via Backorder processing: C006 or via Rescheduling: V_V2
D1.8 Receive Product at Warehouse from Source or Make	Sales and Distribution	MIGO, MB31

CHAPTER 16

Phase 4: Level 4 Process Development and the Storyboard

▶ **How Business Process Improvement Is Like a Good Cartoon**

With the SCOR Level 3 blueprint and SAP transaction scope complete, the project team can begin to work on the SCOR Level 4 process details and the SAP transaction storyboard. Also on the docket is development of process control metrics. Recommendations for organizational changes and finalizing RACI analyses will be covered as part of supply chain strategy (Chapter 18).

In AcceleratedSAP terminology, the SCOR Level 3 blueprint (also referred to as high-level business requirements) is part of the business blueprint Phase 2; in the appendix we are on step eight. The blueprint should reflect how your company wants to do business and operate its supply chain and be consistent with the blueprint templates used as part of the QAdb input process. What many people refer to as SCOR Level 4 processes (or as detailed business requirements) are considered the transition blueprint from AcceleratedSAP business blueprint Phase 2 to realization Phase 3. SCOR Level 5 would be considered the baseline configuration for the system.

In fact, whether involving a system solution or not, SCOR Level 4 process details are necessary for any kind of SCOR process implementation activity to occur. While logical, this discussion is a bit of a misnomer because the SCOR model doesn't standardize definitions for Level 4 processes (Figure 16-1); although the model illustrates the relationship of Level 3 to Level 4, there are no Level 4 definitions to be found in the SCOR dictionary itself.

This chapter, then, is devoted to the concept of creating those definitions—blending system functionality, best practices, and data into a solution storyboard.

The concept of the storyboard is borrowed from the art of animation. At the start of a project, the animation director puts together milestone images on the storyboard. This is where the initial story line is developed, and it serves as a point of reference from which the details of the full-length film are later filled in. Similarly, the

Figure 16-1. SCOR Level 3 and Level 4 definitions.

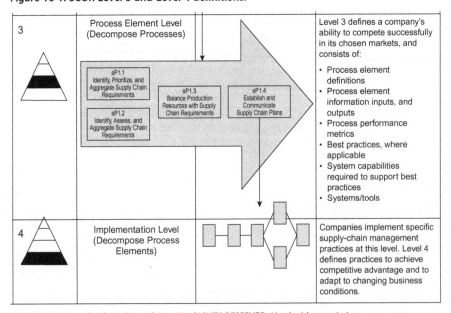

AcceleratedSAP Roadmap (Chapter 17) is the stage at which the solution goes through realization, final preparation, and go-live and support.

Constructing a SCOR Level 4 Process

There are eight steps to building a SCOR Level 4 process. The first four were completed in the last chapter; here is the full list:

1. Find an appropriate leading-practice book that can guide you through best-in-class characteristics.

2. Map your company's "best practice" processes to the SCOR Level 3 process blueprint. (Those who readily admit that they have no leading practices can skip this step).

3. Relate the processes as detailed in the book to appropriate SCOR Level 3 processes.

4. Identify the main system (SAP) transactions to be used, and cross-reference the transactions to the appropriate SCOR Level 3 process; this will help with the inputs and outputs and names for the transactions.

5. Use the transactions to help create a screen-shot storyboard that illustrates the different screens (features and functionality) from the beginning of the process blueprint to its end. The storyboard is relatively easy to produce; the "print screen" key on the computer keyboard allows for easy capture. The storyboard is not intended to replace technical documentation; the goal is to provide the design team and appropriate extended teams with a visual tour of the important functionality.

6. Use the storyboard and the leading-practice book to create the first draft of your Level 4 process.

7. Review the storyboard with appropriate design and extended team members, referencing the process map. The objective is to gain consensus on the features of the solution and understand the degree of change to either the process, the system, or both.

8. Use the feedback from step 7 to set up a system test environment, in which company data can be used to test the new processes and functionality without the risk of messing up the live system. In many cases, these "sandboxes" may have been set up as part of the original implementation effort.

Plan Supply Chain (P1) Level 4 Samples

This chapter includes a generic sample of the Level 4 processes that are commonly used for sales and operations planning. The best-practice resource is based in Thomas F. Wallace and Robert A. Stahl's *Sales & Operations Planning: The How-To Handbook*, 3rd Ed. (T. F. Wallace & Company, 2008). Figures 16-2 through 16-4 illustrate the level process flows for demand planning (P1.1), supply planning (P1.2), and reconciliation (P1.3), respectively.

As an added twist, the Level 4 processes are illustrated in time-phased groupings. In each figure the Level 4 processes are in one of four rows; each row relates to a week of a month (i.e., the first row contains all Week One activities for P1.1, P1.2, and P1.3). That way, a new demand planner can look at Figure 16-2 and understand what work needs to be completed during each week of the month.

Figure 16-5 is an SAP screen shot taken from a P1.1 storyboard that illustrates where the analytical effort from P1.1.4, P1.1.5, P1.1.7, and P1.1.8 (Figure 16-2) would be entered. The shot also illustrates the set of new names for minor transactions: that is, order forecast, marketing adjustment percentage, marketing/sales events, and so on.

(*Text continues on page 199*)

Figure 16-2. P1.1 Level 4 process blueprint for demand planning.

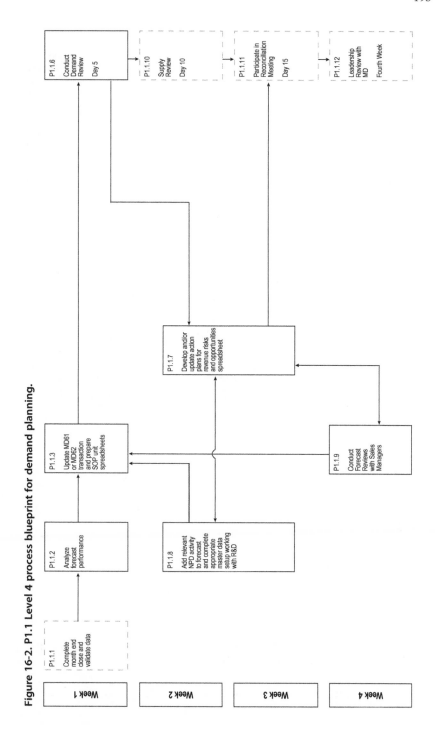

196

Figure 16-3. P1.2 Level 4 process blueprint for supply planning.

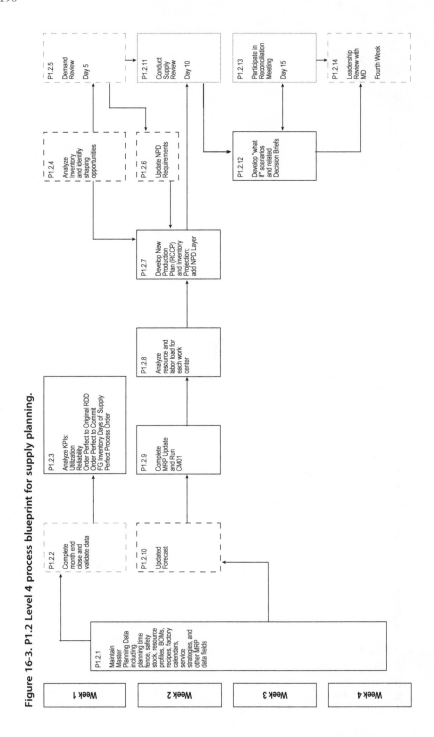

Figure 16-4. P1.3 Level 4 process blueprint for reconciliation.

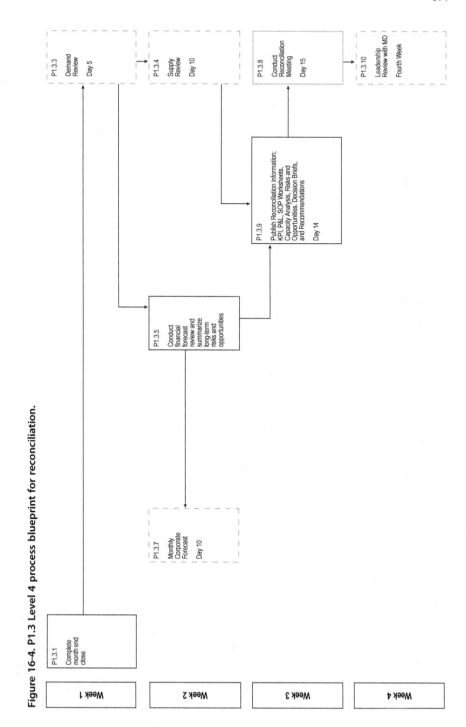

Figure 16-5. Sample storyboard screen shot from P1.1.

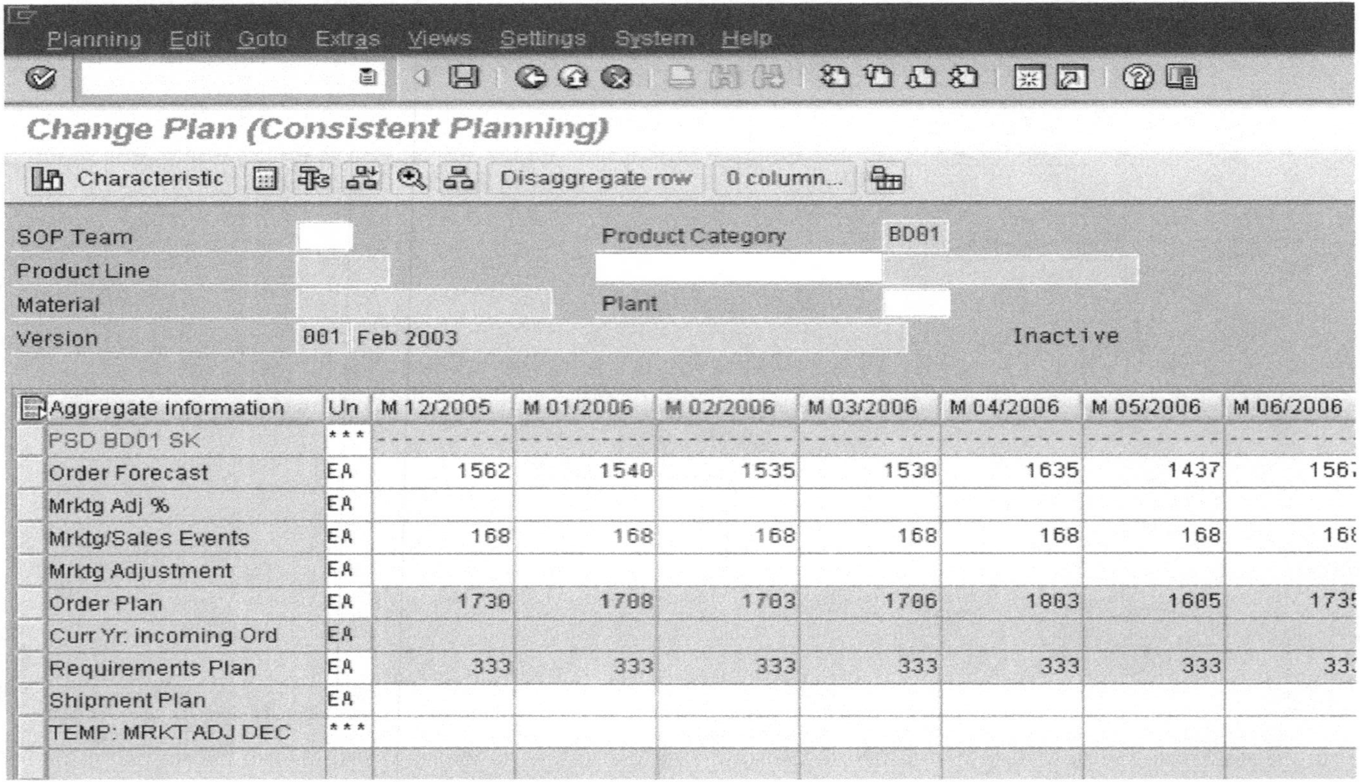
Planning Edit Goto Extras Views Settings System Help
Change Plan (Consistent Planning)
Characteristic
Disaggregate row
0 column...
SOP Team
Product Line
Material
Version
001 Feb 2003
Product Category
BD01
Plant
Inactive

Aggregate information	Un	M 12/2005	M 01/2006	M 02/2006	M 03/2006	M 04/2006	M 05/2006	M 06/2006
PSD BD01 SK	***							
Order Forecast	EA	1562	1540	1535	1538	1635	1437	156
Mrktg Adj %	EA							
Mrktg/Sales Events	EA	168	168	168	168	168	168	16
Mrktg Adjustment	EA							
Order Plan	EA	1730	1708	1703	1706	1803	1605	173
Curr Yr. incoming Ord	EA							
Requirements Plan	EA	333	333	333	333	333	333	33
Shipment Plan	EA							
TEMP: MRKT ADJ DEC	***							

Fowlers P3 Level 4 Processes and Storyboard

Figure 16-6 is Fowlers' P3 PLAN MAKE Level 4 process flow for the Engineer a Tactical Planning Process project. As mentioned, the team members selected *Master Scheduling in the 21st Century* as their best practice resource. They found that it was difficult mapping each of the P3.1, P3.2, P3.3, and P3.4 processes independently, as SAP PP did not behave that way; the flow made more sense by blending the processes on the same page. The process references are consistent with SCOR Level 4.

Capacity Planning for the Storyboard

With the help of the SAP expert, the Fowlers project team started to assemble the resource capacity management storyboard. The first step was to affirm the overall goals—ensure that product will be made with enough lead time to be ready to ship on each sales order, and that adequate capacity, materials, and lead time are available to make this happen.

Second, the team needed to understand how the SAP system is supposed to work. It learned that SAP work centers—or resources—can be used to define the machines and people used to make or assemble materials. In this environment, capacity can be thought of both from a planning and a detailed scheduling point of view.

Capacity planning decisions are typically made for a future time period, commonly 2 to 13 weeks, when it's not yet critical to know exactly when a product will be produced—only that there is sufficient capacity to produce it. Capacity planning answers the question, "Do I have a reasonable chance to make enough product to fulfill a requirement placed on a specific work center within a specific timeframe such as a week or month?"

Detailed scheduling decisions, on the other hand, consider exactly when each product will be produced within the near term, commonly 0 to 2 weeks. The questions a scheduler has to answer are: When exactly (day and shift) do I need the product to be made to fill a specific requirement, such as a sales order or stock transport order? Will I have enough materials to make the product? Will my current production rate achieve the schedule?-And—a favorite of the plant manager and controller: How do I make all of these products and minimize all non-value-added work, such as setup time, changeover time, etc?

Third, the SAP expert worked with the Fowlers project team to piece together the *feature transactions* foundational to the storyboard. The storyboard focused on four areas:

200

Figure 16-6. Fowlers' P3 PLAN MAKE Level 4 process flow for the project: Engineer a Tactical Planning Process.

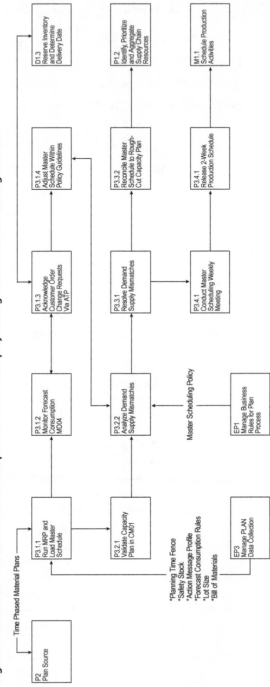

Resources (CRC2), recipes (C202), the capacity planning view (CM01), and the parameter settings for the MRP planning run (MD01). The team selected resource T100 and material F1000 to do a detailed review of the settings.

T100 CRC2 Resource Settings

The capacity formula "Z006" was correct. It calculated the amount of time it took to make one order as Setup Time (defined at Fowlers as the first standard value) plus Machine Time (defined as the second standard value) multiplied by the quantity of product produced (Figure 16-7). The team then checked the standard available capacity (Figure 16-8) and found something wasn't quite right. "We usually only get 85 percent resource capacity utilization but the capacity utilization was set to 100 percent," a team member observed. A note was made to change this field after the review was complete.

F1000 at Plant 2106 C202 Change Recipe

First the team members needed to look at the *Base Quantity* of the recipe to ensure they understood the *run rates* required for each step or operation to make the product. The Base Quantity was equal to 1 (Figure 16-9) The SAP expert explained that this meant the machine run rates would be equal to the amount of time required to make one each of material F1000. The First Standard Value—*setup time*—was equal to 1 hour. The second Standard Value—*machine time*—was equal to 0.1 hours (Figure 16-10).

The SAP expert also explained how capacity was calculated when making material F1000. Using the formula from the resource, he calculated the capacity required to produce one order of 200 Eaches (units) of F1000 as follows:

Setup time = 1.0 hour

Machine Time of 0.1 hour × 200 Eaches (or units) = 20.0 hours

Total time required = 21.0 hours

CM01 Capacity Planning

The first thing the team members noticed was that Week 11 was highlighted in red; capacity requirements exceeded available capacity (Figure 16-11). Clicking on the red line, they drilled down and found that there were two orders planned to be produced that week: orders 12022 and 12103. "Wait a second," one team member exclaimed, "Order 12022 is for a quantity of 1,090 EA of F1000, which would give us a total of 110 hours. But the capacity requirement is only equal to 80 hours. How can that be?" (Figure 16-12). Looking at the dates for order 12022, they were able to determine a start date of Friday, March 11, and completion on Monday, March 21. They went back to the main view of CM01, and by drilling into the prior and post weeks found the "missing" 30 hours. (Figure 16-13).

The capacity problem in Week 11 remained unresolved, but the team agreed it could be addressed when looking at the overall stock requirements for Material F1000, which prompted another team member to notice that there weren't any requirements in any of the future weeks. "We always load forecasts eight weeks into the future to ensure that when we run the MRP for planned orders we can estimate our future capacity requirements," he said. "I've seen planned orders in the future, but where are the requirements?"

MRP Planning Run MD01

To ensure accurate capacity requirements are generated, Scheduling Parameter 2 must be selected when running the MRP planning run (Figure 16-14). When using Scheduling Parameter 1, the system uses information contained within the material master—specifically the scheduling parameters *In-house Production Time, Goods Receipt Processing Time* and the *Scheduling Margin Key*—to calculate the basic start and finish dates for a planned order. Planned Orders created with basic dates do not appear on CM01. The team made a note to change the MD01 Scheduling parameter to "2" for future MRP planning runs.

Figure 16-7. T100 CRC2 resource settings in SAP capacities setup screen.

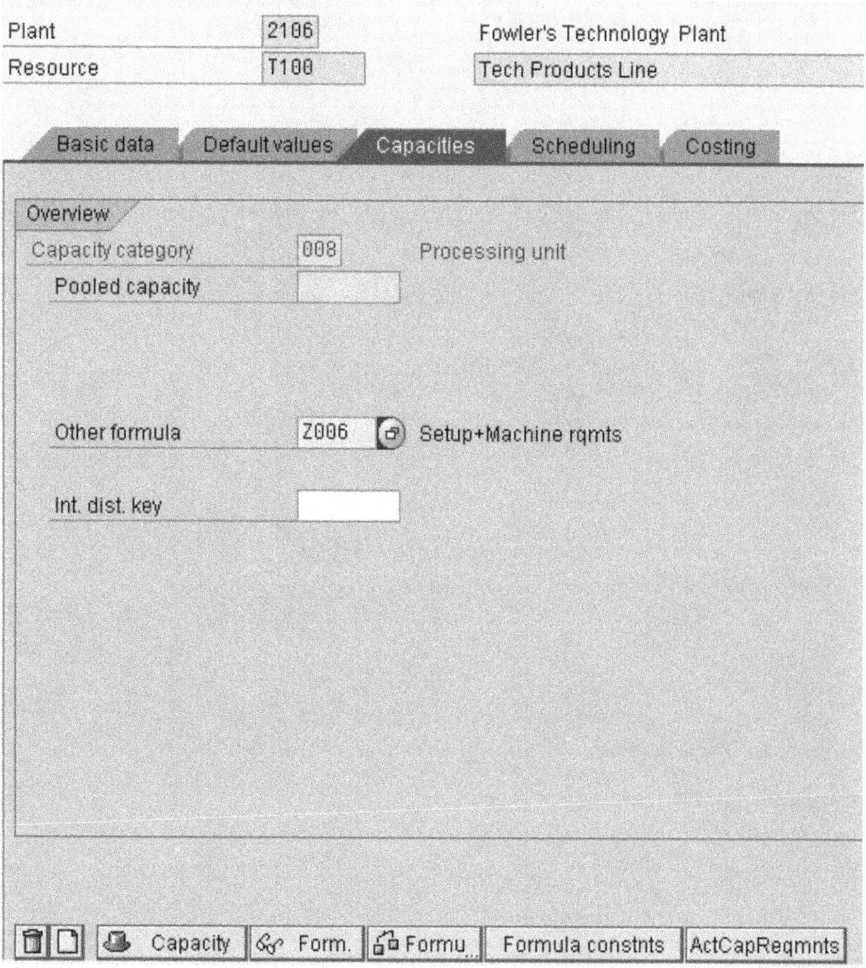

Plant	2106	Fowler's Technology Plant
Resource	T100	Tech Products Line

Basic data | Default values | Capacities | Scheduling | Costing

Overview

Capacity category	008	Processing unit
Pooled capacity		

Other formula	Z006	Setup+Machine rqmts

Int. dist. key

Capacity | Form. | Formu.. | Formula constnts | ActCapReqmnts

Figure 16-8. Standard available capacity in SAP capacity setup screen.

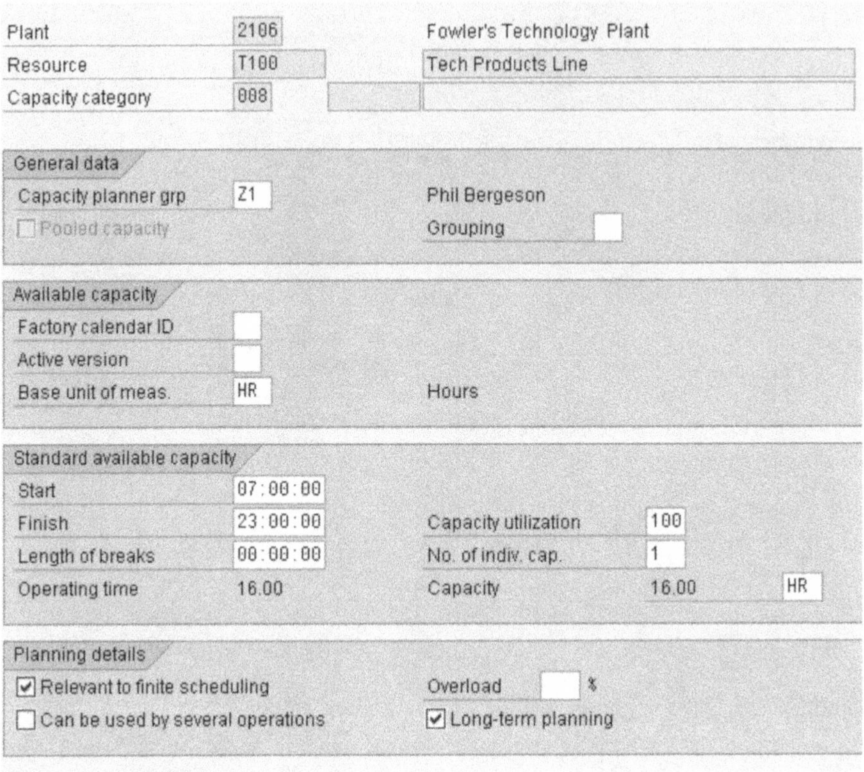

Plant	2106	Fowler's Technology Plant
Resource	T100	Tech Products Line
Capacity category	008	

General data

Capacity planner grp	Z1	Phil Bergeson
☐ Pooled capacity		Grouping ☐

Available capacity

Factory calendar ID	
Active version	
Base unit of meas.	HR	Hours

Standard available capacity

Start	07:00:00		
Finish	23:00:00	Capacity utilization	100
Length of breaks	00:00:00	No. of indiv. cap.	1
Operating time	16.00	Capacity	16.00	HR

Planning details

☑ Relevant to finite scheduling	Overload ☐ %
☐ Can be used by several operations	☑ Long-term planning

Figure 16-9. Setting of base quantity for required run rates.

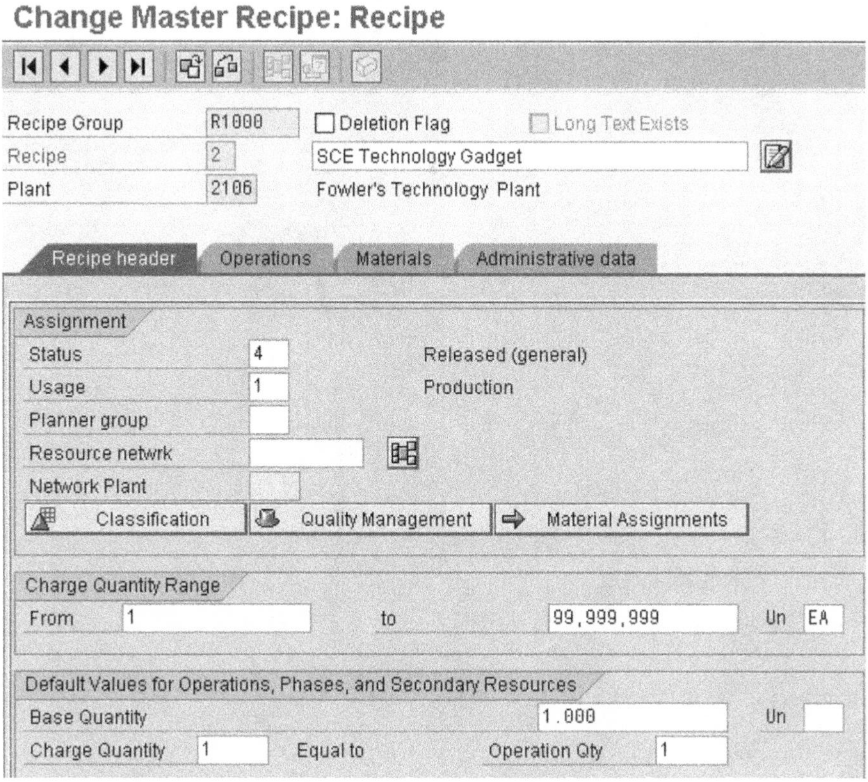

Change Master Recipe: Recipe

Recipe Group	R1000	☐ Deletion Flag	☐ Long Text Exists	
Recipe	2	SCE Technology Gadget		🖉
Plant	2106	Fowler's Technology Plant		

Recipe header | Operations | Materials | Administrative data

Assignment

Status	4	Released (general)
Usage	1	Production
Planner group		
Resource netwrk		
Network Plant		

🗚 Classification | 🖳 Quality Management | ➡ Material Assignments

Charge Quantity Range

From	1	to	99,999,999	Un	EA

Default Values for Operations, Phases, and Secondary Resources

Base Quantity		1.000	Un	
Charge Quantity	1	Equal to	Operation Qty	1

206

Figure 16-10. Settings for set-up time and machine time.

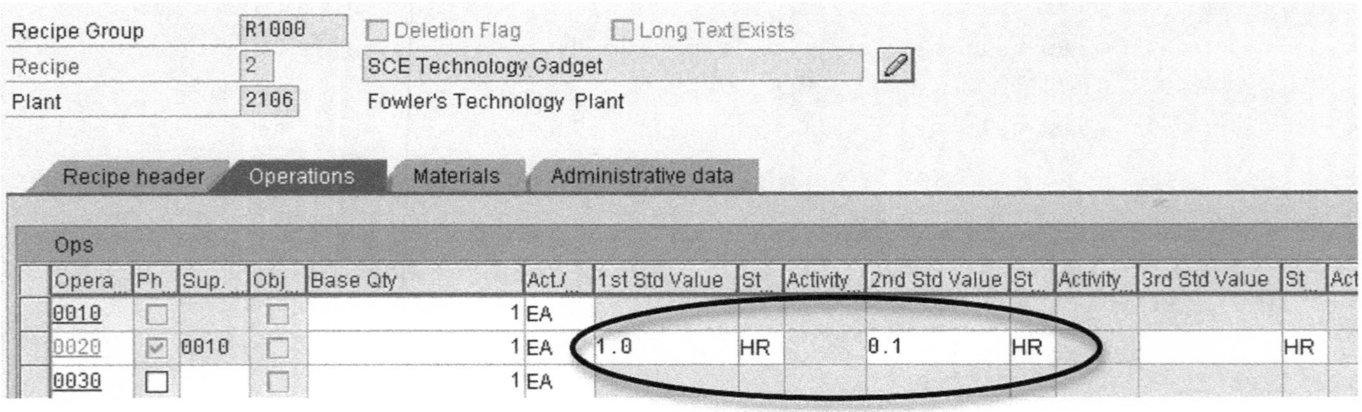

Recipe Group	R1000
Recipe	2	SCE Technology Gadget
Plant	2106	Fowler's Technology Plant

☐ Deletion Flag   ☐ Long Text Exists

Recipe header | Operations | Materials | Administrative data

Ops

Opera.	Ph.	Sup.	Obj.	Base Qty	Act./	1st Std Value	St.	Activity	2nd Std Value	St.	Activity	3rd Std Value	St.	Act
0010	☐		☐		1 EA									
0020	☑	0010	☐		1 EA	1.0	HR		0.1	HR			HR	
0030	☐		☐		1 EA									

Figure 16-11. SAP capacity planning screen showing requirements in excess of capacity.

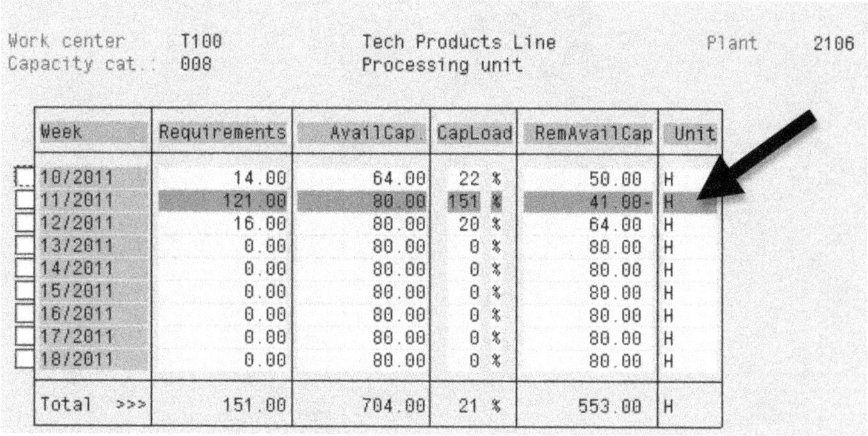

| Work center | T100 | | Tech Products Line | | | Plant | 2106 |
| Capacity cat. | 008 | | Processing unit | | | | |

Week	Requirements	AvailCap.	CapLoad	RemAvailCap	Unit
10/2011	14.00	64.00	22 %	50.00	H
11/2011	121.00	80.00	151 %	41.00-	H
12/2011	16.00	80.00	20 %	64.00	H
13/2011	0.00	80.00	0 %	80.00	H
14/2011	0.00	80.00	0 %	80.00	H
15/2011	0.00	80.00	0 %	80.00	H
16/2011	0.00	80.00	0 %	80.00	H
17/2011	0.00	80.00	0 %	80.00	H
18/2011	0.00	80.00	0 %	80.00	H
Total >>>	151.00	704.00	21 %	553.00	H

Figure 16-12. SAP calendar week 11 capacity planning for Order 12022.

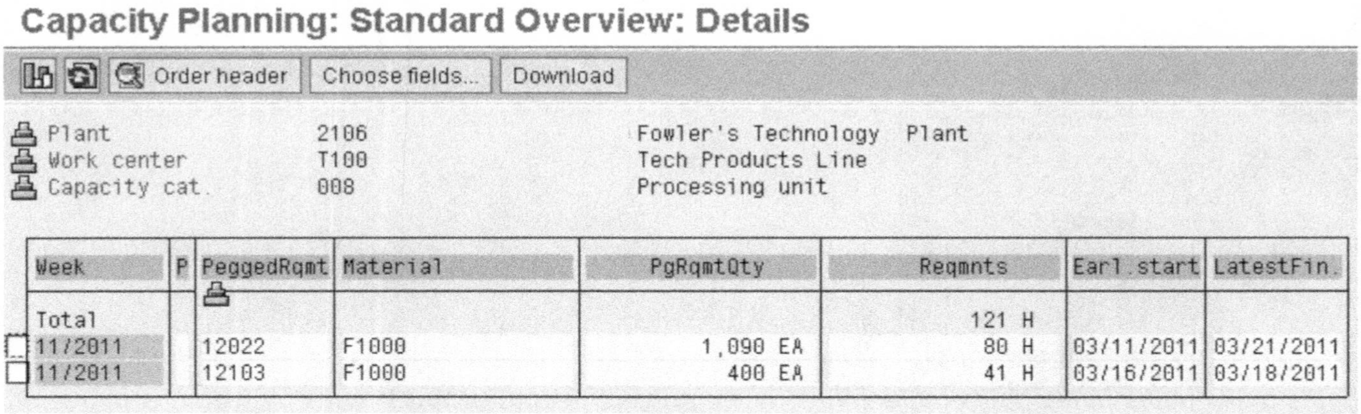

Capacity Planning: Standard Overview: Details

| | | Order header | Choose fields... | Download |

Plant	2106	Fowler's Technology Plant
Work center	T100	Tech Products Line
Capacity cat.	008	Processing unit

Week	P	PeggedRqmt	Material	PgRqmtQty	Reqmnts	Earl. start	LatestFin.
Total					121 H		
11/2011		12022	F1000	1,090 EA	80 H	03/11/2011	03/21/2011
11/2011		12103	F1000	400 EA	41 H	03/16/2011	03/18/2011

Figure 16-13. Finding additional run time needed for Order 12022 in weeks 10 (top) and 12 (bottom).

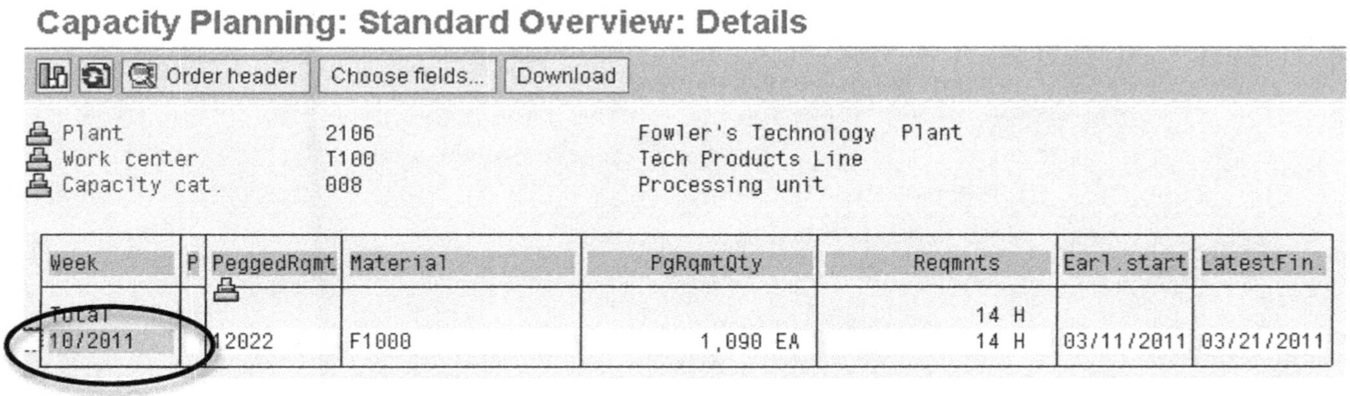

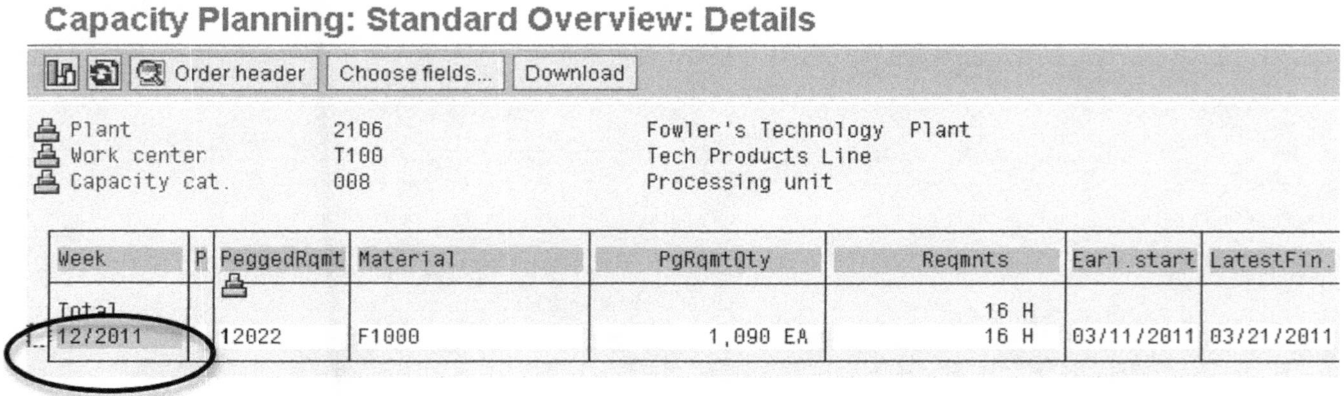

Capacity Planning: Standard Overview: Details

Order header | Choose fields.... | Download

Plant	2106	Fowler's Technology Plant
Work center	T100	Tech Products Line
Capacity cat.	008	Processing unit

Week	P	PeggedRqmt	Material	PgRqmtQty	Reqmnts	Earl.start	LatestFin.
		12022	F1000	1,090 EA	14 H		
Total					14 H	03/11/2011	03/21/2011
10/2011							

Capacity Planning: Standard Overview: Details

Order header | Choose fields.... | Download

Plant	2106	Fowler's Technology Plant
Work center	T100	Tech Products Line
Capacity cat.	008	Processing unit

Week	P	PeggedRqmt	Material	PgRqmtQty	Reqmnts	Earl.start	LatestFin.
		12022	F1000	1,090 EA	16 H		
Total					16 H	03/11/2011	03/21/2011
12/2011							

210

Figure 16-14. Correcting SAP MRP scheduling parameters assures accurate capacity requirements.

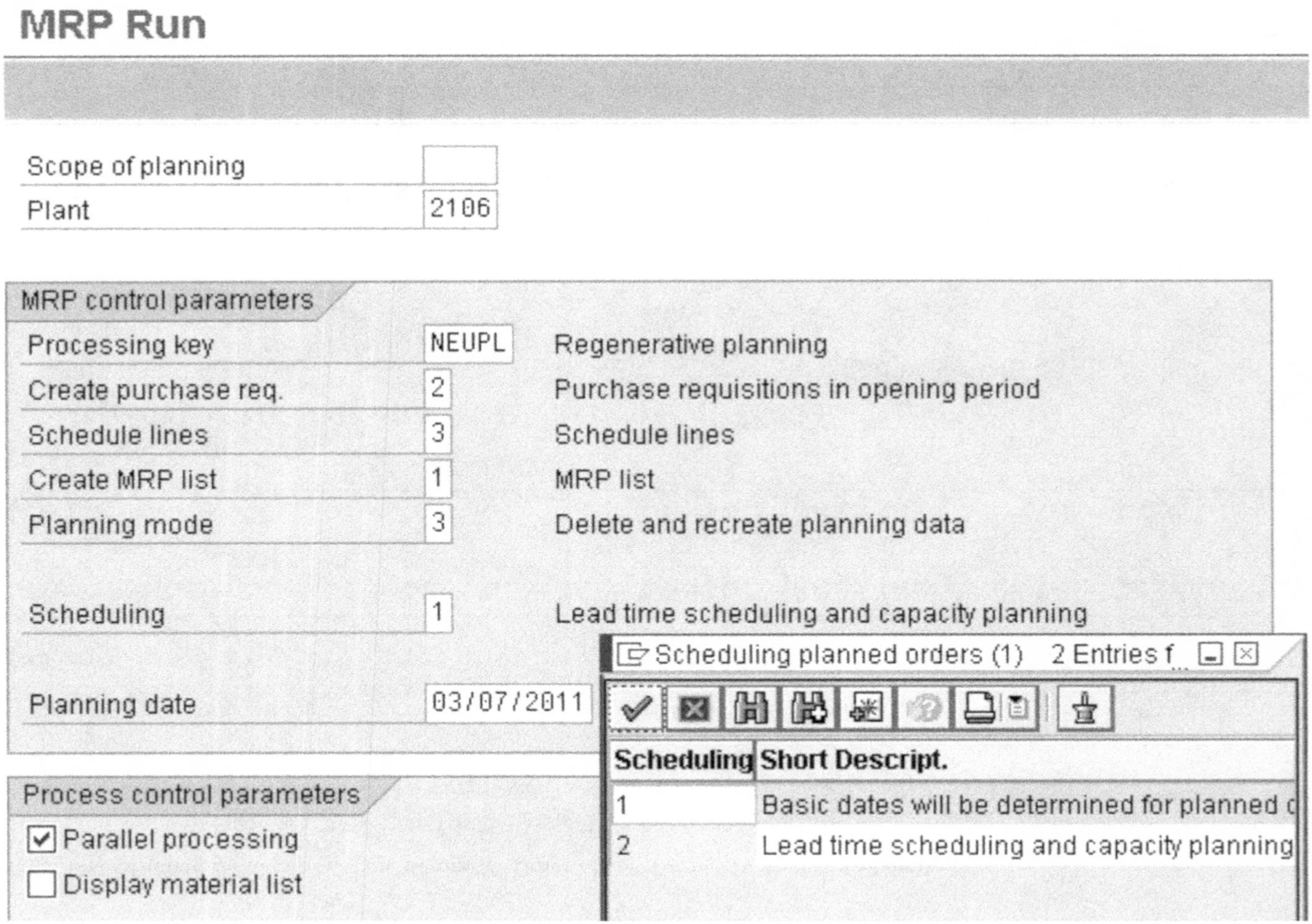

MRP Run

Scope of planning	
Plant	2106

MRP control parameters

Processing key	NEUPL	Regenerative planning
Create purchase req.	2	Purchase requisitions in opening period
Schedule lines	3	Schedule lines
Create MRP list	1	MRP list
Planning mode	3	Delete and recreate planning data
Scheduling	1	Lead time scheduling and capacity planning
Planning date	03/07/2011	

☐ Scheduling planned orders (1)   2 Entries f... ☐ ☒

Scheduling Short Descript.

1	Basic dates will be determined for planned o
2	Lead time scheduling and capacity planning

Process control parameters

☑ Parallel processing

☐ Display material list

Stock Requirements for the Storyboard

Now that the team had the feature pieces of the capacity storyboard (sidebar: Capacity Planning for the Storyboard), the next step was to assemble the feature pieces of the planning process, including demand (requirements) and supply (receipts). The team picked product F1000, a make-to-stock item manufactured at a North American plant (SAP plant 2106) and typically shipped to a distribution center (SAP plant 2105) until required for a customer shipment.

As with all things in the SAP process, the team needed to understand some basic nomenclature. An SAP Material Requirements Planning (MRP) "run" uses *master and transactional data* to generate receipts to fulfill open requirements. Typical requirements are customer orders (*CusOrd*), planned independent requirements (*IndReq*), stock transfer requests to another plant, and safety stock (*SafeSt*). Receipts are represented by purchase requisitions (*PurRqs*) or planned orders (*PldOrd*). All of these MRP elements represent the current and future stock planning situation and can be seen using SAP transaction MD04—the Stock Requirements List (Figure 16-15).

The team first viewed MD04 for SAP plant 2105 and material F1000 and found the following receipt and requirement MRP elements:

Like a checkbook, each receipt (like a deposit) and requirement (like a debit) affects the available stock—SAP terminology is *available qty*. Note, the VSF requirements for 03/07/2011 and 03/14/2011 did not affect available stock; the SAP expert explained that configuration settings for some VSF forecasts, called *planned independent requirements* (PIRs), allow the requirements to be ignored within a specified short-term timeframe. This is helpful when it's desirable to respond only to customer orders in the short term, but do use the VSF forecast (PIRs) to help secure capacity and components.

Working over the same computer, the team members clicked on the summation sign at the left-hand side of the screen and were able to see *weekly aggregated receipts and requirements* (Figure 16-16). The team observed that there were no VSF forecast PIRs in week 12/2011. The SAP expert explained that they were "consumed" by customer orders to ensure that the requirements were not double-counted (900 in the requirements column). The details of this consumption could be found by navigating directly to the *total requirements display* (Figure 16-17) from transaction MD04. SAP Planning Strategy 40—*planning with final assembly*—designated F1000 as a make-to-stock item for which forecasts helped position available stock ahead of customer orders.

The last main feature in the storyboard was that of the planning time fence. On the MD04 screen for F1000 (Figure 16-18) the SAP expert pointed out that the purchase requisitions (additions to stock) would be fulfilled by plant 2106 as noted in the *Deliv/Recv Plant* column, and that the customer ordering the product was "Super Tech" (subtractions from stock). On viewing the stock requirements list (Figure 16-19) for plant 2106, the SAP expert pointed out the *End of planning time fence* listed for date 03/22/

2011. The planning time fence for this material at this plant is set at 10 working days past the current date. Essentially, beyond the planning time fence, SAP MRP can recommend planned orders—*PldOrd*; within the planning time fence, only manual changes can be made by the scheduler. As demand increases within the time fence, planned orders are placed just outside the time fence, as in the case of *PldOrd 03/24/2011*.

Figure 16-15. SAP stock/requirements list for product F1000 at plant 2106.

Stock/Requirements List as of 22:22 Hrs

Show Overview Tree

| Material | F1000 | SCE Technology Gadget |
| Plant | 2105 | MRP type | PD | Material Type | FERT | Unit | EA |

A	Date	MRP element	MRP element data	Rescheduli	E	Rec./reqd qty	Available qty	Deliv./recv. plant	Stor	Customer	Customer
	03/08/2011	Stock					900				
	03/08/2011	SafeSt	Safety stock			100-	800				
	03/07/2011	IndReq	VSF			500-	500-				
	03/14/2011	IndReq	VSF			350-	350-				
	03/17/2011	CusOrd	0010000003/000020/0000			150-	650			10011	SuperTech
	03/24/2011	PurRqs	3000000066/00000			100	750	2106			
	03/24/2011	CusOrd	0010000003/000010/0000			750-	0		0200	10011	SuperTech
	03/28/2011	PurRqs	3000000067/00000			500	500	2106			
	03/28/2011	IndReq	VSF			500-	500-				
	04/04/2011	PldOrd	0000012264/STPO			750	750	2106			
	04/04/2011	IndReq	VSF			750-	0				
	04/11/2011	PldOrd	0000012265/STPO			750	750	2106			
	04/11/2011	IndReq	VSF			750-	0				
	04/18/2011	PldOrd	0000012266/STPO			750	750	2106			
	04/18/2011	IndReq	VSF			750-	0				

Date | GR | ST | On | Vendor | Cust.

Page 1 / 1

Figure 16-16. Product F1000 Weekly Aggregated Receipts and Requirements, with "consumed" PIRs.

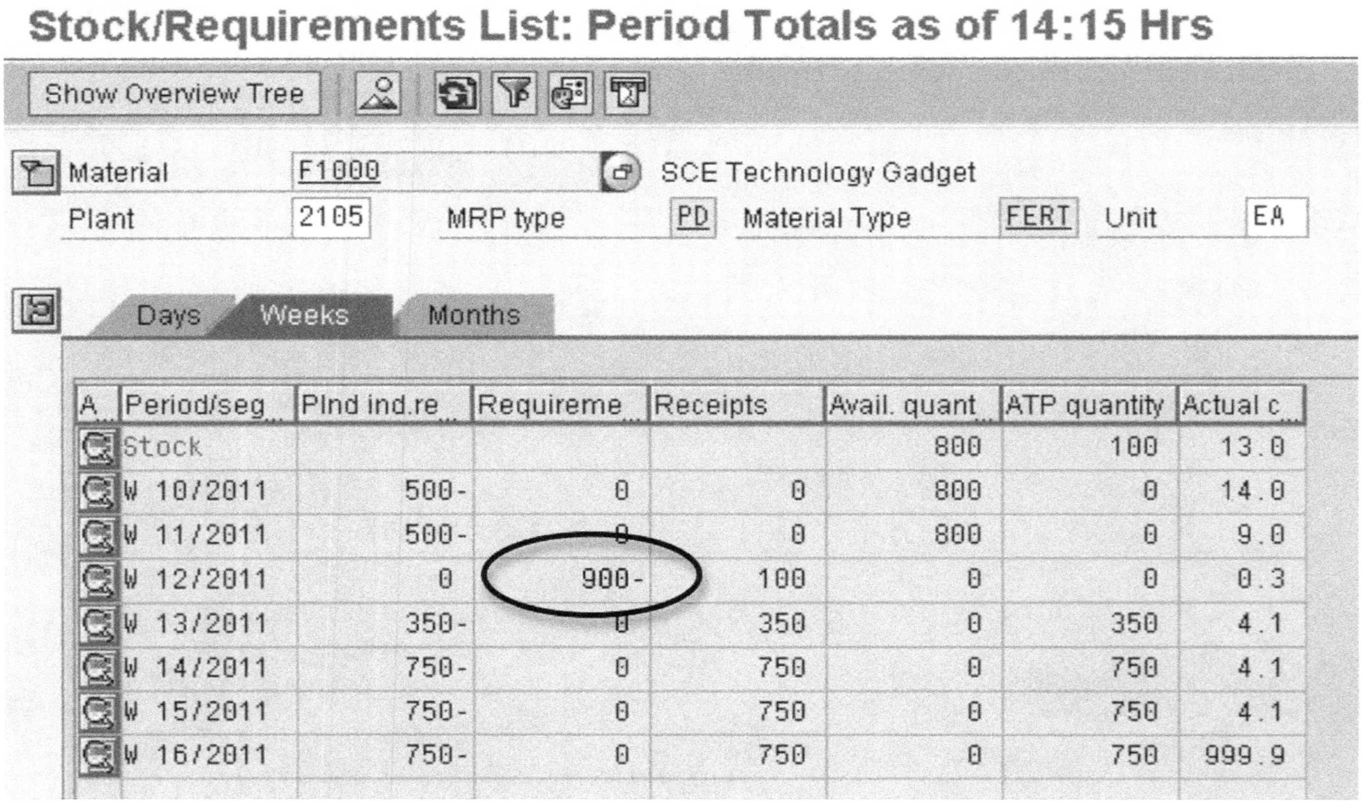

Stock/Requirements List: Period Totals as of 14:15 Hrs

Show Overview Tree

Material F1000 SCE Technology Gadget

Plant 2105 MRP type PD Material Type FERT Unit EA

Days Weeks Months

A	Period/seg	Plnd ind.re	Requireme	Receipts	Avail. quant	ATP quantity	Actual c
	Stock				800	100	13.0
	W 10/2011	500-	0	0	800	0	14.0
	W 11/2011	500-	0	0	800	0	9.0
	W 12/2011	0	900-	100	0	0	0.3
	W 13/2011	350-	0	350	0	350	4.1
	W 14/2011	750-	0	750	0	750	4.1
	W 15/2011	750-	0	750	0	750	4.1
	W 16/2011	750-	0	750	0	750	999.9

Figure 16-17. Total requirements display detailing consumption of PIRs.

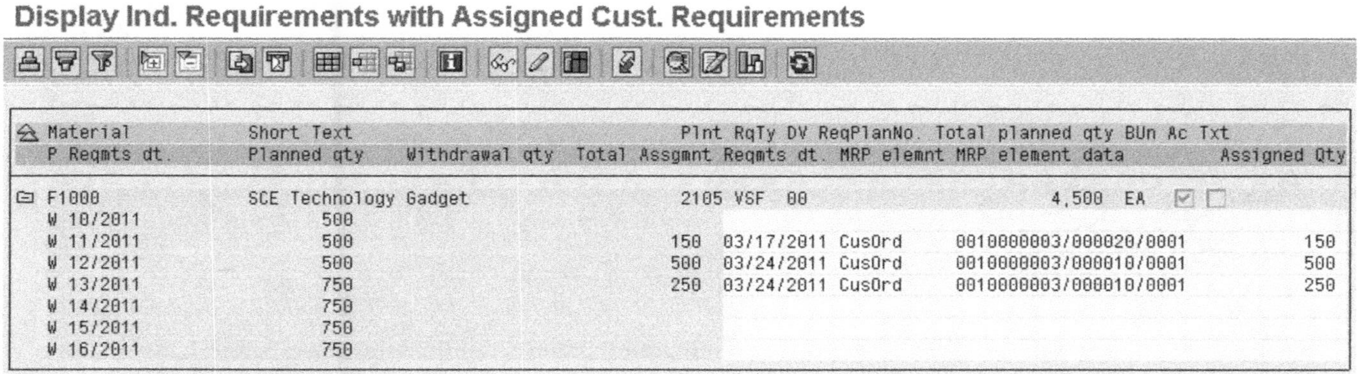

Display Ind. Requirements with Assigned Cust. Requirements

Material	Short Text	Plnt	RqTy	Dv	ReqPlanNo	Total planned qty	BUn	Ac Txt
F1000	SCE Technology Gadget	2105	VSF	00		4,500	EA	

P Reqmts dt.	Planned qty	Withdrawal qty	Total	Assgmnt	Reqmts dt	MRP element	MRP element data	Assigned Qty
W 10/2011	500			150	03/17/2011	CusOrd	0010000003/000020/0001	150
W 11/2011	500			500	03/24/2011	CusOrd	0010000003/000010/0001	500
W 12/2011	500			250	03/24/2011	CusOrd	0010000003/000010/0001	250
W 13/2011	750							
W 14/2011	750							
W 15/2011	750							
W 16/2011	750							

Figure 16-18. Purchase requisitions are fulfilled by plant 2106; customer is "Super Tech."

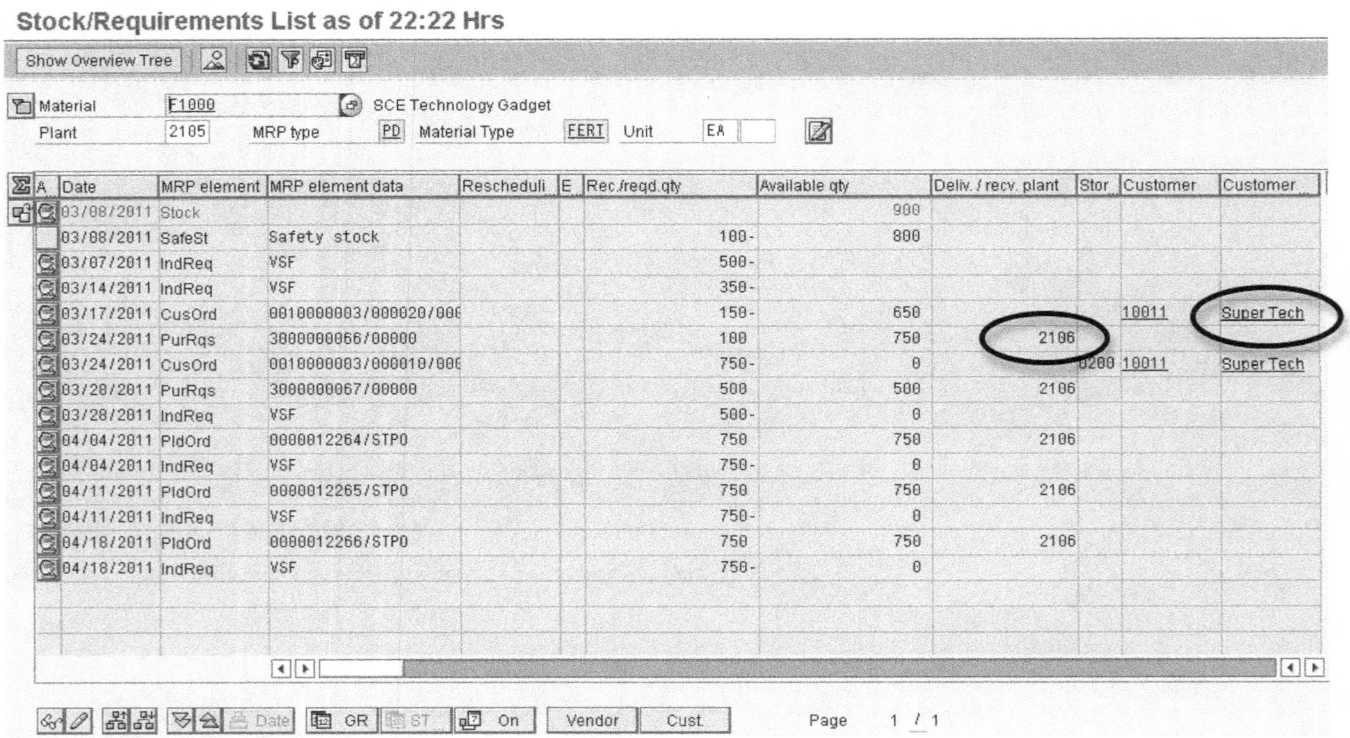
Stock/Requirements List as of 22:22 Hrs
Show Overview Tree
Material F1000 SCE Technology Gadget
Plant 2105 MRP type PD Material Type FERT Unit EA
Date GR ST On Vendor Cust. Page 1 / 1

A	Date	MRP element	MRP element data	Rescheduli	E	Rec./reqd.qty	Available qty	Deliv. / recv. plant	Stor	Customer	Customer
	03/08/2011	Stock					900				
	03/08/2011	SafeSt	Safety stock			100-	800				
	03/07/2011	IndReq	VSF			500-					
	03/14/2011	IndReq	VSF			350-					
	03/17/2011	CusOrd	0010000003/000020/000			150-	650			10011	Super Tech
	03/24/2011	PurRqs	3000000066/00000			100	750	2106			
	03/24/2011	CusOrd	0010000003/000010/000			750-	0		0200	10011	Super Tech
	03/28/2011	PurRqs	3000000067/00000			500	500	2106			
	03/28/2011	IndReq	VSF			500-	0				
	04/04/2011	PldOrd	0000012264/STPO			750	750	2106			
	04/04/2011	IndReq	VSF			750-	0				
	04/11/2011	PldOrd	0000012265/STPO			750	750	2106			
	04/11/2011	IndReq	VSF			750-	0				
	04/18/2011	PldOrd	0000012266/STPO			750	750	2106			
	04/18/2011	IndReq	VSF			750-	0				

Figure 16-19. The planning time fence locks out automated changes during the production run.

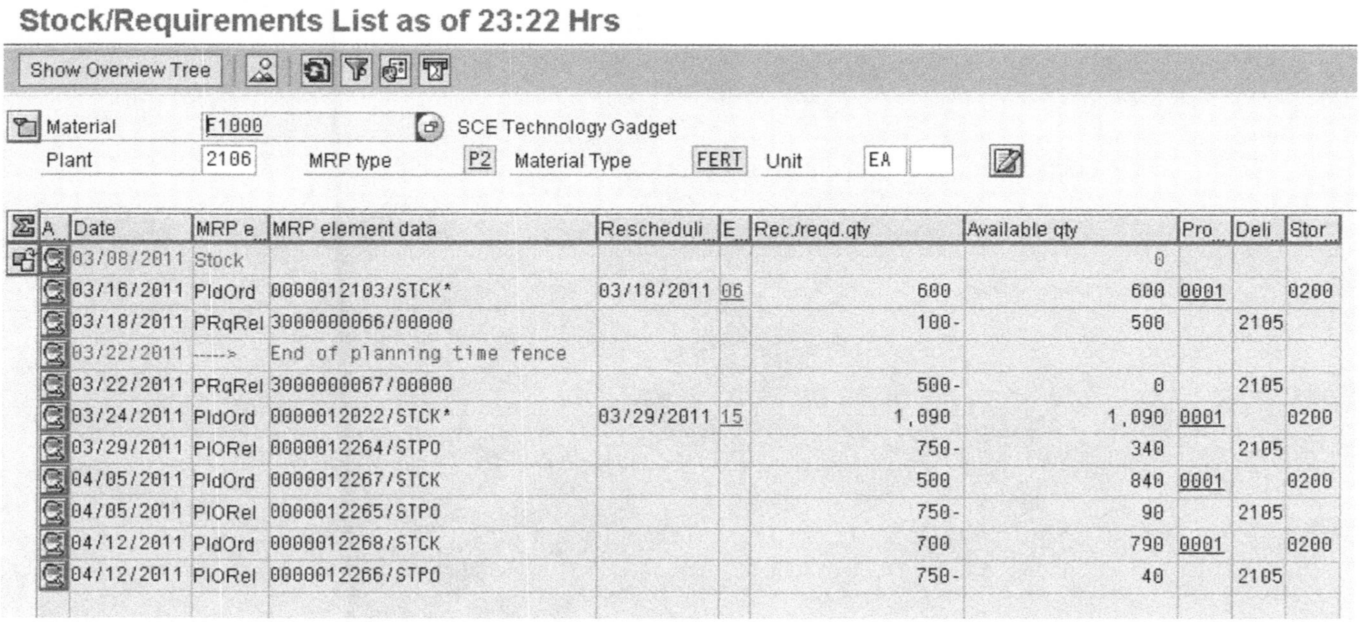

Stock/Requirements List as of 23:22 Hrs

Show Overview Tree

Material F1000   SCE Technology Gadget

Plant 2106   MRP type   P2   Material Type   FERT   Unit   EA

A	Date	MRP e	MRP element data	Reschedul	E	Rec./reqd.qty	Available qty	Pro...	Deli	Stor
	03/08/2011	Stock					0			0200
	03/16/2011	PldOrd	0000012103/STCK*	03/18/2011	06	600	600	0001		0200
	03/18/2011	PRqRel	3000000066/00000			100-	500		2105	
	03/22/2011	---->	End of planning time fence							
	03/22/2011	PRqRel	3000000067/00000			500-	0		2105	
	03/24/2011	PldOrd	0000012022/STCK*	03/29/2011	15	1,090	1,090	0001		0200
	03/29/2011	PlORel	0000012264/STPO			750-	340		2105	
	04/05/2011	PldOrd	0000012267/STCK			500	840	0001	2105	0200
	04/05/2011	PlORel	0000012265/STPO			750-	90		2105	
	04/12/2011	PldOrd	0000012268/STCK			700	790	0001	2105	0200
	04/12/2011	PlORel	0000012266/STPO			750-	40		2105	

CHAPTER 17

Phase 4: Configure, Solution Test, Pilot, Refine, and Roll Out

▶ **Moving the Needle on Performance**

The typical elapsed time to get to this point of project implementation (steps 1 through 8 on the implementation checklist in Chapter 11) ranges from one to three months, depending on the process scope, complexity of the solution storyboard, and the priority of resources assigned. Fully implementing the solution (steps 9 through 13 on the checklist)—meaning rolling it out to all the intended supply chains—typically ranges from six to 12 months, based on the factors already mentioned. In between, there are four approval milestones or "gates": solution test, pilot one, refinement and pilot two, and solution rollout.

From an AcceleratedSAP point of view, this implementation phase aligns to the realization, final preparation, and go-live and support points of the roadmap. Tasks include:

- ◆ Review scope and design all development items
- ◆ Document and complete all functional configuration and programming work

- Baseline configuration
- Fine-tuning configuration

- Conduct system integration testing
  - Unit/functional testing
  - System integration testing
  - User acceptance testing
  - Load and stress testing

- Complete business acceptance and sign-off
- Prepare for production cutover
  - Transport configuration design from development to production system
  - Complete master data integrity check
  - Migrate necessary data from legacy systems
  - Complete final stability, availability, and performance checks

- Go-live
- Support operational stabilization
  - Setup and support process for end-user community
  - Fix bugs, and transport prioritized changes from development to production
  - Measure and respond to SAP performance metrics
  - Measure and respond to business performance metrics
  - Educate user community on standard reports and means to extract data
  - Manage documentation and training

Configuration (or Build)

With the process and system solution (business scenarios) approved, the system's functional experts can begin the process of configuring or building the system to perform the TO BE tasks. Relative to SAP functionality configuration, this involves selecting options that will refine how SAP transactions perform business requirements as defined in the storyboard.

The business team members of the project have other types of configuration tasks. First they must document all SCOR ENABLE process assumptions, policies, performance management, etc., for the process scope as defined. Second, they need to select and train "power users" in the Level 4 processes as well as in the detailed system transactions. Last, they need to publish or update standard operating procedures to accommodate the changes in process.

At Fowlers, the business team members had already built the master scheduling policy, and felt that it served as the basis for the ENABLE PLAN processes and could be refined during the pilot. They picked power-user candidates from the other regions to participate in the pilot as part of the learning process for rollout. They utilized their ISO Quality System change-management and document-control processes to update appropriate standard operation procedures. With an approved solution design (storyboard and SCOR Level 4 process), the SAP PP functional expert went to work. (See "Configuring SAP Functionality" on page 225 for details related to Fowlers' configuration of the tactical planning business process.)

Solution Test

Solution test involves setting up or using an existing system test environment or "sandbox." Essentially, this is a non-production system that has real data, part numbers, customers, suppliers, etc., and is intended to test configuration scripts. The sandbox can be used as early as building the storyboard and viewing TO BE scenarios for individual transactions. In fact, the earlier in the solution design process a sandbox can be used to demonstrate the TO BE, the faster the project team can gain consensus on changes.

For SAP solution test, there generally are four types. First, unit or functional testing validates each step of the storyboard and SCOR Level 4 process to ensure that each performs as expected. Second, integration testing involves walking through all the steps in the blueprint, using real data and business scenarios; the goal is to see if the entire process works together and the process operates effectively within the larger SCOR Level 3 blueprint. Relative to SAP functionality, common integrated test plans may focus on order-to-cash, procure-to-pay, or record to report.

Third, user acceptance testing is a detailed real-world test involving the power users. Ideally, the test scenarios are common and less-common business scenarios that occur on a daily, weekly, and monthly basis. And fourth, load or stress testing is required to ensure that the process is effective under a large volume of users doing their work of managing transactions. Database locking point and responsiveness are two key areas under scrutiny in this last testing phase.

The Fowlers team members felt that their use of the sandbox during solution design, and the results they could observe in the storyboard, met the expectations of the SAP unit test. Integration testing, on the other hand, proved to be more complicated than originally thought. For example, the team needed to ensure that the master scheduling process and transactions worked effectively with the production scheduling transaction. It had been configured as a Z transaction, meaning that it was customized to the plant away from the standard SAP transaction. The TO BE blueprint initially did not operate well with the scheduling transaction. User acceptance testing and load testing were carried out by the power users and functional expert team by the book.

Pilot One, Refine, and Pilot Two

With the testing and business acceptance complete, the next step is to pilot. The first step in a *solution pilot* involves selecting a very small scope on which to run the solution. Examples of a small scope could be one resource (production line) of one plant; one product to one customer; one product from one supplier; or one product family in one business. Next, the team needs to operate the process for at least four weeks; this ensures that the process is tested across a month-end reporting sequence. The third step is for the team to meet formally and conduct a detailed review of the SCOR Level 4 processes—assessing whether the process step was effective and if any changes need to be made to policy, process, system, RACI, etc. Last, a proposed change list is presented to the steering team and, as approved, is incorporated as refinements into the next pilot cycle.

In pilot two, the scope is expanded as appropriate, the processes are operated for another four weeks, and the review and refinement process is followed one more time.

Fowlers Pilot Results

Fowlers' pilot one process yielded some important discoveries that needed to be incorporated into pilot two. First, the team needed better data collection, analysis, and policy for schedule attainment as it related to what the master schedule expected. After the first week of the pilot, an analysis showed that the production line scoped for the pilot achieved 85 percent attainment on overall volume (actual production/scheduled production).

Underneath that number, however, the team discovered that 25 percent of the volume was for items that weren't scheduled. Moreover, another 10 percent of the volume was overproduction. After factoring unneeded volume out of the equation, the attainment was 55 percent (actual production of what was scheduled/needed production as reflected in the schedule).

Second, the team felt that the scope in pilot two needed to go to the entire plant, because one of the process steps was a shared resource among all production lines. It would be difficult to partially capacity-manage that resource. The processes were deemed sound and the SAP transactions worked effectively.

Rollout

At the completion of pilot two, the final step is to plan for and roll out the solution to the rest of the supply chains within the targeted scope.

The Fowlers project team members discussed a strategy that would go through the sequence of educate, pilot one, and pilot two with each of the remaining plants worldwide. They thought the super users from each region would develop a detailed plan, validate master data, translate documentation and standard operating procedures, and review specific regional configuration settings for potential issues.

The power users objected to this strategy for three reasons. First, based on a change-management standpoint, they suggested that the regional leaders needed to understand and buy into this change in the way they would manage plant capacity. Even though their boss was the sponsor, they did not understand the degree of effort and pain that would be needed to change some old habits. Second, the master data cleanup (and more important, maintenance) was too big for one person—whose primary job was to be an SAP transaction expert—to handle. Third, there was no performance baseline and, in fact, little understanding of how to measure the metrics as charted for the project.

The team achieved consensus that the rollout strategy would essentially go through the 13 implementation steps for each plant, with a local plant sponsor, steering team, project leader, and team. Where possible, deliverables could be modified based on previous work, but the plant team needed to address each deliverable for its own location. The kickoff meetings for the remaining plants would be staggered by two months, allowing for a plant to reach pilot two stage before the process was initiated at the next plant.

Configuring SAP Functionality

Trained and experienced professional users may customize SAP functionality to fit business requirements as defined in the SCOR Level 4 process diagram and the storyboard. Transaction SPRO (Figure 17-1) provides access to the *implementation management guide* (IMG), which contains all of the actions required to fully deploy the SAP functionality configurations. The software provides both IMG tracking and change management tools as part of its software solution.

One of the configuration challenges for Fowlers was the *formula* used to calculate capacity for production resources, which included both the actual *run time* (requirements) as well as the *changeover time* (setup). Working through the IMG main screen to production and to capacity planning, the team was able to get to a configuration transaction that allowed for a custom definition of available capacity.

To create the new formula (Figure 17-2), the following inputs were required:

- Unique formula key: Z006

- Description: Setup + Machine rqmts

- The actual formula: SAP_01 + SAP_02 * SAP_09 / SAP_08, which translates into Setup + Machine × Operation quantity / Base quantity (Figure 17-3)

- Then ensure the indicator for *Work Centers for Capacity Reqmts* is checked

The configuration activity is part of the realization phase of ASAP, and is a necessary activity to begin testing activity within modules as well as across modules.

Figure 17-1. The implementation management guide is the portal for customizing SAP functionality.

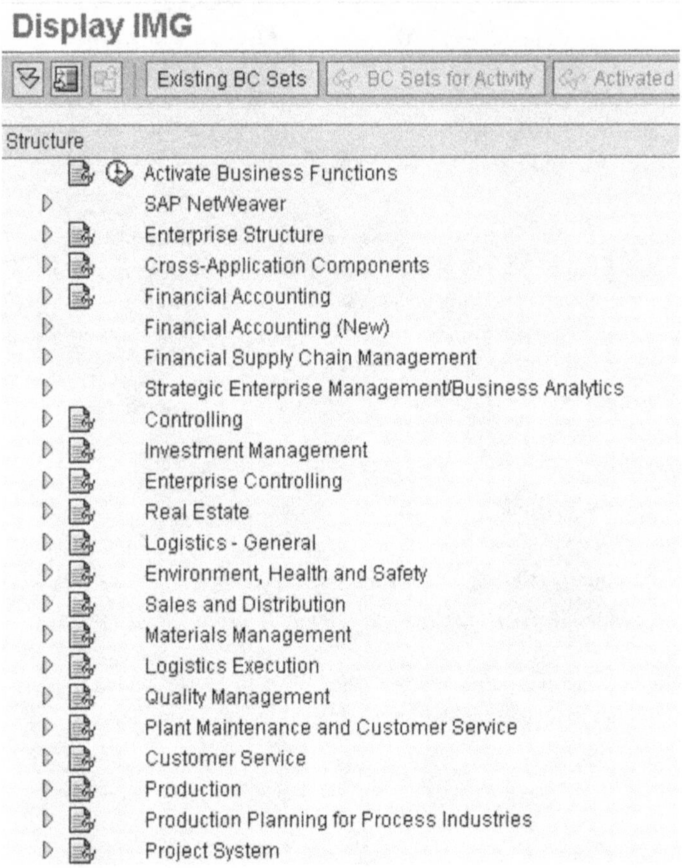

Display IMG

| | | | Existing BC Sets | BC Sets for Activity | Activated |

Structure

- Activate Business Functions
- ▷ SAP NetWeaver
- ▷ Enterprise Structure
- ▷ Cross-Application Components
- ▷ Financial Accounting
- ▷ Financial Accounting (New)
- ▷ Financial Supply Chain Management
- ▷ Strategic Enterprise Management/Business Analytics
- ▷ Controlling
- ▷ Investment Management
- ▷ Enterprise Controlling
- ▷ Real Estate
- ▷ Logistics - General
- ▷ Environment, Health and Safety
- ▷ Sales and Distribution
- ▷ Materials Management
- ▷ Logistics Execution
- ▷ Quality Management
- ▷ Plant Maintenance and Customer Service
- ▷ Customer Service
- ▷ Production
- ▷ Production Planning for Process Industries
- ▷ Project System

Figure 17-2. Fowlers requires a custom formula for capacity planning.

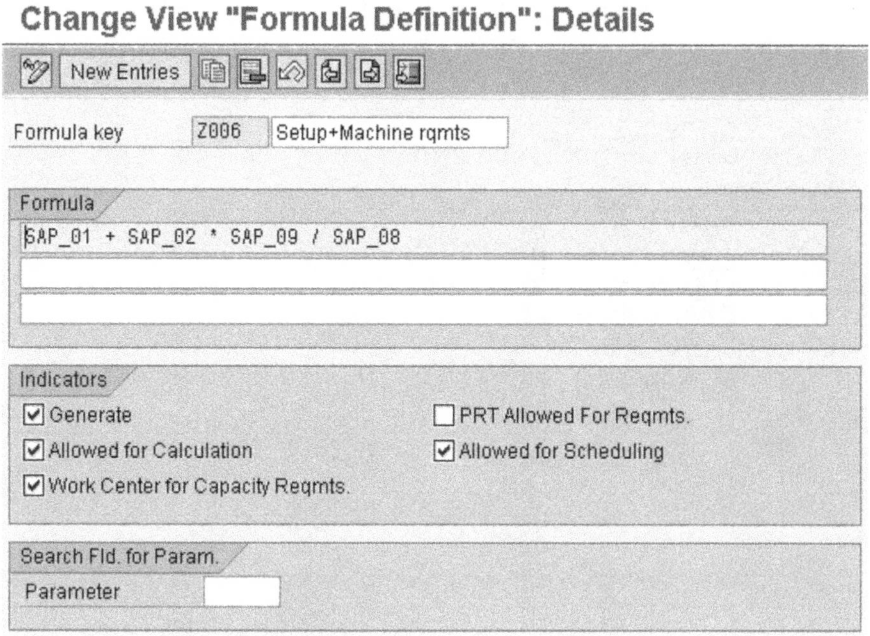

Change View "Formula Definition": Details

| ✎ | New Entries | 🗐 🖫 🗠 🗐 🗐 🗐 |

Formula key   Z006   Setup+Machine rqmts

Formula

SAP_01 + SAP_02 * SAP_09 / SAP_08

Indicators

☑ Generate   ☐ PRT Allowed For Reqmts.

☑ Allowed for Calculation   ☑ Allowed for Scheduling

☑ Work Center for Capacity Reqmts.

Search Fld. for Param.

Parameter

Figure 17-3. Fowlers' customized formula includes both run time and changeover time.

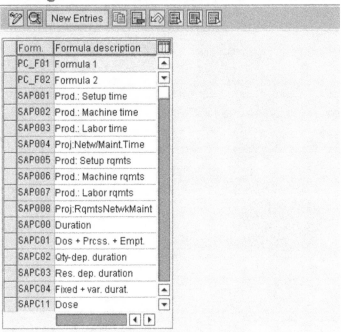

CHAPTER 18

Phase 4: Supply Chain Strategy

▶ **Supply Chain Excellence as a Way of Life**

In this third edition of *Supply Chain Excellence*, we've put to use the concept of "learning by doing." Based on 32 projects undertaken since we completed the second edition of the book in 2007, we have cut the time and resources required to develop the project list by 50 percent. We have eliminated "non-value-added" analysis by moving the material, work, and information flow analysis to the implementation phase, focusing only on those processes and SKUs that are in-scope for the project. We have changed the schedule and mode of meeting interface to accommodate global teams, for which regular travel is expensive and time-consuming, as well as small-business teams, in which a few people wear many hats and the amount of time available to devote to this type of endeavor is limited.

We filtered about 30 percent of the deliverables that, while good ideas in past editions, were not commonly utilized by project teams. And we integrated process and system efforts to minimize the lag time and rework between typical business process engineering and system implementation.

If restating the introduction seems like an odd way to begin the next-to-last chapter, here is the point: In the real world, if something doesn't get used, it atrophies. While most dictionaries start with the figurative definition of atrophy—a gradual decline in effectiveness or vigor due to underuse or neglect—I also like the biological version: to waste away. So in the business world, if we neglect or underuse the skill of Supply Chain Excellence, it will waste away.

How, then, can companies learn from their *Supply Chain Excellence* experience and maintain that continuous improvement mentality so that in five years they can look back and see how far they have progressed on their journey?

Of the five largest companies that have utilized the *Supply Chain Excellence* approach in varying applications since the first edition, all have been through major system implementations (some worldwide); all have global business challenges; each has been recognized by customers as a superior supplier; and though focused on different businesses in different industries, all would say that their supply chain is performing significantly better now than at the beginning of the journey, financially, with shareholders, and with customers. They would also say that with each new learning, they've discovered more opportunities to improve. Finally, they would likely state that they are not satisfied with aspects of their current performance and have plans to address those deficiencies in their supply chain strategy. Keep in mind that these statements are coming from companies that have achieved competitive advantage in their respective marketplaces and have continued to perform in superior fashion against their competitors.

What Is Supply Chain Strategy?

Table 18-1 is a matrix that provides a checklist of essential elements that make up a comprehensive supply chain strategy. The labels in these boxes have changed over the years, but the concept has not.

The theory behind these categories is founded in *Improving Performance: How to Manage the White Space on the Organization Chart*, 2nd ed., by G. A. Rummler and A. P. Brache (Jossey-Bass, 1995). Their theory supports the contention that there are three factors to effective supply chain strategy:

+ Defining appropriate strategy and goals
+ Utilizing effective design techniques to organize businesses, regions, functions, processes, etc.
+ Managing performance measures

Theory supports the belief that there are five supply chain dimensions affected by these factors: (1) trading partners—customers and suppliers alike; (2) your company's organization as defined in the organization chart and business entities; (3) your company's processes relative to supply chain, including SCOR processes, other leading practices, and the physical network, both inbound and outbound; (4) your company's technology—most often fixed assets, but also including supply chain systems specifically; and (5) the job performers, referring to your company's individual contributors.

Table 18-1. Comprehensive supply chain strategy essential elements.

Elements of Effective Supply Chain Strategy	Strategy	Design	Management
Trading Partners	Define Segments, Requirements, and Capabilities	Relationships and Agreements	Joint Metrics
Organization	Supply Chain Competitive Priorities	Global Organizational Design	Balanced Scorecard
Process	Global Process Requirements	Process and Physical Network	Effective Process Measures
Technology	Technology Requirements	Technology Architecture	System Performance
Performers	Job Task Requirements	Job Design	Job Level KPIs

The rest of this chapter highlights key challenges in each dimension that have been addressed by the five large *Supply Chain Excellence* companies, and then summarizes an overall "to do" list for the Fowlers executive team as it begins to strategize for the 2012 fiscal year.

Trading Partner

The simple definition of a trading partner is illustrated on the SCOR model diagram (Figure 1-1), which includes the supplier, supplier's supplier, customer, and customer's customer. A more complex twist comes from Gartner Inc. and AMR Research; they have described the supply chain as a demand-driven value network (DDVN) in which your suppliers can be your customers and your customers can be your suppliers, all in search of the rhythm of the ultimate "pull system"; essentially, a consumer buying something off the shelf.

Trading Partner Dimensional Challenges

- Segment customers based on intended growth, profit, and cost to serve.
- Synchronize with customer and supplier supply chain capabilities.
- Develop, define, and manage effective collaborative relationships with targeted partners.
- Jointly define, measure, report, and manage supply chain metrics.
- Establish effective supplier portals.
- Make use of point-of-sale data in retail and inventory movements in distribution.

Organization

The academic definition of an organization is "a connected body of people with a particular purpose." Organizational theorists offer a more refined version: An organization contains the formal and informal relationships of inputs and outputs between defined groups of people (functions, regions, entities, etc.) who support the achievement of defined goals and strategy. Figure 18-1 illustrates the concept of supply chain execution roles within operating business units in a matrix relationship, with global process ownership at the corporate level. In this case, solid lines indicate primary reporting; dotted lines indicate secondary.

Organization Dimensional Challenges

+ Aligning and prioritizing supply chain competitive requirements and cost-to-serve models with appropriate customer segments; getting away from the one-supply-chain-fits-all mentality.

+ Defining appropriate accountabilities, roles, and responsibilities between business-unit supply chain personnel (who need to operate the supply chain on a daily basis) and supply chain process owners (who need to improve the effectiveness, efficiency, and standardization of the process) across the business units and perhaps across continents. This is the global supply chain organization chart.

+ Defining, developing, and managing a global supply chain scorecard that looks, feels, and operates the same way in every corner of the company, and can be segmented by customers, suppliers, plants, products, and warehouses.

Processes

A business process is a series of steps that, when designed in a particular order, produces a product, service, transaction and/or information. In the case of SCOR, the processes are defined as PLAN, SOURCE, MAKE, DELIVER, RETURN, and ENABLE. In the case of Gartner/AMR, the processes are classified in three broad

Figure 18-1. Supply chain organization scenario with matrix reporting.

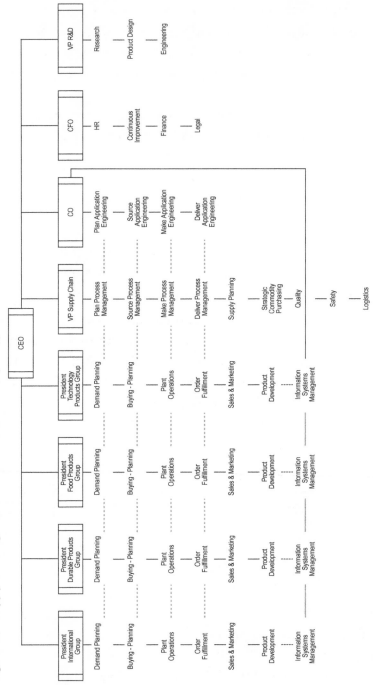

areas—Product, Demand, and Supply—with cross-area processes for Sense, Shape, and Respond.

Other leading practices that have been published also discuss the effective design of supply chain processes, including sales and operations planning, master scheduling, procurement, global sourcing, Lean Manufacturing, distribution requirements planning, demand management, sales forecasting, etc.

Process Dimensional Challenges

+ Translating competitive requirements into effective supply chain process strategy, configuration (MTO, MTS, ETO), and execution; this includes physical network, inventory and service requirements, collaboration requirements, internal processes, and associated transactions.

+ Building a supply chain process blueprint with the appropriate leading practices.

+ Conducting and implementing the conclusions of a physical network study.

+ Linking the global scorecard to process performance.

Technology

For this dimension, I would like to narrow the definition of technology to "supply chain information system technology." This encompasses hardware, software, data (warehouse), and the Internet, where interfaces have a direct impact on supply chain process. The most frequently used types of supply chain information system technology include Internet portals, Enterprise Resource Planning (ERP), advanced planning (AP), manufacturing execution (MES), forecasting, Electronic Data Interchange (EDI), point of sale (POS), warehouse management (WMS), radio frequency (RF), and a data warehouse.

Technology Dimensional Challenges

- ◆ Translating defined process requirements into a technology roadmap supporting the overall supply chain strategy and investment objectives.
- ◆ Effectively designing, configuring, testing, and rolling out integrated technology and process solutions.
- ◆ Linking aspects of system performance to process measures and managing them in the spirit of continuous improvement.

Performers

For this dimension, a performer is defined as someone who carries out his or her work in relation to a specified standard of expectation. I like this definition because in order to succeed, there are two requirements: (1) that the performer carries out the work and (2) that the work is defined in relation to a company standard. SCOR 10.0 contains a section on people. As stated in the manual, this section "introduces standards for managing talent in the supply chain. The key elements of the people section are *skills*, *experiences*, *aptitudes*, and *trainings*. This *skills* management framework within SCOR complements process reference, metrics reference, and practice reference components with an integrated view of supply chain skills in four areas:

1. Baseline skills necessary for the overall process area (e.g., Sourcing or Planning) and for the individual process.
2. Critical skills that differentiate leaders in a particular process area from those who only perform at a baseline level.
3. Performance measures through SCOR metrics that relate to continuous assessment of job performance in each process area.
4. Credentialing of supply chain skills, including training or certification programs, related to the specific process area that tend to indicate superior job performance."

Performer Dimensional Challenges

♦ Organizing job families and job ranges within the supply chain organization to facilitate movement within a process and between processes.

♦ Writing job descriptions that accurately represent the system, process, analytical, and experiential requirements for a supply chain role.

♦ Effectively setting goals, reviewing performance, and identifying growth opportunities.

Implications for Fowlers

The Fowlers executive team had already had an annual top-down strategic planning cycle. The process started in January with the corporate strategy; moved to the business units, which set macro sales and profit targets; and then transitioned into the annual budgeting process, moving in parallel to operations and product development.

The teams that had been involved in the process to this point assembled plans that included capital, labor, and materials. The last stop before the midyear review was finance. The midterm review in July compared the corporate top-down strategy to the business unit bottom-up strategy and annual plan, and worked through a gap-resolution process that, depending on the severity of the issues, could cycle in two to three months. The final piece of the annual budget and strategy review was to be completed in October.

To-Do List

Knowing they couldn't do everything, the team members decided to incorporate the Trading Partner and Organization Strategy, along with the elements of Organization Design, Organization Management, and Technology Requirements, into the executive strategic planning process scheduled to begin in January of the following year (2012).

This decision involved the following objectives:

♦ Task sales, marketing, and procurement to better define customer and supplier requirements, capabilities, and competitive landscape.

♦ Task human resources to understand the role of global process ownership with respect to the operation of supply chain in the business unit.

♦ Assign a designated global scorecard task team to define metrics and collect baselines for each of the business units.

- ◆ Task the CIO with summarizing the Fowlers current technology roadmap.

- ◆ Expect the business units to include baseline and projected performance levels from the global scorecard for the upcoming fiscal year (2012).

- ◆ Target Trading Partner Design and Management, Process Strategy and Design, and Performer Strategy for inclusion in the following year (2013) cycle.

- ◆ Expect that as part of the following-year (2013) cycle each business would have a portfolio that would relate to its projected performance levels.

Extend to the Greater Value Chain

▶ **Analyzing Barriers to Profitable Growth**

Arvid Westergaard, president of the Fowlers Durable Products Group, was speechless after the midyear portfolio review. He had just seen the future leadership of the company collectively present an organized, customer-focused, financially sound review of *Supply Chain Excellence* portfolio projects that were driving real performance—"moving the needle," as a colleague put it. The presentation showed passion, conviction, and confidence. It was the first time he had seen anything like it at Fowlers.

The durable products group had a different set of challenges, and he wondered, "How do I take this approach further into my business?"

Arvid's group was developing a reputation for leaving money on the table. It had premium brands that commanded premium prices, but profits were average at best. Unlike any other operation in the company, its business model was primarily make-to-order and engineer-to-order. Although his business was routinely touted as the future growth driver for the company, Arvid lacked confidence in the team's ability to hit sales projections; there didn't seem to be any "science" behind the numbers.

Further, as sales, order fulfillment, manufacturing, sourcing, planning, and product design teams worked to get product introduced and out the door, they all had their own ways of getting the work done, and "exceptions" were the norm. In one plant tour he had received from a shift foreman, he counted 45 instances in which he was told, "It works like this except when those blankety blank engineers pull us in one direction, then the sales and customer service people yank us in another. How hard can this be?"

For a long time, the durable products group had been an early innovator in quick response and flexibility when faced with customer demands for new products, but the after-sale service business helped support "life cycle management" and showed the most potential for growth. It seemed like both parts of the business should use the same processes but, as the aftermarket business grew, walls were already begin established.

Arvid knew that competitors were catching up—and no one seemed to own the job of "taking it to the next level." Finally, he was under pressure from Jon Park, the chief financial officer, to commit to a plan to improve return on sales. Analysts were not being kind to Fowlers' stock price, and return on sales (ROS) in Arvid's group was a significant factor.

With all this on his mind, Arvid pulled the SCOR coach aside and shared his thoughts. The coach was planning to stay an extra day—so he could join the design team's scheduled celebration. The two agreed to use the full day before the final party to discuss how they might tweak the *Supply Chain Excellence* approach to include more pieces of *the value chain*. Fowlers COO Brian Dowell and David Able caught wind of the meeting and asked if they could join as well.

Value Chain Excellence

The concept of value chain is not new. Both Michael Porter and W. Edwards Deming had developed process frameworks that depicted the entire system of value creation.[1] Supply chain, the derivative of this work, was also not new when the Supply Chain Council released version 1.0 of SCOR in 1996. What was new was cross-industry process detail around common definitions, metrics, and practices, aimed toward the goal of companies using the framework to improve supply chain performance across industries and trading partners. As has been demonstrated, *Supply Chain Excellence* describes an approach for identifying a strategic project list to help drive sustainable improvement.

With the introduction of the CCOR 1.0 (Customer Chain Operations Reference) and DCOR 2.0 (Design Chain Operations Reference) processes, the Supply Chain Council (www.supply-chain.org) is again positioned to support value chain performance improvement through common process definition, metrics framework, and leading practices. The question is how to use these models in a project.

That's the question Arvid asked to start his meeting. The major phases of *Supply Chain Excellence* were adapted by inserting "value chain" as appropriate:

- Build organizational support
- Define value chain project scope
- Analyze performance
- Develop project portfolio
- Implement projects

The next challenge was to figure out how to adapt the major deliverables for each phase. Fresh off the *Supply Chain Excellence* project, the group members were familiar with the key deliverables. They wrote a list and then, for each supply chain deliverable, asked two questions:

♦ Is it necessary for a value chain assessment?

♦ What is the estimated degree of adaptation?

Figure 19-1 summarizes the team's descriptions of key value chain tasks by phase; the rest of this chapter summarizes the team's discussion, highlighting the adaptations for value chain.

Build Organizational Support

The team agreed to describe the deliverables from this phase as (1) identify value chain improvement roles, evangelists, active executive sponsor(s), core steering team, and design team; (2) assemble and deliver appropriate educational content; and (3) gain consensus for a pilot project.

Identify Value Chain Improvement Roles, Evangelists, Active Executive Sponsor(s), Core Steering Team, and Design Team

This task would use the same steps as used in Fowlers' supply chain project. As the discussion turned more philosophical, the coach described the concept of Learning Quotient (LQ)—an organization's ability to acquire knowledge and adapt behavior in response to changes in the business environment. A low organizational LQ (poor adaptability) is like a perpetual "Go to Jail" card in Monopoly. You never pass Go and are stuck watching the game from behind bars unless you get a lucky roll of the dice. The evangelist, active executive sponsor, core steering team, and design team are four key roles that will set the pace of the organization's LQ in relation to value chain improvement; all four roles must be in place to pass Go.

Assemble and Deliver Appropriate Educational Content and Gain Consensus for a Pilot Project

The team members reflected on how they progressed from knowing nothing about SCOR and *Supply Chain Excellence* to constituting

Figure 19-1. Key value chain tasks by phase.

Phase	Deliverable
Phase 0 **Build Organizational** **Support**	TBD
	Value Chain Excellence Overview
	SCOR, DCOR, CCOR Framework Workshop
	Executive Briefing--GO/NO GO
Phase 1 **Define Project Scope**	TBD
	Business Context Summary
	Value Chain Definition Matrix (with data)
	Project Charter
Phase 2 **Analyze Performance**	Kickoff
	Metric Definitions and Data Collection Plan
	Defect Data Collection Plan
	Defect Analysis
	Industry Comparison
	Competitive Requirements
	Benchmark Data
	Preliminary Scorecard
	Scorecard Gap Analysis
	OPTIONAL DEDICATED ON-SITE Staple Yourself to an Order Interviews
	OPTIONAL DEDICATED ON-SITE AS IS Process Diagram
Phase 3 **Develop Project** **Portfolio**	TBD
	AS IS Process Diagram
	Defect Analysis Part 2
	Brainstorm Event and Documentation
	Preliminary Project Portfolio
	Opportunity Analysis
	Assemble and Approve Implementation Project Charters
	Prioritize Implementation Projects
Phase 4 **Implement Projects**	TBD
	Kickoff Projects
	Develop Performance Baselines for Metrics
	Conduct Level 3 and 4 Process Gap Analysis
	Conduct Leading Practice Assessment
	Develop TO BE Process Blueprint
	Assemble Solution Storyboard
	Approve Solution Design
	Build and Test Solution
	Pilot and Verify Solution--Twice
	Define Process Control Measures
	Rollout to Project Scope
	Rollout to Enterprise

the final steering team in six months: light speed compared with other major initiatives. They defined three stages in their organizational learning and agreed that each must occur to move on to the next. They substituted the word "Value" for "Supply" and agreed that the durable products group would need to follow the same path.

Initial Exposure was the first stage; the objective was to investigate the *Value Chain Excellence* framework and the fit of the process models of SCOR, DCOR, and CCOR. The educational content of this phase would be characterized by the phrase "short and sweet." This is the stage at which evangelists and active executive sponsor(s) evaluate the fit of the method and the process frameworks with their business needs.

Learn How to Sell is the second stage; the objective of evangelists and active executive sponsor(s) is to sell core steering team members on the benefits of *Value Chain Excellence* and prepare them to sponsor a pilot project. The educational content of this phase takes the overview content style of the first phase and incorporates real company data in as many places as possible to give the leadership team members the best vision of a project in their own business language.

Implement a Pilot Project is the third stage; the object for the project team—including the evangelist, active executive sponsor(s), core steering team, and design team—is to develop the knowledge, skill, and motivation to successfully execute a project. The educational content in this phase is a mix of detailed "how to" templates and anecdotes that take theory to practice.

The amount of time spent in each phase depends on the organization's LQ. Companies with low LQ spend a lot of time in the first phase, often kicking tires until they're flat. High LQ companies can advance to the last phase in as little as three months; the typical duration is four to six months.

Define Value Chain Project Scope

In addition to the business context document, the team listed the other key deliverables from this second phase as follows: (1) calculate the number of value chains, (2) assemble high-level industry comparison, and (3) decide the scope of the pilot project and finalize the project charter.

Calculate the Number of Value Chains

Defining the number of company value chains requires the same technique as that of defining the number of supply chains (Chapter 3). Figure 19-2 illustrates the durable products group's adaptations. As in the supply chain, the rows represent lines of business or product families, and the lowest level of the row hierarchy is an item or stock keeping unit (SKU). The columns represent customers or customer segments, and the lowest level of the column hierarchy is a customer "ship to" location. The "X" indicates a product or service that is delivered to a customer; the number of X's provides a first draft of the number of company value chains. One adaptation includes growth rate (revenue, unit volume, and gross margin) data for each value chain.

Assemble High-Level Industry Comparison

The industry comparison is assembled using the same steps as for the supply chain, with five new data comparisons focused on the rate of growth from the prior period. These categories are revenue; sales, general, and administration expense; gross margin; operating income; and net income.

Decide on the Project Scope

The phrase "think big, act small, and scale fast" still works for value chain analysis. The value chain priority matrix is assembled in the

Figure 19-2. Durable products group value chains.

Durable Products Group			U.S. Customer/Market Channels		
			Direct-to-Consumer	Home Delivery	OEM-Key Accounts
Lines of Business	Product Family A	Revenue	5.6%	X	X
		Unit	10.0%		
		Gross Margin	-2.5%		
	Product Family B	Revenue	X	X	
		Unit			
		Gross Margin			
	Product Family C	Revenue			X
		Unit			
		Gross Margin			
	Product Family D	Revenue	X	X	X
		Unit			
		Gross Margin			

same fashion as for supply chains. The team brainstormed other categories (columns), including revenue growth rate, percent of new product revenue, and return on sales.

Analyze Value Chain Performance and Project Portfolio Development

The team listed five deliverables for this phase: (1) identify appropriate value chain performance metrics, (2) assemble appropriate benchmark comparisons, (3) assess and prioritize competitive re-

quirements, (4) perform metric defect analysis, and (5) develop a
SCOR, DCOR, and CCOR process oriented project portfolio.

Identify Appropriate Value Chain Performance Metrics and Assemble Appropriate Benchmark Comparisons (Deliverables 1 and 2)

Although the previous scorecard provides a proven baseline to measure supply chain performance, it does not include measures for the
other business processes. The coach suggested the team use a *Balanced Scorecard,*[2] an approach to strategic management developed in
the early 1990s by Dr. Robert Kaplan and Dr. David Norton. The
basic idea is that an organization should measure its performance
from a balanced view against its goals as established in its vision and
strategy. The Balanced Scorecard has four measurement categories:
customer facing, internal process, financial, and individual employee.

The challenge for Arvid, Brian, and David was to pick the right
metrics for each category. The coach discussed two methods to generate the list. The first starts with a blank sheet of paper; we've all
been through that method. The second—which the team ultimately
picked—is to identify relevant metrics from a pool of readily available benchmark sources. The coach suggested some of the same
sources used in the supply chain project. They include the following: the Supply Chain Council (www.supply-chain.org), the Performance Measurement Group (www.pmgbenchmarking.com),
Hoovers (www.hoovers.com), APQC—formerly the American
Productivity & Quality Center (www.apqc.org), and Manufacturing
Performance Institute (www.mpi-group.net). Figure 19-3 is the list
that the team generated. Each metric was assigned to a Balanced
Scorecard category; the team decided not to create employee metrics
before brainstorming with a larger group. Figure 19-4 is a sample of
some of the benchmark data available for select value chain metrics.

Figure 19-3. Value Chain Level 1 metrics and benchmark sources; SCOR metrics shaded.

Benchmark Source	Level One Value Chain Metrics	Customer Facing			Process				Financial		Employee	
		Reliability	Responsiveness	Flexibility	Supply Chain	Design Chain	Customer Chain	Aggregate	Profit	Growth	Performance	Development
APQC PMG	Perfect Order Fulfillment	X										
PMG	Warranty Fulfillment	X										
PMG	Service Order Fulfillment	X										
MPI APQC	Product Quality	X										
APQC PMG	Order Fulfillment Cycle Time		X									
APQC	New Product Development Cycle Time		X									
Data Gap	Selling Process Cycle Time		X									
APQC	Return Process Cycle Time		X									
PMG	Upside Supply Chain Flexibility			X								
PMG	Engineering Change Order Flexibility			X								
PMG	Design Reuse Flexibility			X								
APQC	Total Returns Management Cost						X					
Data Gap	Total Customer Chain Management Cost						X					
ALL	Days Sales Outstanding						X					
PMG APQC	Total Supply Chain Management Costs				X							
ALL	Inventory Days of Supply				X							
APQC PMG	Total Design Chain Management Cost					X						
APQC	Total Warranty Cost					X						
APQC PMG	New Product Revenue							X				
ALL	Cost of Goods Sold							X				
APQC PMG Hoovers	Sales, General, and Administrative Cost							X				
ALL	Cash-to-Cash Cycle Time							X				
PMG Hoovers	Asset Turns							X				
Hoovers	Return on Assets							X				
ALL	Gross Profit Margin								X			
ALL	Operating Margin								X			
Hoovers	Net Profit Margin								X			
Hoovers	Revenue Growth									X		
Hoovers	Gross Profit Growth									X		
Hoovers	Operating Margin Growth									X		

Assess and Prioritize Competitive Requirements

With respect to value chain competitive requirements, the team agreed that a broader framework was needed to assess overall business strategy. The coach suggested a modification of a Michael Porter concept,[3] which describes two basic strategies of competitive advantage: *low cost* or *differentiation*. These two strategies, when applied to a narrowly defined industry segment, create Porter's third

Figure 19-4. Sample benchmark data for select value chain metrics.

Process Model	Metric & Benchmark Source	Sample of Level One Value Chain Metrics	Value Chain Benchmark		
			Performance Versus Comparison Population		
			Parity 50th Percentile	Advantage 70th Percentile	Superior 90th Percentile
DCOR	APQC	New Product Development Cycle Time[1]	245 days	186 days	99 days
DCOR	APQC	Total R&D cost as a percentage of revenue (current reporting period)[1]	17.41%	10.00%	3.04%
DCOR	APQC	Total R&D cost as a percentage of revenue (three reporting periods ago)[1]	16.81%	7.99%	3.44%
DCOR	APQC	Design cycle time in days from start of design, build, and evaluate through completion of test market product/service for new product/service development projects[1]	720.0	437.4	334.5
DCOR	APQC	Total cost of the development cycle as a percentage of revenue[1]	13.00%	11.13%	4.13%
DCOR	APQC	Percentage of sales which is a result of products/services launched during the most recently completed 12 month reporting period[1]	16.50%	25.20%	50.00%
DCOR	PMG	Design Reuse Flexibility[2]	22%	37.15%	42.30%
DCOR	PMG	Total Design Chain Management Cost[2]	9.50%	8.49%	7.47%
DCOR	PMG	New Product Revenue[2]	22.50%	39.20%	55.90%
ALL	Hoovers	Sales, General, and Administrative Cost	19.45%	13.00%	9.06%
ALL	Hoovers	Revenue Growth	13.94%	18.99%	31.31%
ALL	Hoovers	Gross Profit Growth	18.01%	31.55%	39.66%
ALL	Hoovers	Operating Margin Growth	34.29%	63.55%	165.95%

© Copyright 2007 APQC. All Rights Reserved. Used with permission.

[1] APQC is reporting this data on the assumption that lower R&D costs, lower cycle time, lower product development costs, and higher sales due to recent product launches represent superior performance. APQC acknowledges that correlating these measures to various outcomes may support a different perspective. This is published with APQC's permission to present the perspective that best fits the needs of *Supply Chain Excellence*.

[2] Design Reuse Flexibility, Total Design Chain Management Cost (PLM Operating Cost), and New Product Revenue © Copyright 2003 The Performance Measurement Group, LLC, subsidiary of management consultants PRTM. All Rights Reserved. Used with permission.

generic strategy: *Focus*. Put another way, companies must answer two questions: "Will we focus on a broad industry or a narrowly defined segment?" and then, "Will we achieve competitive advantage through low cost or differentiation?" Porter describes companies that try to represent all strategies to all customers as being "stuck in the middle"—and they generally perform at or below parity in all dimensions.

The team also was enamored with the simple assembly and the large impact of the supply chain competitive requirements exercise.

The concept was easy to explain: A company must decide on a supply chain strategy to achieve superior and advantage positions in some metric categories, while maintaining at least parity in others.

So how can the concepts of Porter and SCOR be brought together? Figure 19-5 represents the team's best attempt to mock up an example using the durable products group. The left arrow represents performance in the "cost" strategy, and the right arrow represents performance in the "differentiation" strategy. Specifically, they related the left arrow with process measures and the right arrow with customer-facing measures. The base of the arrow is actual performance; the point of the arrow is target performance.

Arvid talked through one possible strategic scenario: By focusing on niche markets, the durable products group could adopt both cost *and* differentiation tactics to put itself into a better market position. The direction of the arrows suggests that durable products narrow its products and customer focus from "broad industry" to a narrow industry niche, and that it pursue superior cost performance within that niche, while customer-facing metrics operate at parity.

In value-chain metric terms, process measures need to move toward the 90th percentile, and the customer-facing measures need to move toward at least the 50th percentile. They all agreed this chart needed more work, but that the concepts made sense. They

Figure 19-5. Value Chain Competitive Requirements (superior, advantage, parity, below parity).

Competitive Performance	S	A	P	< P	P	A	S
Broad Industry	Low Cost					Differentiation	
Industry Segment	Focus: Low Cost			Stuck in the Middle		Focus: Differentiation	

recognized that if both arrows are in the shaded portion, action is required.

Perform Metric Defect Analysis

The team agreed that the disconnect analysis was critical to uncovering the issues related to performance. Although some templates would need to be created for the new metrics, the steps were identical to the supply chain project.

Develop a Project Portfolio

The team members agreed that this foundational supply chain deliverable would be necessary to help dissect the issues, build projects, and quantify the improvement. They thought the metrics and associated defect analysis would define the brainstorm categories and help the team associate "problems" with not just the supply chain but with the design and customer chains as well. The main conversation centered on determining the level of the process with which the team would associate the problems. All agreed that Level 3 was too detailed. All also agreed that the team needed to discern between Level 1 processes, i.e., Source vs. Research vs. Amend, etc. The main debate was whether to differentiate at Level 2. Did it help to identify problems at the level of make-to-order vs. make-to-stock vs. new product vs. refresh, etc? Their conclusion: Learn by doing.

Implementation Considerations

The team discussed four types of analytical tools that it thought were helpful in the *Supply Chain Excellence* implementation rollout and might also be useful in the value chain project implementation: (1) product-to-market map, (2) Level 2 process diagrams, (3) staple yourself interviews, and (4) TO BE Level 4 process diagrams with information system storyboards.

Product-to-Market Map

This analytical tool was the most difficult to adapt from the *Supply Chain Excellence* process. In the supply chain project, the geographic map was an easy concept to grasp. Although there are material movement aspects to value chains, the team discussed two other layers that needed to be considered as part of the analysis as well.

First, it would be necessary to understand sales by region, as the sales and marketing team views it. Figure 19-6 illustrates the three regions of U.S. sales for durable products. Layering the geographic map on top of the sales-by-region map was both intuitive and logical for the team.

The third layer was not as simple. In fact, a spreadsheet was a better tool than a picture. The concept the team was after was to understand the rate of growth in each sales region between new and existing products, and among new and existing customers. Figure

Figure 19-6. Durable product group's U.S. sales by region.

19-7 is a mock-up of the concept, which the team eventually labeled Value Chain Growth Analysis. The analysis attempts to calculate growth rates for revenue, gross margin, and unit volume for each cell in the matrix. With the use of predetermined criteria, a cell (product and customer) is graded positive (+), negative (−), or neutral (0). The results helped the team understand the issues behind growth. For example, Product Family B has growth issues across the board, whereas Product Family A has particular trouble building sales of existing products to new customers.

The benefit of this perspective is that the next set of "why" questions is not aimed just at supply. Marketing campaigns, pricing strategy, product quality, product life cycle management, sales incentives, and so forth are all in the mix of potential root causes and ultimate projects.

Figure 19-7. Durable product group's U.S. growth rate analysis.

Durable Products - U.S. Value Chain			Western US Sales Territory					
			New Customers			Existing Customers		
			Revenue	Gross Margin	Unit	Revenue	Gross Margin	Unit
North America Lines of Business	Product Family A	New Products	+	+	+	+	+	+
		Existing Products	-	-	-	+	+	+
	Product Family B	New Products	-	-	-	0	0	0
		Existing Products	-	-	-	-	-	-
	Product Family C	New Products	-	-	-	+	+	+
		Existing Products	-	-	-	-	-	+
	Product Family D	New Products	-	-	-	+	+	+
		Existing Products	+	+	+	-	-	-

Level 2 Process Diagrams

As in the supply chain project, the preparation required to create a Level 2 process diagram involved identifying the appropriate processes for each location. Figure 19-8 is a partial list of the choices for each location; one necessary adaptation is the small-letter designation in front of the Level 2 ID; "c" is CCOR, "d" is DCOR, and "s" is SCOR.

Figure 19-9 illustrates the team's work assembling a logical durable products flow. The dotted lines represent both information and product flow. As with any concept drawing, the team had a tough time differentiating the "should be" from "the AS IS." Arvid, David, and Brian also realized they would need to get signed up for DCOR and CCOR framework classes. They needed to affirm their intuitions about the difference between design classifications of "product refresh," "new product," and "new technology"—as well as between the customer classifications of sell to "intermediary," "grouped account," and "named account." For the mock-up, they used both *refreshed* and the traditional *new product* categories for design. For customer categories, they used *grouped account* (direct-to-consumer). Figure 19-10 is the first attempt at putting together a Level 2 process diagram relating the design chain (DCOR) for new products to the supply chain (SCOR) supporting the growing service business. The team decided that one of the necessary adaptations would be to create a set of primary and secondary connection rules among DCOR, CCOR, and SCOR Level 2 process elements.

Staple Yourself Interviews

The team decided that the steps in preparing and conducting the staple yourself interviews would be identical to that of the supply chain. The only necessary adaptation was to brainstorm major transactions for CCOR and DCOR. Here is the first draft list:

Figure 19-8. DCOR, CCOR, and SCOR Level 2 process categories.

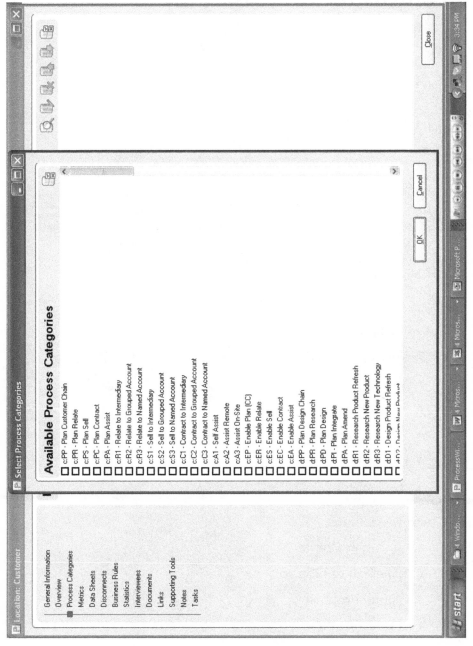

Figure 19-9. DCOR, CCOR, and SCOR Level 2 process categories by location.

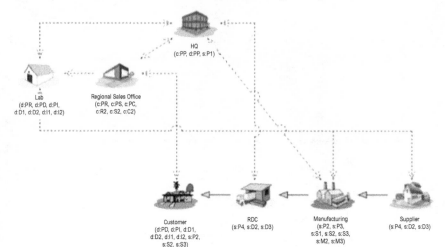

Supply Chain

- ◆ Purchase Order
- ◆ Work Order
- ◆ Sales Order
- ◆ Return Authorization
- ◆ Forecast
- ◆ Replenishment Order

Customer Chain

- ◆ Customer Profile
- ◆ Sales Call to Contract
- ◆ Quote/Proposal
- ◆ Service Request
- ◆ Sales $ Forecast
- ◆ Quota

Figure 19-10. Durable products group value chain Level 2 process diagram first draft.

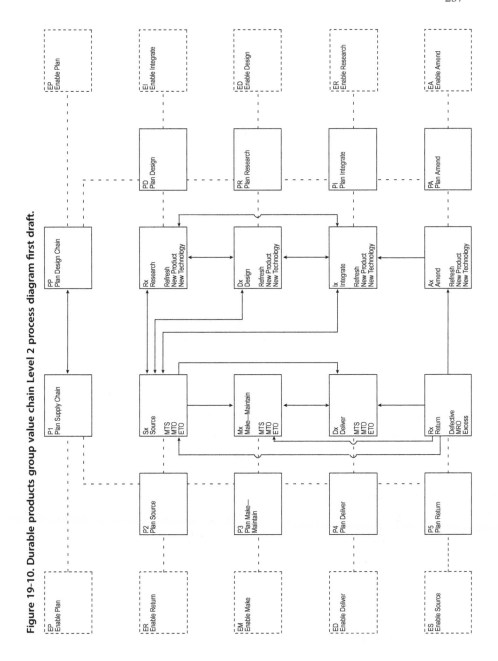

Design Chain

- ◆ Engineering Change Request
- ◆ Product Design Specification
- ◆ Manufacturing Qualification "Certificate"
- ◆ New Product Introduction Plan

TO BE Level 4 Process Diagrams with Information System Storyboards

Like a broken record, the team again found the steps to build Level 4 processes and educate team members through the information system storyboards were a direct application to value chain. No additional adaptations were deemed necessary.

Conclusion

The clock was pointing to 5:30 p.m., and the foursome sat around the conference table, exhausted. They were already a half-hour late leaving for the party that the supply chain design team was holding, but they had that satisfied, head-spinning feeling that a well-prepared college student gets at the end of final exams. Nobody seemed quite ready to move.

Surrounding them were three 12-foot whiteboards full of diagrams, notes, and numbers—each with a great big "SAVE" scribbled in the corner. In one day, they had outlined how to stretch the *Supply Chain Excellence* approach to cover the value chain requirements in Arvid's very different business. They were confident it would work—and just realistic enough to know that the method would have to be adjusted as they progressed.

David and Brian felt as though they'd just gotten two process improvements for the price of one. Arvid felt that great sense of being unburdened from the quiet troubles that had been building within his business.

"When can we get started?" Arvid asked.

Brian smiled and replied, "Can we wait until after the party?"

Notes

1. Michael Porter, *Competitive Advantage: Creating and Sustaining Superior Performance* (New York: The Free Press; 1985); W. Edwards Deming, *Out of the Crisis* (Cambridge, MA: Massachusetts Institute of Technology, Center for Advanced Engineering Study; 1986).

2. Balanced Scorecard Institute, Cary, NC, and Rockville, MD; www.balancedscorecard.org.

3. Michael Porter, *Competitive Advantage: Creating and Sustaining Superior Performance* (New York: The Free Press, 1998).

Fowlers Inc. *Supply Chain Excellence* Project Charter

Organizational Summary

Executive Sponsor: Brian Dowell, COO
Business Sponsor: Jovan Kojcic, President, Technology Products Group
Department: Technology Products Group
Project Manager: David Able, VP Operations—Technology Products
Start Date: March 11, 2011, with executive GO Decision
Approval Date: March 11, 2011
Revision Date: April 18, 2011

I. Introduction

Purpose of the Project Charter

The project charter is created during the initiation phase of a project to ensure that a complete understanding of the project scope and objectives is established. The document allows confirmation of assumptions and expectations with the executive team; project sponsors; stakeholders; project managers; program manager; and project, validation, and resource team members. During the course of the project, change requests may be generated and approved that vary the scope, schedule, or cost of the project. These changes should be documented through the change management process and updates reflected through revisions of the project charter.

Project Charter Contents

The project charter documents the background and business need for the project as well as expectations for the project moving forward. The project overview provides the project scope, business and project objectives, and any assumptions. The project approach outlines the methodology to be used in completing the project along with the schedule, milestones, deliverables, and any project dependencies. A budget for the project is presented, and the organization of the project team is discussed. Project expectations, and the ways in which project success will be measured, are discussed. A plan for communication throughout the project also is presented.

Maintenance of the Project Charter

After initial approval by the project sponsor, the project charter is updated with approved change requests. Each update is noted with a revision date on the cover page.

II. Project Overview

Scope

Definition Matrix

Fowlers North America	Customer/Market Channels						
	Retail Markets	Distributor Markets	Direct-to-Consumer Markets	OEM and Key Accounts	Government	Home Delivery	International
Food Products	X	X			X		
Technology Products	X	X	Developing	X	X		X
Durable Products			X			X	X

In Scope

1. Technology products group including retail, distributor, OEM and key accounts, government, and international markets.

2. Business unit supply chain functions including materials planning, forecasting, purchasing, manufacturing, logistics, customer service, financial control; corporate functions including IT, sales, marketing, and finance.

3. SCOR metrics: perfect order fulfillment, order fulfillment cycle time, upside supply chain flexibility, supply chain management cost, cost of goods, and inventory days of supply.

4. SCOR processes: PLAN, SOURCE, MAKE, DELIVER, and RETURN; ENABLE as necessary.

5. SAP R/3® modules: Materials Management (MM), Production Planning (PP), and Sales and Distribution (SD).

6. All physical locations for the technology products group supply chains, including six regional distribution centers (two each in North America, Asia, and Europe); four manufacturing plants (United States, Netherlands, China, and India); raw material, component and packaging suppliers; and contract manufacturers.

Out of Scope

- The developing technology products direct-to-consumer market.
- Configuration changes to SAP Financial Accounting (FI), Controlling (CO), and Fixed Asset Management (AM).
- Food products and durable products groups.

Business Objectives

- Reduce inventory days of supply by 15 percent.
- Achieve parity level delivery performance.
- Add 10 percent of incremental operating margin.
- Standardize on a global supply chain operational blueprint.
- Improve utilization of SAP functionality.

Project Objectives

- Develop a global scorecard that is consistent worldwide and analytically repeatable on a frequent interval.
- Prioritize supply chain performance targets by region by market.
- Develop and prioritize a global supply chain project improvement portfolio that will help the technology products group rank comparably as one of the top 25 supply chains.

- ◆ Expose all of our global leaders to the process either as providing input, participating directly, and/or reviewing output.

- ◆ Develop internal Fowlers competence in implementing SCOR projects in the future.

III. Project Approach

Methodology

SCOR (Supply Chain Operations Reference) model Version 10.0 will be the basis for this project. The major work tasks will be organized using the discipline highlighted in the *Supply Chain Excellence* book and is summarized by the activities in Phase 0: Build Organizational Support; Phase 1: Define Project Scope; Phase 2: Analyze Performance; Phase 3: Develop Project Portfolio; and Phase 4: Implement Projects. *Supply Chain Excellence* uniquely combines the concepts of Business Process Engineering—Management, Project Management, and SCOR.

Project Schedule

Schedule for Global and Small Business Applications	Deliverable	Classroom Dates
Phase 0 Build Organizational Support	**February 1 to May 1, 2011**	
	Supply Chain Excellence Overview with wide audience	February 7, 2011
	SCOR Framework Workshop	Opportunity
	SCOR Implementation Workshop	Opportunity
	Organizational Briefings	As Needed
	Executive Briefing—GO/NO GO	March 11, 2011
Phase 1 Define Project Scope	**May 1 to July 1, 2011**	
	Business Context Summary	Remote Web-Based Meetings

	Supply Chain Definition Matrix (with data)	Meetings
	Project Charter	April 18
Phase 2 Analyze Performance	Kickoff	April 25
	Metric Definitions and Data Collection Plan	May 2 May 9
	Defect Data Collection Plan	May 16
	Defect Analysis	May 23
	Industry Comparison	May 30
	Competitive Requirements	June 6
	Benchmark Data	
	Preliminary Scorecard	
	Scorecard Gap Analysis	
	IDEALLY DEDICATED ON-SITE Staple Yourself to an Order Interviews	On-Site
	IDEALLY DEDICATED ON-SITE AS IS Process Diagram	June 13 to 17, 2011
Phase 3 Develop Project Portfolio	**July 11 to August 1, 2011**	
	AS IS Process Diagram	
	Defect Analysis Part 2	
	Brainstorm Event and Documentation	On-Site
	Preliminary Project Portfolio	
	Opportunity Analysis	July 11 to 15, 2011
	Assemble and Approve Implementation Project Charters	
	Prioritize Implementation Projects	
Phase 4 Implement Projects	**August 1, 2011, to July 31, 2012**	
	Identify and Approve Project Resource Plan	Combination On-
	Establish Project Schedule, Including Informal Kickoff Date	Site and Remote Management
	Review Project Charter, Background, and Expectations with Project Team	August 1, 2011, to July 31, 2012

Develop Baseline for Metrics Selected as In-Scope
Conduct AS IS Level 3 and 4 Process Gap Analysis
Develop Action Plans to Close "Quick Hit" Gaps
Assemble TO BE Level 3 and 4 Process Based on Leading Practice
Develop and Approve Solution-Design Storyboard
Build and Test Solution
Pilot and Verify Solution
Roll Out Solution to Project Scope and Evaluate Metric Impact
Define Process Control Measures
Scale Implementation to Targeted Supply Chains in the Definition Matrix

Steering Team Meetings

February 7	Introductory Session
March 11	GO/NO GO
May 16	Scorecard Review
June 17	Brainstorm Event Review
July 15	Preliminary Project Portfolio Review
August 1	Implementation Kickoff

Risks and Dependencies

- Active sponsorship
- A Fowlers financial analyst will be available for Phase 2: Analyze Performance
- Availability of Fowlers worldwide raw historical data to collect and calculate actual performance and associated defects

- Consistent availability of steering committee and design team members
- Desire and/or capability to accept the SAP "way of doing things"

Project Organization

Sponsors

Brian Dowell

Jovan Kojcic

Steering Team

Tadeo Morillo

Amanda Messenger

Timothy Ulrich

Girish Naagesh

Jon Park

VP Sales and Marketing—Technology Products Group

Finance Controller—Technology Products Group

Project Leader

David Able

Project Team

Director Applications

Director Customer Service

Director Logistics

Director of Purchasing

Plant Managers from the smallest two technology products group plants

Materials Managers from the largest two technology products group plants

Demand Manager Technology Products Group

Logistics Manager Technology Products Group

Supply Manager Technology Products Group

Finance Control Technology Products Group

Extended Team

SAP super users for MM, PP, and SD

Schedulers from each plant

Buyers from each plant

Production managers from each plant

Warehouse managers from each distribution center

Director Accounts Receivable

Director Accounts Payable

Director Supply Chain

Director Manufacturing

Roles and Responsibilities

Project Sponsor

- Set strategic mission, vision, and direction as context for the project.
- Review team progress against deliverables.
- Provide resource support to project leader and design team.
- Resolve escalated issues.
- Approve budget and schedule.
- Provide final approval for all changes within defined scope.
- Attend steering team review meetings.

Steering Team

- Review and approve design team recommended changes.
- Ensure organizational and functional commitment.
- Resolve cross-functional issues.
- Provide resources to project team as needed.
- Lead change management cross-functionally.
- Initiate and champion projects.
- Attend steering team reviews.

Project Manager

- Recruit project team.
- Serve as liaison between project team and sponsors.
- Measure team progress against deliverables.
- Manage all external resources assigned to the project to contractual commitment.
- Manage all aspects of the project in a manner consistent with company business requirements, policies, project management methodology, and budget procedures.
- Define and plan the project. Responsible for establishing quality standards and acceptance criteria in the statement of work.
- Escalate the resolution of critical issues.
- Obtain necessary approvals.

Design Team

- Commit to class sessions and other blocks of time as required.
- Complete any assigned work (project deliverables) on time.
- Provide subject matter expertise as needed.
- Develop and validate deliverables as needed.

- Define, communicate, and facilitate necessary changes to policies and standards.
- Present results to the steering team.
- Identify extended team members.

Extended Team

- Expected to be available by appointment with advance notice.
- Participate in team meetings, as specified.
- Contribute to all activities of the design team as requested.

Coach

- Provide formal knowledge transfer to the project team regarding *Supply Chain Excellence*, SCOR, etc.
- Provide formal and informal direct knowledge transfer to project leader of all aspects of *Supply Chain Excellence*, project leadership, tools and techniques, and change management.
- Facilitate classroom sessions.
- Provide critique to deliverables.
- Modify instructional method as necessary.
- Ensure curriculum integrity.

Benefits and Measures of Success

Stakeholder Expectations

In addition to the project and business objectives, the following expectations are a summary of stakeholder interviews:

- Improve corporate inventory turns.
- Facilitate *global*, cross-functional process changes, ownership.
- Define a path to superior delivery.

- Increase purchased finished goods (merchandise) turns from 5 to 10.

- Improve transaction process with suppliers.

- Integrate metrics for each area of the supply chain.

- Clearly identify supply chain performance gaps.

- Drive 2011 and 2012 after-tax profit performance.

- Expand supply chain knowledge of the team.

- Develop a repeatable process for future SCOR initiatives in other business units in Fowlers.

- Use SAP functionality more effectively.

Benchmark Sources

- SCORmark™

- Performance Measurement Group

- Hoovers

- Manufacturing Performance Institute

- Warehouse Education Research Center

Benefit Analysis

TBD by July 15. In general, the average *Supply Chain Excellence* portfolio achieves a 3 percent operating income improvement with benefits falling into four areas: revenue growth, improved cash-to-cash, cost reduction, and productivity improvement.

Project Communication

A formal communication plan will be established for each group of stakeholders in this project including the steering team, project manager, design team, extended team and Fowlers at large.

Index

BRITAIN'S BEST REAL HERITAGE PUBS

Pub Interiors of Outstanding Historic Interest

GEOFF BRANDWOOD

Foreword by Simon Thurley
Chief Executive, English Heritage

CAMPAIGN FOR REAL ALE

CAMRA's National Inventory of Historic Pub Interiors

Produced by CAMRA's Pub Heritage Group
www.heritagepubs.org.uk
info.pubheritage@camra.org.uk
With support from CAMRA Books:
Simon Hall and Katie Hunt

Published by the Campaign for Real Ale Ltd
230 Hatfield Road, St Albans
Hertfordshire AL1 4LW
www.camra.org.uk/books

ISBN 978-1-85249-304-2

A CIP catalogue record for this book is available from
the British Library

Printed and bound in the United Kingdom by
Cambrian Printers Ltd, Aberystwyth

Book design/typography: Dale Tomlinson
Maps/plans: Stephen Bere

Photographs: all are by Geoff Brandwood unless otherwise
credited. All were taken in 2012–13 unless otherwise dated

Contents

MAPS

Maps of featured pubs in **England**, **Wales**, **Scotland** and **Northern Ireland** can be found at the end of the book. Also included are city maps of: **London** (Inner) p. 57, (Outer) p. 81; **Manchester** p. 98; **Liverpool** p. 113; and **Edinburgh** p. 217

Acknowledgements

This guide is testimony to more than two decades' work
by CAMRA's Pub Heritage Group (PHG), chaired first
by Dave Gamston and since 2004 by Paul Ainsworth.
The group has always been made up of volunteers who
have given their time and expertise freely to identify
and survey Britain's historic pub interiors. Members
frequently get a (tedious) ribbing with 'it's a tough
job but someone's got to do it – ho-ho!' In fact no-one
has to do it and, if PHG had not taken up the task, it
is highly unlikely any other body would have done
so. In that case many of the pubs in this guide would
remain largely unknown and others would not have
received the all-important protection which successful
listing applications by CAMRA have brought about.

More immediately in terms of this guide, many
people have given help. A small team consisting of
Paul Ainsworth, Dave Gamston, Chris Witt and myself
has been responsible for bringing it together and I
am deeply indebted to my colleagues for reading and
suggesting improvements: Chris's meticulous checking of
the tedious but vital detail of addresses, phone numbers,
websites and pub descriptions has been invaluable and
has saved this guide from no end of error. He also wrote
the features on farm pubs and also that about film and TV
appearances of our historic pubs. Paul Ainsworth drafted
early versions of many county entries. Dave Gamston has
done sterling work in drafting up material for the maps
which, along with the pub plans, have been drawn up by
Steve Bere. Dave also wrote all the entries for Yorkshire.
Dale Tomlinson's skill as a designer has made the book
look what is and it has been a pleasure to work with him.
A good deal of help has been given by Mick Slaughter who
for many years has been a stalwart discoverer of historic
pub interiors and it was he who suggested the basis for
the list of more pubs to try on pp. 260–1: he has also
provided photographs, offered advice on various subjects,
and helped refine the entries on Northern Ireland.
Dave Gamston and Paul Ainsworth kindly drove me on
survey trips in Yorkshire and East Anglia respectively,
David Lawrence did so in the East Midlands, and
Andrew Davison accompanied me around the watering
holes of Leeds. My thanks to Patrick Chaplin for advice
on darts. Support from Simon Hall and Katie Hunt at the
CAMRA Books team has been much appreciated. Finally,
thanks to my partner, Jean Fryer, for granting me leave
of absence for many survey trips and for accompanying
me on others, not to mention carrying the tripod!

Geoff Brandwood
February 2013

Foreword

Pubs are an intrinsic part of British life, and nationwide there are around 50,000 opening their doors every day. But historic pub interiors are something rarer. Across the UK, only some 270 have been identified as having the level of national importance necessary for listing in this guide. The Campaign for Real Ale was instrumental in recognising the need to preserve these rare survivals, and the project that followed has led to listings, list upgradings, and revisions to existing list descriptions.

The list of nationally important pub interiors is of course available on-line, along with its cousin, a database of pubs which hold special regional importance, but do not make the national list. One of those that does make the cut, however, is the Red Lion, Kenninghall, in my own native Norfolk. With its enticing snug, it must surely be one of the best places in England to sup your pint.

English Heritage has been working with CAMRA for 20 years now, and the legacy of that partnership is beautifully revealed within the pages of this book. From wonderful Victorian tiled interiors, through to the simple splendour of Art Deco decoration, the range of pubs recognised through the historic pub interiors project is staggering.

Simon Thurley
Chief Executive
English Heritage

Introduction

The British pub is a wonderful and unique institution. Despite recent horrendous closure rates, over 50,000 remain, offering a rich variety of drinking environments, mostly good, sometimes great, occasionally grim. The *idea* of the 'traditional' pub (whatever that may mean) is mighty appealing and is somehow bound up with a sense of Britishness. Yet this guide about historic pub interiors, which might be expected to embody this sense of tradition, can only muster 270 main entries – that is barely 0.5% of our pub stock. This is all down to an unprecedented amount of change since the 1960s. Like any business, pubs change with time, but frenzied levels of gutting, stripping and refit after refit have meant that incredibly few pubs look anything like they did half a century ago. This is why those in this guide are so important: they are irreplaceable and illuminate aspects of our nation's past and the lives of its people.

CAMRA's awareness of the threats gathered force in the 1980s. A national Pub Preservation Group (a forerunner of today's Pub Heritage Group [PHG]) was set up and pioneered initiatives to identify our most important pub interiors and sowed the seeds for the National Inventory of Historic Pub Interiors (NI). This is the listing of the UK's finest and rarest pub interiors, 270 pubs which were trading as at January 2013 and which formed the core of this guide. In addition, CAMRA has drawn up Regional Inventories covering pubs of lesser intactness or quality but which still possess special historic significance (see the next page).

PHG's work involves achieving better recognition of and protection for these priceless, yet at times vulnerable, buildings which are so much a part of our heritage. Above all, though, this guide aims to convey the pleasure that can be derived from visiting our real heritage pubs – a pleasure which, in most cases, can be amplified with a pint of delicious real ale! We hope this book will encourage you to seek out these pubs, some ornate, some plain, many old but a few more recent, several famous, others little known – but all to be cherished and enjoyed.

Dave Gamston, the first chair of CAMRA's Pub Heritage Group, enjoys a pint in the First Class bar at the Station Buffet, Bridlington, East Yorkshire (196)

CAMRA's National and Regional Inventories of Historic Pub Interiors

The chief focus of the **National Inventory** is pub interiors which remain unaltered since before the Second World War. They do not have to be architecturally splendid because even an unaltered plain pub is now a very rare part of our heritage. The vast majority have multiple rooms, as was the norm until the 1960s. There are also a few early post-war entrants, still built on these traditional lines and which have a *very* high degree of intactness. In addition the NI includes pubs with specific features or rooms of national significance: it may be an intact Victorian snug in an otherwise altered pub, a pub where there is no bar counter at all, or a particularly fine single feature such as superb pictorial tiling or a flamboyant bar-back. The NI is now widely recognised by heritage professionals as the gold standard record of Britain's most important historic pub interiors.

CAMRA's work has also involved identifying pubs which, although falling short of the national list, still have interiors or features of special historic interest. These are included on our various **Regional Inventories**, a selection of the best and most interesting of which is to be found on pp. 260–1. Together, the National and Regional Inventories comprise what CAMRA refers to as the UK's 'Real Heritage Pubs'. Printed guides to them have been produced for Greater London, East Anglia, the North East, Scotland, Wales and Yorkshire. The latter three are still in print (see pp. 285–6). Details can also be found on our website www.heritagepubs. org.uk where clicking on the 'Search Here' facility in the top left-hand corner will take you to easy-to-use drop-down menus.

The Shakespeare, Dudley, West Midlands (179), proudly proclaims its National Inventory status (even if the title isn't quite right!)

CAMRA and English Heritage

CAMRA was not alone in its concerns over the tidal wave of change that was overwhelming our historic pubs. Its work on the National Inventory in the early 1990s attracted close interest from English Heritage, the Government agency for the historic environment in England, which was working on new listing guidelines for the more 'ordinary' types of industrial age buildings, such as mills, chapels and public houses and which had hitherto been largely overlooked for listing. CAMRA was invited in as a specialist working partner to develop guidelines for pubs and undertook a number of pilot studies in various areas – Birmingham, Harrogate, Leeds, Manchester, Walsall and York. They revealed how few interiors were unaltered over the past half-century and built the case both for greater recognition of pub interiors, and greater representation of pubs in the statutory lists (see pp. 11–15).

The result of this collaboration was English Heritage's ground-breaking booklet, *Pubs: Understanding Listing* which was launched at CAMRA's 1994 AGM in Scarborough where EH's then Chief Executive, Jennie Page, provided the keynote address. She affirmed that EH was determined to support more statutory protection for pubs with important historic interiors. Several significant listings followed, not only of architecturally exciting examples, but also of more modest pubs which had now become very rare indeed in terms of their intactness.

The Seymour Arms, Witham Friary, Somerset (145), was built to serve an estate village of the Duke of Somerset. It was listed in 2004 after the importance of its intact 1860s interior became recognised. It was originally part of a farm (see p. 48), hence the buildings on the left

11

In 1998 the EH/CAMRA collaboration was cemented by the jointly-funded, two-year appointment of a part-time caseworker (Geoff Brandwood) to review pubs on the National Inventory with a view to getting them listed, if that was appropriate, reassessing gradings and improving list descriptions. This led to over a dozen completely new listings, including one straight from unlisted to Grade II* – the Art Deco Test Match Hotel, West Bridgford (134) (and p. 14).

Subsequently, CAMRA has maintained a dialogue with EH's designation teams and, as knowledge has increased, this has produced further listings as greater knowledge of the country's pub stock has developed. With the 'discovery' of the superb but unlisted inter-war Eastbrook in Dagenham, Greater London (81), this pub was listed at grade II* in 2009.

The two bodies have continued to work together in other ways. EH is represented among the judges for CAMRA's annual Pub Design Awards in which the conservation category forms a joint award. Furthermore, EH commissioned *Licensed to Sell: the History and Heritage of the Public House*, written by Geoff Brandwood and EH's Andrew Davison with photographs by Michael Slaughter (all long-serving members of CAMRA's PHG), and published in 2004. It went into a new edition in 2011 and remains an ideal introduction for anyone interested in the great history of our pubs.

Beyond England

CAMRA's work also identified public houses in Wales and Northern Ireland which seemed worthy of protection and successful applications for listing have been made to Cadw and the Department of the Environment respectively. Much success in gaining recognition for National Inventory pubs has been achieved north of the Border in collaboration with Historic Scotland: this project is described on p. 228.

When the intactness and quality of the hitherto unlisted Eastbrook, Dagenham (81), was identified by CAMRA, it was given a II* grading. This is the Oak Room

Statutory listing: a short guide

All parts of the UK have systems for protecting buildings of special architectural or historic interest so that they may be passed on to future generations to appreciate and, hopefully, cherish. Contrary to what one often hears – 'it's listed so we can't do anything to it' – the process

is not devised to *prevent* change, rather to *manage* it effectively, working with the grain of the building and not, in a cavalier fashion, against it. Were that not the case then the exemplary additions and/or refurbishments at various pubs in this guide could not have taken place. This in turn would have jeopardised their future as businesses and they might well not be with us today: cases in point are the Five Mile House, Duntisbourne Abbots, Gloucestershire (35 and p. 17), Sun Inn at Leintwardine, Herefordshire (40), Crystal Fountain, Cannock, Staffordshire (148), and King's Arms, Heath, West Yorkshire (214). Work that

Listing in 1993 saved the Railway, Altrincham, Greater Manchester (92), from being swallowed up by a developer's car park

would change the character of a listed building requires permission from the relevant local authority and, in the case of highly graded buildings, will probably involve input from the appropriate national heritage agency. 217 of the 270 pubs in the main gazetteer are listed, along with all twelve in the Closed Pubs section on pp. 256–9.

England

Listings are made by the Secretary of State for Culture, Media & Sport on the advice of English Heritage.

Grade I. This highest of gradings covers just 2.5% of all listed buildings: these are ones that have 'exceptional', perhaps even international interest.

Grade II* (spoken of as 'Two Star'). Covers a further 5.5% of listing buildings. They have 'outstanding' interest.

Grade II. 92% of all English buildings are listed at Grade II. They have what is described as 'special' architectural or historic interest.

Most listed pubs are designated at Grade II. Higher grades apply to some of those in this guide, for example, ones with particularly magnificent Victorian or Edwardian work, such as the II* Bartons Arms, Birmingham (169), or the Garden Gate, Leeds (218). Interwar II* pubs in this guide are the Eastbrook, Dagenham, Greater London (81), the Test Match Hotel, West Bridgford, Nottinghamshire (134), and Margaret Catchpole, Ipswich, Suffolk (155): in all these cases the star was achieved after recommendations from CAMRA. The George, Southwark (77), is the only Grade I pub in this guide, the grading arising not so much from its interior but from the fact that it is, with the New Inn, Gloucester (not in this guide), the last of two galleried inns from the great days of coaching.

The Art Deco lounge at the Test Match Hotel, West Bridgford, Nottinghamshire (134)

Wales

Listing in Wales has the same grades as in England and is undertaken by Cadw on behalf of the Welsh Assembly. The percentage of buildings in each grading is very similar to those in England. No Welsh pubs in this guide are listed at II* or I.

Scotland

Listing is the responsibility of Historic Scotland on behalf of the Scottish Assembly. There are three categories, whereby the proportions of buildings in each is somewhat different from the rest of the UK:

Category A. This category, taking in some 8% of Scotland's listed buildings, covers those of national or international architectural or historical importance, or fine little-altered examples of some particular period, style or building type.

Category B. Approximately 50% of the total. Buildings of regional, or more than local importance, or major examples of some particular period, style or building type which may have been altered.

Category C. Approximately 42% of the total. Buildings of local importance, lesser examples of any period, style, or building type, as originally constructed or moderately altered.

Six pubs in this guide are listed at Grade A: the Café Royal (236), Kenilworth (237), and Central Bar (240), all in Edinburgh; Horse Shoe Bar, Glasgow (244); Bull Inn, Paisley (251); and Feuars Arms, Kirkcaldy (254). A further six are listed at Grade B.

Northern Ireland

Listing is the responsibility of the Department of the Environment which categorises buildings into the following three grades, the proportions of which are very similar to those in England and Wales:

Grade A. Approximately 2.5% of the total. Buildings of greatest importance, including both outstanding architectural set-pieces and the least altered examples of each representative style, period and grouping.

Grade B+. Approximately 6.5% of the total. Buildings which might have merited grade A status but for detracting features such as an incomplete design, lower quality additions, or alterations. Also included are buildings that have exceptional features, interiors or environmental qualities.

Grade B. Approximately 91% of the total. Buildings of local importance and good examples of a particular period or style. A degree of alteration or imperfection of design may be acceptable.

Belfast's magnificent Crown Bar (266) is listed at Grade A and the Boyd Arms, Ballycastle, Co. Antrim (259), at B +.

Saving heritage pubs

The British pub is going through tough times and during 2012 the closure rate varied between twelve and eighteen a week. Since 2008 no less than 4,500 have closed and heritage pubs have suffered along with others. Since 2006, fifteen pubs which would otherwise have featured in this guide have been lost for ever. What can be done to stem this fearful rate of attrition?

Encouraging new ownership

CAMRA's Pub Heritage Group takes active steps to help find new owners for heritage pubs which are on the market, mainly by contacting local breweries and others known to be sympathetic to the cause. Several communities have fended off the threat to their local by buying it themselves. CAMRA has a booklet – *Saving Your Local Pub* – giving detailed advice on how to do this. A number have been saved by the new generation of micro-breweries and are now successful businesses (see p. 175).

Additional uses

Diversification can help improve the viability of pubs, especially rural ones. Many pubs now incorporate small shops, post office counters, meeting rooms, even betting shops and art galleries. The Pub is the Hub organisation (www.pubisthehub.org.uk) offers practical advice and, in some cases, financial assistance with such projects.

Statutory listing

A pub included on the statutory lists of buildings of architectural and historic interest enjoys an enhanced degree of protection (for more see p. 13). Demolishing a listed building or significantly altering its interior, requires planning permission and listed building consent, whereas unlisted buildings can be bulldozed or trashed largely with impunity. At the time of writing, out of the 270 National Inventory pubs that form the core of this guide, 217 were statutorily listed. A number of them have been listed following successful applications by CAMRA and in some instances this has unquestionably prevented destructive change.

Use it or lose it

Arguably the most effective way to save pubs is for them to be well used. CAMRA campaigns strongly to promote pubs and pub-going, through initiatives such as Community Pubs Month. A key aim of this present guide is to stimulate interest in the pubs it covers and so encourage more people to visit them more often.

ENGLAND

The mighty settles in the
tap room at the Five Mile House,
Duntisbourne Abbots,
Gloucestershire (35)

BEDFORDSHIRE

Broom

23 High Street, SG18 9NA
01767 314411
Grade II listed
LPA: Central Bedfordshire

Cock

1

The Cock is a delightful village pub, originally a simple alehouse, but which has expanded over time from one to several rooms whilst still keeping its traditional character. The original public room was to the left of the entrance and now serves as a games room (with a skittle table). Drinks were fetched, as indeed they still are, from the top of the cellar

steps further back up the corridor. Fewer than a dozen pubs in the UK share this total lack of a bar counter or hatch (see p. 41). The room to the right of the entrance was once a shop, hence the cupboards. There is extensive panelling in the front rooms and in the corridor – very atmospheric but much of it was the work of a local carpenter, Richard Beasley, as recently as about 1980. The rear rooms have been developed over stages since 1977 but they really complement the historic area at the front most sympathetically. The floors have extensive quarry-tiling which adds to the atmosphere.

The games room, set up for hood skittles, was the original pub room at the Cock, from which it has subsequently expanded

Luton

79 Hightown Road, LU2 0BW
01582 732815
Grade II listed
LPA: Luton

Painters Arms

2

Rebuilt in 1913, much of the original plan remains. On entering, the key feature is a small, central off-sales or 'Jug Bar' (so described in the door glass): seats on each side were no doubt used by customers having a swift one before leaving with their take-aways (scandalously, these seats have been ripped out recently). The front and right-hand rooms

The saloon and the screen to the 'Jug Bar'

have their original bar-back fittings and counters. To the left, two small rooms were combined many years ago but the names 'Saloon' and 'Private Bar' survive in the door glass. Attractive tiling occurs in both the entrance lobby floors and the dados of some internal walls. Three original fireplaces also survive. Left of the Jug Bar, the counter has a pot-shelf arrangement, as does the room behind. These features look as though they are original and, if so, are remarkable early examples since counters were normally unencumbered with such items until well into the post-war period. A wall at the back was removed in 2000 and a door widened, so now it is possible to circumnavigate the interior, something that people would not have expected back in 1913.

BERKSHIRE

Aldworth

Bell Lane, RG8 9SE
01635 578272
Grade II listed
LPA: West Berkshire

The tap room

Bell   3

A splendid two-room village pub, held by the same family since the 18th century and the winner of many CAMRA awards. The tap room (left) is especially glorious with a great inglenook fireplace, panelling, benches round three sides, quarry-tiled floor, one-handed clock (cf. George, Southwark [77], and chunky scrubbed tables and chairs). This furniture was made in the 19th century at the village blacksmith/ carpentry shop by the same family who owned the pub. It was installed by the present landlady's great-grandmother who was also responsible for the screen to the long corridor. At the heart of the Bell is a glazed-in servery with unusual horizontal sliding windows, one of only a handful

of this type in the country. It is said to have been installed in the 1930s, but may be earlier. The ebony hand-pumps bear the date 1902.

The second room at the Bell wraps around the servery in an L-shape and took this form in 1974 with the removal of a partition. As for the gents' loo, this is outside on the left and known, for obvious reasons after a few beers on a dark evening, as the 'Planetarium'!

BUCKINGHAMSHIRE

West Wycombe
High Street, HP14 3AE
01494 527031
Grade II listed
LPA: Wycombe

Swan   4

An 18th-century pub, run by the same family since 1910, refitted and extended in 1932. There are two well-preserved pub rooms – the saloon (at the front) and public bar – set at right-angles to one another and with an L-shaped servery: note the curtains for providing some privacy between the two bars. Each part of the servery has a mirrored bar-back fitting. In the saloon there is an inglenook fireplace at the far end, plus a brick one which probably dates from the 1932 refit: there is a similar fireplace in the public bar. Both rooms have herringbone parquet flooring. The crisp, white-tiled gents' is a splendid affair, untouched since the 1930s, and sited on the corner of the building with access from both bars (via an 'anteroom' space on each side). On the left side is a door marked 'Reception' (the former jug and bottle) and another door to the dining room. As at a number of pubs in the Chilterns, the casks are stillaged at the back of the servery.

The spick and span saloon and its fittings of 1932

CAMBRIDGESHIRE

Peterborough

12 Highbury Street, PE1 3BE
01733 564653
Not listed
LPA: Peterborough

Hand & Heart   5

Examples of largely intact, small inter-war urban pubs are very rare which is why this small pub of 1938 is to be cherished (cf. the Vine, Wednesfield [186]). The corridor (on the left) retains the original off-sales-cum-drinking lobby with a bell-push and a hinged pane in the glazed screen over the counter (it can still be raised and lowered). The basic public bar retains the original bar counter (with distinctive Art Deco frontage), bar-back and fixed seating. Note the Second World War memorial over the door – one of just 60 such memorials in pubs. At the back of the pub is a smoke room with original seating and a hatch service to the servery – but the fireplace is a Victorian-style replacement, totally inappropriate for a 1930s pub.

The distinctive 1930s counter and surround to the public bar   (Michael Slaughter)

CHESHIRE

Alpraham
Chester Road, CW6 9JA
01829 260523
Not listed
LPA: Cheshire East
🍺

Travellers Rest   6

A wayside pub on the main road through the village. It once comprised just the T-plan building of around 1850 with its Tudor-style windows. This was extended, mainly at the back, in 1937, which is also the date of most of the (quite plain) fittings. Further changes took place around 1970 when the 'Wicker Room' came into use. Back in the old part, the tap room has a fine Victorian fireplace and 1930s mirror; a doorway leads to the tiny public bar which is mostly the result of the 1937 refit. The lounge bar was added at that time and retains its original fittings (but is usually closed – ask the bar staff for permission to view). There's none of that new-fangled electronic gadgetry here – the till is a drawer in the bar counter and the likes of TVs, piped music and fruit machines are nowhere to be found. This pub has been in the hands of the same family for 110 years. The bowling green at the rear is still much used.

The public bar   (Michael Slaughter, 2005)

Barthomley
Audley Road, CW2 5PG
01270 772242
www.whitelionbarthomley.com
Grade II* listed
LPA: Cheshire East
🍺 🍴

White Lion   7

This fine old half-timbered building, opposite the church, dates back to the early 17th century. The oldest part in terms of pub use is the delightful small, beamed tap room in the centre of the building. It had no bar counter and beer was served from the parlour through a hatch: the furniture and fittings are from the 1930s, including a curious high-backed settle which reuses what looks like old wall panelling. Note the glass-covered section of exposed wattle-and-daub on the left-hand side showing the method of filling in the walls between the timber framing. The large room to the left (where the servery now is) has seen use as a court-room and a school-room before becoming part of the pub in 1953 which is the date of most of the fittings. The tiny room at the back was converted from private quarters in 1994.

The tap room with its rustic furniture and inter-war fireplace

Bollington

75 Palmerston Street, SK10 5PW
01625 578017
Not listed
LPA: Cheshire East

The smoke room

Holly Bush

8

Handsomely rebuilt in 'Brewer's Tudor' style around 1935 with a half-timbered upper storey over a brick and stone-dressed ground floor and, like its predecessor, with a three-room layout. In the tap room (left), a bar counter replaced a hatch about 1963 but the original fixed seating and lovely fireplace remain. To the right is the small snug with Tudor-style treatment and especially chunky timbering over the fireplace. Behind all this is, in effect, a drinking lobby in the northern tradition: the servery still has three rising shutters and also a couple

of glazed display cases in the bar-back. In front the smoke room was a walled-off, separate room until 1963 and still retains its original fixed seating, bell-pushes and an imposing fireplace. Panelled walls continue through the lobby to the ladies' which still has some original tiling inside the door. Within the servery is an annunciator box (p. 121) for the bell-push system to show where service was required, but it no longer functions. The rear porch has a tiled floor incorporating the signs of the zodiac. Upstairs a club room is now used for pool.

Gawsworth

Church Lane, SK11 9RR
01260 223325
www.harringtonarmsgawsworth.
robinsonsbrewery.com
Grade II listed
LPA: Cheshire East
🍺 🍴

Harrington Arms   9

An example of a once common way to combine livelihoods: until 2007 the business doubled up as a pub and a working farm run by the same individual, but they are now separate undertakings (see p. 41). The timeless tap room to the left of the entrance is the oldest part and has a red and black quarry-tiled floor, venerable settles, an old fireplace and sundry other vintage furniture. The servery in its present form only dates from 1980. To the right, the snug has a hatch for service, a 1950s fireplace and a settle; the small lounge at the back has a similar period feel. The former kitchen on the rear left became part of the pub in 2007 (the former cooking facilities must have been on a truly industrial scale!). All the rooms have numbers on their doors (p. 147).

Entrance corridor and servery

Haslington

137 Crewe Road, CW1 5RG
01270 582181
Grade II listed
LPA: Cheshire East
🍺 🍴

Hawk Inn   `10`

The star attraction here could easily be missed as it is at the back of the pub. This is the Oak Room, lined with a tremendous display of old panelling, probably of 17th-century origin and likely to have come from a gentry house, rather than an Armada galleon as the hoary old legend would have it. All this was there when Robinsons brewery of Stockport bought the pub in 1929. The room also has a Tudor-style stone fire surround, 1920s fixed seating, bell-pushes and leaded windows. Over the fireplace are three decorative arches in relief, either side of which are paired columns. The rest of the interior has seen much alteration, although some 1930s fittings survive.

The Oak Room

Macclesfield

27 Church Street, SK11 6LB
01625 668863
Grade II listed
LPA: Cheshire East
🍺 🍴

Castle   `11`

Although the building it occupies is 18th-century, the pub was probably created in Victorian times. To the right of the entrance, the charming little tap room has fixed seating and tongue-and-grooved wall benches. Also to the right of the corridor, glazed screenwork incorporates an off-sales/serving hatch, display case and entrance to the servery.

First left from the corridor is a delightful smoke room with early 20th-century fittings (but Victorian fireplace), bell-pushes and a notable ceiling with a pair of lozenge patterns. The room behind the servery has a glazed partition to the corridor and a 1971 bar counter, but older seating. The fourth room at the back is a recent convert to pub use.

The smoke room

Scholar Green

121 Congleton Road North, ST7 3BQ
01782 782272
www.thebleedingwolf.co.uk
Grade II listed
LPA: Cheshire East

The eponymous, ill-starred wolf.
Below: the inglenook fireplace and
exposed, adzed timberwork are a
classic example of 'Brewers' Tudor'

Bleeding Wolf

12

A particularly wonderful and remarkably intact inter-war roadhouse, built in 1936 for Robinsons brewery of Stockport to the designs of architect J. H. Walters. He employed a Vernacular Revival style which aimed to create a nostalgic sense of history and respectability, reinforced by the enormous thatched roof as an emblem of rustic tradition. The hugely ambitious floor-plan of five linked rooms remains, along with most of the original fittings and finishes, notably the adzed tooling on the woodwork to suggest, once again, homely rusticity. The public bar (left) has exposed timbering, rustic fireplace and original counter while the main lounge on the right features the servery and a lovely semi-circular bay to the front of the building; note also the impressive inglenook-style fireplace and the depiction in stained glass of the bleeding wolf (whose legend is told in a panel on the wall). Further to the right is the dining room and to the rear left the fully panelled 'Oak Room' – a splendid period piece. Finally, a former games room now houses the carvery. Lots of superb detailing throughout – for example, the delightful stained glass beer bottles either side of the entrance and the original tiling in the loos. Listed in 2011 following a successful application by CAMRA.

CORNWALL

Falmouth

1 The Moor, TR11 3QA
01326 312111
Grade II listed
LPA: Cornwall

Seven Stars   13

A small town-centre pub, the Seven Stars has been in the hands of the same family since 1868: for 50 of these years, until his death in 2012, the licensee was Barrington Bennetts who was also an ordained Anglican clergyman. At the front, the public bar has various late Victorian fittings, plus metal stillages introduced in the late 1940s.

There was formerly a partitioned-off oyster bar here and its rare, white marble counter-top is still in place. The gas lights at either end of the bar still work. There is also a wood panelled ceiling. A passage, with an off-sales hatch, leads to the rear smoke room which has a hatch/doorway to the back of the bar. The Victorian building was extended to the right in 1912 and an off-sales shop (now defunct) added, but is no longer part of the pub.

The front bar at the Seven Stars in 1953: not much has changed since (Steve Bowie)

CUMBRIA

Bassenthwaite Lake

CA13 9YE
(South off A66, west end of lake)
017687 76234
www.the-pheasant.co.uk
Not listed
LPA: Allerdale

Pheasant   14

The public bar of this Georgian coaching inn, now a smart hotel, has not changed in 70 years. Its layout comprises a small area in front of the counter and a similarly sized alcove, the two being divided by a shallow arch. Inside the arch is, on one side, an early gas fire and on the

An arch divides the public bar into two
(Michael Slaughter, 2005)

other side, a tall thin mirror. The counter is pre-war, as is the bar-back where, unusually, the hand-pumps are positioned. The dado panelling and plastered walls have been much lacquered over the years. Elsewhere, a lounge bar (residents only) has some 1930s features and, in the side passage, there is a two-part glazed hatch inscribed 'Waiters Only', plus two old glazed panels.

Bootle

Main Street, LA19 5TF
01229 718239
Not listed
LPA: Copeland

A bell may be rung to obtain service in the right-hand room
(Michael Slaughter, 2008)

King's Head   15

This austere building of 1753 houses one of the UK's dozen pubs with no bar counter at all (p. 41). A room to the right of the entrance has remnants of fixed seating, whilst the corridor to the left accesses a room which is a bar in the original sense – a private room for the publican from which drinks were served and where valuables were kept. The one here contains hand-pumps (not in use), keg taps, bottles and the till. A room such as this is a very rare survival. The rest of the interior has been significantly changed with the back two rooms and intervening passageway becoming a single space in 1995. Most drinks are served at the table, Customers in  the right-hand room can ring a bell and elsewhere they may summon the landlord by tapping their glasses with coins: this practice has been suggested as the origin of the name 'tap room' (the fact that nearly all tap rooms do *not* have a servery supports this idea, rather than that of being a room where drinks were 'tapped').

Broughton Mills

LA20 6AX
01229 716824
www.theblacksmithsarms.com
Grade II listed
LPA: South Lakeland

Blacksmiths Arms   16

Floored throughout with stone flags, having working gas lights in some rooms and simple furnishings, the Blacksmiths offers a good impression of an old country inn. Only two rooms are genuinely old though. The plain bar counter, with new shelving behind, was installed in the small right-hand room in 1996 – previously there was none. More interesting is the room to the left, divided from the passageway by a solid wooden screen with benches attached. It contains a cast-iron range and a couple of fitted cupboards of the former kitchen, showing how the public house developed out of a private one. The more recent expansions into a shop and private accommodation do not detract from the overall ambience.

The left-hand room
which used to be a kitchen
(Michael Slaughter, 2005)

How old is old?

This book is all about genuine historic pub interiors. But how old are they really? We have all visited churches where the fittings date back to medieval times or a great country house where the family has zealously kept treasures from the days of the Tudors. But when it comes to pubs the story is rather different. Yes, there are plenty of pubs where the structure is centuries old but, when it comes to layout and fittings, there is very little that survives from before the latter part of the 19th century. A very rare exception may be found in London at the George, Southwark (77), the last galleried coaching inn in the capital. In its front room there is very old panelling which might conceivably date back to the rebuilding of the inn in the late seventeenth-century. That would make it an extraordinary survival. Some of the woodwork in the old bar at another London pub, the

Olde Cheshire Cheese in Fleet Street (60), may also be of great (although rather uncertain) age but, again, this is very much an exception.

Even in the 19th century it is not until quite late on that we meet surviving interiors. The earliest virtually intact example in this guide is probably the remarkable Seymour Arms, Witham Friary, Somerset (145), which appears to have been built in 1866 or 1867 for the Duke of Somerset as an estate pub. A very similar date applies to the fittings in a London pub, the Victoria in Bayswater, London (52), which has a superb array of decorative mirrors and a very fancy bar-back. The latter houses a built-in clock which, helpfully, bears a date of 1864. This must surely apply to the whole scheme and that would make it one of the very earliest secure dates for a surviving pub-furnishing scheme anywhere in the country.

A big problem in dating pub interiors is that there is often little or nothing to go on without documentary evidence. At the upper end of the market, schemes can be dated fairly closely on stylistic grounds: for example, etched glass and colourful ceramic work betoken late Victorian or Edwardian work, while 'Brewers' Tudor' designs or Art Deco flourishes can be safely assigned to the two interwar decades. But when it comes to routine work by jobbing carpenters or pub-furnishers, it is often impossible to hazard a date with any reliability. Run-of-the-mill bar counters, settles or dado panelling could look much the same in the 1930s as they did half a century before. Therefore in this guide the temptation has been avoided to suggest dates or periods unless they can be reasonably authenticated.

DERBYSHIRE

Derby

6–7 Queen Street, DE1 3DL
01332 267711
freespace.virgin.net/dmh.derby/
dolphin
Grade II listed
LPA: Derby

Olde Dolphin Inne   17

Derby's oldest pub occupies a late 16th-century building, but what we see inside today (like the external 'Brewers' Tudor' timbering) dates from an inter-war restoration, probably in the 1920s. The four bars are located to the left of a corridor passing right through the building and cluster around an L-shaped servery. At the front left is the main bar with a quarry-tiled floor and beyond, at a slightly higher level, is a 'better' room (hence bell-pushes), Offiler's Lounge, named after the eponymous former owners who brewed in Derby until 1966. Beyond this is the comfortably appointed lounge with its large brick fireplace. Finally, there is a cosy snug which has a part-glazed partition wall to the servery and full-height oak panelling; service is from a hatch to the bar, unlike the other rooms which have counters of varying sizes. Upstairs, the '1530AD Steak Bar' (whose name slightly inaccurately commemorates the date of the building) is open Thurs-Sat evenings and is worth a visit for the massive 16th-century timbers and very old brick fireplace with a brass hood.

The lounge

Elton

Main Street, DE4 2BW
01629 650367
Grade II listed
LPA: Derbyshire Dales

Restricted opening hours

In the public bar

Duke of York   18

This marvellous 200-year-old pub retains its Victorian interior with some minor changes made in 1985. A central tiled corridor leads to the main bar at the rear which is entered through a timber partition wall. It has a quarry-tiled floor, fixed bench seating, wood-panelled ceiling, a stone fireplace and unusual full-height draught screens each side of the door. The bar counter was extended to the window in 1985, albeit using existing panels and which formerly returned at a right angle. Left off the corridor is a plain pool room with a Victorian tiled fireplace and modern hatch to the servery. On the right is a further simply appointed room still with its old fixed bench seating. Upstairs is a large club room. The loos are outside (with old pig sties beyond). Unspoilt village pubs of such simplicity, catering only for the 'wet' trade, are very hard to find nowadays. Opens 8.45pm, also 12–3 Sun.

Glossop

142 Victoria Street, SK13 8JF
01457 862824
Not listed
LPA: High Peak

Crown Inn   19

An end-of-terrace traditional local, built of stone in the 1840s and refitted in later Victorian and interwar times. Beyond the entrance porch is a popular lobby bar with three rooms leading off it. The unusually ornamented bar counter and two sets of bar-back shelves in the lobby servery could be Victorian or even later (in the bar-back a

mirror blocks an outside window which indicates a change at some stage). The front snug retains inter-war fixed seating and a tiled fireplace. The rear snug was a living room until the 1960s but has been fitted out in traditional style by, no doubt, brewers Sam Smiths who own the pub. The long, spacious games room to the left of the entrance extends into the end of the building with fixed seating curving round it: its fireplace has been removed. The three bracket-shaped features round the walls are air vents (with cast-iron grilles outside).

Although modern, the rear room is fitted out in traditional style

Makeney

Holly Bush Lane, DE56 0RX
01332 841729
www.hollybushinnmakeney.co.uk
Grade II listed
LPA: Amber Valley

Holly Bush Inn

20

This marvellous village pub has, like many others, grown from a small original core. Here this was the superb central snug which is formed by a quadrant-shaped partition wall with glazing at the top and a double-hinged door in the middle which, when shut, creates a completely enclosed space. Attached to the inside are benches focusing on the fireplace: this houses a cast-iron range, but note, this was imported as recently as the late 1990s – things in pubs are not always as old as they may seem as owners and publicans strive to create a heritage effect! This wonderful space has a quarry-tiled floor which extends into the corridor. Here a diagonal line in a corner near the snug is said to have marked the site of a counter where beer was served from jugs brought from the cellar before the creation of the present servery in the right-hand room. This room has not changed significantly in the past half-century, although the windows facing the lean-to extension are modern creations replacing a single one in between, the scars of which are still visible. The left-hand room took its present form in 1981 when Holly Bush Cottage, beyond the central post, was incorporated into the pub. The inn sign is painted on the frontage – once a common sight but now a rarity.

The back of the snug, created by two banks of settles

Spondon

Potter Street, DE21 7LH
01332 674203
Grade II listed
LPA: Derby

🍺 🍴

The snug

Malt Shovel   21

A largely 18th-century red-brick building housing an impressive, traditional multi-room pub with off-sales, drinking passageway and three other public rooms. The snug, facing the servery room is especially interesting, being formed by a full-height, part-glazed curved partition wall with seating attached. It is one of very few such spaces to survive (cf. Holly Bush Inn, Makeney (above) and Bell & Cross, Clent, Worcestershire [190]). It has, as does the corridor, a red and black quarry-tiled floor.

The small room further down the corridor has old movable benches. The lounge, on the right, is most unusual in being accessed across a corner of the servery: otherwise it holds little of heritage interest apart from its modest (probably) interwar seating. The large Tudor or Long Room at the front was in use by 1939 although most of the Tudorisation was introduced post-1960. The various rooms are identified by letters, instead of the usual numbers, on the doors (p. 147). The kitchen occupies the former brewhouse which ceased activity in 1918.

Wardlow Mires

SK17 8RW
(at A623/B6465 junction)
01298 872268
Grade II listed
LPA: Derbyshire Dales

🍺 🍴

Restricted opening hours

The public bar
(Michael Slaughter, 2010)

Three Stags' Heads   22

A remote country pub on the A623 which used to be part of a farm but is now linked to a pottery business. The entrance leads to the basic main bar with a stone-flagged floor and huge stone fire surround. The counter was installed in the 1940s (the front is from the 1980s), along with the brown painted shelves which serve as a back-fitting. On the right is a 'music room', only recently brought into pub use but kitted out in a style fully in keeping with the rustic spirit of the main bar. The door on the left of the lobby, with a figure 3 on it, was the original second public room: it is pressed into service when the pub is busy. Sells Abbeydale beers including Lurcher at a thumping 8% and which is only brewed for this pub. Open 7–11 Fri, 12–11 Sat, Sun and bank holidays.

DEVON

Drewsteignton

The Square, EX6 6QN
01647 281224
www.thedrewearms.co.uk
LPA: West Devon
Grade II* listed

🍺 🍎 🍴 🛏️

The ground-floor 'cellar' (right);
left in this picture the original
public bar

Drewe Arms

23

Idyllically situated on Drewsteignton's picture-postcard square,
this pub has evolved out of a series of cottages. The historic core really
comprises just the simply appointed public bar on the left and cellar
behind. This has plain seating round the walls and service through a
hatch from the ground-floor cellar where the casks are stillaged. On the
right is another historic room but for much of its existence this has served
as a dining room. The Drewe Arms is a legend in the annals of historic
rural pubs. For 75 years it was kept by Mabel Mudge who retired in 1994,
aged 99, and is thought to have been England's oldest licensee at the
time. Originally the Druid Arms, the pub name changed in the 1920s at
the instigation of Julius Drewe, tea merchant and founder of the Home
& Colonial grocery stores, who built the fantastic Castle Drogo nearby.

Luppitt

EX14 4RT
01404 891613
LPA: East Devon
Not listed

🍺

Restricted opening hours

Luppitt Inn

24

A rare example of a simple, unspoilt farmhouse pub of the type that
would have been quite common a couple of generations ago, but is now
virtually extinct (see p. 48). It's been in the same family ownership for
over a century and still has a few acres attached for rearing sheep. The
building itself is a modest two-storey Victorian affair, built of local stone.

The entrance is in the yard and the pub part occupies two rooms with a red quarry-tiled hallway between them. The room in regular use is on the right. It is tiny and there is absolutely nothing sophisticated about it – a simple servery with a few shelves and beer drawn direct from casks behind the counter. The left-hand room is used for meetings and overspill from the main bar. Outside gents' and ladies' loos. Opens 7pm, closes Sun.

Mary Wright, aged 91, presides at the Luppitt Inn: through the door are her private quarters

Topsham

Bridge Hill, EX3 0QQ
01392 873862
www.cheffers.co.uk
LPA: Exeter
Grade II listed

🍺 🍴

Bridge Inn   25

Run by the same family since 1897, this glorious old pub is one of the most unspoilt in the country and was even accorded a royal visit in 1998 by HM The Queen. There are two rooms at the front and, across the panelled corridor, is the superb snug which forms the heart of the establishment. A large, high settle with glazed panels over it bulges out into the corridor and effectively forms one of the sides of this intimate room. There is a large stone fireplace, old salt store high up above it, some fixed bench seating and a grandfather clock dating from 1726. On the right is a hatch (immediately post-war) to the parlour through which drinks are brought. Known as the 'Inner Sanctum' this latter area is a private space in which customers may be *invited* to sit: only two other pubs, Ye Horns, Goosnargh, Lancashire (46), and the Arden Arms, Stockport (113), have rooms like this where customers can sit in a room behind what is effectively a working serving area. The former brewery/maltings at the rear is used on occasions.

The lounge at the Bridge
(Nigel Cheffers-Heard)

DORSET

Pamphill

Vine Hill, BH21 4EE
Grid ref. ST994003
01202 882259
Not listed
LPA: East Dorset
🍺 🍎 🍴

Vine

26

This was a bakery until about 1900 when it was fitted out as a pub by the present landlady's grandfather. Until the 1950s it remained a beer and cider house and had a six-day licence (i.e. didn't open on Sunday). The falling site means it is, remarkably, on two levels. The little-altered public bar is on the lower one and, at about 8ft × 8ft in front of the counter, is one of the tiniest in the country. Nine steps lead up to the rather larger tap room which is lined with half-height panelling. On the other side of the public bar, a separate entrance leads into what was grandfather's sitting room – a very small space probably brought into pub use in the 1950s or 1960s. The rooms mostly retain their numbers (p. 147). The gents' is outside at the front of the building; the ladies' is also outside but appears to be a later addition. The building is owned by the National Trust. Lunchtime food only.

The view from behind the bar: the stair (right) leads up to the tap room

Worth Matravers

BH19 3LF
01929 439229
www.squareandcompasspub.co.uk
Grade II listed
LPA: Purbeck
🍺 🍎 🍴

Square & Compass

27

A pub since 1793, the Square & Compass has been run by the Newman family since 1907 and has stunning sea views. Not only is it one of only seven pubs featured in all 40 editions of the *Good Beer Guide* to 2013 (see also the Star, Netherton, Northumberland [130]), it is also one of the very few pubs with no real counter of the usual sort (p. 41). A flagstone passage leads to a servery/cellar at the rear where service is through a hatch/doorway: to the left is a further hatch. Also on the left, wooden partition walls define the venerable tap room, entered via a sliding doorway and fitted out with a flagged floor, solid benches and a large fireplace (opened up 1990 and furnace installed). To the right is the 'Big Room' which amounted to a small parlour until 1935 when it was extended into the stable block (hence two different ceiling heights)

Enjoying the splendid
old tap room

and refitted with a continuous wood-block floor, fielded panelling and, on the left, a hatch for service (the big opening behind the curtains dates from 1978). Outside toilets. A museum of local fossils is in a room to the left. Often sells as much real cider as beer.
Food consists of pies and pasties.

What shaped Britain's pubs – 1: alehouses, taverns and inns

Before the 18th century there were three kinds of establishments in which alcohol was sold and consumed. The most common were **alehouses** which might also offer simple food and accommodation. They were frequently very simple affairs, scarcely distinguishable from ordinary houses. The name survived long after they had switched to serving beer, a development of ale using hops (which had arrived in this country in the 14th century) as a preservative and flavour enhancer. **Taverns** were only found in larger towns and catered for more prosperous customers by providing wine (inevitably expensive) and meals but did not generally provide accommodation. **Inns** were found in towns and on highways and provided meals and accommodation for better off travellers and stabling for their horses.

The George Inn, Southwark, London (77), is the last-remaining galleried coaching inn in the capital

The terms above have little meaning today and most present day public houses are markedly different from all of them. To get some impression of what a simple rural alehouse might have been

like, a visit to some of the simplest pubs in this guide such as the Cider House, Defford (191), or the Red Lion, Ampney St Peter (33), might give some idea. Taverns were always relatively few in number and perhaps the nearest approximation now is the Olde Cheshire Cheese on Fleet Street, London (60). As for inns, we do still have two galleried coaching inns – the fragment of the George, Southwark (77), and (not in this guide) the New Inn, Gloucester. The late 14th-century George, Norton St Philip, Somerset, is thought to be the earliest surviving purpose-built English inn whilst the Angel and Royal, Grantham, Lincolnshire, is a late medieval reminder of the inns that lined our ancient transport arteries (neither are included in this guide since their interiors are essentially modern).

COUNTY DURHAM

Barningham

DL11 7DW
01833 621213
Grade II listed
LPA: Durham
Restricted opening hours

Milbank Arms   28

Customers could almost be forgiven for thinking they had stumbled into someone's house as there is no bar counter of any kind (p. 41). Instead, service is at the top of the cellar steps. Some dispensers are attached to the wall in this area: around the staircase is a collection of over 2,000 spirit miniatures. Only one of the original three rooms, the tap room, is in regular use. It has half-height panelling, fixed seating, a baffle by the door and an old fireplace with new tiles. The Domino Room is occasionally used for meetings but the dining room has been shut since 1969. The pub opened as the Milbank Hotel in 1860 and is named after the local landowning family who still own the pub. There have only ever been three licensees, the present incumbent, Neil Turner, taking over in 1987 from his father who had been in charge since 1939. Opens 7pm and Sun lunchtime.

Landlord Neil Turner pours a pint at the entrance to the cellar

Durham

86 Hallgarth Street, DH1 3AS
0191 386 5269
Grade II listed
LPA: Durham

Victoria   29

The best-surviving historic pub interior in the North East (also great for real ale), built in 1899 to the designs of the successful Newcastle architect, Joseph Oswald. The 'Family Department' (or off-sales: p. 156) is the outstanding feature – a tiny space, accessed from the side entrance, with cut-glass panels, small hatch to the servery and just enough space to stand. Perched on top are old ceramic casks, once used for the dispense of sherry, stingo (a dark, very strong, rich beer), Irish and Scotch whisky. The public bar has a bare wooden floor plus the original ornate bar-back, tiled fireplace, and bench seating. Access to the snug is either from the side passage to the rear or the right-hand entrance. It also has original bench seating with baffles, bell-pushes, a cast-iron and marble fireplace and a sliding hatch for service. The sitting room has a bare wooden floor, small bar counter and signs of bell-pushes in the panelled walls. Most windows have etched glass removable screens in their lower parts. The licensee, who had been here since 1974, saved it from desecration by Scottish & Newcastle Breweries by purchasing it in 1995.

The screened area is the 'Family Department'

ESSEX

Aveley

58 High Street, RM15 4AD
01708 865647
Not listed
LPA: Thurrock

In the private bar

Old Ship

30

The unassuming exterior conceals a four-room pub, the arrangements of which date from the early twentieth century: its stained glass windows are a particular joy. The left-hand saloon bar incorporates a former off-sales compartment (see the disused external door) and is separated from the street-corner private bar by a full-height screen. In the saloon the Victorian-style fireplace is a possible later addition but, on the bar counter, are remains of the shutters, now converted to a pot shelf. The private bar has an old bench, still with its maker's label. In the public bar the counter, with its port-hole decoration, looks as though it was given something of a nautical makeover in the 1960s when such themed fitting out was popular. The fourth (pool) room has a timber screen to the corridor with glazing at the top to provide borrowed light: it has a fairly impressive inter-war-style brick fireplace of around 1930.

Mill Green

The Common
Mill Green Road, CM4 0PT
01277 352010
Not listed
LPA: Brentwood

Viper

31

The star attraction at this splendid rural pub is the small panelled tap room where service is via a hatch-cum-door. Left of its entrance is a partition, behind which is a tiny three-sided seating area, which provides for the now-rare game of toad-in-the-hole in which a coin is tossed at the aforementioned hole: the drawer to collect successfully tossed 'toads' is still there (cf. Red Lion, Snargate, Kent [45]). The wood-block floor and fireplace appear to be of about 1930. To the left the small public bar is a later addition: its counter looks relatively recent.

The room labelled 'Private Bar' was altered in post-war times, when the fourth room came into public use and a counter added to span both rooms. The front window on the far right replaces a door which was closed following subsidence after a hot, dry 1970s summer.

In the tap room
service is via a hatch

A hole and drawer
for toad in the hole

Tolleshunt D'Arcy

The Square, CM9 8TF
01621 860262
www.grayandsons.co.uk
Not listed
LPA: Maldon

The public bar
(Michael Slaughter, 2008)

Queen's Head   32

A visitor from a century ago would feel at home in the small 'Bar Parlour' on the left because great numbers of public bars in country pubs would once have looked like this. The only changes of any significance are the new flooring which was laid on top of the original brick floor in the 1970s, and the more recent brick fireplace. The bar counter and bar-back shelves, though, are very old as is the full-height tongue-and-grooved panelling with bare benches attached. The etched and frosted front window is a 1970s replacement, but to the original design. Elsewhere the pub interior has been much altered although the lounge has a good carved wooden fire surround.

What? No counter?

The bar counter is one of the most characteristic features of the pub. It brings order to the storage and serving of drink with the customers on one side, and staff, drinks for sale (and the takings) on the other, and somewhere to place the ordered drinks while they are being paid for. But it has not always been so. Early drawings of alehouses and taverns commonly show often slightly chaotic scenes, with drink being brought (often over some distance) from elsewhere in the building. Counters helped to bring professionalism to the business of service, and were well-established by the early nineteenth century.

Now there are thought to be just ten pubs with historic serving arrangements which involve no kind of counter or hatch for service. All appear in this guide and all are in England:

Service at the Cock, Broom, Bedfordshire (1), is at the entrance to the cellar

Bedfordshire, Cock, Broom (1): **Cumbria**, King's Head, Bootle (15): **Co. Durham**, Milbank Arms, Barningham (28): **Gloucestershire**, Red Lion, Ampney St Peter (33): **Oxfordshire**, North Star, Steventon (136): **Somerset**, Rose & Crown ('Eli's'), Huish Episcopi (143): Tucker's Grave Inn, Faulkland (142): **Staffordshire**, Coopers Tavern, Burton upon Trent (147): **Suffolk**, King's Head, Laxfield (156): **West Midlands**, Manor Arms, Rushall (182).

At the Britannia, Upper Gornal, West Midlands (184), the old counter-less servery lines one side of the rear room, but a conventional counter has been installed in the front bar.

There are other pubs which have service arrangements not far from those listed above and usually involve a shelf or hatch which represent the rudimentary beginnings of the counter. Those in this guide are:
Devon, Drewe Arms, Drewsteignton (23): **Dorset**, Square & Compass, Worth Matravers (27): **Hampshire**, Harrow, Steep (38): **Sussex, West**, Blue Ship, The Haven (162): **Worcestershire**, Cider House, Defford (191).

Wales: **West Wales**, Dyffryn Arms, Pontfaen (228).

None are known in Scotland or Northern Ireland.

At the Harrow, Steep, Hampshire (38), service in both the bars is through a hatch

GLOUCESTERSHIRE AND BRISTOL

Ampney St Peter

GL7 5SL
01285 851596
Grade II listed

🍺

Restricted opening hours

Red Lion   33

One of the great unspoilt rural classics. Its licensee, John Barnard, only the fourth since 1851, has been here since 1975. The pub occupies two front rooms either side of a central corridor in a 300-year-old cottage. It is remarkable for having no counter (p. 41). Service is in the public bar (numbered '2' on the door: p. 147) on the right where there are a couple of hand-pumps against the back wall and customers occupy

benches round a table: it's impossible not to be drawn into the general conversation. The fireplace is of a type fitted in some 50 Stroud Brewery pubs in about 1950. Note the ring nearby on a piece of string used to summon the licensee if he is out of the room. Across the corridor, which has a hatch for corridor service and off-sales, is the second room. It has simple benches and is used when the main bar is busy. No new-fangled inside loos here – both the ladies' and the gents' are outside on the left. Open 6pm Mon–Sat; 12–2pm Sun.

Landlord John Barnard in the main bar: this is one of the very few pubs to have no counter at all

Bristol: city centre

60 Victoria Street, BS1 6DE
0117 927 7860
Grade II listed

🍺

King's Head   34

A mid 17th-century building housing a wonderful long, narrow, single bar. Along the right-hand wall is a magnificent bar-back of about 1870, with a series of arches and high-level lettering advertising various drinks.

Looking down the bar at the King's Head: the Tramcar Bar is behind the low glazed screen

It has a marble shelf. The ebulliently detailed counter no doubt dates from the same scheme (although the top is from 1998). Most of the rear part of the pub contains the delightful 'Tramcar Bar' – a snug supposedly shaped like – well – the seating area of an old tramcar! Its insertion, presumably in the late 19th or early 20th century, led to the cutting back of the counter, hence the 'stranded' bar-back in this area. Prior to this, apart from the small seated area at the front, this was presumably a largely stand-up drinking establishment. There are two tiny WCs formed by part-glazed partitions adjacent to the rear wall: note the 'Ladies Only' in a glass door panel for the avoidance of any doubt.

Duntisbourne Abbots

Gloucester Road, GL7 7JR
01285 821432
www.fivemilehouse.co.uk
Grade II listed

In the bar, looking through to
the tap room

Five Mile House   `35`

On a dead-end section of the old A417 and tricky to find, but well worth seeking out. The oldest part of the building is on the left and dates back to the 17th-century: it was then extended in the 18th century with a taller block. The pub was kept by the Ruck family for 65 years until Ivy Ruck died in 1995. In Ivy's day it consisted of just two rooms in the older part of the building. These are a true delight; that on the left, the tap room, being especially notable for its two high-backed settles which are the kind of thing that would have graced countless country pubs in days gone by, but which are now extraordinarily rare. The right-hand room of the pair retains its old counter front and around the bay window has a fixed bench which appears to be of considerable antiquity. Downstairs was Ivy's sitting room, now open for public use. From here further steps down and a short passage lead to another additional bar created in 1996 (now the 'Cider Bar'). Back on the ground floor, on the far right, another room was also brought into use.

Purton

GL13 9HU
01453 811262
Not listed
LPA: Stroud

Restricted opening hours

Photo: Michael Slaughter, 2010

Berkeley Arms   36

About 200 yards from the lift bridge over the Gloucester & Sharpness Canal, this is a no-frills, unspoilt rural pub. The central part was extended in the mid-19th century. There is a tiny drinking area in front of a servery which has an old counter and shelves. To the left of this is a separate room with a flagstone floor, a large curved high-backed settle, large stone fireplace and a hatch to the side of the servery. The only recent change was the building of indoor toilets in the 1960s.

HAMPSHIRE

Southampton

55 High Street, SO14 2NS
023 80333595
www.theredlionsouthampton.com
Grade II listed
LPA: Southampton

Red Lion   37

A remarkable medieval interior lies within this long, narrow building. The façade, however, is much more recent: the Tudor-style black-and-white upper storeys probably date from the 1920s while the ground floor was refronted during repairs after wartime bomb damage.

The main bar at the Red Lion occupies a medieval hall

Customers today drink in what was a late medieval hall-house, the hall of which (in the centre of the long building) soars through its full height and displays its massive timber-framing. The pub layout is very largely as it was before the war with the servery located beneath the medieval private upper chamber: the actual fittings in the servery possibly came from another war-damaged pub although the heated (and still-functioning) foot-rail may well be older. A corridor runs down the left-hand side, above which is a gallery (with 16th- or 17th-century timbering) leading to the chamber. At the rear of the hall is a grand Tudor stone fireplace (a less elaborate one is in the dining room behind) whilst a further gallery (screened-off until the post-war repairs) leads to another upper chamber.

Steep

Harrow Lane, GU32 2DA

Grid ref. SU752251

01730 262685

Grade II listed

LPA: East Hampshire

Landladies Claire and Nisa McCutcheon (and Murphy the dog) in the venerable public bar

Harrow 38

A great unspoilt and atmospheric, but hard-to-find, pub (just east of Bedales School) which has been run by the Dodd/McCutcheon family since 1929: they bought it off the brewers Whitbread in 1991. It has two splendid rustic bars, each measuring only about 12 feet × 12 feet. The public bar (left) is the older of the two and has a quarry-tiled floor, bench seating, panelling and a massive fireplace: service is through a hatch from the ground-floor 'cellar' where casks rest on a long wooden stillage. The second room still retains its original name-plate identifying it as the 'Smoking Room'. This too has a hatch for service, a panelled dado, and a miscellaneous collection of seating (not to mention stuffed animals and an old polyphon). This is one of those rare pubs that still has outside toilets - across the road and with a partly open-air gents. Closed Sun evenings in winter.

HEREFORDSHIRE

Kington

22 Victoria Road, HR5 3BX
01544 239033
Grade II listed
LPA: Herefordshire

Ye Olde Tavern 39

This pub was in the hands of the Jones family from 1884 to 2002 and over the years they did little to change it. The entrance leads into a lobby which retains (behind recent glazing) an off-sales facility. To the left lies the public bar which is the chief interest here. This room still retains a Victorian or very early 20th-century feel thanks to the simple fittings – a high counter, bar-back, fixed seating, panelling, and a built-in cupboard to the left of the (probably) interwar fireplace. Right of the lobby is a second room with a flagstone floor. This housed a mighty settle which was destroyed in 2002 to create more trading space (its position is still visible on the floor). Here service is via a stable door. At the rear was a third room but this was converted into toilets in 2002. Closed weekday lunchtimes.

The public bar and, to the right, the former off-sales area with second room beyond

Leintwardine

Rosemary Lane, SY7 0LP
01547 540705
www.suninn-leintwardine.co.uk
Grade II listed
LPA: Herefordshire

'FLOSSIE'
FLORENCE LANE
1914 – 2009
LIVED IN AND
RULED THIS
PARLOUR
PUB
HEREFORDSHIRE CAMRA

A memorial to a
legendary landlady

Sun Inn 40

This pub was kept for 74 years by Florence (Flossie) Lane whose family took over in the early 20th century. She died in 2009 aged 94 years and 11 months and by this time she and her utterly unspoilt pub had

The utterly unspoilt Red Brick Bar

become a legend, so much so that she received obituaries in *The Times* and *Daily Telegraph*. The pub, occupying part of an early 19th-century row of cottages, had certainly been trading since at least the 1860s and was one of the last remaining beerhouses: Flossie only introduced wine in later years. In her time, right of the entrance lobby, there was the 'Brick Bar' (named after the flooring material), equipped with basic tables and benches and a (probably) 1950s brick fireplace. Left of the entrance were 'Flossie's Room' where she sat, and beyond which there was a ground-floor 'cellar' where, in later years, regulars served themselves and put their payments in a tin. Under new ownership all this has been scrupulously preserved but, in the interests of viability, a large but very well-designed extension (with bar counter) was opened in April 2011 with access through the old lobby (see below).

Best of both worlds

Today's trend is towards fewer but bigger pubs. A small pub, particularly in rural areas, often struggles to make ends meet and may well find itself sacrificed on the altar of non-viability. Does this mean inevitable extinction for the small, simple pubs which were once so very common?

Some such pubs survive in town and city centres because lack of space is offset by a steady stream of customers throughout the day – hence we still have the likes of the Circus Tavern, Manchester (102), and the miniscule Nutshell, Bury St Edmunds (154). Out in the country, even many large pubs are finding life difficult so, for the smallest ones, where a food offering is often impossible, the outlook is doubly difficult. A few are hanging on, but readers are advised to visit them whilst they still can.

Enough of the gloom – it *is* possible to make a small, rural pub viable without recourse to the wrecking ball. It takes skill and imagination but some enlightened pub owners have shown what can be achieved. In the following cases the historic core has been kept and other spaces have been brought into use or additions made which do not impact adversely on the historic parts:

the Drewe Arms, Drewsteignton, Devon (23); the Sun Inn, Leintwardine, Herefordshire (40); and the Five Mile House, Duntisbourne Abbots, Gloucestershire (35). Sitting in the old portions, you should be oblivious to the changes made elsewhere.

What's more, the small pub is making a modest comeback with the growth of a new generation of 'micro-pubs'. The first, the Butchers Arms, Herne, Kent (p. 235), opened in a former butcher's shop in 2005 and, as at January 2013, there were twenty such pubs up and down the land with another seven scheduled for opening. Typically, they occupy ex-shops, do not seat more than a couple of dozen people, have low overheads and specialise in real ale. They offer a convivial environment where good drink and conversation are the order of the day in the best tradition of the British pub. Perhaps some will become the heritage pubs of the future!

The new extension at the Sun Inn, Leintwardine (40)

Leysters

HR6 0HW
01568 750230
Not listed
LPA: Herefordshire

Duke of York

41

This modest, beautifully kept country pub still has a smallholding attached (see below) and has been held by same family since 1911. The interior, little altered since before the Second World War, consists of three rooms. The public bar has a fine curved, high-backed settle (which predates 1911) beside the fireplace and some simple dado panelling. Beneath the window is a bench which is equipped for the local version of quoits – four quoits a go, five points for the pin, two for the inner ring, one for the outer (but they must land white side up): easy, or is it? Right is a small darts room with a Victorian tiled fireplace, corner bench and its own hatch. Left is the lounge, added to the public rooms just before the war, and feeling like a domestic sitting room.

Indoor quoits is a popular pub game in Herefordshire

The public bar

Down at the pub, down on the farm

CHRIS WITT

Ever wondered why some rural pubs are so remote, away from habitation? Most probably these pubs developed to serve the local agricultural workers (who were of course much more numerous in the past) and may well have doubled up with farming activity. There are still some pubs attached to working farms or smallholdings but they are now few and far between.

Of those listed in this book the one with by far the largest farming interest is the New Cross Inn, Court Henry, Carmarthenshire

The Duke of York, Leysters, Herefordshire (41), still has a small amount of farmland attached

(227), which still has 780 acres of land attached supporting some 80 head of beef cattle plus 250 of sheep. A remarkable survivor! The only others in this guide which CAMRA is aware of are the Duke of York, Leysters, Herefordshire (41), which still has five acres of grazing land attached; the Luppitt Inn, Luppitt, Devon (24), which has a few acres used for sheep; and the Harrington Arms, Gawsworth, Cheshire (9) which, whilst still part of a farm, is no longer actively worked. How times change!

HERTFORDSHIRE

Flaunden

HP3 0PP

Grid ref. TL015008

01442 832269

www.greendragon.org.uk

Grade II listed

LPA: Dacorum

Green Dragon

42

Most of this country pub comprises modernisations and extensions of between 1976 and 1980, but to the right of the main entrance is a gloriously simple rustic snug retaining its quarry-tiled floor, fixed bench seating and a baffle by the door. Thousands of such basic pub rooms existed until not that long ago, but now only a handful are still with us. Above the fireplace is a gun-rest for three guns, no doubt put to good use by those about to go on, or returning from, a shoot around this remote Chilterns village. The rather crude hatch cut to the servery is an unfortunate recent feature, as is the brick infill to the fireplace. Two famous customers who would have known this room are Joachim von Ribbentrop and the spy, Guy Burgess (no relation to the wartime landlord). The former was Nazi Germany's ambassador to Britain until 1938; the latter made his last known appearance here before defecting to the Soviet Union in 1951.

The tap room now ...

... and then: listening to Churchill on wartime radio. Landlord Bob Burgess stands on the left

KENT

Cowden Pound

Hartfield Road, TN8 5NP
Grid ref. TQ462425
Grade II listed
LPA: Sevenoaks

🍺

Restricted opening hours

The public bar retains its original simplicity

Queen's Arms   `43`

A rural time-warp, in the same family since January 1913 when Henry Long gained his licence, with his daughter, Elsie Maynard, now aged 89, taking over in 1973. Built in 1841 by William Longley of Pound House, the name commemorates the Queen's Royal West Kent Regiment. In the lobby, the door ahead leads to private quarters while that on the right is to a small public bar, untouched since Victorian times (apart from a lick of paint). The counter has just three hand-pumps, recalling the way counters looked before the proliferation of modern fonts – no lager here. Basic shelving forms the bar-back and there is no till – just a bowl for coins with notes placed beneath, whilst simple benches against the walls and window provide the seating. Note the old Bisset dart scorer – finger-operated dials change the score. The saloon (left) was originally a small room but doubled in size in 1953 by taking in a private room. It retains its original Victorian counter (now vivid yellow) and a bell-push. Due to Elsie's advanced age, regulars provide the service. Open 5–10.30 Mon, Tue, Thu, 5–7 Wed, 5–9.30 Fri, 5–8.30 (10.30 if music) Sat, 12–2.30 Sun (could easily change).

Ightham Common

Redwell Lane, TN15 9EE
Grid ref. TQ590559
01732 882383
Grade II listed
LPA: Tonbridge & Malling

🍺

Restricted opening hours

Old House   `44`

A hard-to-find, unspoilt rural pub, with its sign long gone. First licensed as a beer house in 1872, it only obtained a full licence in 1953. The building, partly 17th-century (left) and partly 19th-century, houses two simple pub rooms while the entrance lobby served as an off-sales in former days. The main bar is to the left and appears to be the amalgamation of two small rooms (see the different ceiling treatments), but before living memory. It has a Victorian counter. On the right is a smaller, very domestic-looking public room. All the beer is fetched from the cellar. The pub serves 200 whiskies. Opens 7pm weekdays.

The public bar
(Michael Slaughter, 2011)

Snargate

TN29 9UQ
01797 344648
Grade II listed
LPA: Shepway

Red Lion

45

One of the great rural classics, run by the Jemison family since 1911: Doris has been behind the bar for 62 years and licensee for 27 of them. A century ago the pub consisted of a small public bar (left) and a tap room (right). The former retains its old counter, with a rare marble top (cf. 13, 58, 111, 196, 236, 268) and, on a pewter housing, a set of four hand-pumps dating back to 1870 (but unused as beer is now drawn from casks behind the bar). Beyond the partition is a second room, formerly living quarters, but part of the pub for many decades. The tap room, not used after the Second World War, was converted into a shop which survived until 1974. In the early 1980s it was brought back into pub use with a new quarry-tiled floor and is now a room for games, including toad in the hole (cf. Viper, Mill Green, Essex [31]). Look out for the extensive World War II memorabilia – this pub was situated in a militarily sensitive area at that time.

Doris and Kate Jemison and cheerful customers in the public bar

Beer delivery at the Red Lion *c.*1875-style

LANCASHIRE

Goosnargh

Horns Lane, PR3 2FJ
Grid ref: CR575391
01772 865230
www.yehornsinn.co.uk
Not listed
LPA: Preston

Ye Horns Inn

46

This rather isolated, hard-to-find pub has long been a wayside inn. A stone is dated 1782 but the structure may well be a good deal older. The interior was last significantly changed in the mid-1950s when a partition was taken down between the public bar and a corridor to create what is now the main bar in front of the servery (its brick frontage is probably interwar). The counter still has its functioning sliding screens. However, the star feature at the Horns is the area

behind it, where customers and serving staff actually co-exist in the same space! The door into it is marked 'Private' so as a courtesy ask if it is possible to sit there (it generally is). The only other known surviving examples of this rare arrangement are at the Bridge Inn, Topsham, Devon (25), and the Arden Arms, Stockport (113). This small room has a baffle at the entrance, a brick and wood fireplace, old shelving, a panelled dado and a carved settle. There are some good features elsewhere, notably the fine plasterwork to the small dining room ceiling. On-site brewing began in March 2013.

Landlord Mark Woods pulls a pint in the highly unusual combined service/sitting area

Great Harwood

St John's Street, BB6 7EP
01254 885210
Grade II listed
LPA: Hyndburn

Victoria ('Butcher Brig')

47

This pub of 1905 is a fine example of Edwardian pub-building. The lobby bar, passageway and staircase all have full-height cream and green tiling with flower motifs. The counter too has a tiled front and working screens. Four small rooms lead off the lobby, mostly with original fittings with door panels proclaiming their names – the 'Commercial Room',

The lobby with its counter screens and tilework

a parlour (with notable Art Nouveau fireplace), bar parlour (another fine fireplace), and the 'Public Kitchen'. This name, probably now unique in a pub, may recall how some pubs offered cooking and food heating facilities to the poor. At the end of the passage is a fifth room recently converted to pub use. Above the staircase is a splendid stained glass window. The most altered area is to the right of the entrance where the door opening has been widened. Originally, there was a 'Jug Department' here with hatch service, and its door has been re-sited to the ladies' loo (likewise the smoke room door to the gents'). The nickname comes from a long-gone slaughterhouse and railway bridge. The former bowling green now forms part of the extensive beer garden. Listed in 1997 following a pilot study of Lancashire pubs by CAMRA for English Heritage.

Lytham St Annes

St Annes Road West
St Annes on Sea, FY8 1SB
01253 728252
gkpubs.co.uk/pubs-in-lytham-st-annes/town-house-pub
Not listed
LPA: Fylde

Burlington's Wine & Cocktail Bar
(at the Town House)

48

Burlington's Bar is one of the great pub rooms in Britain – a late Victorian below-ground bar covered from head to foot with tiles and having a magnificent ceramic bar counter. When the St Anne's Hotel was demolished in 1985 and replaced by a modern pub (now called the Town House), the basement bar, once known as Burlington Bertie's, was preserved and became a nightclub. Easily visible through the windows, it was fitted out by Craven Dunnill of Jackfield, Shropshire, probably in the late 1890s. It has a tiled floor, wall tiles (some plain, some flowers and patterns) and an exceedingly long ceramic bar counter in one of the firm's two standard designs. It is identical to that the Red Lion, Erdington, Birmingham (172), and the Crown Bar, Belfast (266). The bar-back is fairly restrained: the lion heads conceal apertures that once held pipes for dispensing spirits. When this guide was prepared Burlington's was open on a limited basis but, as we go to press, it may only now be visited by arrangement with the Town House. It is, however, viewable through the windows.

The glorious ceramic counter and mosaic floor in the public bar. The triple heating pipes would have warmed customers standing at the bar

Of public bars, private bars, smoke rooms, tap rooms and others: naming the parts

Until the latter part of the 20th century the pub almost always had two or more rooms. These were stratified in terms of their ambience, clientele and prices. The most simply appointed room was the **public bar** where beer was a little cheaper than in the better rooms. To over-generalise, it was seen as the bar of the working man. Here there would be a bar counter, no carpet on the floor, lots of smoke in the air and a predominantly male clientele for whom the standard drink would be mild ale in large parts of the country. In the north this room is often called the vault(s).

At the Edwardian Victoria, Great Harwood, Lancashire (47), the Commercial Room was probably a place where commercial travellers might meet with clients and conduct business. The name does not seem to have been prevalent in the south

Also at the Victoria, the 'Parlour' conveys a sense of comfortable, warm and convivial surroundings

Window glass of c. 1930 at the Three Horse Shoes, Boroughbridge, North Yorkshire (202)

Better-appointed rooms went by an almost bewildering variety of names. **Private bars** did not involve a requirement of membership (after all they were in *public* houses) but were smaller than the public bar and the name suggests occupancy by regulars known to one another. The **lounge** and **saloon** tended to be large and one might expect carpets, panelling and waiter service (p. 121). The **smoke/smoking room** is a puzzling name, suggesting it was somewhere where people could smoke. Yet, since smoking was permitted throughout the pub (until legislation earlier this century put a stop to such things), a literal meaning makes no real sense. Smoke rooms tended to be rather smaller than public bars and saloon/lounges, and the idea may have evolved to suggest somewhere where people could take their ease in the way they would have done in a smoking room of a gentleman's residence.

Another paradoxical name is **tap room**. One might be forgiven for thinking that this was where drinks were dispensed but examination of old plans of pubs suggests this was emphatically not the case: sometimes they were at some considerable remove from the servery. One long-serving licensee has suggested to the writer that, unlikely as it might seem, regulars would tap a coin or their glass to summon service. To test this theory it would be interesting to know if tap rooms always/generally lack bell-pushes.

The names above are the most common ones for traditional pub rooms. But there are many more besides. A far from exhaustive list includes news room and commercial room (these two from northern England), sitting room (north-east England and Scotland), snug, parlour, (bar) parlour, vault(s) and (even!) coffee room.

The window of the news room at the Lion Tavern, Liverpool (120), reflecting the offices of the people who probably used it a century ago

Preston

166 Friargate, PR1 2EJ
01772 204855
www.blackhorse-preston.co.uk
Grade II listed
LPA: Preston

Black Horse

49

This pub, with many wonderful features, was rebuilt in 1898 to designs of local architect J. A. Seward for Kay's Atlas Brewery of Manchester. It doubled as a small hotel, which may help explain the superior appointment of the drinking areas, compared to most inner urban locals. From the Friargate entrance, there are small smoke rooms either side of a mosaic-floored corridor and they are replete with original fittings, including the fixed seating. At the heart of the pub is

The rear sitting area

the servery which has a magnificent semi-circular ceramic counter (probably by either Burmantofts or Pilkingtons) in front of which is more mosaic flooring. The overall effect is breath-taking. This area was a public bar accessed from Orchard Street but it was opened up to the rest of the pub about 1995, with the insertion of the elliptical arch. At the back of the servery are glazed counter screens to the main corridor. Originally there was a 'Market Room' at the rear but in 1929 this was replaced by the present U-shaped seating area and indoor toilets (accessed via corridors to the left and right). The upstairs room is largely modernised. Food at lunchtimes only.

The public bar has one of the finest displays of pub ceramics in northern England

LEICESTERSHIRE

Whitwick

11 Leicester Road, LE67 5GN
01530 837311
Grade II listed
LPA: North West Leicestershire

Three Horseshoes
50

This completely unspoilt former coal-mining village local is nicknamed 'Polly Burton's', who started the business well over a century ago. The date of 1882 on the front records the date of its creation out of cottages. The small entrance lobby, still with its off-sales hatch, leads to the public bar on the left. This has evidently been its present size since the building was converted to pub use, as indicated by the all-over quarry-tiled floor and extensive bench seating which straddles the two former cottage rooms. It retains its original servery fittings and pair of fireplaces. The only change seems to be the boxing-in of the seating in the late 20th century. There is nothing as fancy as a till: the takings simply find their way into pint glasses. Right of the lobby is a small snug with a bare wooden floor, a Victorian fireplace and basic bench seating: service is from a hatch to the back of the bar servery. Outside loos.

The public bar

LINCOLNSHIRE

Scunthorpe

Doncaster Road, DN15 7DS
01724 842333
Not listed
LPA: Scunthorpe

Berkeley
51

One of Britain's best surviving roadhouses (p. 129) and a well-known local landmark on the outskirts of the town which will be familiar to generations of trippers to the Lincolnshire coast. Opened in 1940 and designed by West Midlands architects Scott & Clark of Wednesbury, it still preserves its original layout of three main rooms (one now a dining room), spacious entrance foyer, impressive ballroom and (disused) off-sales. Some fittings have been renewed in recent times by present owners, the brewers Samuel Smiths of Tadcaster, but with an emphasis on careful and sympathetic restoration. The foyer and the public bar (the latter separately accessed, in keeping with its era) are still largely as-built and, elsewhere in the building, the joinery, ceilings, plasterwork and windows are mostly original too. The main lounge retains its original counter, back-fitting and bench seating but the entrance screenwork and Art Deco-style lighting are careful re-creations of how they might have appeared in 1940 whilst the prominent fireplace, although genuinely of the Thirties, is an import from elsewhere.

The ballroom

GREATER LONDON – INNER

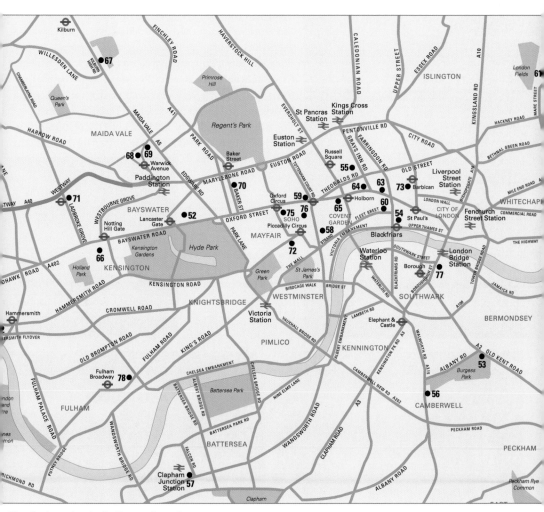

The featured pubs in **Inner London**

Bayswater

10A Strathearn Place, W2 2NH
020 7724 1191
www.victoriapaddington.co.uk
Grade II listed
LPA: Westminster

⊖ Lancaster Gate

Victoria   `52`

This Fuller's-owned, corner-site pub has some very spectacular early fittings. Such was the amount of pub renovation at the end of the 19th century and subsequently, that any earlier fittings are incredibly rare. At the Victoria a date of 1864 is suggested by the dated clock in the bar-back fitting: as such they make up one of the oldest, securely datable Victorian pub-furnishing schemes in the country. We even know the man responsible for the work as, below the clock, is an inscription, 'S. Hill Fitter New St. Boro' Rd. Southwark'. The back-fitting, together with a side wall, has large mirrors with really intricate gilding and coloured decoration (one of the panels has been replaced and it is not

hard to work out which). In the angle of the building is a delicate Regency-style fireplace containing a print of a famous picture of 1846 by F. X. Winterhalter of Queen Victoria, Prince Albert and their numerous progeny. The counter is, no doubt, of 1864 too (the a pair of brass water-dispensers for diluting spirits are modern replacements). The prints of soldiers, tiles with Dickens characters and various roundels are thought to date from the 1960s or 1970s. In Victorian times the interior would have been divided up into a series of compartments. The decorative ceiling is made of Lincrusta.Upstairs the Theatre Bar has ornate fittings imported from the Gaiety Theatre about 1958.

A date of 1864 on the clock suggests the age of the magnificent painted and gilded mirrors

Detail

What is now a single space would have been divided into compartments in Victorian days.

Bermondsey

386 Old Kent Road, SE1 5AA
020 7701 8510
Grade II listed
LPA: Southwark
⊖ Borough then bus 21 south

Lord Nelson

This Victorian pub has seen better days, yet it does retain some spectacular fittings. Pride of place goes to a large painted and gilded mirror of the eponymous admiral receiving the surrender after the Battle of Cape St Vincent in 1797 from the shifty, swarthy Spanish types. There are two other vast mirrors but one is badly cracked. There is also what is probably a unique pub feature – an impressive timber arcade striding across the servery with two bays sitting atop the counter and a third spanning a walkway between two counters. The screen and bar-back have wonderful detail including coloured panels advertising all manner of drinks and the name of the licensee when all this work was carried out, John Bastow. The serving area has an extraordinary shape, so laid out to reach a whole variety of small compartments which survived until about 1968. The semi-circular entrance to the saloon (at the side) has a mosaic floor with the name of the pub and stained glass: the saloon itself also has a huge timber superstructure on the counter.

Nelson accepts the surrender after the Battle of Cape St Vincent

The mighty screen in the main bar is probably unique

Blackfriars

174 Queen Victoria Street, EC4V 4EG
020 7236 5474
www.nicholsonspubs.co.uk/
theblackfriarblackfriarslondon
Grade II* listed
LPA: City of London

🍺 🍴

⇌ Blackfriars, City Thameslink
⊖ Blackfriars

Black Friar

The Black Friar is amazing and quite unlike anything else. This wedge-shaped pub, now dwarfed by later buildings, dates from 1873 but was given a make-over from about 1905 under architect H. Fuller Clark and with much decoration by artist Henry Poole. The theme was the Dominican friary established here in 1278. The friars – or rather, jolly, reinvented versions of them – appear everywhere in sculptures, mosaics and metal reliefs, and engage in the serious business of eating, drinking and generally having a good time – for example, in singing carols in the copper relief over the magnificent inglenook fireplace, or in a scene showing eels and fish being collected for (meatless) Friday. The most remarkable part is the barrel-vaulted area at the back of the pub, under the adjacent railway, and added as a snack bar in 1917–21 with more reliefs 'mixing monkery with Aesop and nursery rhymes.' The richness of the interior is enhanced by much alabaster and marble, including the top and front to the counter. The exterior is worth a good look too: a couple of friars helpfully point towards the 'saloon' and so, clearly, what is now a single bar was originally divided into two: it's easy to work out where the division was.

Enjoying a tipple

Variations on a monkish theme

Bloomsbury

7 Roger Street, WC1N 2PB
020 7242 7230
www.dukepub.co.uk
Grade II listed
LPA: Camden

⊖ Russell Square

Duke (of York)   `55`

An Art Deco treasure, now a trendy gastro-pub. It is part of Mytre House, a development of 1937–8 by architect D. E. Harrington. There are two rooms which retain their original fittings almost intact and show how many inter-war pubs would have looked before modern changes. Decoration is pared down and the fittings are sleek and undemonstrative. The most prominent feature is a series of small open drinking booths in the far room with timber and reeded glass partitions between them.

The similar seating in the larger bar, however, seems a later addition, probably from around 1960 when the Double Diamond window glass must have gone in. Don't miss the loos which are also amazingly intact.

The Duke: a rare survival of 1930s fittings in central London

Camberwell

181 Camberwell Road, SE5 0HB
020 7703 4007
Not listed
LPA: Southwark

⇌/⊖ Elephant & Castle then
buses 12/35/40/45/68 south

The saloon

Corrib Bar   `56`

A remarkably unaltered street-corner pub, rebuilt in 1937 as the Duke of Clarence (see the large tiled sign outside) by East End brewers Charringtons. It is now an Irish bar, hence the name taken from a river and lough in Galway. What makes it special are the three unspoilt, separate rooms: public bar on the corner, then a cosy snug, and finally a saloon. The 'higher' status of the saloon is shown by the slightly superior panelling compared to the other rooms. The fittings are all low-key, as was usual in the 1930s. The most striking feature is the band of terrazzo in the snug looking like an over-sized piano keyboard. The bar-back has unusual dimpled glazing and strips of green glass. In the 1960s this was a haunt of the notorious Richardson gang, the south London counterpart of the Krays.

Clapham Junction
(Battersea)

2 St John's Hill, SW11 1RU

020 7228 2076

www.nicholsonspubs.co.uk/the
falconclaphamjunctionlondon

Grade II listed

LPA: Wandsworth

🍺 🍴

⇌ Clapham Junction

Falcon

A splendid, showy (and usually busy) pub of 1887, handily placed for Britain's busiest railway station. The interior is extraordinary and its island servery (with office in the middle), at slightly over 125ft around the outer circumference, is the longest in the UK (the nearest challenger is the Horse Shoe Bar, Glasgow [244], at just over 104ft). Much of the original arrangements survive. At the corner is a large public bar (originally with partitions) and at the rear a luxuriously panelled room (pity about the garish modern glass in the skylights). On the left-hand side is a snug enclosed by a glazed screen. Adjacent is a lobby where the original glass has portrayals of the eponymous falcon and the words 'private bar'. The most interesting glass is in the rear room, showing the pub in its humble pre-1887 state and its grander, present manifestation. You can see funeral corteges stopping off at 'Death's Door', the nickname for the pub when the landlord was a Mr Death!

The 125ft circumference of the island bar counter makes it the longest in the UK

Covent Garden

90 St Martin's Lane, WC2N 4AP

020 7836 5863

www.taylor-walker.co.uk/pub/
salisbury-covent-garden/c3111

Grade II listed

LPA: Westminster

 🍴

⊖ Leicester Square

Salisbury

58

In the heart of Theatreland, the Salisbury has an impressively lavish interior. The pub opened in 1898 and takes its name from Lord Salisbury, three times Prime Minister between 1885 and 1901. The 'SS' in the lavish window glass is for the original name, 'Salisbury Stores' – 'stores' being a not uncommon tag in pub names at the time. There is a good sense of how pubs around 1900 were divided up (each outside door would have led to its own drinking compartment). There is a small snug along St Martin's Lane (named as a saloon on the brass door-plate) formed by glazed screenwork and typical of the intimate spaces that many late Victorian London drinkers liked. In the main bar the counter has a rare, white marble top (see also 13, 45, 111, 196, 136, 268) and original metal statuette lamps with nymphs: they preside over semi-circular seating arrangements. In contrast to the glorious Victorian glass, the modern etched glass is sadly feeble.

One of the distinctive lamps
at the Salisbury

The snug

Fitzrovia

6 Oxford Street, W1D 1AN
020 7636 8324
www.nicholsonspubs.co.uk/the
tottenhamoxfordstreetlondon
Grade II* listed
LPA: Westminster

🍺 🍴

⊖ Tottenham Court Road

Tottenham   59

Built in 1892 in a flowery Flemish Renaissance style by well-known pub architects Saville & Martin for Baker Bros Ltd, successful publicans who owned a chain of London pubs. The long, single space is the result of the amalgamation of at least two spaces. There is a great deal of decoration to admire although the skylight at the rear is marred by unpleasant modern glass. The right-hand wall has mirrors and paintings of ladies representing three of the Four Seasons, painted by the artist Felix de Jong: they are Spring, Summer and Autumn (did

Winter lie behind the boxed in work by the entrance?) There are tiled panels between the paintings and mirrors and fringes of tiling at high level and round the skylight. The cheap-looking window frontage is a modern feature and seems to be set back from the original position.

Decorative riches at the Tottenham
(Michael Slaughter, 2009)

Fleet Street

145 Fleet Street, EC4A 2BU
020 7353 6170
Grade II listed
LPA: City of London

🍺 🍴

🚆 City Thameslink
⊖ Blackfriars

Olde Cheshire Cheese   60

What really counts at this famous old London pub is the pair of rooms either side of the entrance corridor. On the right is a small bar with what appears to be very old panelling, simple bench seating, a huge fireplace and a possibly Victorian counter. Over the entrance is a notice from less egalitarian days – 'Gentlemen only served in this bar' (p. 133). Under the adjacent hatch it says 'Waiter service' – no doubt the waiters in question would have been serving the 'Chop Room' across the corridor, a panelled eating area which is the nearest thing we have to the atmosphere of an eating area in an old tavern. Next to the hatch is a tiny pewter-lined sink with a still-working tap (to rinse glasses or provide drinking water for diners, or both?) The upper floors are in restaurant use and have panelling of various dates, much of it 20th-century. The pub was much extended to the east and a new part added in about 1991 by architects Waterhouse & Ripley for owners Sam Smiths.

The corridor at 'the Cheese', nostalgically recalling the good(?) old days of spit and sawdust

The old bar which has changed little since this view was published in Edward Callow's *Old London Taverns* of 1909

Hackney

165 Mare Street, E8 3RH
020 8985 3727
Grade II listed
LPA: Hackney
⚡ London Fields

Dolphin

61

Although much altered internally, the great thing here is the wall-tiling, installed perhaps in the 1890s by W. B. Simpson & Sons who tiled many a London pub. The star feature is the right-hand wall which lined a former corridor (see evidence of it on the floor). There are blue and white tiles with pairs of birds and swirling Arabesque patterns, but near the entrance is a vast tile panel depicting the legend of Arion, a young Greek who was thrown overboard by thieving sailors but saved by a friendly dolphin. On the other side, a panel by the entrance depicts Diana the Huntress: then come more blue and white bird-and-foliage panels. The servery fittings are largely late Victorian. At the rear-left is a separate room although its panelling seems modern. Other screenwork shows how the front part of the pub would have been divided into separate drinking spaces.

A Greek legend in Victorian tiles
(Michael Slaughter, 2010)

On the tiles

One of the great glories of late Victorian and Edwardian pubs is the use of ceramics and this guide draws attention to the very best examples in the country. As early as 1850 the billiard room at Gurton's in Old Bond Street, London, was decorated with pictorial ceramic panels, but it is likely that such work was not common until the 1880s: in any case, little survives in the way of pub furnishings and fittings before that time (see p. 29).

Ceramics were employed in various forms, ranging from their mundane, but very necessary use in toilets, through plain floor and wall tiling, to rich mosaic flooring, pictorial panels, and even ceramic bar counters. Tiles were more expensive than wood but had the great advantage of being hard-wearing and – useful in the smoky atmosphere of the pub in bygone days – hygienic, as they were easily cleaned.

Although a great many have been destroyed as pubs were refurbished in the second half of the 20th century, we still have a significant numbers of **tiled paintings**. Important examples in this guide are at pub numbers 61, 160, 168, 169, 173, 220, 234, 236, 240 and 254. There is no particular theme that is characteristic of pub tiling. A depiction of the Battle of Hastings at the General Havelock in Hastings (160) seems an obvious choice. Although the legend of Arion is little known today, its appearance in a huge tiled panel at the Dolphin,

The shepherdess is the companion-piece to the jester at the Feuars Arms, Kirkcaldy, Fife (254)

Hackney in London (61) is explained by the fact that it was dolphins who saved this young Greek poet after he had been kidnapped and cast into the sea by pirates. On the other hand, there seems no particular reason why the Bartons Arms, in an industrial inner suburb of Birmingham (169), should have a huge tiled panel with a hunting scene. The owners of the Café Royal in Edinburgh (236) seem to have preferred a more educational theme by commissioning panels of inventors and their inventions for the main wall downstairs. At the Mountain Daisy,

General Havelock presides over the entrance of the Hastings pub named in his honour (160)

The interior tiling at the General Havelock is proudly signed by its creator

Durham Cathedral sandwiched between the Tyne and Wear in the Buffet Bar at the Mountain Daisy, Sunderland (168)

Sunderland (168), the choice was scenes from Northumbria. Tiled paintings seem to have dropped out of fashion by the First World War but a rare, late appearance in 1920 occurs at the Rose Villa Tavern in Birmingham (173).

The other spectacular use of ceramics of pubs is for **bar counters**. There are thought to be fourteen

Dado tiling by Maws of Broseley, Shropshire, at the Cemetery Hotel, Rochdale (109)

faience (glazed coloured earthenware) counters in the country. All feature in this guide apart from those at the Gunmakers Arms, Gerrard Street, Birmingham; Castle, Oldham Street, Manchester; Towler, Tottington, Greater Manchester; and Waterloo Hotel, Alexandra Street, Newport, Gwent. It seems unlikely that there were ever many more. Occasionally the patterns repeat: those at Burlington's Wine & Cocktail Bar, Lytham St Annes (48), the Red Lion, Birmingham (172), and the Crown Bar, Belfast (266) were all created by the makers, Craven Dunnill, to the same design. Another Craven Dunnill design reappears at the Mountain Daisy, Sunderland, the Gunmakers, Birmingham and the Golden Cross, Cardiff (220). Tiled counters are to be found at the Prince Arthur, Liverpool (124), and

the Feuar's Arms, Kirkcaldy (254). At the Philharmonic Dining Rooms, Liverpool (122), the counter is made spectacular through the use of its mosaic facing.

Other pubs in this guide with good displays of tilework are numbers 49, 65, 104, 105, 106, 118, 139, 171, 199, 200, and 237.

Counter at the Black Horse, Preston (49)

Hammersmith

20 Macbeth Street, W6 9JJ
Grade II listed
LPA: Hammersmith & Fulham
⊖ Hammersmith

Hope & Anchor   62

Closed since this guide was prepared. A good example of a modest Truman's pub of about 1932, probably designed by architect A. E. Sewell and planned as part of a housing development, it retains its public bar and saloon essentially intact. Both bar-backs have an Art Deco clock. The saloon has an excellent example of a spittoon trough and typical Truman's advertising lettering on the woodwork. The one big change is the loss of the off-sales compartment – traceable in the closed doorway on the (puzzlingly named) Riverside Gardens side and the stopped-off spittoon trough.

The saloon: note the tiled spittoon trough at the foot of the counter
(Michael Slaughter)

Hatton Garden

1 Ely Court
Ely Place, EC1N 6SJ
020 7405 4751
www.yeoldemitreholburn.co.uk
Grade II listed
🍺 🍎 🍴
⇌ Farringdon
⊖ Farringdon or Chancery Lane

Ye Olde Mitre   63

A remarkable, fine pub tucked away up an alley. The building dates from the late 18th century but what we see inside is a complete scheme from the inter-war period. Either side of the central servery are two bars, each with extensive Tudor-style panelling and exposed ceiling timbers. Leading off the rear room is a cosy little snug, known as 'Ye Closet'. The front bar has three outside doors, suggesting it was once divided into small compartments (but a single space certainly since the 1930s). The upper part of the servery opening has attractive glazed screening. The gents' can only be accessed from outside – a very rare thing for a London pub. The upstairs room was fitted out about 1990 and is known as the Bishop's Room which, like the name of the pub and its address, is a reminder that the bishops of Ely had their London residence nearby until 1772.

Ye Olde Mitre as seen from the rear room

Holborn

22 High Holborn, WC1V 6BN
020 7242 7670
Grade II listed
LPA: Camden

🍺 🍴

⊖ Chancery Lane

Baronial splendour
in the rear room

Cittie of Yorke

A truly extraordinary pub, rebuilt in 1923–4 to replace a shop owned by wine merchants Henekey & Co.: the architect was probably Ernest R. Barrow. The elegant Tudor façade has a wide, flagstoned passage on the right leading to a pair of rooms. The front one is conventional enough but that at the rear is a wonderful evocation of a medieval hall with a mighty open roof and clerestory (a more modest example occurs at the contemporary Black Horse, Birmingham [175]). The high-level window from which the lord of the manor might have kept an eye on proceedings bears SS motifs for Samuel Smiths of Tadcaster, the present owners. It has a series of drinking booths which seem unique in an English pub at this date but found in Northern Irish pubs and imitated, for example, at pubs in the Wetherspoon chain. As for the vats, they are said to have been in use until the Second World War when the owners were still Henekeys (the iron columns to the gallery are no doubt Victorian). The triangular stove is said to have come from Gray's Inn and to date from about 1815. The brick cellars (open Tue–Fri evenings) are a survival from the earlier building.

Drinking booths down the side of the main bar: in the foreground is the early 19th-century cast-iron Gothic stove

Holborn

208–209 High Holborn, WC1V 7EP
020 7405 8816
Grade II* listed
LPA: Camden

🍺 🍴
⊖ Holborn

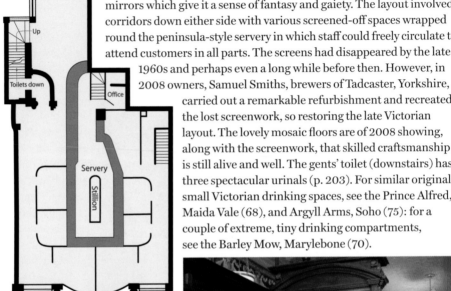

Princess Louise

65

A visit here is an amazing experience and shows how late-Victorian London drinkers and publicans liked their pubs when there was money to spend. The 1870s building seems to have been remodelled in the 1890s, whence the sumptuous display of tiling (by W. B. Simpson & Sons) and mirrors which give it a sense of fantasy and gaiety. The layout involved corridors down either side with various screened-off spaces wrapped round the peninsula-style servery in which staff could freely circulate to attend customers in all parts. The screens had disappeared by the late 1960s and perhaps even a long while before then. However, in 2008 owners, Samuel Smiths, brewers of Tadcaster, Yorkshire, carried out a remarkable refurbishment and recreated the lost screenwork, so restoring the late Victorian layout. The lovely mosaic floors are of 2008 showing, along with the screenwork, that skilled craftsmanship is still alive and well. The gents' toilet (downstairs) has three spectacular urinals (p. 203). For similar original small Victorian drinking spaces, see the Prince Alfred, Maida Vale (68), and Argyll Arms, Soho (75): for a couple of extreme, tiny drinking compartments, see the Barley Mow, Marylebone (70).

The glorious gilded mirrorwork
(signed by R. Morris of Kennington)

Screenwork installed in 2008
during a faithful re-creation of
the Victorian interior (John Cryne)

The rear left area and its
reinstated screenwork

Kensington

114 Campden Hill Road, W8 7AR

020 7243 8797

www.thewindsorcastlekensington.co.uk

Grade II listed

LPA: Kensington & Chelsea

🍺 🍴 ⑂

⊖ Notting Hill Gate

Windsor Castle

66

A remarkable example of Victorian-type drinking arrangements surviving well into the interwar years, this plain two-storey late Georgian building was refitted about 1933. We know this because there is a plaque in the 'Sherry Bar' which helpfully explains that the oak used to furnish it was felled between April 1930 and December 1932. The refitting created three small compartments separated by screens: they are named in the contemporary door glass. There is much panelling throughout and a pair of screens separating the spaces: that between the 'Sherry Bar' and small 'Private Bar' is a floor-to-ceiling affair with a low service door. The screen between the Private Bar and 'Campden Bar' is much lower and has, unfortunately, lost its door. The mahogany bar-back is the sole survivor from the Victorian era. To the right and opened up to the 'Campden Bar' is a further room (in two parts) known as 'The Ordinary', which may be private quarters brought into pub use at a later date.

This plaque in the Sherry Bar explains the sources of the woodwork

THE ENGLISH OAK

USED IN PANELLING THIS ROOM

WAS GROWN IN THE FOLLOWING PLACES:-

THE ½" PANELS FROM WARESLEY PARK, HAMPSHIRE. CUT DEC.1932.

THE ¾" RAILS AND MOULDINGS FROM MILTON ABBEY, DORSET. CUT APL.1930.

THE 1" FRAMING AND OTHER THICKNESSES FROM READING, BERKSHIRE. CUT DEC.1930.

In the private bar, with the Sherry Bar left and Campden Bar right seen through the service doorways

Kilburn

274 Kilburn High Road, NW6 2BY
020 7624 1424
www.blacklionguesthouse.com
Grade II* listed
LPA: Camden

🍺 🍴 🛏

⊖ Brondesbury
⊖ Kilburn

Metal reliefs and mirrors
on the south wall

General view of the main bar:
a screen survives on the
left-hand side

Black Lion

67

An imposing corner-site pub built in 1898 to designs by architect
R. A. Lewcock. It has a light, spacious interior enriched with some
spectacular decoration. Pride of place goes
to the series of four copper relief panels
by designer F. A. Callcott showing 18th-
century folk at leisure at the supposed
predecessor of the present pub. There is a
superbly ornate Florentine frieze in both
main rooms and a richly decorated ceiling.
Originally the main space would have been
subdivided – see the names public bar,
private bar and saloon above the doors
– and there is still one screen surviving
which was moved to its present position
in 2003. There is also a long, panelled bar
counter (note the doors to service the beer
engines in former times) and the original
bar-back. The large right-hand room was
originally a music room (now a restaurant).
There are some fine etched windows in
the side elevation. Opens 3pm weekdays.

Maida Vale

5a Formosa Street, W9 1EE
020 7286 3287
www.theprincealfred.com
Grade II listed
LPA: Westminster

🍺 🍴

⊖ Warwick Avenue

Prince Alfred

An astonishing survivor. The Prince Alfred has the only peninsula-style servery to retain all of its original surrounding drinking areas – no fewer than five of them, each with its own external entrance (see the Princess Louise, Holborn (65), for a superb re-creation). The building went up in about 1865 but was given a complete refit around 1898. Outside one can see the exposed ceiling on the ground floor and how timber and glass screenwork has been inserted later, cutting across the patterned decoration. Note the tiles and mosaic in the entrance. The main space is divided up by timber and glass screens, each with a low service door for the use of, say, pot boys and cleaners. The smallest compartment has a set of snob screens to offer customers a sense of privacy. In the middle of the servery is a wonderfully tall, carved stillion, which is secured to the ceiling by ironwork. All this late Victorian work gives the pub a delicate Rococo feel. A refit in 2001 transformed the character into a café-restaurant establishment with an over-prominent kitchen and dining room: the counter was refronted at this time.

A series of unique original drinking compartments radiate from the peninsular servery

Maida Vale

93 Warrington Crescent, W9 1EH
020 7286 8282
www.faucetinn.com/warrington
Grade II listed
LPA: Westminster

🍺 🍴

⊖ Warwick Avenue

Warrington

One of London's most opulent pubs, now part of Faucet Inns' small chain, built in 1857 but refitted, probably in the 1890s. The glorious tiled columns to the entrance porch and a huge mosaic floor bearing the name of the pub give a foretaste of the riches inside. The main room (right) has a grey marble-topped counter with unusual, bulging pilasters and lozenge decoration. Grey marble also appears in the columns of the arcade marching across the room and embracing the generously scaled staircase up to the restaurant. Some of the windows have lively stained glass, while over the servery is a semi-circular canopy, decorated with Art Nouveau-style paintings of naked ladies. More such paintings, with the signature 'Colin Beswick 1965', appear on the back wall and evoke the unlikely story that this was once a brothel. The left-hand room was once clearly divided into three as the patterning in the ceiling shows. The lowest status part has matchboard wall-panelling and an ornate, much decayed, mirror advertising Bass Pale Ale.

This is one of the grandest historic rooms in any London pub

Marylebone

8 Dorset Street, W1U 6QW
07967 484596
www.thebarleymowpub.com
Grade II listed
LPA: Westminster

🍺 🍴

⊖ Baker Street

Barley Mow

70

This tall four-storey building of 1791 houses a Victorian interior of great interest. What is now unique is the survival of a couple of small drinking boxes attached to the counter on the left-hand side – a perfect example of how, in times gone by, Londoners liked to drink in intimate cosy surroundings. The spurious claim that they were intended for pawnbroking transactions is probably a late-20th-century explanation for features which have become inexplicable with changed drinking

traditions (that is not to say, of course, that a few dodgy deals may not have taken place therein over the years). Screwed to the counter top is a worn brass plate displaying the prices of liquor with rum at 15 shillings (75p) a gallon! There is another on the counter alongside the snugs. Note on the bar-back a tap marked 'Old Tom', an extremely popular gin, which was once dispensed from an overhead barrel. The existence of three entrances in the frontage is clear evidence of other internal subdivisions, which have now gone.

Two tiny drinking boxes are attached to the end of the counter

Notting Hill

96 Ladbroke Grove, W11 1PY
020 7229 5663
www.geronimo-inns.co.uk/
theelgin
Grade II listed
LPA: Kensington & Chelsea

🍺 🍴

⊖ Ladbroke Grove

Parts of the Elgin have extraordinarily rich Victorian decoration

Elgin

71

A pub with some spectacular Victorian features. Three distinct rooms are still clearly discernible although they are now interlinked. The star performer is the one in the northern part of the building, which is screened off from the corner bar by a timber and glass screen of exceptional exuberance. Also in this room is a bar-back of rare richness, embellished with 17th-century detailing, gilded mirrors and a coved frieze of apples in low relief. Finally, on the side wall are coloured tile strips (with an EA monogram for Elgin Arms) and gilded mirrors and painted glass displaying foliage, butterflies and birds in flight.

The counters are original too and have doors to allow the servicing of the beer engines in times gone by. At the rear is a large lounge with a skylight. The bar-back in the corner bar is modern. Behind the servery is an office (now used as a kitchen) with some fine decorative glass.

St James's

2 Duke of York Street, SW1Y 6JP
www.redlionmayfair.co.uk
020 7321 0782
Grade II listed
LPA: Westminster

 🍴

⊖ Piccadilly Circus

Red Lion   `72`

One of the most spectacular late Victorian pub interiors anywhere. The trading area is extremely small and surrounds a central servery; yet a century ago, small as it is, the pub would have been divided up into various separate areas. The three outside doorways are proof of that, as are two surviving room names –'public bar' and 'private bar' – in the door glass. The front part was probably divided into three whilst the bar area at the rear was always a single space. What makes this part

so special are the superlative etched and cut mirrors which create brilliant, glittering reflections, and make the pub seem larger than it is. The counter at the front has drop-down panels for servicing the beer engines in former days (you can see the keyholes). Don't be fooled by the gantry on top of the counter which is modern work (as with nearly all such features).

Etched and cut mirrors create a sparkling, fantasy-like atmosphere in the rear room

Smithfield

1 Middle Street, EC1A 7JA
020 7600 0257
Grade II listed
LPA: City of London

 🍴

⊖ Barbican

Hand & Shears   `73`

An unpretentious interior with simple woodwork of fairly indeterminable date and unlike anything else in central London. The island servery is still surrounded by a series of drinking spaces, including a cosy little private bar (so named, along with a saloon,

in the door glass which looks like work of the 1950s or early 1960s). A sensitive refurbishment in 1989 expanded the gents' slightly into the rear bar area, installed the diagonal shelving over the servery and replaced the iron columns but, thankfully, the overall traditional character was kept. The pub name comes from the cutting of the first cloth by the lord mayor at Bartholomew Fair, England's greatest cloth fair from 1133 until it was suppressed in 1855 amid fears of public disorder.

The tiny private bar: there is nothing else quite like it in central London

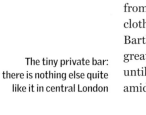

Smithfield

126 Newgate Street, EC1A 7AA
020 7600 1863
www.viaducttavern.co.uk
Grade II listed
LPA: City of London

🍺 🍴
🚆 City Thameslink
🚇 St Paul's

Viaduct Tavern

74

Built in 1874, although the wonderful fittings are from a remodelling by architect Arthur Dixon in 1898–1900. The former separate drinking areas (suggested by the three sets of double doors) have gone, but there is still an amazing amount of excellent and very eclectic decoration. At the rear of the peninsula-style servery is a small, glazed-in office with fine etched glass and delicate woodwork: there is similar work to the right of it forming a canopy. Delicate too is the small stillion in the middle of the servery with its arched woodwork and ornamented glass. The ceiling, no doubt unaltered from 1874 with its swirling relief panels, is a fine sight. On the right-hand wall are paintings in marble surrounds depicting allegorical ladies although what they represent is less than clear: the one left holds a wheatsheaf (agriculture?), right stands beside a vine, centre two figures with London landmarks in the background: the panels are signed by one 'Hal'. At the head of the stairs is some rich red tiling and a lavish Victorian mirror advertising Bass (big advertising mirrors, common in Scotland, are fairly rare in England). A final curiosity is the heavily carved sliding door at the rear, leading to the private quarters above.

The Viaduct was fitted in lavish style in 1898–1900

Soho

18 Argyll Street, W1F 7TP
020 7734 6117
www.nicholsonspubs.co.uk/the
argyllarmsoxfordcircuslondon
Grade II* listed
LPA: Westminster

🍺 🍴
⊖ Oxford Circus

A screened drinking area,
looking through to the corridor

Argyll Arms
75

An astonishing survival within yards of bustling Oxford Street.
With the Prince Alfred, Maida Vale (68), it is the best example of a
late-Victorian London pub divided up into multiple compartments by
screenwork. The building dates from 1868 but the fittings are probably
from the 1890s. At the front there are two entrances, the right-hand
one leading to a screened space while the left one leads to a corridor to
the rear of the building, and from which other spaces are accessed.
Along the corridor mirrors enhance the sumptuous atmosphere with
reflections of the rich etched and cut glazed screens opposite. At the
back the 'saloon and dining room' has another glittering display of
mirrors. The bar-back is elaborate and contains a little office in the
middle (cf. Winchester, Highgate [87], for a much grander example).
A magnificent, swirling iron stair-rail sweeps up to the restaurant (all
modern apart from the ornate orange breccia fireplace and its overmantel).
Other features to relish are the highly decorated ceiling, an immensely
deep, decorated cornice and a big ornamented column in the rear parts.

Soho

18 Bateman Street W1D 3AJ
020 7494 0697
www.nicholsonspubs.co.uk/the
dogandducksoholondon
Grade II listed
LPA: Westminster

🍺 🍴
⊖ Tottenham Court Road

Dog & Duck

A lovely small (and usually busy) pub, built as a hotel in 1897 to designs by architect Francis Chambers. The exterior has glazed brick upper floors and a carving of the eponymous fauna which appear again in a delightful but sadly mauled mosaic at the Frith Street entrance and in the wall tiling. Tiles are an important element in the decoration, lining the back wall of the left-hand part of the pub, and forming the dado and framing two fine advertising mirrors on the right side: interestingly neither promotes alcohol, rather cigarettes and cigars, seltzer and mineral waters (the craftsman, S. Trenner, signs his creations). Originally the pub would surely have had a division between the two very different halves and quite possibly divisions within the right-hand side. It is hard to envisage where the servery would have been: the present one, probably introduced in the post-war period, straddles one of two blocked external doorways: the superstructure on the counter is clearly reused work.

The eponymous dog and duck

The advertising mirrors
promote tobacco and, curiously,
non-alcoholic drinks

Southwark

77 Borough High Street, SE1 1NH

020 7407 2056

www.nationaltrust.org.uk/main/
w-georgeinn

Grade I listed

LPA: Southwark

🍺 🍴

≠/⊖ London Bridge

George

An amazing survivor from the days when Southwark was a major terminus for the coaching trade between London and southern England. The George was rebuilt in 1676 and is the last galleried inn in London: even this is but a fragment, as the other parts which helped make up a courtyard were demolished in 1889. Most of the interior is modern work but the first room you encounter from the High Street – the Parliament Bar – has remarkably old woodwork (might some of it be late 17th-century?). This space was evidently two rooms at one time. Nearest the street there is full-height horizontal boarding and simple fixed seating plus an ancient fireplace with a wooden hood and also a large one-handed clock that reminded travellers of the time. At the other end of the room is a mighty fireplace and a remarkable glazed-in servery with a now-disused, rare set of Victorian 'cash-register'-style hand pumps.

The Parliament Bar and its clock

West Brompton

1 Billing Road, SW10 9UJ
020 7352 2943
Not listed
LPA: Kensington & Chelsea

🍺 🍴

⊖ Fulham Broadway

Fox & Pheasant   `78`

This lovely, small pub is an inter-war time warp. It lies in a private road and was built as part of a terrace in 1896. Originally known as the Prince of Wales, it became the Bedford Arms some ten years later, and finally the Fox & Pheasant in 1965. It was licensed simply as a beer house until 1953. It was fully refitted some time around 1930 when the ground floor exterior was faced with tiles (now sadly painted over). There is a

lobby with an off-sales hatch at the entrance, and doors to the public bar (left) and a rather larger saloon (right). Everything is quite low-key and this is typical of pub-fitting between the wars. The servery has glazed areas on each side, housing spirits, glasses etc. The rear doors and windows have attractive dimpled glass with green bands. Remarkably, much of the loose furniture still survives from the time of the refit: a real rarity.

The public bar looking through to the saloon with the servery in between. The furniture seems to date from the interwar refit

GREATER LONDON – OUTER

The featured pubs in
Outer London

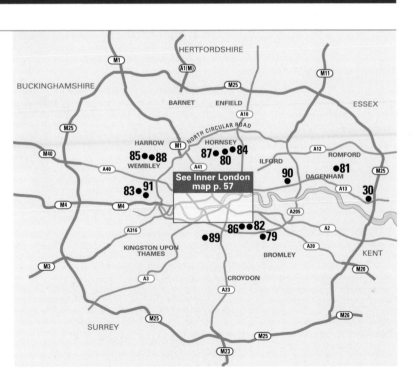

London pub heritage

Greater London has over 8 million people living in 32 boroughs and something like 5,000 pubs to serve them: 40 of these make it onto the National Inventory of Historic Pub Interiors and hence into this guide. A goodly number are in the very centre and offer ample opportunities for several superlative historic pub crawls. Pubs like the Black Friar (54), Salisbury (58) and Olde Cheshire Cheese (60) are actually tourist destinations in their own right.

London was at the forefront of the great pub-building boom at the end of the 19th century as brewers, in particular, sought to expand and improve their estates (see p. 92). Pubs such as the Salisbury (58), Warrington, Maida Vale (69), Argyll Arms, Soho (75), Queens, Crouch End (80), and Kings Head, Tooting (89), stunningly demonstrate the expense poured into pub development and embellishment at the time. Such pubs provided vast opportunities, not only for builders, but also for armies of ceramic and ornamental glass manufacturers, wood-carvers and decorators. The splendid Forester, West Ealing (91), is an instructive pub in representing a halfway house between Victorian glitz and glitter and the more restrained taste that was developing in the early 20th century.

Inter-war pubs are also represented in this guide. In the centre the great star is the Cittie of Yorke (64) rebuilt by a wine merchant in the 1920s and with a huge, echoing 'baronial hall' at the rear. This was the era when the principle of 'few but better' (see p. 92) really came to the fore. Pubs for new housing developments tended to be few, but were large and catered for a wide spectrum of clients. As elsewhere, not

The Forester, West Ealing (91), is one of our finest pubs from the years immediately before the First World War

many of these 'super-pubs' have survived intact but this guide includes two good examples, the magnificent Eastbrook, Dagenham (81), and the more modest Windermere, South Kenton (88).

A century ago English pubs were multi-room establishments but London drinkers seem to have been particularly partial to occupying very small spaces. The extreme example is the unique pair of tiny boxes at the Barley Mow, Marylebone (70), rather like heightened box-pews from a Georgian church. The Prince Alfred, Maida Vale (68), is the best example in the country of screened-off compartments radiating from a peninsula-shaped servery: it also has a set of now very rare snob screens. Amazingly the Argyll Arms, Soho, has also kept a series of screened compartments between its entrance corridor and the servery. At the Princess Louise, Holborn (65), facsimile screenwork was, miraculously, reinstated in 2008.

Very rare snob screens survive at the Prince Alfred, Maida Vale (68). They were intended to give a little extra privacy to 'better class' customers

Bellingham

Randlesdown Road, SE6 3BT
020 8697 2522
Grade II listed
LPA: Lewisham
🍺
⇌ Bellingham

Fellowship Inn

79

A gigantic pub of 1923–4 by F.G. Newnham who was in-house architect to brewers, Barclay Perkins. Sadly it has seen distinctly better days, but is still almost entirely intact. Only one room remains in use – the spacious, panelled saloon bar on the right-hand side with original bar fittings and a small office behind. The odd open screens and the pot shelf over the counter are modern work but affect the character little. At the rear is a folding screen behind which is a huge function room, added in *c*.1926 (referred to as a ballroom and used as such into the 1960s) but in a very poor state. Beneath is another big room, again very run down – a theatre, still with its box office and fitted up with rows of seating. Also on the lower level is an off-sales on a truly epic scale, facing the housing estate at the rear. Upstairs once again, the left-hand room was the public bar.

The saloon, the only part of this vast pub still in public use

Crouch End

26 Broadway Parade, N8 9DE
020 8340 2031
www.thequeenscrouchend.co.uk
Grade II* listed
LPA: Haringey
🍺 🍴
⇌ Hornsey then bus 41 south

The restaurant (right)

Sumptuous glass
fills the front windows

Queens

80

This sumptuous pub of 1899–1902, originally called the Queen's Hotel, is the sister of the Salisbury on Green Lanes (84), both built and designed by John Cathles Hill, a Dundee man who came to London aged 21 and made his fortune as a successful developer. Both pubs share a roughly similar layout. There is a large servery in the centre encircled by a series of screened-off spaces. On the right there is what the door glass suggests was a restaurant, which has a couple of alcoves and a

spectacular plaster ceiling: indeed the ceilings and deep friezes throughout are all lavishly decorated. There is so much to admire, notably the wonderful Art Nouveau-style window glass. The bar counter is original although the central fitting has much modern work in it. Also noteworthy is the circular entrance in the corner with a mosaic floor, bearing Mr Hill's monogram and Q for Queens. A regrettable feature is the overpowering modern fitting atop the bar but, overall, this is a great place to appreciate late Victorian pub-building at its most ebullient.

Dagenham

Dagenham Road, RM10 7UP

020 8592 1873

Grade II* listed

LPA: Barking & Dagenham

🍺 🍴

⊖ Dagenham East then
    bus 103 north

Glass in the Music Room
Below: The Walnut Room

Eastbrook

81

One of the very best and most complete inter-war interiors in the country. The Eastbrook is a large estate pub, built in 1937 for G. A. Smith & Sons, wine merchants and off-licence proprietors (their name can still be seen on the adjacent and still-functioning off-sales premises). Behind the lively exterior are two separate and very different bars – the Oak Room (right) and Walnut Room (centre) plus a large Music Room on the left which is divided off by a folding screen. The Oak Room forms the public bar and is an exercise in 'Brewers' Tudor' style with imitation beams and exposed joists, Tudor arches and oak veneer wall-panelling. The Walnut Room is more opulent and the abundant use of the eponymous wood gives it an unusual character: it has prominent fluted columns supporting a joist across the front. Columns also frame the stage in the Music Room which has a backdrop of delightful stained glass. The fittings throughout are a remarkably complete assemblage from the day the pub opened over 70 years ago. It was unlisted until 2009 but when its importance was recognised by CAMRA, a successful application to English Heritage promptly resulted in grading at II*.

East Dulwich

2 Forest Hill Road, SE22 0RR

020 8299 9521

www.theherne.net

Not listed

LPA: Southwark

🍺 🍴

⇌ Peckham Rye then bus 63 south

Herne Tavern

82

The original building is mid-Victorian but was given a thorough, interwar makeover and is remarkably unaltered since then. The window glass tells us the left-hand room was the public bar, while the right-hand one was the saloon lounge – and which was apparently extended out as a single storey from the original building. There is a third room at the rear left, linked by an arch to the area at the front. There is much panelling, several inter-war fireplaces, loose chairs and

some very attractive window glass with clear textured panes enlivened by others with mottled green glass. The servery fittings are from the same scheme but are quite conventional: on the saloon lounge side there was a dumb waiter (now reused for wine bottles). The only changes, possibly from the 1980s, are the introduction of a doorway between public bar and saloon lounge, and the addition of a conservatory at the rear.

The servery in the saloon

Hanwell

110 Uxbridge Road, W7 3SU

020 8567 2370

Not listed

LPA: Ealing

🍴

⇌ Hanwell

Kings Arms

83

A large, fairly plain high street pub, rebuilt in 1930 by brewers Mann, Crossman & Paulin. On either side there are two rooms, one behind the other and between them, at the front, a small private bar.

On the left the public bar has what is now a games room behind it: the only real change is the loss of double doors between the two. The same layout (and loss of doors) occurs on the right but the hierarchical distinction between the two sides is reflected in the greater elaboration of the saloon counter. In the middle of the servery is an example of a publican's private office. The toilets on the left-hand side retain their original tiling. On the far right externally is a staircase leading to an upstairs function room and further right is a former off-sales shop.

The cosy snug

Harringay

1 Grand Parade, Green Lanes, N4 1JX
020 8800 9617
Grade II* listed
LPA: Haringey

🍺 🍴

⇌ Harringay Green Lanes
⊖ Turnpike Lane then
   bus 29/141 south

The front bar: the flooring
was installed in 2003

Salisbury   84

This glorious landmark pub was built in 1898–9 by John Cathles Hill, who laid out much of the surrounding area and designed this pub and the Queens (80). Both have very similar plans. Rich ironwork, tiling and mosaics in the generous porches give a foretaste of what to expect inside. The most lavish room is the richly appointed saloon with its attractive alcoves. Behind is the former billiard room (now a restaurant) with its lovely skylight. The rest of the pub is taken up with two bars surrounding an island servery of epic proportions. Originally there would have been more drinking areas within the large L-shaped bar on the corner. The servery has a large, original back fitting with delicate Art Nouveau details. In 2003 the black and white marble floor was added as part of an excellent refurbishment and the magnificent etched and gilded mirror by the right-hand entrance (by Cakebread, Robey & Co), which had been stolen, was replaced with a modern copy.

Harrow-on-the-Hill

30 West Street, HA1 3EF

020 8422 3155

www.castle-harrow.co.uk

Grade II listed

LPA: Harrow

🍺 🍴

≷/⊖ Harrow-on-the-Hill then
   bus 258/H17

Castle

85

The Castle probably dates back to the early eighteenth century and was rebuilt as we see it today by Fuller, Smith & Turner in 1901. It has kept most of its original layout, the only major change being indicated by a disused side door which must have led to a separate drinking space or off-sales. Now it has four rooms, with the largest of these split by a timber screen with a low service door to enable staff to get from one side to another. On the right are a pair of smaller rooms with a large hatch to the servery. At the back is the final room with wood-block flooring and imitation panelling. The counter is original, as is the simple back fitting. Parts of the fireplaces are modern insertions. Outside there is highly attractive ironwork over the main entrance and a mosaic floor panel with the pub's name.

Screen with a low service door divides the main bar at the Castle

Herne Hill

10 Half Moon Lane, SE24 9HU
020 7274 2733
www.halfmoonpub.co.uk
Grade II* listed
LPA: Southwark

🍺 🍴

🚆 Herne Hill

Half Moon

This architectural extravaganza went up in 1896 – the same year as the equally flamboyant Kings Head, Tooting (89). At both pubs there is a good sense of how the spaces were originally divided into separate rooms. At the Half Moon they were arranged around an L-shaped servery, whose original fittings survive. The greatest attraction is the snug bar, tucked away at the back with its six lovely painted mirrors of birds in watery surroundings: a pair of small labels helpfully tell us that the makers were W. Gibbs & Sons of Blackfriars. Here the screen to the servery had snob screens (but sadly they are gone). Two other screens have etched, cut and coloured glass with pretty lozenges showing barley, hops and foliage. Four hefty iron columns with Corinthian capitals support the upper floors. Now very much a music venue.

The small snug is lined with painted mirrors featuring water birds

Highgate

206 Archway Road, N6 5BA
020 8374 1690
www.winchester-hotel.com
Not listed
LPA: Haringey

⊖ Highgate

Winchester

`87`

Built in 1881 as part of a very distinctive parade of shops with residential accommodation above. The great feature here is the massive, glazed-in office surrounded on three sides by the servery. Its windows have remarkably lovely, delicate etched glass with trails of foliage and depictions of flowers and birds. Originally there would have been multiple rooms and drinking areas. Most of these have been swept away but the top part of one screen survives with yet more attractive glazing.

At the rear, through an arch from the main bar, there is a room with a diagonally boarded ceiling. The counter is original and has a number of doors for servicing beer engines in times gone by. The porches have some wonderful decorative ironwork and that on the right also has some attractive tiling.

The glazed office which is the principal feature at the Winchester

South Kenton

Windermere Avenue, HA9 8QT
020 8904 7484
www.windermerepub.com
Grade II listed
LPA: Brent

⊖⊖ South Kenton

Windermere

`88`

A rare, largely intact example of a big inter-war suburban pub, built in 1938 or 1939 by the Courage brewery. There are three rooms. The public bar, facing Windermere Avenue, is only used for parties and functions. On the station side there is a saloon with a lounge behind. Original features include the large inner porches, bar counters, back fittings, wall panelling, wavy cornices, doors between the saloon and

The saloon

lounge, fireplaces (charming pictorial tiles with windmills in the saloon fire surround), tiles and fittings in the gents' and, in the saloon, an advertising mirror over the fireplace with a Courage cockerel and a (now non-functioning) clock. The only significant change is the loss of the off-sales compartment, now incorporated into the public bar. The fixed seats are additions and the superstructures on the saloon and lounge counters, bearing the name of the pub, look like work of the 1950s or 1960s.

Tooting

84 Upper Tooting Road, SW17 7PB
020 8767 6708
www.taylor-walker.co.uk/pub/
kings-head-tooting/c1215
Grade II listed
LPA: Wandsworth

🍺 🍴 🍽️

🚇 Tooting Bec

The King's Head retains its 1896 sumptuous fittings and many traces of its original layout

Kings Head   89

The Kings Head is an architectural riot on the main road through Tooting, mixing styles with gay abandon. Built in 1896 to designs by prolific pub architect W. M. Brutton, one can still get a very good sense of how a lavish late Victorian pub was laid out around a central servery. Originally the numerous outside doors would each have led into a separate drinking space, those on the right being quite small. Down both sides of the pub are tiled corridors which led to various separate compartments. The original servery fittings, including a delicately detailed bar-back plus an octagonal display feature survive, together with a good deal of the screenwork and decorative glass. Timber and plaster arches straddle the servery. At the rear is a large, screened-off room with skylights that would have served as a billiard room or restaurant.

Upton Park

1 Barking Road, E6 1PW
020 8472 2182
Grade II listed
LPA: Newham

⊖ Upton Park

Boleyn   `90`

One of the more spectacular late Victorian pubs in London, built in 1899–1900 in free Renaissance style to designs by prolific pub architects Shoebridge & Rising. The interior is a *tour de force*. The door glass would suggest there were, unusually, two or three spaces termed 'private bar'. Over the saloon is a small skylight with lovely stained glass. Beyond lies a vast and spectacular billiard room with a much larger stained glass skylight, a space for a stage and a rich, coved frieze. Other old features include the bar counter, cast-iron columns and lots of etched decorative glass, although the servery back-fitting is modern. The pub is right beside West Ham's football ground so avoid match days for your visit.

The stunning skylight over the billiard room

West Ealing

2 Leighton Road, W13 9EP
020 8567 1654
www.theforesterealing.com
Grade II listed
LPA: Ealing

⊖ Northfields then bus E2/E3 north

Forester   `91`

One of England's finest Edwardian pubs, built in 1909 for the Royal Brewery, Brentford, by well-known pub architect, T. H. Nowell Parr, and showing a shift away from late Victorian opulent glitz. Behind the distinctive gabled and columned porch exterior are five splendid intact rooms, all with fine mahogany and oak woodwork by Maples. There are two public bars (on the corner and the next along Leighton Road), a saloon and, at the back, a restaurant: even the former off-sales (disused) along Seaford Street remains. The only major changes are the loss of double doors between some rooms and the insertion of loos at the north end of the main public bar. Attractive stained glass in many windows. Note the bell-pushes in the saloon (very rare in London pubs), one with the word 'BELL' to avoid any doubt!

Two of the bars with their original fittings

What shaped Britain's pubs – 2: the golden age of pub building

The end of the 19th century and the first few years of the 20th saw the most magnificent age of British pub-building, of which there are many examples in this guide. Various factors came together to bring this about.

The need for reform. During the Victorian years there was much concern about the evils of drink and the places where it was consumed. To somewhat oversimplify, the pub came to be seen by the 'better classes' as a place where drunkenness was rife, morality was usurped and the principles of true religion endangered. There had been a vast explosion of beerhouse numbers following the 1830 Beer Act which made it possible for any ratepayer to open one on payment of just two guineas: over the next two years more than 33,000 of them did just that. The new beerhouses were nigh-on impossible for the authorities to supervise adequately and were a source of widespread concern. It took 40 years for control to be brought back into the hands of licensing justices.

The Temperance Movement. Into this arena stepped the Temperance Movement, originating in the United States and appearing on our shores in 1829. By 1889 its Band of Hope had no less than two million members. Although the most radical anti-drink campaigners – teetotallers and abolitionists – failed to secure prohibition, the movement had immense influence in its demands to improve public house facilities and the closure, or threat of closure, of badly run and inadequate premises.

Fewer and better. Licensing justices made use of powers granted in 1872 to reduce pub numbers. Anyone seeking to open new ones had to convince the justices of the suitability of the premises and often had to surrender two or more licenses in exchange for the new one. The net effect was to gradually improve the stock of pubs at a time when they needed to appeal to their customers as never before.

Competition. At the start of the Victorian period there were few opportunities for most ordinary people to enjoy themselves other than at the pub. By the end of the 19th century things were very different.

The Salisbury, Harringay, north London (84), is one of many grand pubs erected about 1900

There was more money and leisure time and no shortage of opportunities to spend them – organised sport, personal recreation such as cycling, excursions, working men's institutes and clubs and music halls, to name but a few. The pub needed to offer not just drink but an appealing environment where people would want to consume it.

The brewers' rush to build. At the end of the 19th century there was a major move by brewers, especially in London, to expand their estates to tie up the trade. Capital was more freely available than ever before (especially thanks to the flotation of joint stock companies) and this was used to enlarge pub estates and the quality of the buildings within them.

A fair political climate. The hand of the brewers and other pub owners was strengthened at the end of the century when the 1895 general election saw the Conservative Party sweep to victory. It was supportive of the drink interest whereas its rivals, the Liberals, were allied with the Temperance lobby and had drastic proposals to clamp down on drink and the places where it was sold. In this climate those making investments in pubs could feel confident at least for the next few years.

The Temperance Movement offered sober alternatives to the pub. Ironically, this one in Battersea, London, probably built in the period 1906–11 by Temperance Billiard Halls Ltd, *is* now a pub

MANCHESTER, GREATER

Altrincham

153 Manchester Road
Broadheath, WA14 5NT
0161 941 3383
Grade II listed
LPA: Trafford
🍺
🚉 Navigation Road

The tap room

Bury

6 Bolton Street, BL9 0LQ
0161 764 2641
www.guesthouse-bury.co.uk
Not listed
LPA: Bury
🍺 🍴 🛏
🚉 Bury

Railway   92

A small and appealing but unpretentious Victorian pub, saved from demolition in 1996 and now marooned in the parking area of the retail centre that was planned to destroy it. It has a multi-room layout and a recent modest refurbishment has only enhanced its attractiveness. Either side of the entrance are the tap room (left) and bar parlour, named in the cut and etched glass door panels, both with fixed seating and bell-pushes. A black and white quarry-tiled passage leads to the bar parlour, which has an attractive late Victorian fireplace with a pretty tiled border. In the heart of the building is a small drinking lobby, dominated by the curvaceous panelled bar counter and with bench seating along the walls: the bar-back fittings, unfortunately, are modern. Behind all this are two rooms brought into pub use quite recently: the door proclaiming 'Vault' came from another pub. Threats of demolition were successfully averted by listing in 1993 following a pilot study of Greater Manchester pubs by CAMRA for English Heritage.

Old White Lion   93

The splendid Oak Room at the rear right is the reason to visit this late-Victorian pub. It was refitted in the period 1910–20 and has wall-panelling with 17th-century motifs. A splendid Tudor-style fireplace has tiles and a carved wood surround while the decorative plaster ceiling includes Tudor rose symbols, animal faces, lions, and birds in relief, plus a cornice of luscious grapes. The party wall to the bar side comprises a screen of painted glass with lion masks and swags. There is fixed seating with bell-pushes above. A rather remarkable feature is the hinged baffle beside the door: why it was so constructed is hard to imagine. The former commercial (now pool) room (rear left) has a stained glass window but nothing else of note, while the two front rooms have been knocked into one. The Oak Room is not normally open but access is usually allowed if the pub is not too busy. At the front of the pub are the sad remnants of a former revolving door.

The beautifully appointed Oak Room

Eccles

439 Liverpool Road
Peel Green, M30 7HD
0161 789 6971
www.joseph-holt.com/Joseph-
Holt-Pubs-53-Grapes.aspx
Grade II listed
LPA: Salford

🍺 🍴
⇌ Patricroft

Grapes

94

One of three wonderful pubs built in Eccles for Joseph Holt's brewery between 1903 and 1906 by local architects Hartley, Hacking & Co. (the Lamb Hotel (95) and the Royal Oak (96) being the others). This is the most spacious of the three and the most extravagant in its use of mahogany and decorative glass. The drinking passage is arguably as impressive as any in the country with its terrazzo floor, deep-etched glazed door panels and superb glazed screenwork to the servery. The Art Nouveau tiling throughout is very special: the dado of green tiles continues up the staircase. The bar parlour and rear smoke room also have many original features, though the latter has been extended into former private quarters. A billiard (now pool) room still has its raised seating (as at the Lamb Hotel [95]), a tiled and wood surround fireplace, bell-pushes and a hatch to the bar. The public bar absorbed the off-sales some time ago and most of its fittings are modern: also its counter has been truncated, hence the 'stranded' screenwork to the corridor. Listed in 1994 following a pilot study of Greater Manchester pubs by CAMRA for English Heritage. Food consists of sandwiches.

The corridor at the back of the servery

Eccles

33 Regent Street, M30 0BP
www.joseph-holt.com/Joseph-
Holt-Pubs-63-Lamb-Hotel.aspx
Grade II listed
LPA: Salford

≥ 🚉 Eccles

Lamb Hotel   95

A classic Edwardian red brick and terracotta extravaganza rebuilt in 1906 and designed by Mr Newton of Hartley, Hacking & Co. for Holt's brewery (cf. Grapes (94) and Royal Oak [96]). It has superbly preserved fittings throughout, including elaborate Jacobean-style mahogany door surrounds and chimneypieces, Art Nouveau wall-tiling and mosaic flooring. From the entrance lobby, with its terrazzo floor and dado of green tiles, a door to the right leads to the vault. This has seen some changes, including incorporation of an off-sales (see the blocked door outside on the right-hand side street) and a replacement bar counter. The bar parlour retains fixed seating with bell-pushes and a wood-surround fireplace. Second on the left, the rear smoke room, entered through a wide arch from the lobby, also has its Edwardian fixed seating plus a Jacobean-style chimneypiece. The billiard room is quite amazing, complete with full-size snooker table (supplied by Burroughs & Watts of London when the pub opened) and seating on raised platforms for spectators to watch the play. The other star feature is the screened, curved mahogany bar in the lobby with brilliant-cut glazed hatches, still with sliding windows and over-lights. The lobby also has a dado of Art Nouveau glazed tiles which continues up the stairs. Listed in 1994 following a pilot study of Greater Manchester pubs by CAMRA for English Heritage.

The magnificently preserved billiard room: note the heating pipes beneath the seat

The lobby with its screenwork in front of the servery. The billiard room is through the door on the left

Eccles

34 Barton Lane, M30 0EN
07971 835029
www.joseph-holt.com/Joseph-
Holt-Pubs-98-Royal-Oak.aspx
Grade II listed
LPA: Salford

⇌ 🚌 Eccles

*The corridor here in use,
as such corridors are
in the north, for drinking*

Royal Oak

The Royal Oak has undergone minimal change since construction in 1904 – even the stable block in the yard has escaped attention. Built of red brick with terracotta dressings, it was designed by Mr Newton of Hartley, Hacking & Co. for Holt's brewery (cf. Grapes [94] and Lamb Hotel [95]). The lobby bar has a terrazzo floor, a dado of dark green Art Nouveau tiles and an impressive screened servery with mostly intact sliding hatches. Leading off the lobby are the news room, bar parlour and (former) billiard room. The large vault on the corner has its own separate entrance (as was so

often the case with public bars in times gone by), terrazzo floor and long bar counter, richly detailed and endowed with mahogany screens. In one corner it is clear where the former off-sales has been incorporated. The other rooms retain much fixed seating and the bar parlour still has its bell-pushes and original fireplace. Listed in 1994 following a pilot study of Greater Manchester pubs by CAMRA for English Heritage.

Eccles

295 Liverpool Road, M30 0QN
www.joseph-holt.com/Joseph-Holt-
Pubs-130-Stanley-Arms.aspx
Not listed
LPA: Salford

⇌ Patricroft

*The corridor divides the pub into
the vault and servery (right) with
two further rooms to the left*

Stanley Arms

A small, simple street-corner local with etched windows throughout. It was purchased by Joseph Holt's brewery in 1909 so the work we see today no doubt dates from shortly after this. The drinkers' lobby-corridor is L-shaped, separating the front vault and servery from the rear two rooms. This corridor features green tilework and glazed counter screens to the servery. The small vault has two old benches and an irregularly shaped counter. Across the passage, a smoke room has original fixed benches and bell pushes. A former cottage has been incorporated to create a back room out of a former kitchen, hence the impressive cast-iron fireplace.

Farnworth

1 Glynne Street, BL4 7DN
01204 578282
www.bravoinns.com
Grade II listed
LPA: Bolton
⇌ Moses Gate

The woodwork around
the opening to the servery
in the commercial room is
a quintessential piece of
1920s design

Shakespeare

98

Built in 1926 for Bolton brewers
Magee Marshall and largely
unchanged since. Beyond the main
entrance is a spacious drinking
lobby, whose rich counter is topped
by a carved shield (one of several
such adorning the woodwork).
The tilework, unfortunately, has
been papered over. The lounge to
the left has good panelling and a
Tudor-style fireplace. At the front
right is the 'News Room' (so named
on a door-plate), complete with
richly decorated counter, fixed seats
and the original coat hooks. The
back room is described on the
door-plate as the 'Commercial Room'
and has another fine counter.
A door at the side of the pub accesses
the off-sales, now lost in most pubs but here untouched, albeit unused.
The final ground-floor room (rear left) seems to be a private room
brought into pub use and now houses a pool table.

Gorton

927 Hyde Road, M18 7FB
0161 223 5565
Grade II listed
LPA: Manchester
🍺
⇌ Belle Vue

The tiled corridor and
hatch to the servery

Plough

99

A basic, but friendly, drinkers' pub of red brick with some terracotta
details, whose layout is virtually unaltered since the building was
constructed in 1893. The main entrance leads to a black and white
floored corridor/drinking lobby with lots of lovely green tiling in
the dado. To the right is the vault which is a splendid example of a
late-Victorian public bar. It has a richly carved bar counter, ornate

bar-back in the Jacobean style,
and plain, bare-bench seating with
raked back-rests. The corridor
leads on to what is now termed the
snug (front left) and lounge (rear)
which have historic features such
as bell-pushes. The pool room
has been stripped of any historic
interest. On the side road is a
doorway to the former off-sales
compartment and upstairs is a
meeting room. Listed in 1994
following a pilot study of Greater
Manchester pubs by CAMRA
for English Heritage.

Heywood

Peel Lane, OL10 4PR
01706 369705
Not listed
LPA: Rochdale

Grapes

A 1920s estate pub which has kept most of its floor plan and fittings. The entrance has plentiful tiling and mosaic floors, and leads to a drinking lobby with original bar counter (but new top) and bar back. The two screens around the doors to the toilets off the lobby are most unusual and no comparable examples are presently known. A corresponding screen surrounds a phone booth but this seems to be new work, probably installed by the owners, Sam Smiths, who have a strong record for introducing period/historicising features. The room to the right of the bar has been slightly reduced in size to create a passageway. The vault in the south-east corner has basic bench seating plus the original counter, whilst in the pool room are baffles by the door and more bench seating. Mounted on the counter fronts are horizontal metal bands – is this original Art Deco work or something introduced by Sam Smiths?! The Art Deco-style toilets, with simple coloured tilework, are worth a visit.

The drinking lobby

The featured pubs in
Manchester city centre

Manchester: city centre

50 Great Bridgewater Street,
M1 5LE
0161 236 5895
www.britonsprotection.co.uk
Grade II listed
LPA: Manchester
🍺 🍴
⇌ Oxford Road
🚏 St Peter's Square

At the angle of the L-shaped corridor
enveloping the public bar and servery

Detail of the tiling in the corridor
showing typical decoration of *c.*1930

Britons Protection

Remodelling around 1930 bestowed extensive amounts of tiling and
quality woodwork to the interior here. The public bar is along the
front, surrounded by a terrazzo tile-floored corridor, beyond which
are a pair of back rooms (smoke room and snug) served by a double-
doored hatch with screens at the back of the servery. Especially good
features are the moulded ceiling and bar furniture in the public
bar and corridor, the 1930s copper fireplace in the smoke room
and the tiling in the passage, which also runs up the staircase. The
massive 1930s urinals and tiled walls in the gents' are also worth
inspection. The pub opened in 1811 and is said to have been used for
recruitment during the Napoleonic wars hence, it seems, the name.

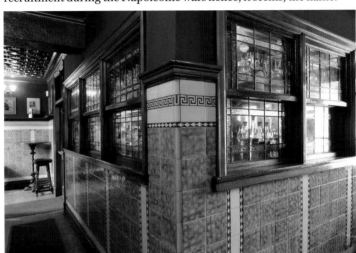

Manchester: city centre

86 Portland Street, M1 4GX
Grade II listed
LPA: Manchester
🍺
⇌ Oxford Road
🚏 St Peter's Square

The front room looking towards
the servery

Circus Tavern

A tiny pub in the very centre of
bustling central Manchester. The
building, originally a house, is just
one bay wide. A corridor on the
left leads to two tiny, simply-fitted
public rooms, separated by a
vertically boarded partition. The
miniscule servery is under the
stairs and large enough for only
one person to serve. Its design,
with its glazed superstructure,
suggests a 1930s origin. Both
rooms have old fixed benches:
until very recently there were
baffles at the entrances to the
rooms but unfortunately all but

one have been destroyed. The fireplaces are replacements. More than 40 customers and the place is packed. Sadly the interior is heavily cluttered with photographs, making full appreciation difficult. Listed in 1994 following a pilot study of Greater Manchester pubs by CAMRA for English Heritage.

Manchester: city centre

46 Shudehill, M4 4AA

0161 832 4737

Grade II listed

LPA: Manchester

≈ Victoria

☖ Shudehill

The drinking lobby, looking towards the rear room

Hare & Hounds

103

An exceptionally complete interior, from a remodelling of 1925, when the blue-brown ceramic frontage was also installed. The entrance leads to a through corridor which bulges in the centre to form a drinking lobby in front of the servery (just as at the Swan with Two Necks, Stockport [114]). The half-height wall tiling here is similar to that in the Britons Protection (101). The front bar has similar tiling and a counter which supports a glazed superstructure modelled to resemble sash windows. Above the counter in the central lobby are hatches and glazed panels (but not the lower screens – although the pulleys which operated them are still visible). The back room retains fixed seating and other features from the 1925 refit. The porches serving both front and back entrances are also lavishly tiled.

Manchester: city centre

73 Rochdale Road, M4 4HY
0161 832 5914
www.marblebeers.com/
marble-arch
Grade II listed
LPA: Manchester

≷ Victoria
🚇 Shudehill

The most lavish display of tilework
inside a Manchester pub

Marble Arch   104

Built in 1888 to designs by local architects Darbyshire & Smith, the
ground-floor is faced with granite and its Gothic detailing is very
unusual: the style was more associated with churches and, therefore,
seemed inappropriate for pubs. The interior is truly impressive – a long,
narrow room whose walls are lined with glazed bricks in shades of
yellow, cream and green. Above is a wonderful frieze flourishing a
litany of alcoholic (and cordial) delights. The ceiling features more
glazed bricks forming low jack-arches on iron girders, at the ends of
which are ceramic brackets. Beware the sloping floor, especially as you
may be distracted by its blue and cream mosaic work inset with flower
motifs. After a tasteless refurbishment in 1954 the arches, walls and
mosaic flooring remained concealed until revealed again in 1989 and
the present counter, fireplace and seating were installed. The Marble
Brewery was established at the rear of the building in 1997 although
brewing now takes place off-site.

Manchester: city centre

52 Cross Street, M2 7AR
0161 832 2245
tomsmanchester.
thevictorianchophousecompany.
com
Grade II listed
LPA: Manchester
🍺 🍴
🚃 Market Street

Mr Thomas's Chop House

105

An exuberant example of *fin de siècle* architecture in an ornate
Jacobean style. The interior comprises four spaces, one behind the
other, demarcated by blue-green ceramic arches. A similarly coloured
dado runs along much of the walling and the third compartment
from the front also has plain cream tiling, reaching up to the ceiling.
The small area at the back has an outstanding ceramic fireplace.
Tiled flooring runs throughout the pub. The main changes have
been to the bar furniture, which is mostly modern: a photograph
in the historic picture gallery in the gents' shows how the servery
was formerly located in the third compartment from the front.
Over half of this fine interior operates as a classy restaurant. The
painter L. S. Lowry was a regular here in its less upmarket days.

Looking towards the rear

Manchester: city centre

127 Great Bridgewater Street,
M1 5JQ

0161 236 6364

Grade II listed

LPA: Manchester

🍺

⇌ Oxford Road

🚃 St Peter's Square

The whole of the exterior is
covered with ceramic work

The glorious fittings in the public
bar (Michael Slaughter)

Peveril of the Peak

106

An amazing sight with its ceramic-faced outside walls, but the interior
is very special too. A dog-leg corridor serves as a drinking lobby,
lined with a dado of green and cream tiles and defined on the west
side by a glazed screen forming the back of the servery. The most

impressive room is that facing
Great Bridgewater Street – it has
baffles by the door, fixed seating,
bell-pushes, a Victorian fireplace
and a bar counter with fielded
panels and pilasters. The stained
glass screen over the counter only
dates from 1982 but was skilfully
crafted to match the panels in
the lobby. The rear lounge and
smoke room have fixed seating
and bell-pushes, the latter also
having an elaborate Victorian
marble fire surround. The pub was
saved from demolition (for a road
scheme) after campaigning by
CAMRA and others in the 1980s.

Manchester: Withington

520 Wilmslow Road, M20 4BT
0161 445 4565
Not listed
LPA: Manchester

Turnpike

107

Something of a rarity in this guide, being one of the *very* few post-war interiors in this book (cf. 135, 194 and 245). This is because pubs built or refitted between 1945 and 1970 came to be regarded as unfashionable and were invariably altered again. The work here dates mainly from the early 1960s when the pub expanded into the shop next door and gained its partly stone frontage. The left-hand bar formed the original pub and the ply-panel bar counter is likely to date from the 1930s. However, the bar-back shelves, quirky fire surround faced with cobblestones, and also the radiators with wood surrounds have a distinct 1960s flavour. The lounge has full-height, characteristically *c.*1960 corrugated wall panelling. Its counter, with its leatherette padded sections, is a 2002 copy of the lost sixties original – Sam Smiths, the owning brewery, has a considerable track record for reinstating features removed from their pubs in less enlightened times. The fixed seating is original as is the random-coursed green slate fireplace.

1960s chic in the lounge

Oldham

178 Union Street, OL1 1EN
0161 633 2642
Not listed

🚉 Oldham Mumps

Royal Oak

108

A three-storey brick pub close to the centre of Oldham and which was given a major refit about 1930. The key feature here is the servery, a splendid semi-circular structure which projects forward into what is, in effect, a variant of the typical regional drinking lobby arrangement. It is a stunning piece, fully provided with counter screens. The back of the servery fits squarely on to the lounge at the front, to which it is linked by a hatch with counter screening. The *c.*1930 work provided large expanses of two-tone tiling on the walls, a good deal of which has been papered over. The two rooms on the left have been amalgamated into one. On the side street there is an entrance to a rare, complete off-sales compartment which has a hatch to the servery. There is a large upstairs bar with an original servery and mock half-timbering but it is just used for functions. Attractive stained glass on the landing.

The servery and its remarkable curved screen

Coloured window lighting the stairs

Rochdale

470 Bury Road, OL11 5EU
01706 645635
Grade II listed
LPA: Rochdale
🍺 🍴
🚆 Rochdale then Bus

Cemetery Hotel

109

Largely unchanged since Edwardian times, the pub takes its dark-sounding name from the nearby cemetery. The entrance porch and drinking lobby are both richly tiled, including lovely Art Nouveau-style wall panels and friezes in shades of green, blue and orange. The front left parlour (no. 2 on the door) is expensively fitted-out with four seating areas, created by substantial part-glazed mahogany baffles with Classical columns. This splendid room also sports a distinctive fireplace with a rich blue ceramic surround and a wooden overmantel: there is also one original etched and cut window. On the front right, a small pool room (no. 1) is rather plain, with fixed seating, a window advertising 'Crown Ales', and a full-blown range with the maker's name on it (but surely this room was never a kitchen?). The snug (no. 3) retains fixed seating with a baffle, but its fireplace is a replacement. All three rooms have attractive Art Nouveau-style decorative glass in their upper parts. In the heart of the pub is the servery and drinking lobby, but the former consists largely of modern work.

Edwardian elegance in the parlour

Salford

350 Eccles New Road, M5 5NN
0161 736 1203
Grade II listed
LPA: Salford
🚋 Weaste

Coach & Horses   110

An unusually intact multi-roomed locals' pub built in 1913 for the Rochdale & Manor brewery. The public bar occupies the right-hand corner, surrounded by a corridor, off which rooms lead to left and right. First (on the right-hand side) comes the 'Outdoor Department', normally locked and sadly now used for storage, but essentially intact. Next, the lounge has original fixed seating with bell-pushes though the doorway is now smaller than it once was, as can be seen from the still-existing old door-frame. A small smoke room has, like the other rooms, lovely etching in the glass door panel but little else of interest. The corridor itself has a fine black and white quarry-tile floor and a dado of green tiles. The servery has an imposing timber and glass screen. Another three sections of this screen are in the public bar along with old fixed seating with baffles – but the fireplace has gone. Statutorily listed in January 2012 following a successful application by CAMRA.

The servery and drinking lobby

Stalybridge

Stalybridge Railway Station
Rassbottom Street, SK15 1RF
0161 303 0007
www.stalybridgebuffetbar.co.uk
Not listed
LPA: Tameside
 🍴
≷ Stalybridge

Station Buffet

111

Housed in platform buildings that were part of this busy station's reconstruction in 1885, this is one of only two largely intact licensed buffets on the national rail network that date from before the Second World War (the other is at Bridlington, East Yorkshire [196]). The old core here, the little-altered main Buffet Bar, has the original warming hearth at one end, a practical, straight bar counter with marble top (a rarity in itself, but cf. 13, 45, 58, 196, 236 and 268) running the full-length of the room and ornate little back-fitting units between

the outside windows behind the servery. Until 1996, when the establishment was greatly extended into adjacent sections of the old station buildings (a scheme which won the national CAMRA/ English Heritage Pub Refurbishment Award in 1998) it consisted only of the main Buffet Bar plus a conservatory extension. The present conservatory is a modern replica dating from 2009.

The main bar (Michael Slaughter, 2005)

Stockport: centre

195 Northgate Road
Edgeley, SK3 9NJ
0161 476 0097
Grade II listed
LPA: Stockport
🍺
≷ Stockport

Alexandra

112

In this fine 1911 building, only the bar-back and off-sales area have suffered alteration, though the latter still exists intact between the bar back and a locked door. The spacious hall, much used for stand-up drinking, has multi-coloured Art Nouveau-style tiling and, beneath the carpet, a marble mosaic floor (how wonderful if this could be revealed once more, as it was at the Stork Hotel, Birkenhead [118]). The servery has a curved mahogany bar with screenwork above but

the bar-back fitting has been replaced and a low suspended ceiling inserted. Rooms lead off from each corner, all with their names etched in the door glass – tap room, smoke room, bar parlour and commercial. All the rooms have fixed seating, coloured glass and original fireplaces. Decoration continues up the stairs which are lit by a wonderful window with coloured glass. An attached billiard room has a vestibule entrance, painted glass skylight and bay window with billiard balls etched in glass. Listed in 1994 following a pilot study of Greater Manchester pubs by CAMRA for English Heritage.

The servery and drinking lobby with rooms radiating off

Stockport: centre

23 Millgate, SK1 2LX
0161 480 2185
www.arden-arms.co.uk
Grade II listed
LPA: Stockport
🍺 🍴
⇌ Stockport

Remarkably, the Arden Arms
has a public room only
accessed through the servery

Arden Arms

113

This fine 19th-century town centre pub has
a well-preserved interior, replete with
simple wooden panelling, bench seating
and quarry-tiled floors plus, in the lobby,
a floor-to-ceiling screened bar – still with
its rising sashes. Three rooms open off this
lobby whilst the fourth, the snug, offers a
most unusual arrangement as it can only be
accessed by passing through the bar – with
permission from the staff. Only two other
pubs are known to have rooms like this –
the Bridge Inn, Topsham, Devon (25), and
Ye Horns Inn at Goosnargh, Lancashire (46).
In the vault are rare 'bell tables' where bell-
pushes sit in the centre of tables rather than,
as is usual, on the walls. The fixing of hand-
pumps to the bar-back, rather than the counter, is also a rarity. Some
structural alterations have taken place in recent years, notably the
incorporation of the once private rear right-hand room to make a larger
pub space, but the integrity of the historic interior remains largely intact.

Stockport: centre

36 Princes Street, SK1 1RY
0161 480 2341
Grade II listed
LPA: Stockport
🍺 🍴
⇌ Stockport

The smoke room at the rear is a
delightful panelled space

Swan with Two Necks

114

A long, narrow pub which has changed little since being rebuilt in 1926,
just before it was bought by local brewers Robinsons. The interior is
simply organised and the extensive use of wall panelling is typical of
inter-war pubs. To the left of the tiled and panelled entrance lobby is

the vault, with plentiful panelling, a portion of which was added quite recently to cover up a fireplace. The other door from the entrance leads into a drinking lobby, which is essentially an expansion of the corridor and faces the servery. Beyond this is the delightful smoke room which, with its Tudor-style fireplace and oak panelling, has a particularly warm and comfortable atmosphere. A small room at the back came into pub use during the 1960s.

Stockport: Heaton Norris

258 Green Lane, SK4 2NA
0161 432 2044
www.hydesbrewery.co.uk
Grade II listed
LPA: Stockport

Nursery Inn   115

Built in 1939, this genteel pub lies in a delightful, quiet neighbourhood. It is virtually unchanged, sporting a clean sub-Georgian design and its original multi-room layout. As well as a large lounge (front left), there is a bar lobby area, smoke room (rear centre), vault with a separate side entrance and a plain, upstairs function room – plus an immaculate, very well-used bowling green at the rear. Light oak is used generously throughout and the windows in all three main rooms are charmingly embellished with stained glass horticultural motifs such as a spade, watering can and rose. Also notable are the rows of 'silk glass' panels over the serveries in the lounge and vault, with paintings of drink-related items: for example, glasses of beer, a tankard, a glass and bottle of wine, a water jug and hand-pumps – all very much in the 1930s style. There are bell-pushes in the lounge and smoke room but not, of course, in the vault. The Nursery was CAMRA's national Pub of the Year in 2001 and was statutorily listed in 2011.

A large, genteel lounge is located at the front

Westhoughton

2 Market Street, BL5 3AN
01942 811991
www.joseph-holt.com/Joseph-Holt-
Pubs-118-White-Lion-WH.aspx
Not listed
LPA: Bolton

The 1920s servery in the
public bar with its tiled front
and counter screens

White Lion   116

This corner-site pub
was bought by the
Joseph Holt brewery
in 1925 and the fittings
no doubt date from
very shortly after that.
The servery is the
centrepiece, with its
still-working etched
glass rising sash screens
and tiled counters
which, together, form
the most impressive

features of this pub. It is surrounded by a drinking lobby, the vault
and the so-called 'Ugly Room'. There is also a small bar parlour
(the 'John Hyde Suite', commemorating a former regular) and a
refitted darts room. Bell-pushes for table service survive in three
rooms, as does a good selection of etched glass.

Wigan

47 Springfield Road
Springfield, WN6 7BB
01942 201203
Grade II listed
LPA: Wigan

⇌ Wigan North Western or Wallgate

Springfield   117

An opulent Edwardian pub-cum-hotel of 1903 designed for the Oldfield
Brewery of Poolstock, Wigan by local architects Heaton & Ralph. The
main entrance leads to a spacious drinking lobby with an extraordinary,
multi-tiered counter screen: it has columns, glazed sashes and is partly
curved. There is also lots of decorative dado tiling. Much original layout
survives: a small public bar along Rylands Street; commercial room
(front right, named in the etched glass); news room (front left, once
so-named in the glass), now amalgamated with a sitting area behind a
broad arch to the lobby and leading to the spacious billiard room; and

another room left (now crudely opened
out). A bell-box in the lobby has various
room names (including 'Front D[oo]r' but,
puzzlingly, there are anomalies: no news
room, for example). Changes, probably in
the 1970s or 1980s, involve the remarkable
screenwork being reproduced (without
sash provision) on the public bar side of the
servery; linking of the front two spaces left
of the main entrance; and the opening up
of the rear left room (possibly originally
gents' only). There was an off-sales on the
side street but this has been lost as, sadly,
has a massive bowling green.

The screen to the servery in the lobby area
(Michael Slaughter)

Riches around Manchester

The Manchester area has a fine variety of historic pubs. The city centre alone offers half a dozen in this guide, all within walking distance of one another. They range from the tiny two-room Circus Tavern (102), through fine inter-war refits at the Britons Protection (101) and Hare & Hounds (103) to the glorious Victorian tiled interior at the Marble Arch (104). Another remarkable knot of unspoilt interiors is in Eccles where Joseph Holt's brewery built three pubs in the period 1903–6 which feature in this guide: they all retain their multiple rooms and deploy the various arts of pub-building that came to fulfilment in the late 19th century – tiles and mosaics, etched glass and carved woodwork. The still-functioning billiard room at the Lamb Hotel (95) is one of the best surviving in any pub.

Many pubs have drinking lobbies. A common northern plan is for there to be a lobby placed in front of the servery which sits between two rooms (see p. 195 for such a plan): examples are at the Hare & Hounds, Manchester, and the Swan with Two Necks, Stockport (114). Another common plan, as in Liverpool, was for the public bar to be sited on a street corner with an L-shaped corridor wrapping round the back of it, as at the Lamb Hotel, Eccles, and the Britons Protection, Manchester. Public bars are often known as (the) 'vault(s). Other room names following northern practice are 'commercial room' (e.g. Shakespeare, Farnworth [98]) and 'news rooms' (e.g. Springfield, Wigan [117]). An unusual name for an off-sales is found at the Alexandra, Stockport (112) – 'order department'.

A particular treasure is the Nursery Inn at Heaton Norris (115). Built in 1939, it epitomises the 'improved pub house' of the interwar years. Its multi-room interior remains intact and is elegantly fitted out with some charming details. Outside there are beautifully

The Swan with Two Necks, Stockport (114), where the corridor expands to form a drinking lobby in front of the servery

cared-for, well-used bowling greens. Pubs like this would not be built again. For something completely different, Stalybridge (111) is home to one of the two largely intact historic licensed station buffets, along with Bridlington, East Yorkshire (196) – and famous as a haven of real ale and cider.

At Altrincham the appealing community pub, the Railway (92) (p. 13), is proof of the importance of statutory protection for saving pubs with historic interiors. Promoters of a great Behemoth of an out-of-town shopping centre wanted to demolish it, but an enlightened Grade II listing in 1993, on English Heritage's recommendation, proved the saviour of this popular local.

The bowling greens at the Nursery Inn, Heaton Norris, Stockport (115), are still very much is use

MERSEYSIDE

Birkenhead

41 Price Street, CH41 6JN
0151 647 7506
Grade II listed
LPA: Liverpool

🍺 🍴

⇌ Hamilton Square or
   Conway Park

Stork Hotel

118

A splendid example of lavish Edwardian refitting, carried out by
Threlfalls' brewery of Salford around 1905. The external tilework gives
some idea of the superb interior which is laid out with a public bar on
the street corner, enclosed by a corridor with other rooms leading off
as at the Lion Tavern (120) and Prince Arthur (124), both in Liverpool.
The best place to admire the pub is from the cosy semi-circular alcove
where the mosaic-floored corridor sweeps in a curve through 90 degrees.
The back of the servery is formed by a screen with a dado covered in

blue, yellow and buff tiles with
Art Nouveau detailing, above
which is a glazed screen with
richly decorated glass. The tiling
was made by George Swift Ltd
of the Swan Tile Works,
Liverpool and extends to other
parts of the pub too, even down
to the loos (the gents' tiling may
be inter-war). Leading off the
corridor are two other rooms,
named as a news room and bar
parlour. There is extensive
original seating and bell-push
arrangements. Note the lovely
fireplace where the corridor
turns. Mostly modern fittings in
the public bar although the
dado tiling, with a dominant
brown colour rather than blue,
is original.

The corridor which wraps round
the back of the servery

The featured pubs in
Liverpool city centre

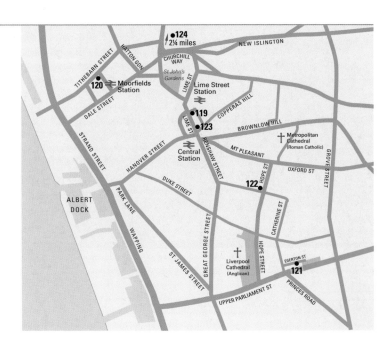

Liverpool: city centre

43 Lime Street, L1 1JQ

0151 707 6027

www.thecrownliverpool.co.uk

Grade II listed

LPA: Liverpool

🍺 🍴

≋ Lime Street

The front bar

Crown Hotel   `119`

The Crown, with its riotous decoration, is a dramatic sight on emerging
from Lime Street station. It was built about 1905, at the height of
Liverpool's prosperity, by Walkers of Warrington. There are now two
ground-floor rooms. That at the rear seems intact but the front one is
now a large open area, the two disused doors indicating that it would
have had three partitioned areas originally. The finest features are the
amazingly ornate plasterwork in the ceilings and cornices. At the front,
the bar counter has a copper front and an interesting bar-back with

mannered detail (the mirrors are clearly modern). On the right is a mightily impressive ceramic fireplace. Sadly, this room has lost nearly all its once-superb decorative window glass (some survives facing the station). The rear room (named, unusually, as 'Bar Room' in the door glass) is fitted out with high-quality panelling all around plus a fine fireplace with a copper central facing, tiled strips either side and a mirror above. A winding staircase, under a glazed dome, leads to an upstairs room: it has a modest frieze of crests and nice stained glass windows but the servery is new.

Crown Hotel: front room fireplace

Liverpool: city centre

67 Moorfields, L2 2BP

0151 236 1734

www.liontavern.com

Grade II listed

LPA: Liverpool

🍺 🍴

🚊 Moorfields

Lion Tavern   120

This richly appointed pub has a layout similar to others on Merseyside, notably the Stork Hotel, Birkenhead (118), and the Prince Arthur, Liverpool (124); that is with an L-shaped corridor enclosing the public bar on the street corner, and with spaces leading off it. A plan of 1903 shows the public bar as now, but in 1915 the Lion expanded into the building next door. The corridor was then created along with a news room (so-named in the window glass) in the newly acquired area, and a lounge beneath a skylight (the dividing walls were taken down in 1967). The corridor has a mosaic floor and a lovely Art Nouveau tiled dado, above which is a timber and etched glass screen with openings allowing service to drinkers in the corridor. The back fitting in the public bar seems to be Victorian: the dado tiling here is to the same design as in the corridor. There is a fine set of old carved screens in the front windows carrying advertising, something that is occasionally seen in Scotland but rarely in England. The eponymous Lion was a locomotive built for the Liverpool & Manchester Railway in 1838 and is displayed at the Museum of Liverpool.

The back of the servery, which is enveloped by the L-shaped corridor

Liverpool: city centre

2–6 Egerton Street, L8 7LY
0151 709 3443
Grade II listed
LPA: Liverpool

Peter Kavanagh's

This quirky interior was refitted in 1929 by Peter Kavanagh, licensee from 1897 to 1950. The historic core has the common northern layout of front and rear rooms with a drinking lobby/servery in between. Both rooms have fixed seating, above which are large murals commissioned by Kavanagh from Scottish artist Eric Robinson: at the front are scenes from Dickens and at the rear by Hogarth. There is also much attractive stained glass made by artist William English, with seafaring themes in the 'Dickens Room' and a miscellaneous selection in the 'Hogarth'. Kavanagh also introduced much jokey woodwork, including four panels with scenes set in what seems to be the 16th century, and numerous faces, including ones resembling Peter K. himself. He was an inventor, for example, of the highly distinctive tables with grilles covering bowls for water to extinguish cigarette ends. The pub was extended in 1964 with a new lounge and again in 1977, taking in 6 Egerton Street. Formerly the Grapes, it was renamed after the remarkable Mr Kavanagh in 1978.

A bench-end caricaturing its creator

The Dickens Room: the tables were designed by Peter Kavanagh himself

Liverpool: city centre

36 Hope St, L1 9BX
0151 707 2837
www.nicholsonspubs.co.uk/the
philharmonicdiningroomsliverpool
Grade II* listed
LPA: Liverpool

⇌ Lime Street or Central

Philharmonic Dining Rooms

This spectacular pub is rivalled only by the nearby Vines (123) and Belfast's Crown Bar (266). Built about 1900 for Robert Cain's brewery at the height of Liverpool's fortunes to designs by local architect Walter Thomas, the exterior is waywardly eclectic, the high point being the glorious gates (the best such Art Nouveau work in Britain). They lead into what is, in effect, an up-market version of a northern drinking lobby, off which other rooms radiate. The customer is met by the whole gamut of embellishment that makes the 'the Phil' so special – plasterwork, mosaic (even on the counter), mahogany, copper reliefs (by German-American artist H. Bloomfield Bare) and stained glass. In the delightful fireplace-alcove the drinker is presided over by stained glass heroes of the Boer War (being fought as the pub went up).

Splendour on Merseyside

The golden age of British pub-building was around 1900. This coincided with the height of Liverpool's prosperity as an international port and trading centre, when it was one of the richest and most splendid cities on Earth. Not surprising then that it produced pubs to match. This is the context of the Philharmonic (today with Dining Rooms added to the title [122]) and Vines (123) which are only rivalled in the UK by the Crown Bar, Belfast (266). Both were built by brewer Robert Cain (1826–1907) whose family settled here from Ireland in 1827. Cain rose to become one of Liverpool's most

St Cecilia, patron saint of music, presides in the news room at the 'Phil'

successful businessmen. The drinks sold in these places were, no doubt, rather more expensive than in more modest pubs – and the ordinary working man would probably not have felt welcome. Over the road from Lime Street station is the Crown Hotel (119) which has some truly spectacular Edwardian décor.

Down the social (and architectural) scale there are other pubs on Merseyside which are still

very ornate and have a distinctive layout. These are represented here by the Lion Tavern (120) and Prince Arthur (124) in Liverpool and the Stork Hotel in Birkenhead (118) which were all refitted in ambitious schemes at the start of the 20th century. They have street-corner public bars enclosed by an L-shaped drinking/service corridor off which other rooms lead. Each pub is splendidly enriched by tiles, decorative glass and woodwork.

Another facet of Merseyside pub culture is the survival (although only just) of table service. The bell-pushes on the better rooms of our pubs are mostly defunct, but a few pubs do still have the civilised practice of serving customers at their tables. One of these is the Volunteer Canteen at Waterloo (127). The bell-pushes in the end room at the Scotch Piper, Lydiate (125) work, but are not responded to.

Another localism is a room name – the news room. It is not exclusive to Merseyside but seems rather more prevalent here than elsewhere. Examples are at the Lion Tavern and Philharmonic in Liverpool and the Stork Hotel in Birkenhead. It conjures up the idea of sitting down in one of the better-appointed rooms of a traditional pub, in pre-TV days, and perusing the happenings in the world (or picking the winners at Aintree) whilst enjoying a pint.

Ebullient tilework characterises the exterior of the Stork, Birkenhead (118), which was remodelled about 1905

Facing the counter are two magnificent panelled rooms, originally a smoke room (left) and news room (right, with St Cecilia, patroness of music, in stained glass). Further small (now linked) spaces line the angle of the streets. A small office lies within the servery. At the back is a vast room, said to have been a billiard room (or was it a restaurant?), sumptuously embellished with a huge frieze incorporating the crowning of Apollo (over the door) and 'The Murmur of the Sea' (opposite) by artist Charles Allen: lavish fireplaces, panelling and copper reliefs (again by Bare). Finally, the gents' – the best in any British pub (when not in use, ladies may inspect).

Ceramics, wood, plasterwork and copper panels create an interior of extraordinary richness

The huge rear room is opulently fitted out with woodwork, plaster reliefs and copper panels

Liverpool: city centre

81 Lime Street, L1 1JQ
Tel: 0151 709 3977
Grade II* listed
LPA: Liverpool
🍴 (lunchtime)
🚆 Lime Street
Restricted opening hours

The lounge and its fireplace

Vines

123

The Vines was built in 1907 and is, like its elder sister the Philharmonic (122), one of the great show pubs of the country. Both were designed by local architect Walter Thomas for Liverpool brewer, Robert Cain, and was named after Albert B. Vines who opened a pub here in 1867. Behind the extravagant Baroque exterior is a magnificent sequence of rooms with opulent embellishment. On the right is the public bar: less lavish, of course, than the rest and altered in 1989 by the incorporation of a snug and the cutting back of the bar counter (which can be readily made out). The decorative ebullience explodes in the lounge to the left with its columns, copper-fronted counter and caryatid-flanked fireplace. The latter is back-to-back with that in the smoke room, which carries Viking ships in relief. Here customers, comfortably seated in the alcoves, are surrounded by wood panelling and deep ornamented friezes populated by busy figures of chubby cherubic figures. Here they would have been served at table (hence the bell-pushes): all this is presided over by signs of the Zodiac in the ceiling. Beyond the corridor, which runs behind the servery, is a vast high-ceilinged room (as at 'The Phil'), now called the 'Heritage Suite'. This magnificent room (not always open) has giant Corinthian pilasters, an oval skylight, panelling and an enormous marble fireplace. Closed Tue–Thu.

Liverpool: Walton

93 Rice Lane, L9 1AD
Grade II listed
LPA: Liverpool
⇌ Rice Lane

Wall tiling in the corridor and public bar

Screenwork round the servery

Prince Arthur　　124

This is an out-of-town drinkers' pub, probably refurbished at the very start of the 20th century. The decorative glass and insignia outside reveal that this was done by Walker's of Warrington and give a hint of the tremendous exuberance within. Pride of place goes to the public bar, set on the street corner. Here bright red tiles line the walls, the stubby screens and even cover the counter front. The tiling continues round the L-shaped corridor which wraps round the public bar in a typical Merseyside arrangement, as at the Stork Hotel, Birkenhead (118), and Lion Tavern, Liverpool (120). This has highly unusual openings to the servery with lovely jewel-like glazing. At the rear is a large smoke room. Gents should not miss the hefty triple urinals.

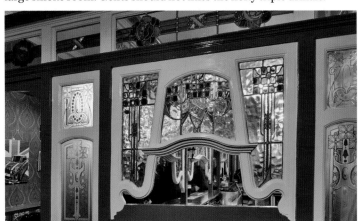

Lydiate

Southport Road, L31 4HD
0151 526 0503
Grade II* listed
LPA: Sefton

The public bar

Scotch Piper　　125

Claimed as the oldest inn in Lancashire, this whitewashed, thatched and cruck-framed building has been dated by dendrochronology to around 1450 (extended north in the 18th century). It is said to have been in pub use since the 15th century but this is perhaps a matter of wishful thinking. A sequence of three rooms runs the length of the building with the public bar on the left. Here a cruck truss is exposed and there is simple bench seating against two of the walls: until 1997 service was via a hatch. Two other rooms are reached from the corridor. The far one was originally a storage area/animal shed and later a living room: it still retains working bell pushes from the days of table service. The fittings are mostly quite simple and the pub still has outside loos. It was taken over by Burtonwood brewery in 1945, after which the brick fireplaces and the concrete 'half-timbering' over the fireplaces were put in.

Sutton Leach

Mill Lane, WA9 4HN
01744 813994
www.thewheaty.com
Not listed
LPA: St Helens

🍺 🍴   The public bar

Wheatsheaf   126

Designed in 1936 for brewers Greenall Whitley, this brick- and half-timbered roadhouse retains much of its original multi-room layout. The rooms, ranging from public bar (front left), a buffet (front right) to a small dining room (rear right) are named in etched glass in the doors. The bar fittings, fire surrounds and seating are mostly original. A former verandah (the long, narrow bar at rear centre) overlooks a beautifully

maintained bowling green area, but has been truncated at one end for the present 'cellar'. The original cellaring was on the first floor, serviced by a hoist behind the now blocked entrance in the frontage. The Wheatsheaf has suffered dramatically from mining subsidence – hence the disconcerting (non-alcohol induced!) sense of disequilibrium caused by the sloping floors. Much of the interior is concealed by the vast collection of football and rugby shirts.

Waterloo

45 East Street, L22 8QR
07891 407464
Grade II listed
LPA: Sefton

🍺

 Waterloo

Volunteer Canteen   127

A pub since 1871, the Volunteer Canteen was refurbished by Higsons of Toxteth in 1924 since when there have been few major changes. The brewer's name lives on in the window glass. A central entrance leads into a panelled corridor, to the right of which is an opening to the servery and either side of this are service hatches with glazed panels above. On the left is a wide arch which is contemporary with the rest and opens

into the lounge. The bell-pushes were recently removed but this is still a rare example of a pub where customers are served at their tables except, of course, at busy times (see right). The cupboards and rather crude mirror on the back wall are modern work although the fire surround and seating are evidently of the 1920s. The toilets retain their original 1924 doors, each labelled with the appropriate gender in the glazing. Opens 2pm weekdays.

The servery

Of table service, bells and prices

In days gone by customers could order drinks in the 'better' rooms of pubs by pressing a bell and a member of the serving staff, or a dedicated waiter, would come over and take the order. Where there were several rooms to be served, a disc (or similar) would oscillate in a little window in an annunciator box which was labelled with the names of the rooms. Not all pubs had bell systems and in some waiters would walk around looking for likely customers, as this writer can testify from his student days in Manchester in the early/mid 1960s.

By the 1960s table service was only widespread in West Yorkshire and the North West. It is still practised at a number of pubs on Merseyside, such as the Volunteer Canteen, Waterloo (127). It is also found at the Kings Head, Bootle, Cumbria (15), and in Scotland at the Clep Bar, Dundee (256). As in the past, a small tip is expected.

It is a curious thing but there is a definite geography of bell-pushes in English pubs. They are common from the Midlands northwards but very rare in the south. It is impossible to conjecture why this should be so because we know that waiter service did take place in many London pubs a century ago. In London CAMRA knows of only one pub with historic bell-pushes and this is at the Forester in Ealing, west London (91): perhaps the device was so unfamiliar to customers that, when the pub was put up in 1909, it was felt necessary to add the word 'BELL' beside it!

Drinks in 'better' rooms attracted a slightly higher price than in the public bar, which also reflected a higher standard of furnishing and the possibility of table service. Nowadays everything is one price throughout the pub and today's drinkers would probably be shocked if they discovered they were paying more in one room than another. Until 2010 there was such a difference at the Cricketers, Woodford Green in north-east London, but now the only pub CAMRA knows where such differential pricing still takes place is at the White Swan, Reading Street, Broadstairs in Kent, where it stands at 4p on the price of a pint (neither pub is in this guide).

Bell-push at the Forester, West Ealing (91), with explanatory caption!

A bell-push in the magnificent smoke room at the Vines, Liverpool (123)

No need to go up to the bar at the Volunteer Canteen, Waterloo (127) (Michael Slaughter)

The 1930s annunciator box and its associated bell at the Holly Bush, Bollington, Cheshire (8)

NORFOLK

Kenninghall

East Church Street, NR16 2EP
01953 887849
www.redlionkenninghall.co.uk
Grade II listed
LPA: Breckland

Timber partitioning
creates the snug

Red Lion

128

The snug, to the right of the entrance, is one of Norfolk's finest old pub rooms and creates a wonderful, intimate drinking space. It has curved partition walling formed by high-backed settle seating (cf. Holly Bush Inn, Makeney (20), and Malt Shovel, Spondon (21), both in Derbyshire, and the Bell & Cross, Clent, Worcestershire [190]). Until recently the timbers were painted white but, unfortunately, have been stripped by rather savage blasting. The metal grille on the corner is a modern insertion, presumably to aid supervision. More curious is the little, rectangular, hinged opening over the doorway for which no logical explanation has been put forward. The floor of the corridor is laid with traditional large Norfolk terracotta tiles known as pamments. The pub is a remarkable survival having been shut for seven years until 1997. Many of the fittings in the public bar and restaurant area date from that time.

NORTHUMBERLAND

Berwick-upon-Tweed

75 Castlegate, TD15 1LF
01289 306498
Grade II listed
LPA: Northumberland

Free Trade

129

This is a wonderful survival of a traditional small urban pub, said to date from 1767 (the 1849 datestone to the left refers only to buildings constructed at the rear). The pub was refitted around 1910 and displays what is believed to be the only remaining example of a very unusual pub layout. This features a partition, with iron stays attached to the ceiling, forming a corridor down the left-hand side, thereby enabling customers to access the off-sales in the middle of the pub without having contact with whoever was in the main bars at the time. The front bar, formerly two small rooms, is basic and wood-panelled; retains an original bar counter, bar-back (with drawers and shelves held up by fluted pilasters), seating with bell-pushes and period fireplace with green tiles and touches of Art Nouveau-style detail. The narrow off-sales is intact but now used for storage. A rear smoke room (used for pool) has a small continuation of the 1910 servery and some contemporary panelling: this room has bell-pushes and an attractive brick and tile, probably inter-war, fireplace.

The Free Trade was refitted in 1910. Partitioning separates the public bar from a corridor which heads to an off-sales compartment in the middle of the pub (behind the white radiator)

Netherton

NE65 7HD
01669 630238
Not listed
LPA: Northumberland

Restricted opening hours

Star 130

A pub is known to have existed here since 1788 but the present building consists of a 19th-century wing and a much bigger block added in 1902 containing the public bar. The pub was bought in 1917 by the grandfather of present owner, Miss Vera W Wilson-Morton. From the entrance, a hallway leads to a tiny servery, from where the landlady serves beer from the cellar at a hatch. The public room – and there is only one – is a classic of its kind, though there is nothing fancy about it. Large, plain and square, it has bare-slatted fixed seating round all sides plus a few tables and chairs. Above a 1950s-style fireplace is a huge mirror advertising Ushers' pale ale. There is actually another room directly behind the servery but this only comes into use on rare occasions when the pub is busy. This is one of only seven pubs to have appeared in every edition of the *Good Beer Guide* to 2013 (see also Square & Compass, Worth Matravers, Dorset [27]).
Open 7.30–10.30, Tue, Wed (10), Fri–Sun (but best to check).

The plain Edwardian public room looking through to the servery   (Michael Slaughter, 2003)

NOTTINGHAMSHIRE

Arnold
8–10 Mansfield Road
Daybrook, NG5 3GG
0115 926 8864
Grade II listed
LPA: Gedling

Vale Hotel

`131`

In the Vale and Test Match Hotel, West Bridgford (134), Nottinghamshire has two of the three best Art Deco pub interiors in England (see also the rather more modest and smaller Three Pigeons, Halifax [213]). Both reveal the kind of civilised, 'improved public house' arrangements that interwar clients, customers and licensing justices alike thought desirable. Built in the late 1930s for the nearby Home Brewery to designs by T. Cecil Howitt, the Vale retains features such as the rounded projections on either side of the building and its original metal windows. Also surviving is much of the sleek, Art Deco interior. Pride of place goes to the central parts. Here there is a lovely glazed entrance lobby and, left of this, a wonderful smoke room with original wall-panelling, counter and bar-back, and roundels bearing the Home Brewery initials: all this could be at home on a trans-Atlantic liner. Only very careful inspection will show that in 2011 the entrance directly from the lobby has been blocked and its doorway transferred to the far end to create a link to what was the public bar (where the counter and panelling are not original). On the right is a spacious lounge, entered through what is now a wide opening from a drinking lobby area (relatively modern counter and fitment above). The rear room (now a carvery) was added in period style in 1964.

The smoke room, and detail of the Home Brewery monogram

Nottingham: city centre

1 Brewhouse Yard
Castle Road, NG1 6AD
0115 947 3171
www.triptojerusalem.com
Grade II listed
LPA: Nottingham

Olde Trip to Jerusalem

132

Parts of this remarkable building are 17th-century – but *not* from the 12th as the made-up date outside would have us believe! What makes it special is a series of rooms burrowing into the soft sandstone of Castle Rock. Alterations in 1997–8 did not impact adversely on the historic core and, indeed, won a CAMRA/English Heritage design award. A flagstone passage leads to the Ward Room (named after licensees between 1894 and 1989), hollowed out of the rock. Opposite is the servery which seems of varied but fairly indeterminate dates. Beyond is a tiny rock-cut snug created during the alterations. Up a staircase is 'Mortimer's Room', a cavernous lounge refitted around 1930 with a quarter-circle counter and brick fireplace: beware the 'cursed galleon' which has not been cleaned for over 50 years following the mysterious deaths of the last three people who tried to! From here, a passage through the rock (again from 1997–8) leads to another small room, previously an office. Back downstairs, room no. 3 may have been a kitchen in the past and is known as Yorkey's Room after 'Yorkey' Ward, licensee 1894–1914 (see his inn sign on the wall). The adjacent snug was converted from living accommodation in 1996.

Mortimer's Bar, upstairs at the Olde Trip

Nottingham: Sherwood

Edwards Lane, NG5 3HU

0115 926 5612

www.johnbarras.com/pub/
five-ways-nottingham/c3453

Grade II listed

LPA: Nottingham

🍺 🍴

The smoke room

Five Ways

133

A prominent 'Brewers' Tudor' roadhouse of 1936–7 for Warwick & Richardsons of Newark to designs by architect A. E. Eberlin. The off-sales has been lost (blocked doorway at the front) but the layout is otherwise intact, ranged around an L-shaped panelled corridor (with sashed screens to the servery and a former telephone booth). The front two rooms comprise a corner public bar and, on the left, a smoke room, now called the 'Ken Yarwood Room' with panelling, a Tudor fireplace, and formerly sashed screen to a narrow servery. On the far side of the corridor is a large lounge (right) covered by a fine segmental plaster ceiling with decorative bands, and a long function room which now serves as the main bar. This shift of focus leaves the rest of the pub with a rather isolated feel and this is matched by generally cheap, modern furnishing schemes.

West Bridgford

Gordon Square
Gordon Road, NG2 5LP

0115 981 1481

www.testmatchhotel.com

Grade II* listed

LPA: Rushcliffe

🍺 🍴

Test Match Hotel

134

In the Test Match and the Vale Hotel, Arnold (131), Nottinghamshire has two of the three best Art Deco pub interiors in England (see also the rather more modest and smaller Three Pigeons, Halifax [213]). It was built in 1938 to the designs of A.C. Wheeler for brewers Hardys & Hansons of Kimberley and the name derives from the nearby cricket ground at Trent Bridge. The revolving door sweeps you into a glorious two-storey, ash-panelled lounge where the ceiling lighting is reminiscent of a great interwar cinema. The (later) wall-paintings by local artist

T. L. B. Hutchinson have a cricketing theme. To the right is the former gents-only smoke room with a striking arched approach to the toilets (obviously no provision for ladies): as elsewhere in the pub they are as built. A wide staircase from the lounge leads up to the beautifully preserved Boundary Bar (originally a cocktail lounge) with its semi-circular counter. During a major but sensitive refurbishment in 2001 the lounge was linked to what was an assembly room at the rear. A side entrance leads to the remarkable public bar, complete with its jazzy terrazzo floor, tiered counter and angular slate fireplaces. The Test Match was unlisted until its importance was recognised by joint CAMRA/ English Heritage fieldwork and was promptly graded at II* in 2000.

The fireplace (now blocked) and engraved mirror in the upstairs bar

Going to the gents' 1930s-style

The striking public bar

What shaped Britain's pubs – 3: between the wars

Pub architecture between the wars was very different from the period around 1900. Around the First World War there was already a reaction against late Victorian glitz and glitter, interesting examples of which are the Forester, Ealing in west London (91), of 1909 and the Rose Villa Tavern, Birmingham (173), of 1919–20. However, multi-room plans with public bars and better quality ones continued to be built and would be until the 1960s.

In terms of architecture and fitting out, one new strand was nostalgia for the good old days of the 16th and 17th centuries, expressed in what is known as **'Brewers' Tudor'** and characterised by half-timbering and exposed beams, as at the vast King & Queen, Brighton (158), and the Black Horse, Northfield, Birmingham (175). In terms of architecture, self-conscious nostalgia also lies behind essays in the **Vernacular Revival**, the best examples of which in this guide are the Bleeding Wolf, Scholar Green, Cheshire (12), with its huge thatched roof, and the Margaret Catchpole, Ipswich (155), characterised by sweeping tiled roofs and tall chimneys. In complete contrast there was the occasional use of up-to-the-minute **Art Deco**, the finest English examples of

The Black Horse, Northfield (175), is a vast 'Brewers' Tudor roadhouse dating from 1929

which are the Vale Hotel, Arnold (131), and Test Match Hotel, West Bridgford (134), both in Nottinghamshire, and the smaller, rather more modest Three Pigeons, Halifax (213). Scotland is well-endowed with Art Deco pub interiors, the most spectacular being the Crook Inn, Tweedsmuir, in the Borders (p. 259). Visits to the Steps Bar (247) and Portland Arms (248), both in Glasgow, and Frews Bar, Dundee (257), will also richly reward enthusiasts. The term **Moderne** is sometimes used to describe Art Deco at its most modest and can be applied to fittings like those at the Crystal Fountain, Cannock, Staffordshire (148), the New Inn, Selby, North Yorkshire (204), and the Clep Bar, Dundee (256).

Between the wars, the principle of 'fewer but better' was very evident in large public houses built on new estates and beside major roads, the latter being referred to, predictably, as 'roadhouses' and catering for a generation of newly mobile motorists (then untroubled by drink-drive laws). Such pubs were large and, in addition to offering a hierarchy of rooms, they provided a wide variety of facilities which made them 'destination pubs' (to use a present-day term) where

women and, indeed, whole families were welcome. This is what lies behind large and well-appointed pubs such as the Bleeding Wolf (below), the Berkeley, Scunthorpe (51), and Eastbrook, Dagenham (81). Some pubs still retain their bowling greens from pre-war days as at the Nursery Inn, Heaton Norris, Stockport (115), Black Horse, Northfield, and Margaret Catchpole (both mentioned above). Grand statements such as these are almost entirely absent from the pub stock of Wales, Scotland and Northern Ireland.

A pair of seats and table in the main bar at the Clep Bar, Dundee (256)

A large Vernacular Revival roadhouse in Cheshire – the Bleeding Wolf, Scholar Green (12)

OXFORDSHIRE

Oxford

16 Glebelands
Lye Valley Estate
Headington, OX3 7EN
01865 763448
Not listed
LPA: Oxford

Fairview Inn

135

The 'Cotswold Lounge' is a remarkable survival. The Second World War devastated Britain economically and post-1945 reconstruction did not include the frivolous business of pub-building. This only restarted in the mid-1950s, and was mostly cheap and pretty dismal (hence so little survives) – see also 107, 194 and 245. Brewers H. & G. Simonds of Reading built the Fairview for a large housing estate in 1958–9 (architect Reginald Southall) and its Cotswold Lounge is a piece of up-to-the-minute pub furnishing of that time. The walls are lined with hardwood panelling and the quadrant-shaped counter has vertical lapped boarding (until the 1980s it had a thatched canopy, the sort of thing that was popular in late 1950s and 1960s pubs): one wall has Cotswold stone facing which gives the room its name. A coal-effect fire with chrome surround (seems original) with stone mantelpiece completes the period feel. The intact gents' has seven mighty urinals, tiled walls and floor, and sinks with bizarre taps. The off-sales has been absorbed into the public bar, but its 1950s counter remains, as does the main counter and seating.

The late 1950s Cotswold Lounge

Steventon

Stocks Lane, OX13 6SG

Grade II listed

LPA: Vale of White Horse

Restricted opening hours

North Star   136

The main bar is one of the great rural pub rooms of Britain. Its arrangements would have once been common enough, but are now all incredibly rare. It has settles in the centre, focusing on the fireplace: the attached ironwork formerly carried curtains for greater privacy and warmth. There is no bar counter and this too is a great rarity (see p. 41). Service is via a stable door from the ground-floor 'cellar'. Many locals stand drinking in the passageway around the settles and, at busy times, getting a drink can be a challenge. The second room (rather more modern) is served from a hatch to the cellar. There is another plain room across a corridor further back in the pub. The timber porch has some fixed seating and now doubles as the smoking shelter. Outdoor loos. The pub was in the hands of the Cox family for 150 years: Jack Cox, a railway enthusiast, changed the pub sign to show a GWR locomotive, rather than the heavenly body. Opens 5pm Mon–Thu, 3pm Fri, noon Sat–Sun.

Settles such as this, facing a warm fireplace, were once a common feature of rural pubs

SHROPSHIRE

Selattyn

Glyn Road, SY10 7DN
01691 650247
www.thecrosskeys-selattyn.co.uk
Not listed
LPA: Shropshire
🍺 🛏 (self-catering)

The public bar

Cross Keys

137

A modest four-roomed village pub just a mile from the Welsh border
and which doubled as the village shop until 1994 (hence the big window
on the right). There have been only two owners since 1939. The old
core of the pub is the delightful small bar on the right of a passageway:
it has some Victorian or early 20th-century fittings (fireplace perhaps
of *c.*1970) and red and black quarry-tile flooring. Across the corridor is
the 'Music Room', so-called since it hosts Irish music every Thursday:
the inglenook fireplace may date from the 1930s. Further back are two
rooms which have been brought into use in modern times: one serves
as a games room, formerly a living room, where the only old fittings are
the wall cupboards. A large function room occupies the former stables.

Shrewsbury

1 Church Street, SY1 1UG
01743 360275
www.theloggerheads.co.uk
Grade II listed
LPA: Shropshire
🍺 🍴

Loggerheads

138

A wonderfully unspoilt pub in an 18th-century building in the old
heart of Shrewsbury, still with four separate rooms. Off the left-hand
passageway are a serving hatch (right) and the venerable (former)
'Gents Only' bar (now an outlawed feature of pub life! – see right)
formed by a timber and glass partition which doubles as a high-backed
settle: the outside wall is lined with reused 16th- or 17th-century oak
panelling. Here there are some old (non-working) bell-pushes and a
traditional slate shove ha'penny board. The tiny front bar in the centre
is a homely room with plain furnishings and at the rear left is a tiny snug
(Poet's Room) with old padded bench seating. The corridor runs around
the back of the servery to the lounge bar which occupies a (probably)
interwar extension and which has a parquet floor, fixed seating on two
sides, a brick fireplace and service from a hatch at the side of the servery.

The former gents' only bar at the Loggerheads

Gents only

Time was when male drinkers could cut themselves off from the other half of humanity in their own domain within the pub. The plan of the Black Horse, Northfield, Birmingham (175), shows a capacious 'gents' smoke room' to the rear right: had menfolk wished to take their wives or lady friends out for a drink then they would have used the 'mixed smoke room' at the front. At the other great Birmingham inter-war pub in this guide, the British Oak, Stirchley (176), men could find themselves a single-sex space in the lounge on the left at the front of the pub. Village pubs in this guide with such provision were the

NO LADIES SUPPLIED IN THIS BAR

PLEASE BRING 'YOUR OWN!!!'

Couldn't be clearer! A notice from the demolished Happy Haven, Maryhill, Glasgow, now in the Laurieston Bar (245). The gloss, needless to say, is modern

Rose & Crown at Huish Episcopi, Somerset (143), where the right-hand front room is still known as the 'Men's Kitchen', and the Bell & Cross, Clent, Worcestershire (190), where there was a men's

smoke room. Over the entrance to the old bar at the Olde Cheshire Cheese in London (60) is the legend 'Gentlemen Only'. In Aberdeen the Grill (229) was an entirely gents only pub. And so things remained in many pubs up and down the land until the Sex Discrimination Act of 1975 (which took effect on 1 January the following year) and put a stop to such things. If you go to the Loggerheads, Shrewsbury (138), you will see at the entrance to the left-hand room, lettering on a baffle beside the door which reads 'Gents only (until 1975)'. Is this just a matter of historical record or is there a hint of wistful, masculine regret – who dares say?!

Telford

Plough Road,
Wrockwardine Wood, TF2 7AW
Grade II listed
LPA: Telford & Wrekin

Tiles cover the walls and floor in the public bar

Bull's Head   139

This pub, with its thrilling and colourful display of tiles and glazed bricks, probably dates from about 1904. The ceramics are by Maw & Co. of Jackfield (in the Ironbridge Gorge) which was possibly the world's largest manufacturer of decorative tiles in the late 19th century. The frontage has bands of green and yellow glazed brick on the upper floor and strips of mosaic below. In the front room the tiling extends from floor to ceiling, in various designs and colours. The floor too is tiled in patterns of brown, buff, blue and white. Some of the window glass is contemporary, including the windows on the first floor and the door glass inscribed 'Bar'. A change is that there used to be a corridor from the right-hand doorway to the rear. The counter (with unusual strips of low relief carved decoration) and the bar-back are, no doubt, Edwardian as well. The rear and left-hand parts were created in 1982.

SOMERSET

Bath

12 Green Street, BA1 2JZ
01225 448259
Grade II listed
LPA: Bath & North East
Somerset

Old Green Tree   140

This small, cosy pub is part of a late 18th-century terrace right in the heart of Bath. It was extended to the rear in 1926 and refurbished in a very restrained way by local architect, W. A. Williams: the shop-like frontage dates from this time. It consists of two panelled rooms plus a drinking lobby in front of the servery at the centre of the building, an arrangement that is common in many a northern pub (e.g. 103, 114, 208) but most unusual in the south. All these spaces are panelled and have herringbone wood-block floors. At the front is a small lounge with service via a doorway to the servery, and at the rear is a smoke room with a similar arrangement. All the doors still bear the numbers that were used to identify the rooms for licensing purposes (2 for the front bar, 4 for the cellar etc). The gents', down eleven steps, still has its 1926 urinals (although the lurid wall tiling seems modern).

The popular drinking lobby at the Old Green Tree

Bath

23 The Vineyards
Paragon, BA1 5NA
01225 425072
www.star-inn-bath.co.uk
Grade II listed
LPA: Bath & North East Somerset

Star Inn

Occupying a Georgian terrace and first licensed in the 1760s, the Star is a fantastic survival, completely refurbished and extended into half of no. 22 next door in 1928 by local architect W. A. Williams. It has scarcely altered since and consists of four rooms plus an entrance lobby. On the left is an attractive, panelled lounge, still with bell-pushes. To the right is a small snug where the long bench is nicknamed (in anticipation of elderly customers) 'death row'. A timber screen separates this from the so-called 'Glass Room' which has a remarkable, fold-up slate shove ha'penny board. Finally comes the screened-off public bar in front of the servery where two casks of Bass (for which the pub is famous) are stillaged. Note the annunciator box at the back of the servery and a vintage telephone near the counter in the snug. The Star serves as the brewery tap for Abbey Ales. Food consists of rolls.

The well-used slate shove ha'penny board in the 'Glass Room'

Looking from the public bar to the 'Glass Room' beyond.

Faulkland

Wells Road, BA3 5XF
01373 834230
Grade II listed
LPA: Mendip

Tucker's Grave Inn   142

This remarkable three-roomed rural pub lies on the main road east of
the village of Faulkland and is part of an 18th-century cottage which
has housed a pub for over 200 years. The strange name comes from a
suicide, Edwin Tucker, who killed himself in 1747 and was buried
nearby (commonly suicides were buried in unconsecrated ground,
often near a crossroads). The pub has no bar counter at all (p. 41) and
casks of beer and polycasks of cider are stacked in the bay window in
the public bar. To the right is the splendidly unspoilt tap room: the
Georgian-style lettering on the door dates from the early 19th, if not
the late 18th-century, and is surely amongst the earliest pub lettering
in the country. A third room to the far left was formerly a living room
and was brought into use in 1985. At the end of the passage is a door
leading to the outside gents' and ladies' on the rear right of the building.
There is a skittle alley in a separate stone building at the rear.

The ground-floor cellar.
There is no counter:
immediately behind
the camera is one of the
main public rooms

Huish Episcopi

Wincanton Road, TA10 9QT
01458 250494
Grade II listed
LPA: South Somerset

Rose & Crown ('Eli's')   143

The simple Gothic windows here suggest a rebuilding in the late
18th century or very early 19th. The Rose & Crown was known by this
name by 1835 and is also affectionately known as 'Eli's' after Eli Scott,
grandfather of the present family members running the pub. Its special
feature is the sunken cellar area, a unique layout where customers freely
wander in to order drinks: it has a stone-flagged floor and shelving with
hand-pumps attached to it (see p. 41 for pubs without bar counters).
Surrounding it is a series of small rooms. One of these, on the front
right of the building, is the 'Men's Kitchen', once a male-only retreat.
Another historic room is the (now piano-less) 'Piano Room' at the front
in the middle of the building. On the left end are two rooms brought
into use: the front one was the family parlour (or living room) and the
rear was created in 1984 on the site of the original gents' outside toilets.

The heart of 'Eli's' is the servery where customers and staff mingle freely

Midsomer Norton

The Island, BA3 2HQ

01761 418270

Grade II listed

LPA: Bath & North East Somerset

The public bar

White Hart

A town-centre Victorian pub which retains its original arrangement of public bar, snug (formerly lounge) and former off-sales (with its hatch). The public bar has kept various historic features such as the wooden partition near the door, simple bench seats under the windows and the bar counter. Part of the latter bulges out to create space to serve the lobby hatch: at the other end it was altered in 1985 to accommodate the door to the new gents' toilets. The snug on the right of the entrance retains its original panelled dado with some wall benches attached, and an old fireplace with mirrored surround above. The new lounge to the rear was created in 1985 and is a combination of a former beer store, situated where the present servery stands, and a private lounge. A skittle alley to the rear right has been part of the pub for many years but the bar there was added in the 1960s.

Witham Friary

BA11 5HF
01749 850742
Grade II listed
LPA: Mendip

Seymour Arms

145

Owned by the same family since 1943, this pub is a truly amazing survival. It was purpose-built, along with farm buildings, in 1866 or 1867 for the Duke of Somerset's estate – illustrating how rural pubs were combined with other functions in times past: the farm was sold in 1980 (see p. 48). It has a dignified exterior, with a splendid wrought-

iron inn sign on a corner, and a surprisingly spacious interior of two rooms astride a large central corridor leading to a glazed-in servery/'cellar', in front of which many customers like to congregate. Within the servery is a bank of four brass taps formerly used for service and a number of built-in drawers, no doubt dating from the building of the pub. On the left is the main public bar with simple bench seating and service via a hatch from the 'cellar'. To the right is the 'Commercial Room' with its early 20th-century fireplace. The only major change has been the addition of inside toilets in 1981.

As much cider is sold as beer – something that would have been true of so many rural Somerset pubs until the mid-20th century. Another very similar pub was built for the Somerset estate, the Somerset Arms at Maiden Bradley, now greatly modernised.

The central corridor and servery
with its sliding sashes

STAFFORDSHIRE

Audley

18 Church Street, ST7 8DE
01782 720486
Not listed
LPA: Newcastle-under-Lyme

Butchers Arms   146

Rebuilt in 1933, this attractive brick-and-half-timbered pub (not far off the M6) has changed little since. The entrance leads to a spacious corridor with panelling and quarry-tiled flooring and the latter continues into the small public bar (right). This has an impressive ceiling, divided into three deep compartments and with rich cornices bearing grapes and Tudor roses. The counter is original, albeit with a new top. The lounge (rear right and named in the door glass) is larger and also has a triple-compartmented ceiling and the same frieze as in the public bar. There is a Tudor-style fireplace (with heraldic crest above), good dado panelling, and a counter ornamented by fleur-de-lys (again the top is new). The smoke room (rear left and also named in the door glass) still has its original fireplace, fixed seating and bell-pushes: here the rather simpler ceiling has a border with oak leaves. In the large upstairs function room, the fireplace is the only original feature. The pub was built with an early form of electric-powered air conditioning, and the vents can be seen in all the public rooms. The only major loss is the off-sales on the right side, formerly connected to the servery. Opens 7pm Mon–Thu, otherwise normal hours.

The 'Brewers' Tudor architecture is underlined inside by the design of the fireplace, the frieze and the use of heraldry
(Michael Slaughter, 2011)

The Lounge

Burton upon Trent

43 Cross Street, DE14 1EG

01283 532551

www.joulesbrewery.co.uk

Not listed

LPA: East Staffordshire

Coopers Tavern

This remarkable pub is famous as the former Bass brewery tap and for the fact that it has no real bar counter (p. 41). It began life as an overflow store for special malts and by 1826 was a store for Bass's Imperial Stout. It evidently had attractions for senior members of the brewery who used it as a kind of personal pub. In 1858 it became licensed as a public house but the back area remained the fiefdom of the selected few until about 1950: the *hoi poloi* were served at a hatch door between this 'cellar' and the passage beyond. Now anyone can drink there, sitting on three benches and a raised area in the corner: within the same area a large variety of beers, ciders, perries and other drinks are stored, so creating a drinking environment unlike any other. At the front of the pub is a large lounge, in which the two different types of quarry tiles suggest it may once have comprised two separate spaces: it has old benches and even still-working bell-pushes. The snug (front left) is a fairly modern creation out of private quarters. Excellent Bass is still dispensed on gravity. Food only served Sunday lunchtime.

There is no bar counter at the Coopers

Cannock

35 St John's Road, WS11 0AL
01543 574812
Grade II listed
LPA: Cannock Chase

The public bar with a pair of
heating pipes at the foot

Crystal Fountain   148

A plain neo-Georgian brick pub built in 1937. It retains its original
four-room layout and Moderne-style fittings, the only significant change
being the opening of a link between the public bar and the snug at the
front, and the addition of a small counter in the lounge. The latter is to
the rear left and to its right is a function room (originally named in
now almost blanked out lettering 'Non-smoking dining room') with
large windows opening to the garden. Lots of period features survive,
notably in the counter, the bar-back, bench seating, sleek doors, and
the fitting out of the loos on the left. The right-hand gents' is not now
used: there never was a ladies' on this side of the pub but, after all, the
adjacent public bar was largely a male preserve. After over a decade's
chequered history the pub was very carefully refurbished by Black
Country Ales (who have also made a success of the Vine, Wednesfield,
West Midlands [186]), and reopened in May 2012.

High Offley

Peggs Lane, Old Lea, ST20 0NG
(by bridge 42 on Shropshire
Union Canal)
01785 284569
Not listed
LPA: Stafford

Restricted opening hours

Anchor   149

Perhaps the most unspoilt example of a canal-side pub, with the front
door facing the water rather than the road. It was built around 1830 to
serve the Shropshire Union Canal, England's last trunk narrow canal
(completed in 1835) and the last major project of the great engineer
Thomas Telford. The pub has been in the same family since 1903.
The right-hand room is particularly memorable, with its quarry-tiled
floor, two high-backed settles, window bench and scrubbed tables;
the ensemble creating a truly timeless atmosphere. The left-hand
bar was refitted in the early 1960s in the 'taste' of the time. The bar

counter was also installed then and is decorated to resemble a narrow boat. The Wadworth's 6X is normally served on hand-pump but, on request, can be fetched from the cellar in a jug. In winter only opens Fri and Sat lunchtimes and evening plus Sunday lunchtime.

Landlady Olive Cliff at the bar of the Anchor

Rugeley
19 Market Street, WS15 2JH
01889 586848
Grade II listed
LPA: Cannock Chase

Dominoes in the public bar

Red Lion

150

Last refitted in the interwar years, this popular three-room drinkers' pub occupies a 16th-century timber-framed building. The small public bar in the centre has some very old re-used panelling, a red quarry-tiled floor and a beamed ceiling. The fireplace was modified in the 1970s when the metal inset with the Banks's brewery lion was installed (the same feature recurs in the two other rooms). The tiny cupboard on the left of the fireplace was to keep valuable items, such as salt, dry. The counter appears to be interwar work while the bar-back with its turned shafts seems earlier. To the left, a snug has some modern fittings but an interwar fireplace. The games room on the right has panelling and old bench seating but a modern tiled floor.

Games at the pub

Pubs are places for pleasure and relaxation so it is hardly surprising that they have been venues for the playing a multitude of games over the centuries. Some, such as cards, dominoes or that post-war invention, the pub quiz, require no special provision whereas, at the other end of the scale, substantial investment is required for long alley skittles or outdoor bowling.

The game most associated with the pub is, no doubt, darts. Although not as popular as it was 30 or 40 years ago, the game is thought to be played by over two million people on a regular basis, with pubs as prime locations for their activity. A survey in 2006 concluded that 53 per cent of Britain's pubs had a dartboard. No special facilities are required for the game, other than the dartboard itself and a clear space for throwing the darts. At the Punch Bowl, Worcester (194), one of the few post-war pubs in this book, there is a long projection off the public bar where the game can be played.

Billiards and snooker have a long association with the pub and many Victorian and Edwardian ones were provided with a purpose-built billiard room. Billiard rooms are illustrated in this guide for the Lamb Hotel, Eccles (95), and Douglas Arms, Bethesda, Gwynedd (224). Nowadays the pool table, which arrived from America after 1960, overwhelmingly outnumbers its larger billiard cousin in our pubs.

A fairly rare game surfaces at two pubs in this guide. This is toad in the hole in which coins or other metal discs are tossed at a hole. The game had all but died out by the 1990s but was revived in the Lewes area where, in 2009, it was believed to be played at 35 pubs in a 15-mile radius of the town.

The game of quoits, like skittles, takes various forms. The outdoor variety is now quite rare but the indoor game is popular in the Herefordshire/Forest of Dean area. An illustration of the game appears under the entry for the Duke of York, Leysters, Herefordshire (41).

Sadly many outdoor bowling greens have been lost, as at the Victoria, Great Harwood, Lancashire (47), and Springfield,

Toad in the hole at the Red Lion, Snargate, Kent (45)

Wigan (117). However, they may be found at the following pubs in this guide: the Travellers Rest, Alpraham, Cheshire (6), Margaret Catchpole, Ipswich (155), Nursery Inn, Stockport (115), Wheatsheaf, Sutton Leach, Merseyside (126), Black Horse (175) and British Oak (176), both in Birmingham.

This automatic darts scorer saves on mental arithmetic at the Drewe Arms, Drewsteignton, Devon (23)

Bowls at the Margaret Catchpole, Ipswich (155)

Of glass and glazing

One of the defining features of Victorian pubs is magnificent glass, whether in windows, doors, or mirrors. At its richest, it involved embossing and brilliant cutting. Embossing involved etching a pattern with acid, while the part to be embossed was unaffected thanks to a protective coating: then the embossed portions were ground to remove the transparency. Brilliant cutting was undertaken by a rotating stone wheel, after which the cut was polished. Particularly good examples of such work is to be found at the Red Lion, St James's (72), and the Kings Head, Tooting (89), both in London, and the Garden Gate, Leeds (218). Gilding and other colouration was sometimes applied.

Until the post-war period pub windows were never clear as it was not considered fitting for passers-by to be able to see the drinkers and drinking inside: in any case licensing magistrates would not have allowed such visibility. Instead, the windows of the pub provided a translucent veil between the pub and its pleasures, and the mundane world beyond.

Embossed and cut glass at the Kings Head, Tooting, London (89)

Advertising at the King's Head, Bristol (34)

Mirrors often assumed considerable prominence in the pub and took various forms. They might have brilliant cutting to produce a stunning, glittering effect as at the Red Lion, St James's, or have back painting, of which fine examples illustrated in this guide are at the Lord Nelson, Bermondsey (53), Tottenham, Fitzrovia (59), and Half Moon, Herne Hill (86), all in London. Advertising mirrors were used to promote drinks of all kinds: a good example is illustrated here in the Star at Netherton, Northumberland (130). Such mirrors are a particular feature of many Scottish pubs.

Stained glass also found its way into the pub and various examples are shown in these pages. Perhaps the most striking display is in the vast skylight over the billiard room at the Boleyn, Upton Park, London (90).

Stained glass at the Princess Louise, Holborn, London (65)   (John Cryne)

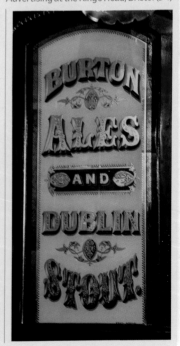

Stoke-on-Trent: Hanley

65 Lichfield Street, ST1 3EA
01782 262158
Not listed
LPA: Stoke-on-Trent

Coachmakers Arms　　`151`

An early Victorian mid-terrace pub, which retains its layout of a central drinking passage with two rooms on either side of it. The passage has a tiled dado by Mintons, a red and black tiled floor and a hatch to the side of the servery. The tiny snug bar (front left) retains old benches but the original counter is somewhat marred by the over-large modern top. The lounge (front right) has fixed bench seating and a fireplace.

At the rear right the small 'Piano Room' is quite plain except for a highly attractive, possibly Edwardian, fire-surround with pretty Art Nouveau touches: the red and black flooring is the same as in the corridor. Rear left is the most altered room which has been extended back into former private quarters, perhaps in the 1960s or 1970s. At the time of writing, the pub was under threat of demolition due to redevelopment plans for the area.

The lounge

Stoke-on-Trent: Tunstall

13 Naylor Street
Pitshill, ST6 6LS
01782 834102
Grade II listed
LPA: Stoke-on-Trent

Vine　　`152`

An archetypal small, unspoilt, back-street Victorian local with three small rooms. In northern towns and cities, hundreds, if not thousands of pubs like this existed at one time for working people, but only a handful remain. A passageway runs from the front door with, on its left, a partly glazed partition and two small rooms – a lounge at the front and a games room at the back, both with their original fixed seating and 1950s tiled fireplaces. Opposite the games room is a hatch with a sliding window. The small public bar on the right has an etched window inscribed 'Vaults' and original bar-back shelves, bar counter and fixed seating. The bar top and tiled fireplace, however, are more recent additions.

This multi-room, back street local is characterised by simple, straightforward fittings

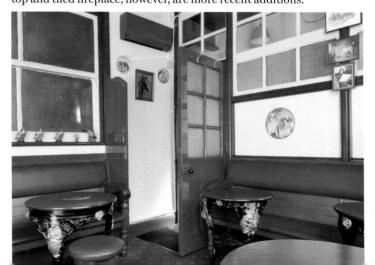

SUFFOLK

Brent Eleigh

Lavenham Road, CO10 9PB
01787 247371
Grade II listed
LPA: Babergh

Cock

A lovely thatched building, probably 18th-century, although the timber-framing behind the rendering could well be older. The smaller bar on the right has wooden panelling in the dado, a small bar counter with old woodwork and a set of old bar back shelves, complete with till drawer. The quarry-tiled floor, tongue-and-groove panelled ceiling, old fireplace and bare wall benches all add to the atmosphere. The main room on the left saw changes in 1976 which created a servery out of part of the off-sales area (half of which remains). The counter and the bar-back date from this time. Note the hole in the end of one bench for the now-rare pub game of tossing the penny which you can play using George III pennies loaned for the purpose by the pub (see also the Viper, Mill Green, Essex [31], and the Red Lion, Snargate, Kent [45]). A 1989 book called *The Perfect Pub* by Nick & Charlie Burt opined that this indeed was it.

The right-hand bar
(Michael Slaughter)

The scores on the doors

Close inspection will reveal numbers on, over and beside doors in many historic pubs: '1' might be the public bar; '2' the smoke room; '3' the cellar, and so on. Until relatively recently (probably the 1960s) it was a legal requirement for every licensee to 'make entry' of his premises with HM Customs and Excise, so that they

A typical pub room number: this one is at the Harrington Arms, Gawsworth, Cheshire (9)

could check his or her premises complied with the law. This process included listing all the rooms used for the storage and consumption of alcohol. Although rooms might be identified by their names, they usually seem to have been denoted by numbers or sometimes, especially around Merseyside, by letters.

Bury St Edmunds

The Traverse, IP33 1BJ
01284 764867
www.thenutshellpub.co.uk
Grade II listed
LPA: St Edmundsbury

A few customers (plus dog) soon fill the miniscule Nutshell

Nutshell   154

The Nutshell is an extraordinary little pub. It is thought to have opened as a beerhouse in 1873, having previously been used by newspaper vendors. With an interior measuring just 15ft by 7ft it is the most authentic claimant to be the UK's smallest pub. Another aspirant, the diminutive Lakeside, Southport, Merseyside – not originally a pub – was a mighty 22ft × 16ft and even this has been extended. The bar-back shelves may be Victorian but the counter is of more uncertain age and, indeed, looks quite recent. Old benches run around some of the walls. As far back as 1884 the pub made much of its collection of curiosities and some still adorn this tiny establishment, not least a mummified cat. The record number of people to have been squeezed inside is claimed to be 102 plus a dog called Blob.

Ipswich

Cliff Lane, IP3 0PQ
01473 252450
Grade II* listed
LPA: Ipswich

Margaret Catchpole

For a combination of quality and intactness this is the finest 1930s pub in all England. Built in 1936 for a housing estate, this precious survival embodies all that inter-war pub builders sought to achieve – refined architecture, high-quality, restrained furnishings, and community facilities (in this case a still well-used bowling green). The large sweeping roofs, prominent dormers and tall chimneystacks draw on vernacular traditions. Inside are three unaltered rooms plus an off-sales (intact but used for storage). The spacious public bar has parquet flooring, a solid curved counter, fine stone fireplace, lots of panelling and a bay window looking out to the bowling green. The only change is a 1970s link to the gents', formerly outside. A small, panelled saloon (right) has its own quadrant-shaped bar counter but is only open for meetings and functions: it has bell-pushes and another polished stone fireplace. An annunciator box still shows the names of the rooms requiring service. The smoke room (rear) also has a curved counter and a bar-back with original cupboard and drawers, along with a wood-block floor, panelled walls, original fireplace in an alcove and more bell-pushes. Margaret Catchpole was a horse-stealer and gaol-breaker – a true Suffolk heroine! Upgraded to Grade II* as a result of joint CAMRA/English Heritage casework in 2001.

The smoke room at the rear of the pub

Laxfield

Gorams Mill Lane, IP13 8DW
01986 798395
www.laxfieldkingshead.co.uk
Grade II listed
LPA: Mid-Suffolk

King's Head ('Low House')   156

A superlative, unspoilt country pub, and which features a truly remarkable main bar. The building was started in the 16th century and extended to the left in the 18th. Its unspoilt nature results from its being run by the Felgate family from 1882 to 1979. The front doorway leads into the main bar which is dominated by high settles on three sides, the backs of which define a corridor running round the room – a rare, historic arrangement (cf. North Star, Steventon, Oxon [136]). The settles face a fire-place at the sides of which are cupboards for keeping items dry (cf. Red Lion, Rugeley, Staffordshire [150]). To the right is a further room with fixed seats and a tiled floor. Behind comes another room with plain panelling and a large multi-drawer cupboard, which was probably at one time on the left-hand side of a corridor. Finally, this all leads to the servery, which is in fact also the cellar and has no counter (see p. 41) – beer is served direct from casks on the stillage. The dining room in the left-hand portion came into public use relatively recently.

Looking towards the 'cellar' with a high settle on the left

Pin Mill

The Quay, IP9 1JW
01473 780764
www.debeninns.co.uk/
buttandoyster
Grade II listed
LPA: Ipswich

Butt & Oyster

157

Picturesquely situated on the Orwell estuary, the pub occupies a
17th-century building which was enlarged both in the 19th century and
again in 1932. The public bar with its red floor tiles and high-backed
settles is especially attractive, containing some 17th-century fielded
panelling and an early 20th-century brick fireplace. The bar counter is
thought to be late Victorian – it was moved back some 18 inches in 1988
but nothing else here has changed for over 50 years. Also enjoying fine
views across the river is the dining room, doubled in size in 1932 but
with a section of raised floor from 1997, when the panelling and seating
in this area were renewed. Across the quarry-tiled corridor which runs
through the building is a small smoke room – over the brick fireplace
is a 17th-century carved panel with naïvely treated figures and
contemporary ornamentation. Casks are stillaged within the servery.

Paul Ainsworth, chair of
CAMRA's Pub Heritage Group,
savours a pint in the public bar

SUSSEX, EAST

Brighton

13 Marlborough Place, BN1 1UB
01273 607207
www.thekingandqueen.co.uk
Grade II listed
LPA: Brighton & Hove

King & Queen

158

Behind the exuberant exterior is a stunning evocation of a great Tudor
hall, dating from the rebuild of 1931 by local architects Clayton & Black
for Edlins Ltd, drink retailers (the gatehouse range is from 1935–6).
Originally the saloon (left) and public bar were divided by a screen
(removed c.1967). Also gone is a ladies' parlour which appears to have
been at the front left. Another change is the unpleasing 'Royal Box'
added over the servery. The counter is partly original but the back-fittings
are probably from the 1960s. Despite these changes, the overall character
is still very much as Edlins intended for the delight and astonishment
of their customers. On the first floor at the front is a minstrels' gallery,

The olde worlde splendour
of the King & Queen

open to the hall, and also an enclosed bar, all of which adds to the
visual excitement. Overlooking the courtyard is the 'Tudor Room'
with a barrel-vaulted ceiling. At the rear left is a small panelled room
(originally a billiard room) with a red tiled floor. The interior is full of
joyous detail, too rich and extensive to describe in detail here – stained
glass, carved foliage and beasts, painted emblems on chimney breasts,
grand fireplaces and much more. It now operates as a sports bar with
many TV screens and live events, so time your visit judiciously!

In days of old when
knights were bold

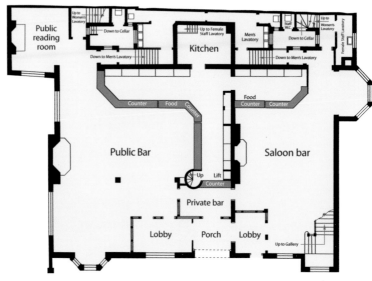

Hadlow Down

TN22 4HJ
07909 904870
Grade II listed
LPA: Wealden District Council

New Inn

A roadside hotel-cum-pub rebuilt in 1885 by the Southdown & East Grinstead Breweries Ltd: the hotel function is firmly proclaimed in the glass of the central doors. The pub part is on the right and is a long room with spartan fittings. These are much as they were in Victorian times with a wood-block floor, wall seating, panelled counter and bar-back fitting (with cash drawers including two slots for notes) and ceramic spirit casks. Note the hatch on the left of the servery for hotel customers and waiters who would have served the restaurant on the left (now a function room). The small room at the rear has split doors with a hatch/shelf to the back of the servery. Closed weekday afternoons.

The public bar

Drawers often served as tills in times gone by and spirits were dispensed on draught, in this case from ceramic casks

Hastings

27 Havelock Road, TN34 1BP
01424 719048
Grade II listed
LPA: Hastings

General Havelock

This central Hastings pub features here for one reason only –
it has Britain's most resplendent pictorial pub tiling, rivalled only
by Edinburgh's Café Royal (236). An existing pub was renamed after
Henry Havelock, a hero in the Indian Mutiny of 1857, and was refitted
in 1889–90 with tilework, designed by Alfred T. S. Carter who duly
signs his creations. Lining a former corridor are scenes depicting
Hastings Castle (centre), a mightily energetic Battle of Hastings (left),
and a sea engagement where stout-hearted English fishermen set
about some wicked French pirates. Since one of the English vessels is
titled 'Conqueror, Hastings', the correct outcome is beyond doubt!
Below is a tiled dado while the floor has black-and-white geometrical
designs and the pub name. At the Havelock Street entrance is a fine
panel depicting Havelock astride a white horse. Otherwise the pub has
been totally modernised: it was simply called the Havelock until 2012.

1066 and all that

Sturdy Brits lay into some
French pirates (detail)

SUSSEX, WEST

Ball's Cross

GU28 9JP

01403 820241

www.staginn-ballscross.co.uk

Grade II listed

LPA: Chichester

Stag Inn

161

The two-rooms in the centre of the present pub, a simple beerhouse from the late 18th century, form its historic core. This was extended in the late 19th or early 20th century when the former post office cottage of 1880 (on the right) was added, whilst the fourth room (left), the former beer store, became a games room in the mid-1990s. The public bar is floored with large Horsham flags and has an inglenook fireplace

and half-height, horizontal panelling: the counter is inter-war. So is the quarter-circle counter in the second room to the right (it appears in an old newspaper photo of 1938 on show here). The post office cottage was converted to dining use in the 1990s. Outside toilets for both sexes.

A regular (plus dog) in 1939

Looking through to the public bar

The Haven

RH14 9BS
Grid ref. TQ084305
01403 822709
www.theblueship.co.uk
Grade II listed
LPA: Horsham

🍺 🍴

Once countless country pubs would have looked like this: now this scene at the Blue Ship is very rare

Blue Ship 162

A rural classic. The pretty red-brick and tile-hung Victorian exterior conceals an 18th century, if not earlier, structure. The public area used to be much smaller because the left-hand rooms are relatively new additions, being taken in from private quarters in about 1973 (front) and around 1986 (rear). The real focus is the splendid old room on the right with exposed beams, simple seating, scrubbed pine tables, bare brick floor and an inglenook fireplace with seats (but modern stove). Originally it appears to have consisted of two rooms, which were knocked together when the pub was established about a century ago. Service seems then to have been at a tiny hatch to the right of the present doorway-cum-hatch. A stone-flagged corridor leads to the much smaller bar at the rear and which also only has a doorway-cum-hatch to the servery (where beer is drawn direct from the cask).

Wineham

Wineham Lane, BN5 9AY
01444 881252
www.horshampub.co.uk/royal-oak-wineham.php
Grade II listed
LPA: Mid Sussex

🍺 🍴

Royal Oak 163

An attractive, partly half-timbered village pub run by the Peacock family for 60 years until 2007. After they came a number of changes were made in 1946 or 1947, notably alteration of a straight counter to the current polygonal shape. The left-hand side of the main bar has basic bench seating partly made from old barrel staves, an inglenook fireplace, exposed beams and a brick floor. Beer is served from casks on stillage, clearly visible from the counter. Unusually, there is a small brick fireplace within the servery area. At the rear is a simply appointed room, with a wood-block floor and a narrow passage to the right at the end of which is a hatch to the back of the servery. The right-hand side of the main bar was created in 1946/7 out of a former shop, the door to which now provides service to outdoor customers. To the right of the pub is a separate corrugated iron function room. Outside gents' but ladies' inside with a blocked spyhole in the door – this being an exterior door until 1947!

The simply appointed main bar at the Royal Oak

Taking it home with you

Where did you last buy drink to take home? Chances are it was a supermarket, perhaps a convenience store or possibly a high street drinks shop. It's hardly likely to have been down at your local pub. But 50 years ago or more it would have been a very different story. Pubs sold drinks of all kinds for customers to enjoy at home and often there was special provision in the layout of the building to cater for this. Then legislation changed in the early 1960s to enable supermarkets to sell alcohol freely and the rest is history.

The unusally named off-sales at the Alexandra in Stockport (112)

The 'off-sales' at pubs went under a bewildering variety of names – off-sales (of course), jug and bottle (and vice versa), outdoor department, family department, order department, retail department and perhaps several more. Such names can still sometimes by seen fossilised in etched glass or doorplates. Occasionally there was a bench in the space in question: typically this would be occupied by women popping down to get beer for their dad or husband and stopping for a quick one with their friends. Where there was no special enclosed small space for off-sales, there might be a hatch facing the front door, or one in a corridor, and many examples will be found in the pages of this guide.

With the demise of off-sales from pubs, so many small rooms or compartments devoted to the purpose have been incorporated into an adjacent pub room, turned

The snug/off-sales at Bennets Bar, Edinburgh (235), with its typical small hatch to the servery

over to storage and occasionally converted into a small kitchen. So, when next you see what appears to be a spare door on the outside of a pub, ask yourself the question – was this where the off-sales was?

TYNE & WEAR

Gateshead

Half Moon Lane, NE8 2AN
0191 478 2543
www.theheadofsteam.co.uk/
gateshead
Grade II listed
LPA: Gateshead

The late Victorian Buffet Bar
at the Central

Central

164

The intact 'Buffet Bar' is the star attraction of this grand mid-Victorian hotel-cum-pub situated between the Tyne and High Level Bridges. It was refitted in the late Victorian period and the building was the subject of sympathetic alterations in 2010 and is now a haven of real ale and cider. The U-shaped counter in the Buffet Bar has an impressive front with broad segmental arches and its bar-back is highly ornate. There is also fixed seating, half-height panelling, etched glass in the doors, a fine ceiling and plasterwork frieze. Elsewhere, panelling survives in the hallway staircase whilst the public bar has further panelling and a partially old bar counter. The sharp angle of the site explains the unusual triangular shape of the sitting room behind the Buffet Bar (cf. Bath Hotel, Sheffield [211]). If it is closed, please ask the staff to open up for you.

Newcastle upon Tyne

31 The Side, NE1 3JE

0191 232 1269

www.sjf.co.uk

Grade II listed

LPA: Newcastle

Stained glass window at
the front of the pub

Crown Posada

165

Rebuilt in 1880 for local brewer John Sanderson, this long, narrow pub retains its three drinking areas, one behind the other. At the front, impressive Pre-Raphaelite-style stained-glass windows depict a lady serving a drink, and a Tudor gent about to consume it. Inside, the ceiling sports ornate moulding and the mahogany bar-back has four bays. Behind the wallpaper are some wall paintings, which only see the light of day when the pub is redecorated. The wall mirrors, fixed seating and much other woodwork are modern replacements, installed during recent careful refurbishment. A delightful small, screened-off snug can be found near the entrance.

South Shields

45–47 Fowler Street, NE33 1NS

Grade II listed

LPA: South Tyneside

The unusual upstairs bar

Stag's Head

166

The really unusual feature at this Victorian pub of 1897 is the two-storey arrangement with bars one above the other – clearly the result of the narrow, shallow site. Many pubs have upstairs public rooms but most of these were function rooms, or often came into service at a later date and/or did not have their own servery. On the ground floor the entrance

lobby, to the left, has floor to ceiling tiling and the inner door has stained glass. In the small public bar, the wide, four-centred arch spanning the servery is an oddity and there is also a vast Victorian fireplace topped with a stag's head. The counter and bar-back are original and most impressive. This room was extended in the 1970s, into part of the rear yard. The upstairs room has also seen some changes, notably moving of the bar fittings and (possibly) shortening of the bar counter in the process. However, the counter and bar-back are original, as is the fixed seating, frieze and ornate fireplace. This room is only open Friday and Saturday evenings or at other times on request.

Sunderland

9 High West Street, SR1 3HA

0191 565 3534

Grade II listed

LPA: Sunderland

Dun Cow 167

An impressive building of 1901–2, designed by architect B. F. Simpson. A good sense of the original layout remains, despite the filling in of a corner doorway and removal of a wall to the sitting room. The bar-back is one of the most stunning in the country. It has three sections, divided by semi-circular projections, and is richly decorated with delicate Art Nouveau-style woodcarving and curious plaster reliefs. The formidable bar counter also has strong detailing. The side entrance may have led to a lobby – the curved screen dividing it from the main bar is still there, though partly opened up for easy access.

The Dun Cow has a particularly impressive bar-back fitting

Sunderland

150 Hylton Road, SR4 7XT
0191 597 7261
Grade II* listed
LPA: Sunderland

The Buffet Bar has one
of the most spectacular
of all tiled pub rooms

Mountain Daisy

168

This imposing pub was rebuilt in 1900–2 by local architects
W. & T. R. Milburn. Some original windows survive but the interior was
substantially remodelled in the 1970s, apart from the truly spectacular
Buffet Bar. This offers a visual feast of ceramic work, manufactured by
Craven Dunnill & Co. of Jackfield, Shropshire. The walls are tiled from
floor to ceiling and a wonderfully decorated mosaic covers the floor.
The quadrant-shaped ceramic bar counter is stunning, one of only
fourteen such left in the country. Seven ceramic pictures, also by Craven
Dunnill, depict scenes in the North East – clockwise from the right of
the window, the High Level Bridge, Newcastle; Durham Cathedral;
Wearmouth Bridge, Sunderland; Finchale Abbey; Marsden Rock with
its grotto; Bamburgh Castle; and Cragside, Rothbury. Completing the
cornucopia of delights are a floral-tiled fireplace with mirror above and
three stained glass windows, showing scenes of merriment. The main
bar retains some attractive sinuous Art Nouveau-style glass. Upstairs,
a large function room still has old bar fittings, fireplaces and stained
glass windows but is viewable only on request.

WEST MIDLANDS

Birmingham: Aston

152 High Street
Newtown, B6 4UP
0121 333 5988
www.oakhamales.com/
bartonabout.asp
Grade II* listed
LPA: Birmingham

Bartons Arms

169

One our most impressive *fin-de siècle* pubs, the Bartons dates from 1900–1, designed by James & Lister Lea of Birmingham for Mitchells & Butlers whose monogram recurs in the glasswork. It is built of stone and red brick in a loosely Jacobean style, with shaped gables and a tall clock tower. Alterations in 1980 created interconnecting spaces but

The staircase hall

The smoking room,
now set up for dining

nonetheless these are still spectacular, due especially to the grand display of Minton Hollins tiling. Two tiled vestibules at the sharp end of the building lead into the public bar, originally divided into three by partitions. The more up-market areas were entered via a vestibule (also tiled) facing the main road. Right of this was a saloon where the snob screens, giving better class clients a sense of privacy, survive (cf. Prince Alfred, Maida Vale [68]). More snob screens occur in the great staircase-hall with its large pictorial tiled hunting scene. Left of the vestibule is a big smoke room with a projection to one side (now used for dining). On the stairwell is a grand window dated 1901. Upstairs, the club and billiard rooms are still used for functions and meetings. The pub was reopened by Oakham Ales of Peterborough in 2003 after three years' closure.

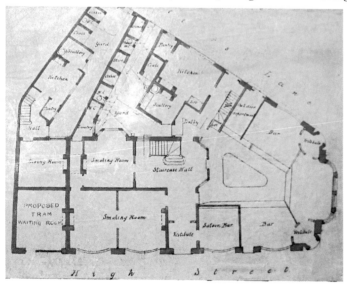

Plan of the original layout

Birmingham: Digbeth

308 Bradford Street, B5 6ET
0121 622 4516
www.anchorinndigbeth.co.uk
Grade II listed
LPA: Birmingham

Anchor

170

A red-brick and terracotta pub of 1902 for Ansells' brewery, designed by James & Lister Lea. It retains a timber and glass screen dividing the main space into two: a plan of the intended pub (in a frame in the smoke room) shows this screen was but one of several that divided the space into small compartments, including an off-sales accessed from Rea Street (its blocked doorway can still be seen). The original counter and bar-back remain, making up an L-shaped servery: heating pipes run along the foot of the counter. Behind is a smoke room (now called 'lounge') with a hatch and modern counter. It has etched panels in the doors and fixed seating with baffles and bell-pushes. A delightful small drinking area sits between the smoke room and the Rea Street entrance. The windows are interesting with Art Nouveau-style detail in the upper parts plus geometric-patterned glass in the lower ones – typical of many pubs of this date in the city. Does this quasi-Art Deco glass really go back to c.1900? It reappears in the similarly dated White Swan (171) further along Bradford Street and at other Birmingham pubs.

Glass in the public bar windows

The public bar is divided by a screen

Birmingham: Digbeth
276 Bradford Street, B12 0QY
0121 622 2586
Grade II listed
LPA: Birmingham
🍺 🍴

White Swan

171

An ambitious, red-brick and terracotta corner-site pub of 1899–1900
for Ansells brewery, designed by prolific pub architects James and
Lister Lea and retaining most of its original floor plan and extensive
tile decoration. The main changes are the loss of two low partitions
(which no doubt resembled the extant one at the Anchor [170]) within
the public bar and insertion of a modern servery in the smoke room.
The L-shaped public bar sits in the angle of the roads whilst a superbly
tiled corridor on the left-hand side widens into a stand-up drinking
area with a serving hatch. The public bar has its original counter and
bar-back, the latter with a distinctive balustrade on the top. Tiling
covers the walls, including a pretty, swirling cornice similar to that in
the corridor, whilst the ceiling is covered in copper-tiles, as at the
Waggon & Horses, Oldbury (181), but, sadly, like the latter it has been
covered over with modern paint. Also unfortunate is the modern
superstructure on top of the bar counter. The off-sales (closed in 2005)
is still in evidence to the rear right but is now used for storage.

The tiled corridor

Birmingham: Erdington

105 Station Road, B23 6UG

0121 373 0373

Not listed

LPA: Birmingham

The design of the ceramic bar counter reappears at Burlington's Bar, Lytham St Annes (48), and the Crown Bar, Belfast (266)

Red Lion

172

A corner pub of 1899 with a prominent square clock tower, designed by Wood & Kendrick for their regular clients Mitchells & Butlers. The public bar has a superb servery sweeping round through 90 degrees and featuring a stunning ceramic bar counter by Craven Dunnill of Jackfield, Shropshire. The bar-back is a lavish affair with a corner clock and glittering ornamented glasswork and a large, unusual mirror promoting 'Cragganmore Liqueur Scotch Whisky'. The floor in this bar is modern. To the right it is evident, as a sharp tap will prove, that the wall is a flimsy stud partition and it is said that, until fairly recent times, an off-sales lay beyond and that the counter has been cut back. How this fits together is hard to understand. It looks as though the large saloon/smoke room beyond is little altered but this surely cannot be (there is certainly a disused external doorway on the right but it is far-removed from the supposed off-sales). The saloon/smoke room has a good bar-back (but apparently modern counter) and generous semi-circular-plan seating units.

Birmingham: Jewellery Quarter

172 Warstone Lane, B18 6JW

0121 236 7910

www.therosevillatavern.co.uk

Grade II listed

LPA: Birmingham

Rose Villa Tavern

173

An interesting building of 1919–20, built for Mitchells & Butlers by their regular architects Wood & Kendrick and interestingly poised between florid late-Victorian taste and the simpler architecture of the inter-war years. The interior has undergone much change so that it is now possible to circumnavigate the central servery. The great attraction here is the extensive tilework by Carters of Poole. This is at its most dramatic in the small room behind the servery with its floor-to-ceiling tiling and the embellishment around the inglenook fireplace. Other notable features in this area are the tile painting over the fireplace and the stained glass in the skylight. The main front bar has plenty of tiling too, including panels depicting scantily-clad young damsels (alas, the panels are covered over). The other highlight is the exterior window glass with its colourful representations of galleons (why galleons in the middle of England?). The bar counters are mostly new. The pub reopened in 2011 following a refurbishment which added various contemporary design features. Listed in 1998 following a pilot study of Birmingham pubs by CAMRA for English Heritage.

Birmingham's distinctive pubs

Like the rest of the country Birmingham experienced a pub-building boom at the end of the 19th century, driven by social pressures to improve the quality of public houses, the desire by brewers to develop their estates to attract custom, and the fact that the pub was facing unprecedented competition for people's leisure time and spending money. Architecturally the distinctive Birmingham development was the building of prominent red brick and terracotta pubs, the first of which appeared in 1896 as the Coach & Horses, Bordesley Green. Designed by prolific pub architects James & Lister Lea, its ground floor was entirely of terracotta. Over the next decade dozens of such buildings, with considerably varied detail, appeared invitingly on Birmingham's street corners and provided excellent business for the Hathern Station Brick & Terracotta Co. Ones in this guide

The White Swan, Digbeth (171), is one of Birmingham's characteristic red brick and terracotta pubs

are the Anchor (170), White Swan, Digbeth (171), and Villa Tavern (174). Typically, the corner bar was divided up by timber screens (e.g. the Anchor) with 'better' rooms placed behind the servery. They were very often embellished

with lavish internal tilework. 1896 also saw the start of the Birmingham Surrender Scheme, organised by Arthur Chamberlain, chairman of the licensing bench. This did much to boost the building of better pubs in the city by demanding the surrender of licences in the inner areas in exchange for permission to build pubs in the growing suburbs. This policy was energetically pursued after the First World War as brewers and magistrates acted in concert to carry the policy forward under the slogan 'Fewer and Better'. This produced a remarkable and enormously varied collection, often of considerable magnificence. These still form landmarks on major roads in the city, but sadly nearly all have been wrecked inside since the 1960s. Just two make it to this guide, the Black Horse, Northfield (175 and p. 129), and the British Oak, Stirchley (176).

Tiles cover the walls and fireplace in the back room at the Rose Villa Tavern

Birmingham: Nechells

307 Nechells Park Road, B7 5PD
0121 326 7466
Grade II listed
LPA: Birmingham

The lobby between the servery and
the club room (behind the camera)

Villa Tavern

174

A red-brick and terracotta corner
pub built for Ansells' brewery in
1924–5 to designs by architect
Matthew J. Butcher. As usual, the
public bar occupies the angle of the
site and retains its counter and bar-
back, the latter with round arches
and mirror glass. The lobby area
between the bar and club room has
typical 1920s dado tiling. Behind
the servery lies a small smoke room,
complete with fixed seating, bell-
pushes and fireplace (but a new bar
counter). Some original seating
survives in the club room. Beware
the sign outside saying 'Built 1897' –
simply not true as building
regulation plans in the Birmingham
Archives prove! Listed in 1999
following fieldwork by CAMRA and
English Heritage.

Birmingham: Northfield

Bristol Road South, B31 2QT
0121 477 1800
www.jdwetherspoon.co.uk/
home/pubs/the-black-horse
Grade II listed
LPA: Birmingham

Black Horse

175

Without doubt one of the greatest and most magnificent pubs created
between the wars, this enormous 'Brewers' Tudor' roadhouse dates from
a rebuilding in 1929 for Birmingham brewers Davenports by Francis
Goldsbrough of architects Bateman & Bateman. The extravagantly
half-timbered exterior (p. 129) has gables, carved woodwork,
leaded glass and barley-sugar chimneys. Inside, the ground floor has
experienced much change, especially at the front, including some
refitting in its latest incarnation as a pub in the J. D. Wetherspoon chain,
which took over in 2010 after a period of closure. The most notable
spaces on the ground floor are the former gents' smoke room (rear right)
and the dining and assembly room (rear left): the first is a romantic
evocation of a baronial hall with a sturdy tie-beam roof (the servery is
modern), while the latter has a series of low ceilings punctuated by tall
two-light windows. Among the details to enjoy on the ground floor are
three grand and varied fireplaces. The first floor is less changed and
definitely worth a visit. The first space is a barrel-vaulted lobby area
which leads to a huge function room (with three-sided ceiling) and
beyond this is a conference room with a fine circular plaster ceiling.
Don't miss the spacious bowling green at the back.

Baron John Davenport, the inspiration behind the Black Horse:
bust in the upstairs function room

Upstairs at the Black Horse

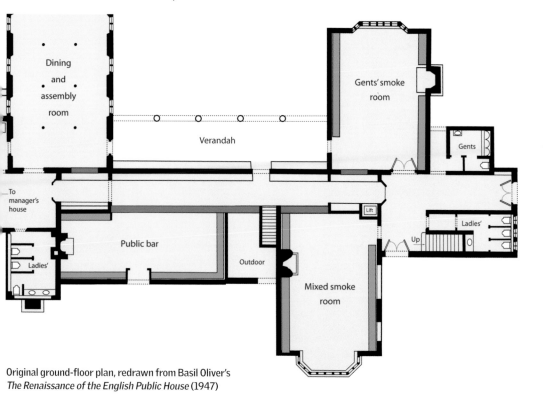

Original ground-floor plan, redrawn from Basil Oliver's
The Renaissance of the English Public House (1947)

Birmingham: Stirchley

1364 Pershore Road, B30 2XS

0121 458 1758

Grade II listed

LPA: Birmingham

British Oak   176

Designed for Mitchells & Butlers by prolific pub architects James & Lister Lea of Birmingham and built in 1923–4, this large, brick pub has an asymmetrical frontage in a 17th-century domestic style, behind which are no less than five substantially intact public rooms. Double doors in the centre lead into a lobby with tiled dado, behind which is the large public bar with a terrazzo floor, original fixed seating and oak bar counter; the bar-back is also of oak behind the yellow paint. Front left, the narrow lounge (formerly 'gents only') has its original fireplace and panelling, fixed seating with bell-pushes and a couple of baffles. The assembly room at the rear has a parquet floor, marble fireplace and small hatch to the servery. Also at the back is the smoke room with an alcove, wall-panelling to two-thirds height, and a three-sided servery (but is the latter original?). Finally, back to the front of the pub, where the right-hand room again has its original fireplace and seating. Both gents' toilets have their original tiling, as has the ladies' on the right. The bowling green is still in use. Listed in 1998 following a pilot study of Birmingham pubs by CAMRA for English Heritage.

The public bar

97 Elmore Green Road, WS3 2HN

Grade II listed

LPA: Walsall

Romping Cat

177

A corner local of 1900 which retains its three-room layout and 'outdoor department' (still with functioning original sliding sash windows). In the bar on the right occupying the rounded corner of the building are an unaltered counter, bar-back and fixed seating plus etched and frosted windows advertising 'Banks's Noted Ales & Stouts'. The small smoke room on the left has a hatch to the servery and original curved bench seating, but a modern fireplace within the old wooden surround. A passage with colourful mosaic flooring runs round the back of the servery to a further bar which has an etched window inscribed 'Coffee Room', an intact old fireplace plus original, if shortened, fixed seating. The pub was formerly known as the Sandbank Tavern but its sign showed a heraldic lion from the arms of Sir Gilbert Wakering, the Elizabethan lord of the manor: the resultant nickname became official in 1957. The Grade II listing in 2004 was prompted by an application from CAMRA.

The smoke room has a hatch to the servery

Bloxwich

13 Wolverhampton Road, WS3 2EZ

01922 407745

Grade II listed

LPA: Walsall

Restricted opening hours

Turf Tavern

178

Few, if any, Victorian terraced pubs have experienced so little change as the Turf which has been owned by the same family since 1871. The simple two-storey frontage has a bay window either side of a central entrance leading to a quarry-tiled passage. A couple of hatches to the servery line its right-hand side. The public bar has more quarry-tiling and a simple Victorian bar-back (with drawers) and counter (but with a 1960s Formica top) plus hand-pumps dating from 1927. There is bare seating and a couple of simple, moveable low benches. The front left-hand room has window glass inscribed 'Smoke Room', 'Wines' and 'Spirits', and unusual fixed seating with padded benches divided into individual seats by arm rests. The rear left-hand room has leather-covered bench seating with baffles. The outside gents' are worth a visit for their massive old urinals and among the other outbuildings are a malt room (part of the former home brewery) and three pig-sties. The rarity of such unaltered, modest public houses led to the Turf being Grade II listed in 1996 following a CAMRA/English Heritage study in the West Midlands. Open 1–2.30 Fri–Sun, 7–10.30 (10 Mon).

The public bar

Dudley
74 Stafford Street, DY1 1RT
01384 213461
Grade II listed
LPA: Dudley

Shakespeare

179

Hundreds of Black Country pubs would once have resembled this simply-appointed, three-room drinkers' establishment. In the centre a corridor, with red and black quarry tiles, leads to the back past a tiny hatch to the servery and on to the outside toilets. Off to the left at the front, behind a match-boarded partition, is a very small bar with a plain panelled counter and basic shelving to serve as a bar-back. This is actually called the tap room and it is one of the very rare cases where that name is used for a room where drink is actually dispensed (see p. 54 for this paradox). Behind this is a long plain room with an irregular plan reflecting the shape of the site. A further room on the right is once again very plainly appointed. Fixed seating throughout.

The Shakespeare was listed at Grade II in 1999 as a result of joint CAMRA/English Heritage casework, showing the growing recognition of the rarity of such small, basic pubs.

The tap room (see p. 54 for discussion of this name)

Netherton

89 Halesowen Road, DY2 9PY
01384 253075
Grade II listed
LPA: Dudley

Old Swan ('Ma Pardoe's')   180

One of only four surviving brew-pubs when CAMRA was formed in 1971. It takes its nickname from Mrs Doris Pardoe, licensee until 1984, after taking over from her late husband in the early 1950s. Brewing stopped in 1988 but restarted in 2001. The wonderfully evocative front bar seems unchanged since Victorian times, apart from the gloriously over-the-top red paint. The enamel-panel ceiling is an extraordinary rarity and its eponymous swan a stunning feature, as are the old stove (still used) with its flue running across the room, and the old weighing machine. A rear smoke room also has its historic fittings: originally it was entered from a corridor door on the right. The drinking area to the right of the smoke room, known as the 'ladies' room', was converted out of a former office during 1980s changes. A tiny off-sales-cum-snug lies between the two old bars and has a single bench for customers sneaking a swift one while making their purchases. In the 1980s, the pub expanded into a former shop next door, but without compromising the historic core.

No false modesty at 'Ma Pardoe's'

The brightly coloured public bar with its enamelled ceiling

Oldbury

17a Church Street, B69 3AD
0121 552 5467
Grade II listed
LPA: Sandwell
🍺 🍴

The entrance corridor with a
hatch to the servery

Waggon & Horses

181

A small, friendly corner pub built
by Holt's brewery of Aston about
1900 using the brick and terracotta
so prevalent for pubs in this area at
that time. The extensive use of
internal tiling puts it in the same
stable as certain Birmingham pubs
(169 and 171). On the corner, as
usual, is the public bar where the
walls are lined with mainly cream
tiles, and the counter with its richly
treated bar-back no doubt date
from the building of the pub: the
ceiling is remarkable for being clad
with sheet copper tiles (cf. White
Swan, Birmingham [171]) – sadly
these have been painted over on
more than one occasion. The side
entrance leads to a tiled corridor
with a hatch to the servery, which
makes an L-shape round a smoke

room where there are fixed seats, bell-pushes and a fireplace and which
appears to be partly of *c*.1900 and partly interwar (if not a little later).

Rushall

Park Road
Daw End, WS4 1LG
01922 642333
Grade II listed
LPA: Walsall
🍺 🍴

The Manor Arms is one of those
rare pubs lacking a counter (p. 41)

Manor Arms

182

This is one of the very few pubs in the country with no bar counter
(see p. 41). It is a three-room canal-side establishment opened as a
beerhouse in 1895 within an 18th-century building. The central corridor
is a favourite place for a drink with many regulars and on its left is the
public bar, where the hand-pumps and taps are set against the back wall

beneath rows of shelving for glasses and bottles. Customers and serving staff are therefore not segregated as happens with a conventional bar counter. This warm and welcoming room has simple dado panelling, a boarded ceiling, a fixed bench and a (possibly) interwar brick fireplace. The front right-hand room has an old quarry-tiled floor, fixed seating (possibly from the 1930s) and a modern brick fireplace in an old inglenook. At the back is the lounge, a small room brought into pub use in relatively recent times and with no historic fittings.

What shaped Britain's pubs – 4: after the war was over

In 1945 Britain was bankrupt. The Second World War had been far more devastating than the First so that, whereas pub-building was in full swing again in the early 1920s, it would be another ten years before precious resources were allowed to be directed to the far from essential business of building and refurbishing public houses. By the mid-1950s, when things did get going again, there was an inevitable spirit of economy so that the solidity which characterised 1930s architecture and fittings was replaced by meagre design and a general sense of tightened belts. Not surprisingly, as the century wore on and Britons 'never had it so good', such work was replaced so that we have the paradoxical situation in this guide that pub interiors from the 1950s and 1960s are almost wholly absent (135, 194, 231 and 245 are the rare exceptions) and are hugely outnumbered by ones twice as old.

Until the 1960s multi-room interiors continued to be built but since then the single-room, open-plan pub has become the norm. Several reasons underpin this. Society has become less stratified and, in a de-industrialised society, there are no longer hordes of thirsty, dirty steelworkers and coalminers who need to be confined to the public bar. Licensing magistrates

The lounge at the Laurieston Bar, Glasgow (245), the most intact example of a pub interior from about 1960

and the police, long-concerned with public order and illicit goings-on in pubs, have been only too happy to encourage pubs where the sight lines allow for improved supervision. Furthermore, the more open the pub, the larger the trading area.

It is against this background that CAMRA's National Inventory of Historic Pub Interiors came into being. About 1970 there was vastly more of what we might regard today as pub 'heritage' and so it was unnoticed, unloved and ripe for redevelopment. Breweries and pub owners are commercial businesses and have, with few exceptions, been more interested in profits than the finer points of heritage. It is undoubtedly

the case that quite a number of pubs in this guide would not be here were it not for the statutory listing system. It is also true to say that a fair number of them are here solely because they have been (or were) in the hands of private families who, with no shareholders to satisfy and often with no mortgage to pay, were happy to leave them unaltered. A long, but by no means exhaustive, list of such pubs includes those numbered in this guide as follows: 3, 9, 13, 15, 18, 24, 25, 26, 27, 28, 33, 35, 36, 38, 41, 43, 45, 46, 129, 130, 136, 142, 143, 145, 149, 152, 178, 180, 187, 191, 195, 221, 222, 224, 227, 228, 230, 253, 255, 260, 261, 264, 265, 268, 269, 270.

Sedgley

129 Bilston Street, DY3 1JE
01902 883380
www.sarahhughesbrewery.co.uk
Grade II listed
LPA: Dudley

Beacon Hotel

183

An incredibly rare survivor – an unspoilt gem of a four-room
pub with a mid-Victorian tower brewery attached at the rear.
Sarah Hughes bought the business in 1921 and little has changed
since the Twenties, apart from additional rooms being created at the
back. The most remarkable feature is the small glazed-in cubicle for
service which sits between the front snug and the larger rear smoke
room. Both these rooms have a small hatch for service as does the
adjacent corridor and at all three of these hatches customers have to
bend down to communicate their requirements to the staff. The largest
room is the smoke room which is boarded all over but this boarding
had been covered up and was only revealed during refurbishment
in 1987: it may possibly be Victorian. The tap room at the front right
may once have been a kitchen (see the range) and some of the fittings
look Victorian. The brewery lay idle from the 1950s until 1987
since when, under new ownership, it has produced award-winning
ales whose names honour the redoubtable Sarah Hughes. Food
consists of cobs. Listed in 2010 after an application by CAMRA.

In the smoke room, showing the
highly unusual glazed servery

Micro-brewers and National Inventory pubs

The rise and rise of the micro-brewer is one of the exciting features of the recent British beer scene. In 2012 the number of UK breweries topped 1,000, the highest figure for 60 years, and this is all down to the opening up of new ventures supplying the market with quality ales. Where better to appreciate their wares than in genuinely historic pub surroundings? And it's not just the view of those of us in CAMRA involved with the present guide. Several brewers have already worked it out! In preparing the guide it became evident how many are in the hands of small breweries. In a few cases they've been capitalising on the asset for years, in others they have turned basket cases into thriving businesses which are quite simply a great place for a drink. Where the big pubcos and lacklustre lessees and managers have failed, others have succeeded. Often there's nothing fancy involved – just damned good ale, enthusiastic and committed staff and management, and a welcoming environment in traditional surroundings.

Here is the list as we go to press of these small brewery-owned or run National Inventory pubs: brewing is *not* on-site unless stated.

Lancashire, Goosnargh, Ye Horns Inn (46): on-site brewing began in March 2013.

Manchester, Greater, Manchester, Marble Arch (104): owned by Marble Beers.

Somerset, Bath, Star Inn (141): the brewery tap for Abbey Ales.

Staffordshire, Cannock, Crystal Fountain (148): owned by Black Country Ales.

Brewing at the Prestoungrange Gothenburg   (David Whyte)

West Midlands, Birmingham, Bartons Arms (169): owned by Oakham Ales of Peterborough. Netherton, Old Swan ('Ma Pardoe's') (180): on-site brewing ceased in 1988 but was started again in 2001 by the Olde Swan Brewery. Sedgley, Beacon Hotel (183): on-site brewing was restarted by the Sarah Hughes Brewery in 1987. Wednesfield, Vine (186): owned by Black Country Ales.

Yorkshire, West, Halifax, Three Pigeons (213): owned by Ossett Brewery. Heath, King's Arms (214): leased by Ossett Brewery. Leeds, Garden Gate (218): owned by Leeds Brewery.

Wales, North-West, Conwy, Albion Ale House (225): leased by a consortium of four micro-breweries: Conwy, Great Orme, Nant and Purple Moose.

Scotland, Edinburgh and the Lothians, Prestonpans, Prestoungrange Gothenburg (242): the Demonbrew Brewery (independent of the pub) is viewable from the main bar which sells its beer.

On pp. 256–9 we also present the dark side – closed pubs looking for new owners. Any imaginative brewers out there who want to take on one of these a love-lorn historic pubs? They might well repay your affection!

Upper Gornal

109 Kent Street, DY3 1UX

01902 883253

Not listed

LPA: Dudley

🍺 🍴

The Britannia in about 1929 with joints of meat hanging in the window: the girl in the centre is Sallie Perry who would go on to be the landlady from 1942 to 1991

Britannia ('Sallies') 184

At the rear left of this pub is a very special room, possibly fitted out in the 1920s. The 'wood' panelling is, in fact, imitation (like embossed wallpaper) and there are fixed benches together with some stained glass. But the real points of interest, however, are the shelving, drawers and bank of four hand-pumps (with pewter drip tray) set against the corridor wall – a now very rare arrangement of a servery without a counter (and still used on Saturday nights). The hatch with pewter ledge to the corridor would probably have been used as an off-sales and also by customers in the former second room (now in the area of the ladies' toilet). The pub has had a very interesting development. It opened as a beerhouse about 1832. Then, after he purchased it in 1864, Henry Perry opened a butcher's shop at the front and had his beerhouse at the rear. Beer was brewed in the buildings behind (until 1959). The Perry family kept the pub until 1991 and it is still sometimes known as 'Sallie's' after the landlady from 1942. It was purchased by Batham's brewery in 1997. Now customers have to be content with a roll and a pint in the front bar rather than stocking up with a pound of sausages!

The old servery forms one side of the rear room

Wednesbury

Wood Green Road, WS10 9AX
0121 556 0464
Not listed
LPA: Sandwell

The public bar has a rare
ceramic bar counter

Horse & Jockey

185

Built in 1898 to designs by Wood & Kendrick, this pub is included for
one reason only – the servery in the public bar. This has a ceramic bar
counter which is organised in a series of layers as if on a cake, each with
a different colour and different detail. It also has brown pilasters, each
terminated by a grotesque mask with a protruding tongue, dividing the
counter front up into a series of bays. Unfortunately the counter has
been cut back on the left to create space for an entrance from the
corridor. Behind the servery there is an elaborately treated back-fitting
of five bays housing some fine mirrorwork. The large rear room is almost
wholly modern and represents an expansion of the original smoke room.

Wednesfield

35 Lichfield Road, WV11 1TN
01902 733529
Grade II listed
LPA: Wolverhampton

The public bar

Vine

186

A rare and intact example of a simple inter-war, urban, working-class
pub. It opened in 1938 and remains complete apart from the loss of the
off-sales hatch opposite the front door and the insertion of a tiny counter
in the smoke room. The public bar on the left has a colourful terrazzo
floor plus the original bar counter, seating and fireplace. On the right is
a smoke room, with a parquet floor, Tudor-style fireplace and fixed
seating with bell-pushes. A second smoke room lies at the back across
the terrazzo-floored hallway and has similar original features to its
namesake. The toilets are scarcely
altered since they were built. An
unfortunate addition has been the
anachronistic Victorian-style
embossed paper applied to the dadoes.
Listing at Grade II in 2002 following
an application by CAMRA recognised
that even straightforward locals such
as this are precious survivals if they
remain essentially unaltered.

WILTSHIRE

Easton Royal

Easton Road, SN9 5LR

01672 810216

www.thebrucearms.net

Not listed

LPA: Wiltshire

🍺 🍴 (weekends)

🛏 (caravan and campsite)

Bruce Arms ('The Gammon') 187

This traditional roadside pub, built about 1850, lies on the B3087 to the west of the village. Until 1997 it was kept by Rose Raisey, who died in 1993 aged 87, and her long tenure helped preserve the historic core over the years. At the entrance is a small snug with a counter and a red and black quarry-tiled floor. On the right is a simply-appointed public bar which has a red-brick floor and scrubbed Victorian tables and benches. The counter is thought to be from a refit in the 1930s, a date which would accord well with the brick fireplace. The utterly basic shelving in the servery is believed to be later. Beyond, on the right, Rose's kitchen has been brought into public use and further on still is an extension of 1996 which serves as a games room. On the left of the pub is the lounge with a hatch to the servery: it is furnished with domestic sofas and chairs and also a piano bought for Rose when she was 13. The inside toilets (left) were added in 1952. The nickname is said to come from a pub that stood opposite but which burned down about 1830.

The redoubtable Rose Raisey kept the Bruce Arms unaltered. The public bar below

Salisbury

1–5 Minster Street, SP1 1TB
01722 411313
www.haunch-salisbury.com
Grade II* listed
LPA: Wiltshire

The rare spirit cocks on the counter in the snug

Haunch of Venison

188

A pub of great antiquity and character in the heart of Salisbury and long-styled (outside) as 'An Old English Chop House'. Right of the lobby, a narrow door leads into a tiny room, sometimes referred to as the 'Ladies' Snug' (no doubt they popped in for a swift one, away from male gaze). It has a quarry-tiled floor, panelled walls with benches attached, and a rare pewter counter top. Note the wooden arch housing seven spirit taps (with a brass plate inscription, 'Gravity fed spirit taps fitted by H. Neale, Plumber, Salisbury' and dated 1909). Only four other examples are known – two in this guide, the Bull Inn, Paisley (251), and Crown Bar, Belfast (266), and two others, Shipman's, Northampton; and Queen's Head, Stockport. The public bar (the 'House of Commons') has more quarry-tiling, panelled walls, benches and another pewter counter-top: hand-pumps are fixed to the bar-back. Up the stairs the 'House of Lords' (left) has a low, beamed ceiling, panelled walls and inglenook fireplace (with bread oven containing a grisly, mummified hand, supposedly that of a cheating card-player). The restaurant, incorporating part of a 16th-century merchant's house, includes a fine ceiling.

The public bar

WORCESTERSHIRE

Bretforton

The Cross
Bretforton, WR11 7JE
01386 831173
www.thefleeceinn.co.uk
Grade II listed
LPA: Wychavon

🍺 🍎 🍴 🛏️

The 'Dug Out'

Fleece

189

This legend of a pub, occupying a 17th-century building, was in the hands of the same family for generations. The last of the line, Miss Lola Taplin, lived here for all of her 77 years and on her death in 1977 she left the property to the National Trust. It has three stone-flagged rooms which retain Lola's extraordinary assemblage of old furniture and other artefacts. The 'Pewter Room' is named after an impressive collection of antique pewterware and has a large settle (note the doors at the back for storage): note also the 'witches circles' near the inglenook fireplace which were supposedly efficacious in preventing witches from entering down the chimney. The 'Dug Out' – down two steps and with a stone fireplace – is the former games room, popular for darts in Lola's day. The most impressive room is the 'Brewhouse' which has a vast inglenook fireplace and two indentations in the wall through which water from the well outside was fed in the days of home brewing. After fire damage in February 2004 the Fleece was carefully restored and reopened in May the following year.

The Brewhouse Bar

Clent

Holy Cross, DY9 9QL
01562 730319
www.bellandcrossclent.co.uk
Grade II listed
LPA: Bromsgrove

Bell & Cross   190

This has been a pub for nearly 200 years, growing over time to five
separate rooms. Although there is much emphasis on food, a good sense
of a traditional small village pub can still be recaptured. The central
quarry-tiled corridor runs to the rear and has a tiny hatch on the left
which, no doubt, was used for off-sales. Behind this is the small public
bar with a possibly Victorian counter, bar-back and some old fixed seating:
the fireplace is probably interwar. Right of the entrance is a delightful
snug created by a pair of full-height timber partitions which form the
backs to the fixed seating within. This cosy space appears as many
thousands of pub rooms must have once done up and down the land.
Room '6' (see p. 147 for room numbering) beyond is believed to have
been the landlord's living room. Room '4', facing it, was the gentlemen's
smoke room. At the rear is a further room created out of a barn in
1998. These last three rooms have been refitted in modern times.

The snug with its screens which
incorporate bench seating

Defford

Woodmancote
Defford, WR8 9BW
(on A4104 west of the village)
01386 750234
Grade II listed
LPA: Wychavon

Restricted opening hours

Cider House ('Monkey House')   191

Unique – that's the Cider House, one of the country's most unspoilt
pubs and part of a 17th-century thatched, half-timbered building. The
drink is cider – for this is one of only four remaining cider-only houses
in the country (no beer is served). It has been in the family of landlady
Gill Collins for 150 years. The main bar is actually outside – it's the
front garden! And if the weather isn't too good, customers drink in the
former bakehouse at the side. Service is not over one of those new-
fangled bar counters but through a hatch in a stable door on the left of

the cottage. The casks of cider are stillaged behind in a ground-floor 'cellar'. Outside loos – the gents' (roofless), the ladies' (roofed). Why the nickname? Many years ago, a well-mellowed customer is said to have returned home covered in cuts and scratches inflicted by a tribe of monkeys, rather than a self-induced collapse into a bramble patch.

To the left, the old bakehouse is the only under-cover space: to its right, the servery

Hanley Castle

Church End, WR8 0BL
01684 592686
Grade II listed
LPA: Malvern Hills

Three Kings

192

This pub has been held by the same family since 1911. It is named not after the biblical Three Wise Men but, it is said, three brothers surnamed King who owned the building in the late 17th century. The oldest part is to the left where, to the right of the corridor, there is a gloriously unspoiled public bar. Entered through a sliding door, it has

The public bar with its open fire, settle and bare tile floor (viewed from behind the servery)

a quarry-tiled floor, high-backed settle (doubling as the partition to the corridor), a huge fireplace (with a copper hood), and a hatch to the servery. Left of the corridor is a little-used smoke room, also with a sliding door. The right-hand side of the pub houses 'Nell's Lounge', added in 1982 and named after schoolmistress Nell Creese whose house it was. It retains the range in her former kitchen and, at the front, a high-backed settle and an inglenook fireplace with a bread oven.

Worcester

4 Bull Ring
St Johns, WR2 5AD
01905 863598
Not listed
LPA: Worcester

Bush

193

A small corner site pub built in 1879 and containing two old rooms and some good fittings. The public bar was once divided into three as scars on the counter reveal: it has a couple of bell-pushes and original seating. This room is served from an L-shaped servery which has a particularly fine L-shaped bar-back, incorporating on the corner twisted columns and a clock that helpfully names the bar fitters, Yates & Greenways of Birmingham, whose names also appear in a little plate on the counter. On the left is a now-closed tiled corridor with an off-sales hatch to the servery. The corridor leads to a small smoke room (also reached from the side door and corridor) at the rear with fixed seating and bell-pushes. Upstairs is a former billiards room (duly named in etched glass).

The public bar servery

Worcester

Lichfield Avenue
Ronkswood, WR5 1PE
01905 863054
Not listed
LPA: Worcester

Punch Bowl

194

That rare thing, a post-war pub which remains very little altered (see also 107, 135 and 245). The Punch Bowl was built with an irregularly shaped plan and four rooms plus off-sales in 1958 for a housing estate. In a characteristic piece of contemporary town planning, it is located on a circular development in the centre of the estate with a church in the middle and shops round the perimeter. The relatively small public bar faces on to the circle and is as it was fifty years ago with simple fixed seating, quarry-tile flooring, brick fireplace, counter, and bar-back. On the right is an unusual projection, evidently for playing darts and including a fixed seat for the players and spectators. To the rear right of the public bar is a small pool room and at the back of the pub is a large function room, extended to provide a skittle alley. Finally, on the left is a small smoke room and a former off-sales compartment, now converted to form an office. The fittings are all very plain and simple, reflecting the austerity and desire for simple clean lines at the end of the Fifties.

In the public bar at the Punch Bowl

YORKSHIRE, EAST

*All Yorkshire entries are by **Dave Gamston***

Beverley

22 Hengate, HU17 8BN
01482 861973
www.nellies.co.uk
Grade II* listed
LPA: East Riding of Yorkshire

🍺 🍴

White Horse ('Nellie's')   `195`

Something of a Yorkshire institution, 'Nellie's' is one of the must-see highlights of this historic county town. A vernacular gem, it has evolved into a warren of varied and distinctive rooms, still with gas lighting and warmed in winter by blazing fires in the old hearths. It takes its popular nickname from Nellie Collinson, whose family acquired the pub in 1927 and who was its long-serving and redoubtable licensee until the 1970s when the current owners, Samuel Smith's brewery of Tadcaster, took over. Changes made by them include a modern servery in the main bar whereas Nellie had made do with just a simple table and pulled the beer from two hand-pumps against a wall, the remnants of which can still be seen. Also a new, over-wide opening was created to the front parlour, and a sizeable modern extension built. Among many positives, the old semi-private kitchen has been brought into regular pub use and the old-fashioned front snug (right), second parlour and entrance corridors from Hengate have been left largely untouched.

**The interior of Nellie's is an amazing time-warp
with many rooms and interesting vistas**

Bridlington

Bridlington Railway Station
Station Approach, YO15 3EP
01262 673709
www.stationbuffet.co.uk
Grade II listed
LPA: East Riding of Yorkshire

In the first class area of
Bridlington's Station Buffet

Station Buffet

One of only two working licensed railway buffets on the main national rail network to have survived largely intact from before the Second World War (see also Stalybridge, Greater Manchester [111]). It occupies part of a two-storey block designed in 1922 (built 1925) by the North Eastern Railway's last serving company architect, Stephen Wilkinson, as a careful addition to the 1912 station concourse of his predecessor, William Bell. It retains all the main elements of its original interior and its layout of two rooms was to cater separately for the two 'classes' of passenger: the first class customers had the benefit of being served nearer the tracks! Both rooms preserve their original bar-counters with rare marble tops and plinths, ceilings and terrazzo flooring. Most of the joinery is original too – windows, door-frames, the chimney breast pilasters and the lobby screen-work in first class room – but both rooms have lost their old fireplaces. The entire station was statutorily listed in 2003 following a successful application by CAMRA.

Hull: city centre

150 High Street, HU1 1PS
07894 254043
www.yeoldeblackboy.weebly.com
Grade II listed
LPA: Hull

Olde Black Boy

A rare survivor of the many pubs that lined what was once old Hull's principal thoroughfare. The premises has had many uses over the years, including tobacco dealing (traditionally symbolised by an Indian Chief – 'black boy'!) but the key interest lies in its transition from Victorian wine merchant to public house, whilst retaining much of the layout of the former. The refitting was done in 1926 for local company T. Linsley

& Co. – the former wine merchant's office became the front smoke room, the warehouse became the rear bar, and the cosy upstairs rooms continued their function for meetings. Original fittings from 1926 include the downstairs panelling (that upstairs is more recent), bar-counters and front fire surround. Threats of alterations in 2001 were averted following CAMRA's successful application for statutory listing.

Musicians play each Wednesday afternoon in the front room at the Olde Black Boy, which was refitted in the 1920s

Hull: city centre

25 Silver Street, HU1 1JG
01482 326363
www.yeoldewhiteharte.co.uk
Grade II* listed
LPA: Hull
🍺 🍴

Olde White Harte

198

The impressive Olde White Harte has been a licensed premises since the 18th century and has parts dating back to the 17th. Its historic interest as a public house, however, derives from a major refurbishment of 1881 by local architects, Smith & Brodrick. Their designs for the downstairs rooms (smoke room to the left, and public bar) used various elements of the original domestic interior, but incorporated them into

The 17th-century staircase

The idea of an 'Olde Englishe' inn as recreated in 1881

an idealised re-creation of a 17th-century 'Olde Englishe' inn, complete with massive brick fireplaces – a striking example of a 'theme pub' by the Victorians! Only one of the downstairs serveries is now in regular use: both have copper counter tops, possibly from the 1960s. The old panelled upstairs rooms, now reserved mainly for dining and functions, were left largely untouched by the 1881 scheme. One is dubbed the 'Plotting Room', a Civil War reference to be taken with a large pinch of salt, since the building post-dates that conflict!

Hull: city centre

109 Alfred Gelder Street, HU1 1EP
01482 228136
www.thewhiteharthull.co.uk
Grade II listed
LPA: Hull

Restricted opening hours

White Hart   199

Rebuilt in 1904 for the Hull Brewery Co. (architects Freeman, Son & Gaskell), the White Hart was given a classy frontage to the newly opened Alfred Gelder Street and a well-appointed interior in the manner of a small Edwardian drinking 'palace'. Its beautifully preserved front bar boasts a fine mahogany back-fitting with glazed, towered cupboards, which is probably unique. There is also a spectacular ceramic-fronted

The ceramic counter and glazed cabinets in the back-fitting. The counter has the same design as that at the Garden Gate, Leeds (218)

counter, one of only fourteen such examples in the whole UK and probably a product of the Burmantofts company of Leeds: another, by the same architects for the same brewery client, can also be found in Hull at the Polar Bear (200). As well as these lovely fittings, the White Hart's front bar also retains all its wood panelling and seating, while the entrance lobby too is complete with its original doors and floor tiling. The back section, however, which had its own small ceramic counter until the 1970s, has succumbed to modern alteration.

Hull: Spring Bank

229 Spring Bank, HU3 1LR
Grade II listed
LPA: Hull

Polar Bear

200

The stand-out feature at the Polar Bear is its magnificent ceramic-fronted bar counter, one of only fourteen surviving in the whole UK and the largest of any with a curved front. Its manufacturer was probably Burmantofts of Leeds, and Hull can proudly boast of another example, at the White Hart (199). The pub itself, whose name reflects its proximity to Hull's one-time zoological gardens, was built in 1895 by prolific local architects Freeman, Son & Gaskell and later extended and refitted by them in 1922 (for the Hull Brewery Co.), adding elements like the 'orchestra' area with its the splendid domed skylight, the fitted bench seating, and the striking stone signage outside. Modern alterations in the early 1980s retained the separate back smoke room (now a games room) but swept away a small partitioned-off saloon from within the large front bar. Statutorily listed in 2005, following a successful application by CAMRA.

The Polar Bear has one of the two ceramic counters in Hull pubs

YORKSHIRE, NORTH

Beck Hole

YO22 5LE
01947 896245
www.beckhole.info
Grade II listed
LPA: North York Moors National Park

🍺 🍴

Restricted opening hours

Birch Hall Inn

201

A unique timewarp, lovingly preserved, comprising two simple rooms either side of a tiny village shop. The Birch Hall is an absolute gem, a mile north of Goathland and nestling in an idyllic valley setting which is hard to imagine having an industrial past. Yet, back in the 1860s, Beck Hole rang to the clamour of ironstone mines, furnaces, quarries and the railway. The three-storey, right-hand half of the premises was built (by the pub landlord of the time) as a shop, with lodgings above for the influx of workers. The original pub was no more than a single room (essentially the 'Big Bar' of today) in the 18th-century cottage to the left, and it was not until after the Second World War that a second public room, the 'Little Bar', was created from part of the Victorian shop. The present owners are dedicated to keeping the pub unaltered and to preserving its old-fashioned simplicity; indeed, when they took over in 1981, they gladly accepted a condition of sale to do exactly this – imposed by former landlady, Mrs Schofield, whose home it had been for 53 years. Closed Mon eve and all day Tue in winter.

One of the two small rooms at the Birch Hall Inn

Boroughbridge

Bridge Street, YO51 9LF

01423 322314

www.
threehorseshoesboroughbridge.
co.uk

Grade II listed

LPA: Harrogate

🍷 🍴

Three Horse Shoes   202

This is one of the best-preserved examples of a small inter-war road-house and one whose revival has been a recent success story. Originally built to serve traffic on the old Great North Road, which then ran straight through the town, it was sold-off in 2003 by its long-time family owners and narrowly escaped conversion to a Chinese restaurant! Thanks partly to its statutory listing, successfully sought by CAMRA in 2000, it has re-emerged relatively unscathed. Apart from losing original fitted seating and sustaining two enlarged openings between rooms (one now sensitively hung with double doors) its interior differs only slightly from the 1929 plans by architect Sydney Blenkhorn of Knaresborough. The fittings, which include quality oak bar structures, oak fire surrounds and excellent stained and leaded glass are all from the original building scheme by Hepworth & Co., a small Ripon brewery for whom this would doubtless have been a prestige project.

Screened counters, as here, were a feature of some pubs in the north (cf. pub nos 103, 116, 117, 195 and 209)

Middlesbrough

9 Zetland Road, TS1 1EH

01642 242155

Grade II listed

LPA: Middlesbrough

Restricted opening hours

Zetland   203

The Zetland was built around 1860 as a pub-cum-hotel to serve the railway station opposite and the mosaic floor panel at the entrance and cast-iron columns outside are from that time. The principal interest here, however, is the spectacular tiled and mirrored lounge which was added at the rear in 1893, designed by local architect J. M. Bottomley for a private client and described as 'luncheon bar' on the earliest plans. To this day it retains its superb display of round-arched mirrors with surrounding tilework in cream, browns and light blue together with a plaster ceiling with geometric patterns and ornamented cornice and frieze. The servery is modern, however, as are the fittings in the main front bar. Commonly opens Fri and Sat evenings but opening times are complicated (check before visiting).

The amazing tiled and mirrored rear room is now used as a night-club (hence the bright lights) but may be inspected on request

Selby

4 Gowthorpe, YO8 4ET
Grade II listed
LPA: Selby

New Inn   `204`

The New Inn is a town-centre pub of long standing, which was completely remodelled in 1934 and preserves an outstanding remnant from that inter-war scheme in its front smoke room. Sometimes dubbed 'The Vatican' (for which there are differing theories), this charming little room has fine wood panelling, stylish built-in settles,

original bell-pushes and a striking bow-windowed counter screen with intact sashed serving hatches. The decorative leaded windows are striking too, with 'sporting' scenes that may reflect the enthusiasm of members of the Middlebrough family, the pub's local brewer-owners of the time. Their architect for the 1934 refurbishment was John Poulson, then just 24 years of age and as yet untainted by the national scandals that would lead to his later shaming and jailing. Poulson had begun his career with the Pontefract firm of Garside & Pennington who were experienced pub designers, but this may be one of few pub commissions he undertook in his own right.

Inside 'The Vatican'

Settle

Market Place, BD24 9ED
01729 822561
www.theroyaloakhotel-settle.co.uk
Not listed
LPA: Craven

Royal Oak Hotel   `205`

Once a flourishing 18th-century inn on the Keighley-Kendal turnpike road, the Royal Oak was acquired by the Blackburn brewers, Dutton's, in 1902. It was extensively remodelled by them in the interwar years and given an idealised 'Olde Englishe' panelled interior, to create an enticing stopping-off place for the new breed of motorised tourists on their way to Morecambe or the Lakes. Some of this panelling was executed with canny economy, using plasterwork to imitate timber, but to impressive overall effect. The lavish display can still be appreciated today, although the pub's layout was much altered in the mid-1960s when the former snug and smoke-room were merged and the tap room became the gents' toilet. There is still a separate dining room with yet more panelling. The revolving entrance door is a noteworthy rarity.

Neo-Tudor panelling
at the Royal Oak
(Michael Slaughter)

York: city centre

53 Fossgate, YO1 9TF
01904 654904
Grade II* listed
LPA: York

Blue Bell

The compact and intimate Blue Bell is a true national treasure and one of very few public houses to have the distinction of Grade II* status for the outstanding importance of its interior (the listing was upgraded in 1997). It is the result of a refurbishment in 1903 by local wine merchants, C. J. Melrose & Co. and consists of a public bar at the front, a smoke room to the rear and a side corridor modestly widened into an early version of a northern drinking lobby. All the Edwardian fittings survive and include engraved and frosted glass in the doors and windows, glazed screens with sashed service hatches to the back room and corridor, and varnished matchboarding to the walls and ceilings. The unusual little tip-up seat in the corridor lobby might be part of the 1903 works too. The Blue Bell's preservation in such an unaltered state has had much to do with its tenancy remaining in the same family throughout most of the 20th century. It has subsequently had to weather three major ownership changes but, thanks to enthusiastic and caring licensees, it continues to thrive.

An unusual seat in the corridor

The smoke room
looking towards servery

York

2 Cromwell Road, YO1 6DU
01904 652211
www.goldenball-york.co.uk
Grade II listed
LPA: York

Golden Ball

This 1929 'improvement' of a small Victorian back-street local is thought to be the most complete surviving inter-war scheme by John Smith's, the Tadcaster company who became one of the UK's biggest regional brewers and pub-builders. Their remodelling here raised the ceiling heights of the cramped old interior and incorporated the adjoining corner building to create a more generous layout. The resulting interior is unusual in its planning, with a single main entrance, public bar to the rear, and an intimate little seated alcove beside the servery. The 1929 scheme also created the corner off-sales (now defunct) and left a distinctive ceramic signature in the glazed brick and tiled exterior and also in the rare tiled counter front. The only substantial post-war change has been the 1990s formation of an extra room, left of the entrance. The Golden Ball was statutorily listed in 2010 following a successful application by CAMRA and, since late 2012, its running has been enterprisingly taken over by a local community cooperative.

The public bar has a rare tiled front, the design of which is continued on the walling

York

16 Bishopgate Street, YO23 1JH
01904 634968
www.bishyroad.net/shop/
the-swan
Grade II listed
LPA: York

Swan

208

The Swan is a near-intact 1930s remodelling of a small Victorian corner local and has one of the best-preserved interiors of its kind in the country. It was designed in 1936 for the Leeds brewer Joshua Tetley by architects Kitson, Parish, Ledgard & Pyman, also of Leeds, who were responsible for much of Tetley's work between the Wars. Their design here centres on a room-sized stand-up lobby (one of the best surviving examples of this distinctly northern feature) with a room at either end of the central servery, each served by a hatch. Modern touches are few in number and, as well as the unaltered layout, it is authentic fabric like the fitted seating, bell-pushes, leaded and glazed screenwork, terrazzo flooring – even the toilet ceramics – that help make this a memorable 1930s survival. The Swan was statutorily listed in 2010 following a successful application by CAMRA.

The central lobby at the Swan exemplifies a distinctly northern tradition (cf. pub nos 103 and 114)

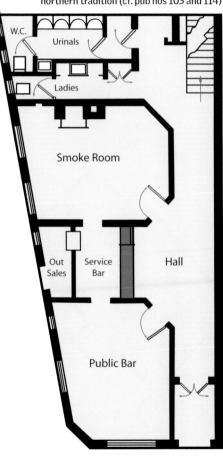

YORKSHIRE, SOUTH

Barnburgh

High Street, DN5 7EP
01709 892306
Grade II listed
LPA: Doncaster

Coach & Horses   209

The Coach & Horses is a suburban-style pub in a village setting, built in 1937 and hardly altered since. For a 1930s layout to survive so completely in a pub of this type and size is quite exceptional and makes this a true national rarity. As an 'improved' pub of its time, it was designed to look and be respectable, offering varied facilities – a commodious smoke room (right of the lobby) with bell-pushes, a 'refreshment room' (far left) for non-alcoholic comforts, an entirely separate public bar and that notably northern feature of a stand-up lobby. It was designed by Doncaster architects Wilburn & Atkinson for the brewers Whitworth, Son & Nephew of nearby Wath upon Dearne, whose wheatsheaf logo appears on the lovely glazed counter screens that are such a signature feature throughout. As well as this sashed screenwork, all the ceilings, doors, fitted seating and tiling are from the 1937 scheme, as is the substantial bar

The Thursday Club poses for the camera in the smoke room where the counter still has its sashed counter screens

back-fitting with its multiple drawers. The counter fronts have been renewed, however, apart from that in the refreshment room. Statutorily listed in 2010 following a successful application by CAMRA.

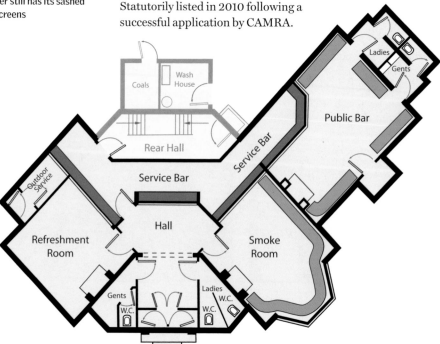

Doncaster

8 West Laith Gate, DN1 1SF
01302 738310
www.thelittleplough.co.uk
Not listed
LPA: Doncaster

Plough

`210`

Known locally as the 'Little Plough', this is an unassuming two-roomed pub near the railway station with a well-preserved interior created under plans of 1934 (displayed in the corridor) for a remodelling by the Grimsby brewers Hewitt Brothers Ltd who were Doncaster's biggest pub owners for many years. Their legacy here is a straightforward but pleasing design of front bar, back lounge and side corridor. Apart from the modern fireplaces in both rooms and missing side panels from the serving 'hatch' to the lounge (called a 'music room' on the plans), there is little to detract from the pub's authentic 1930s character. Leaded glasswork, wall-coverings and fittings typical of the period are much in evidence, including the fixed seating with bell-pushes in the lounge and the bar-counter with its horizontal banding which appears to have been built larger than shown on the plans.

The Plough was refitted in the 1930s

Sheffield: city centre

66–68 Victoria Street, S3 7QL
0114 249 5151
www.thebathpub.co.uk
Grade II listed
LPA: Sheffield

Bath Hotel

`211`

The Bath Hotel stands at the sharp-angled corner of a mid-Victorian terrace and close to the eponymous (Glossop Street) baths. Acquired by the Burton brewers Ind Coope in 1914, it was remodelled and extended next door by them in 1931 and, except for the loss of its off-sales (hence one disused outside doorway), its layout and fittings are scarcely altered since. The lounge-snug at the very corner is a real delight, with simply-patterned leaded windows, curving leatherette bench seating and hole-in-the-wall serving hatch. The larger main bar has some original fitments too, while the angled corridor, with its service opening for stand-up drinking, is just as it ever was. The Bath was statutorily listed in 1999 following casework by CAMRA and a sensitive refurbishment two years later won it a prestigious national Pub Conservation Award (awarded jointly by English Heritage, the Victorian Society and CAMRA).

The main bar

(Rob Vevers)

YORKSHIRE, WEST

Bradford

169–171 Westgate, BD1 3AA

01274 721784

www.newbeehiveinn.co.uk

Not listed

LPA: Bradford

🍺 🍎 🍴 🛏

Chalking up the ales of the day in the hatch to the 1936 lobby

New Beehive Inn

212

The New Beehive blends elements of its original late Victorian-style interior with a 1936 remodelling by William Whitaker & Co, one of Bradford's leading brewers of the inter-war era. It was rebuilt in 1901 as part of the municipal improvement of Westgate (replacing an old coaching inn) and the plans for its construction were drawn up by the city architect and surveyor of the time, J. H. Cox. The original three rooms are to a typical 'house' plan, with the central corridor elaborated into a drinking hallway. In the front public bar, the curved counter, arcaded back fitting and bench seating are all fittings from the 1901 scheme. The old fabric and décor elsewhere is from the 1936 refurbishment and seen at its best in the back-left smoke room and hallway. The gents' toilet, the tiled corridor to it, and the back concert room (now lacking in original fittings) are also of 1936. Food consists of snacks.

Halifax

1 Sun Fold
South Parade, HX1 2LX
01422 347001
www.ossett-brewery.co.uk
Grade II listed
LPA: Calderdale

Three Pigeons

213

A marvellous 1930s survival which combines Art Deco internal styling with one of the best, and most interesting, examples of the northern 'drinking lobby'. Rebuilt in 1932 for Samuel Webster & Son, one of Halifax's leading brewers of that time, and designed by local architects Jackson & Fox (who undertook all of Websters' commissions between the Wars) the Three Pigeons preserves an interior that is rare and remarkable. Its layout is probably unique, with the drinking lobby as a superb centrepiece from which three rooms and the servery all radiate. The lobby itself, moreover, is the only octagonal version of its type now known to survive. There is much else to delight: flush panelling in oak veneer, stylish metal-ribbon signage on doors, geometric patterning in the lobby's terrazzo floor and stepped plasterwork to its 'dome' (echoing the room cornices). Also noteworthy are the timber fire surrounds, fitted seating throughout, and a good bar back-fitting with mirrored panels, one featuring a vintage advertisement for 'Green Label' beer. A sensitive restoration won the Three Pigeons a prestigious national conservation award in 2007 and it was statutorily listed in 2010, following a successful application by CAMRA.

A central lobby, with rooms leading off, forms the heart of the Three Pigeons

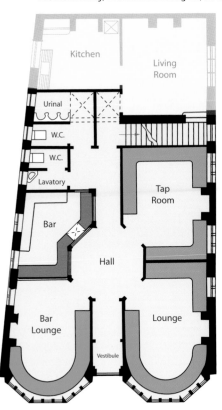

Heath

Heath Common, WF1 5SL
01924 377527
www.thekingsarmsheath.co.uk
Grade II listed
LPA: Wakefield

King's Arms 214

Almost a textbook example of how a pub can undergo enormous
enlargement without seriously compromising its historic core.
The old core here is the time-worn, wood-panelled arrangement of
front bar, corridor entrance and front snug, which together formed
the entire extent of the pub before the Second World War. It still
functions as the 'pub' heart of a pub-restaurant that has expanded
into adjoining domestic accommodation, stabling and barn
conversions, as well as spawning a huge conservatory. The lounge
to the right, although a post-war conversion, has some attractive
adornments of its own – fireplaces made of salvaged materials
from Heath Old Hall and a carved coat of arms of 1980s vintage.
The King's Arms has more than 30 working gaslights – most of
them modern, but possibly the largest number in any UK pub.

The front snug   (Michael Slaughter)

Leeds: Burley

364 Kirkstall Road, LS4 2HQ
Grade II listed
LPA: Leeds

Cardigan Arms 215

Built in 1896 with an eye on the affluent new housing developments of
Lord Cardigan's Leeds estates, the 'Cardy' is outstanding for the overall
completeness of its compartmentalised interior. With four rooms of
different sizes off a large L-shaped drinking foyer, a separate vaults and
an upstairs function room, it is the most internally complex of a surviving
local trio of substantial Victorian pubs designed by Leeds architect
Thomas Winn (q.v. the Adelphi [216] and the Rising Sun [closed]).

It retains much of its as-built décor and fittings with extensive use made of etched glass, fine woodwork and ornamented ceilings and wall-coverings. There are also signs of a 1930s makeover – the tiling in the right-hand corridor and gents', and woodwork in the Oak Room – and the bar-fittings are from restoration work in the 1980s by its long-time owners, Joshua Tetley & Son. The old outbuildings include a (disused) tower brewhouse. Statutorily listed in 1998 following a pilot study of Leeds pubs by CAMRA for English Heritage.

In the northern tradition, rooms lead off the drinking lobby

Leeds: city centre

3–5 Hunslet Road
Leeds Bridge, LS10 1JQ
0113 245 6377
www.theadelphileeds.co.uk
Grade II listed
LPA: Leeds

Adelphi

216

Built 1901 in the majestic style of a high-Victorian drinking 'palace' (few of this type were ever built in Yorkshire's cities), the Adelphi was designed by Leeds architect Thomas Winn for the local Melbourne Brewery. Its highly-ornate, multi-roomed interior was carefully looked after for many years by Melbourne's powerful successor, Joshua Tetley & Son, and it has survived wonderfully well to this day (although the effect has been superficially diminished of late by some 'café-bar' décor). Four spacious rooms open off a drinking foyer from which a lavish staircase rises grandly to a former ballroom, and there is a rich array of original tiling, etched glasswork and mahogany fittings on display. The sub-division of the large public bar with a sympathetically designed screen was done by Tetley's in the 1980s. The Adelphi was statutorily listed in 1998 following a pilot study of Leeds pubs by CAMRA for English Heritage.

The 'No. 2 Smoke Room' and its original screens, seating and fire surround

Leeds: city centre

Turk's Head Yard
Briggate, LS1 6HB
0113 245 3950
www.whitelocksleeds.com
Grade II listed
LPA: Leeds

Whitelock's Ale House

217

Described by John Betjeman as 'the very heart of Leeds', Whitelock's is one of that special breed of old-style luncheon bars that only a few of the UK's biggest cities can boast. Tucked away up an old alley, it has been licensed since 1715, but the pub of today is essentially late Victorian – the result of a major re-modelling in 1895 by local architects Waite & Sons for the Whitelock family, its owners from 1880. A combination of long, narrow plan-form (reflecting the plot's medieval origins), dark wood panelling, glittering copper and brasswork, plus a rich display of old mirrors, creates a unique environment that has changed little in over 100 years. The tile-fronted bar counter is a rarity in itself. Whitelock's today continues in its busy role as a pub and eating place, although the rear section is no longer presented as the separate, distinctive dining area it once was. The 'Top Bar' (further up the yard) is a modern conversion dating only from the 1980s.

The glittering interior at Whitelock's

Of natural functions

As night follows day, a few drinks in the pub will be followed by a visit to the loo. Pub toilets thus assume a place of huge importance in providing comfort and relief to humanity. Most are pretty ordinary affairs but historic examples can sometimes be quirky and very occasionally downright magnificent. The gazetteer points out cases which are rather more than run-of-the-mill.

In times past our less delicate forebears were not too troubled about having to exit the pub to relieve themselves. There are still a few cases where this trip outside is still the order of the day: examples are the North Star, Steventon, Oxfordshire (136), and the Bell, Aldworth, Berkshire (3), where star-gazing gents gave the blessed facility the nickname of 'The Planetarium'. At the Harrow, Steep, Hampshire (38), you have to go (sorry!) over the road.

At the other end of the spectrum, two pubs in this guide have especially magnificent examples. The finest loos of the lot are at the Philharmonic in Liverpool (122), which are provided with a mosaic floor, marble and urinals with imitation Veronese marble. Those at the Prince Louise, Holborn, in London (65) are also splendid – they are proudly signed by their makers, J. Tylor & Sons of London and Sydney.

North of the Border, at the Feuars Arms, Kirkcaldy (254), the loos were supplied by Doultons and in the gents you can see the water gurgling away in a

glass-sided cistern. The Crook Inn, Tweedsmuir, in the Borders (p. 259), is closed at the time of writing but is expected to reopen in due course when customers will be able to inspect the spectacular 1930s Art Deco facilities.

Lavatorial splendour at the Princess Louise, Holborn, London (65)

The gents' at the Feuars Arms, Kirkcaldy, Fife (254), boasts a glass-sided cistern

---

Leeds: Hunslet

3 Whitfield Place, LS10 2QB
0113 277 7705
www.gardengateleeds.co.uk
Grade II* listed
LPA: Leeds

Garden Gate   218

Probably the jewel in the crown of historic pub architecture in Yorkshire, the Garden Gate is a treasure trove of Edwardian decorative design. Apart from the loss of its original off-sales (on the right) the layout and internal fittings are virtually untouched since 1902–3, when it was rebuilt for a private owner by Stourton architect W. Mason Coggill. It combines a very traditional small-pub layout (central through-corridor, counter in the vault, and hatch service to other rooms) with resplendent decoration, inside and out, to rival the great city drinking 'palaces' of the period. Its riches include etched glass with Art Nouveau motifs, lavish tiling, mosaic floors, moulded plasterwork and ornate mahogany fitments. The undoubted highlight is the vault, a *tour de force* of the decorative tiler's art and centring on a magnificent curved ceramic bar-counter – almost certainly a product of Burmantofts of Leeds. It is

The corridor leads to the side rooms and has a hatch to the servery

The spectacularly appointed vaults the counter has the same design as that at the White Hart, Hull (199)

a sobering thought that, but for action by enlightened local protesters in the early 1970s, this superb pub would have been lost forever to an urban clearance scheme. Positive developments in 2010 were its upgrading to Grade II* listing, following a successful application by CAMRA, and its acquisition by the local Leeds Brewery.

Norwood Green

Village Street, HX3 8QG
01274 676645
www.oldwhitebeare.com
Grade II listed
LPA: Calderdale

Old White Beare

219

The old snug here is surely as good as any of the best historic pub rooms in England. With its high-backed settles, old stone fireplace and low-beamed ceiling; and divided off by matchboard partitions (partly curving and partly top-glazed for borrowed light) it is a little gem. This remarkable survival is set inside a country 'destination' pub which, although most pleasant, has undergone its share of recent change and has few other old fittings or features of great note. Its back tap room has made way for toilet accommodation in recent years while the main front bar room has been considerably altered and modernised. The counter here, for instance, dates from about 2000.

Inside the snug

WALES

The smoke room at the
Albion Ale House, Conwy (225)

GLAMORGAN

Cardiff

282 Hayes Bridge Road, CF10 1GH

029 2034 3129

www.sabrain.com/golden-cross

Grade II listed

LPA: Cardiff

Golden Cross

220

Built in 1903 for Brains' brewery, this city-centre pub is the most spectacularly decorated pub in Wales and is famous for its ceramics by Craven Dunnill of Jackfield, Shropshire. The façade proclaims the Brains name and gives a foretaste of the riches within. Here the L-shaped counter on the left is one of fourteen remaining ceramic bar counters in the UK and the design, featuring grotesques, is one of three made by Craven Dunnill: the others are at the Mountain Daisy, Sunderland (168), and the Gunmakers Arms Birmingham (not in this guide). There are also two original pictorial tiled panels, that in the public bar showing Cardiff Castle, and the one in the left-hand room showing the Old Town Hall as it was in 1863. The impressive bar-backs remain in the public bar and in the lounge (to the right), but the counter in the latter is modern. In 1978 the pub was threatened by road widening but a vociferous campaign saved it and it reopened in 1986: the modern lobby panel of Brains' brewery dates from that time. Popular as a gay pub in the evenings.

The ceramic bar counter and tiled painting of Cardiff Castle

MID-WALES

Llanidloes (Powys)

41 Long Bridge Street, SY18 6EF
01686 412398
Grade II listed
LPA: Powys

Crown & Anchor

221

An unspoilt small-town pub in the hands of the same family for over 100 years with the present licensee, Ruby Holmes, running it since 1965. It now consists of five simply appointed rooms which are divided by a panelled corridor down the centre. The room at the front right was a haberdashery shop until around 1948. The tiny snug on the middle right

is the original public bar and retains a (probably) Victorian counter and shelving behind: it has a glazed screen to the corridor and it is this screening which is the defining characteristic of the pub. In this room an old mirror advertises 'Ind Coope Burton Ales'. Another old mirror, for 'Truman's Burton Ales', survives in the rear right-hand room.

A rear room (with landlady Ruby Holmes)

Rhayader (Powys)

West Street, LD6 5AB
01597 810202
www.lionroyal.co.uk
Not listed
LPA: Powys
Restricted opening hours

Lion Royal Hotel

222

A former coaching inn, this is an old-fashioned small-town hotel where the main bar has remained unchanged since 1921. It is on the left of the entrance corridor where there are three vertically sliding sashes to the servery with etched and frosted leonine faces: a door announces the 'Bar' in similar glass. The room has a wood-block floor plus a rather exotic bar counter with Jacobean detailing. In the bar-back are two sets of shelves with a display of now-defunct ceramic spirit vessels while on the counter are two glorious 1920s hand-pumps with a brass label, 'Gaskell & Chambers Lt Prize Bar Fitters Birmingham'. Also from the 1920s are the glazed brick and marble fireplace and two sections of bench seating. The lounge at the front left, not normally open, has a large stone fireplace, The bar may be visited on application in the week and is open Friday and Saturday evenings.

The 1920s servery

NORTH-EAST WALES

Ysceifiog (Flintshire)

CH8 8NJ

01352 720241

Grade II listed

LPA: Flintshire

🍺 🍴

Restricted opening hours

Fox

223

This appealing village pub has four small rooms and is relatively little altered since the 1930s. Beyond the entrance is a slate-floored drinking lobby with a tiny hatch in the leaded screen around the servery. A sliding door on the left leads to the most important room; the small, panelled front bar which is no doubt the oldest part of the pub. It has bare bench seating – some of it, remarkably, attached to the front of the counter. At the rear left the dining room has a disused glazed, sliding hatch to the servery, and retains interwar fixed seating. The rear right room caters for overspill dining. At the front right is a small games room with a cast-iron fireplace. Opens 4pm Mon–Fri (closed Wed), 1pm Sat–Sun.

The public bar

NORTH-WEST WALES

Bethesda (Gwynedd)

London Road, LL57 3AY
01248 600219
www.douglas-arms-bethesda.com
Grade II listed
LPA: Gwynedd
🍺

Restricted opening hours

In the billiard room looking
towards the servery (centre) and
former hotel reception (right)

Douglas Arms   224

Built as a coaching inn around 1820 to serve Thomas Telford's new road
to Holyhead, the Douglas Arms has been in the hands of the Davies
family since 1913. It is little changed since the 1930s and has four public
rooms. A projection into the entrance corridor, once a hotel reception
area, is now incorporated into the billiard room behind: this acquired
its full-sized billiard table about 1934. The public bar (rear right) was
once two small rooms until a partition was removed in the 1950s.
It has a bentwood bench, a red leather bench and two old settles: the
(probably) Victorian bar-back contains many drawers and a display of
spirit jars, although the counter has modern refronting. At the front
are two rooms, a function/dining room (left) and a smoke room (right)
with a 1930s Art Deco fireplace. Closed lunchtimes Mon–Sat.

Conwy

6 Uppergate Street, LL32 8RF
01492 582484
Grade II listed
LPA: Conwy
🍺 🍴 (Food consists of snacks)

Albion Ale House   225

By far the best example of an unaltered inter-war pub in Wales
and a great pub to visit, having been revived by a consortium of four
Welsh micro-breweries, who reopened it in February 2012. Re-built
in 1921, it has a brick ground floor with pebble-dashed first floor and a
touch of half-timbering. A corridor, with attractive green tiling, gives
access to three well-preserved rooms. The public bar (right front)

The public bar at the Albion Ale House

has retained its 1920s fittings, including the long bar counter and fine mirrored bar-back. The off-sales which occupied the right-hand bay of the counter has gone and the screen between it and the public bar has been placed against the wall. On the corner is a smoke room with some Art Nouveau touches in the glazing and a mightily impressive baronial-style fireplace set behind a timber and brick canopy. The seating and bell-pushes survive. A second smoke room at the rear retains a large brick fire-surround, fixed seating and a hatch to the servery: the herringbone flooring incorporates an unusual diamond-shaped feature in the centre. The restoration in 2011 was a model of its kind.

Llansannan (Conwy)

High Street, LL16 5HG
01745 870256
www.redlioninn.cabanova.com
Not listed
LPA: Conwy

🍺 🍴 🛏

Restricted opening hours

An old settle at the front of the pub focuses on the hearth

Red Lion Inn   226

The great feature here is the delightful snug and its low, curved settle sweeping round through 90 degrees in front of the fire and a large iron range. The settle is fixed in place by iron stays to the beams above. Up to 40 years ago the lounge at the rear, with its stone fireplace, was half its present size. In the 1960s the pub expanded when the house next door was purchased by Lees' brewery (primarily to add indoor toilets): the pool room (front right) was also created and retains a period bare counter. At the front left is a plain, modern dining room. Closed weekday lunchtimes.

WEST WALES

Court Henry (Carmarthenshire)

SA32 8SD

(1 mile north of A40 at Court Henry)

01558 668276

Not listed

LPA: Carmarthenshire

🍴 (Sun)

Restricted opening hours

The public bar

New Cross Inn

227

A truly remarkable survivor, and still part of a 780-acre livestock farm. It celebrated its 100th birthday on 18 March 2009, as invitations to the original opening dinner show. The small public bar with its red and black quarry-tile floor retains a matchboarded counter, simple shelving behind and a wooden fire-surround: with a 'Truman, Hanbury & Buxton & Co Burton Ales' mirror above. When built there was also a smoking room (note a door on the left of the porch) but this became part of the living quarters in the 1960s. At this time the old stables to the right were converted into a large restaurant/new lounge that can hold 100 diners, mainly for functions, but this impacts scarcely at all on the historic public bar. Open 7pm Thu and Sat eve, Sun lunch.

NEW CROSS HOTEL, LLANEGWAD.

A

House Warming Dinner

WILL TAKE PLACE AT THE ABOVE HOTEL,

On THURSDAY, the 18th of MARCH, 1909.

Dinner on the Table at 3 o'clock p.m.

Ticket, 2/6.

T. J. BLAKEMAN, Proprietor.

NEW CROSS HOTEL, LLANEGWAD.

A

House Warming Dinner

WILL TAKE PLACE AT THE ABOVE HOTEL,

On THURSDAY, the 18th of MARCH, 1909.

Dinner on the Table at 6.30 o'clock p.m.

Ticket, 1/-

T. J. BLAKEMAN, Proprietor.

Announcing the opening in 1909   (Photos: Michael Slaughter, 2009)

Pontfaen (Pembrokeshire)
Gwaun Valley Road, SA65 9SG
01348 881305
Not listed
LPA: Pembrokeshire

Dyffryn Arms

228

One of the great survivors among rural pubs and a reminder of how simple most of them would have been in days gone by. This pebble-dashed building of 1845 looks more like a private house, as there is no hanging inn sign. It has always been in the same family ownership and is affectionately known as 'Bessie's' after the present octogenarian

licensee. The heart of the pub is a squarish public bar with a medley of furniture, including an old high-back seat/box settle and basic bench. There is no counter as such – just an opening with horizontally-sliding sashes to the ground-floor cellar. The lounge (occasionally brought into use) lies across the central corridor. These days the entrance is down a side passage, complete with dado tiling from 1938. Outside toilets. Together with the Cresselly Arms, Cresswell Quay (also Pembrokeshire), this is one of only two Welsh pubs that serve beer from the cask via a jug into the glass.

A simple sign advertises this classic rural pub   (Rob Vevers)

The main bar and hatch to the servery   (Michael Slaughter, 2002)

SCOTLAND

Leslie's Bar, Edinburgh (241):
the lounge with its unusual
'ticket booth' openings
to the servery, and a
small snug at the far end

ABERDEEN AND GRAMPIAN

Aberdeen
213 Union Street, AB11 6BA
01224 573530
www.thegrillaberdeen.co.uk
Grade B listed
LPA: Aberdeen

Grill

229

A fine pub behind an unprepossessing exterior in a grey granite terrace of the early 1830s. It was a restaurant from the 1870s, but was turned into a pub in 1926 by architects Jenkins & Marr. The mainly stand-up bar retains its fittings of that date, including a fine mahogany gantry with three glazed cabinets. The long counter carries the letter 'G' along its various sections and also has brass match-strikers from the good(?) old days of smoke-filled pubs. The walls are covered in mahogany veneer and the tables, with cast-iron bases, are inscribed 'The Grill'. A striking feature is the ceiling, with large oval (front) and circular (rear) moulded plasterwork designs. This was a men-only bar until the Sex Discrimination Act came into force on 1 January 1976 and there was no ladies' toilet until as late as 1998, when the gents' WC experienced a sex-change. The nearby Bridge Bar, another former men-only bar, still has no ladies' toilet and there is a sign on the door warning customers of this fact! The Grill stocks over 300 single malt whiskies (menu available). Food consists of snacks.

Looking from the front to the rear of the Grill

(Michael Slaughter, 2003)

Craigellachie

AB38 9RR
01340 881239
Grade C listed
LPA: Moray

Fiddichside Inn `230`

A marvellous rural survival, picturesquely sited by a bridge over the River Fiddich and which has been in the hands of the present family since November 1919. The tiny bar is at the end of a cottage and measures a mere 10ft x 15ft. It has a panelled counter running down the length of the room and leaving only half the space for customers – there is only room for some bar stools and a couple of benches. Behind the bar is a simple gantry and the walls have half-height panelling: there are also mirrors advertising William Younger's and Robert Younger's IPA. Listed in 2008 as a result of survey work by CAMRA.

Joe Brandie presides at the small, single-bar Fiddichside Inn
(George Howie, 2006)

ARGYLL AND THE ISLES

Lochgilphead

Lochnell Street, PA31 8JL
01546 602492
Grade C listed
LPA: Argyll & Bute

Commercial ('The Comm') `231`

This plain, early 19th-century building houses a three-room pub with a rare and untouched example of immediately post-WWII pub-fitting. The work was carried out in 1945–6 and all the rooms have bench seating. In the small public bar there is a curved panelled counter, a gantry with mirrored shelving, and a brick fireplace with an Art Deco mirror above. Along a passage and through the multi-pane door is the smoke room. At the rear is the lounge with a large brick fireplace, brick canopy and the original tables. There is a curious door between the smoke room and the servery – it's open when it's closed and closed when it's open! Another fun feature is the tiny gents' loo and its sliding door with glass inscription (for the avoidance of any doubt) 'Gents Lavatory – Slide it Chum'!

A door that opens two ways (left) and another with clear instructions as to how to get to the gents'
(Michael Slaughter, 2007)

EDINBURGH AND THE LOTHIANS

Edinburgh: Abbeyhill
21 Cadzow Place
London Road, EH7 5SN
0131 661 2855
Not listed
LPA: Edinburgh

Station Bar   232

Virtually unaltered in over 40 years, this is a basic inner suburban pub on the ground floor of a four-storey tenement building. The public bar retains its 1890s gantry and counter with a heating rail at the foot. There is extensive wall-panelling and a massive mirror advertising Dryborough's Pale & Mild Ales (protected with cardboard when Hibernian are playing at home!). The most interesting feature is the rare survival of a tiny jug and bottle compartment on the right. At the far end of the public bar, where the counter ends, is an arch beyond which the bar opens out and it seems the layout was always like this. At the rear is the small Safari Lounge, cheaply refitted in the 1960s. However, this may be lost under plans for new toilets and an extension of the drinking area. Opens 9am Mon–Sat.

The jug and bottle compartment
viewed from the public bar

The featured pubs in
Edinburgh city centre

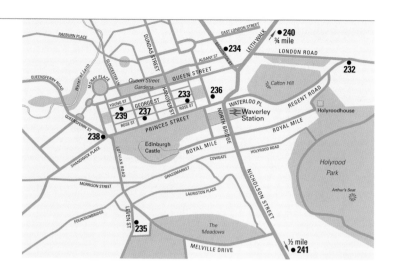

Edinburgh: city centre

3–5 Rose Street, EH2 2PR

0131 225 5276

www.theabbotsford.com

Grade B listed

LPA: Edinburgh

The ornate island servery

Abbotsford   `233`

One of the finest examples of the quite common Scottish arrangement of an island-style servery. The Abbotsford was built in 1902 to designs by one of Edinburgh's most prolific pub architects, Peter Lyle Henderson, for Charles Jenner of Edinburgh's famous department store. Unusually there is no gantry in the middle of the servery which no doubt explains the mahogany superstructure on top of the counter. Although such features, usually designed to hold pot-shelves, are now very common in pubs, they are usually no older than the 1960s and this example is a very early and ornate precursor of the type. The panelled walls have inlaid mirrors, and there is a richly decorated high plaster ceiling. In the far left corner is the original snack counter, with a fine balustraded

and mirrored gantry and various drawers. On the back wall opposite Rose Street is an annunciator box which indicates that at one time (in addition to the main bar) there was a dining room, a private room and a smoking room. Alterations took place in the 1970s when the first floor was acquired for pub use and a staircase inserted. The Abbotsford is one of a handful of pubs in Edinburgh still using the traditional Scottish method of dispense – the tall fount (the 'u' is silent) – to dispense its range of real ales.

Edinburgh: city centre

81–83 Broughton Street, EH1 3RJ

0131 558 2874

Grade B listed

LPA: Edinburgh

Barony Bar

234

A relatively small L-shaped, single-bar pub with a luscious interior. Located in an 1804 four-storey tenement, it wraps around other property on the street corner and has an attractive teak frontage. The interior is notable for its 1899 decorative scheme by John Forrester. The multi-coloured tiled dado includes small pictorial panels of rural Scottish scenes (sadly, mostly hidden by seating – why were they placed so low? – this must always have been a problem). The counter, ornate gantry and two tiled fireplaces (with mirrored overmantels) are all from the late Victorian scheme. As with so many historic Scottish pubs, there are advertising mirrors, in this case a massive pair proclaiming McLaughlan Bros' wares and also, around the corner, one promoting William Younger's India Pale Ale. Originally, the right-hand front door led to a jug and bottle, and there were a couple of snugs at the rear.

The 1899 refit provided the fittings we see today, including the low-level tiling

Edinburgh: city centre

8 Leven Street
Tollcross, EH3 9LG
0131 229 5143
Grade B listed
LPA: Edinburgh

Bennets Bar

`235`

Edinburgh's finest pub interior after the Café Royal. The pub was designed in 1891 by George Lyle and refitted in 1906. The main bar stretches back from the street and down the left-hand side is the servery, which has a flamboyant five-bay gantry housing four spirit casks, the last to survive in an Edinburgh pub: the counter top has two still-functioning water dispensers while at the base is a marble spittoon trough. On the right, above the seating, is a four-bay mirrored and arcaded feature with tilework populated by cherubs and figures in Classical dress (made by W.B. Simpson & Sons of London). A particular delight, to the immediate left (as you enter) of the porch, is a tiny snug with a hatch and a door into the servery. The glasswork is varied and interesting, such as the swirly Art Nouveau windows to the street and door panel advertisements offering the blandishments of Jenkinson's beers and aerated waters, not to mention Jeffrey's lager. At the end of the bar an enormous mirror advertises Bernard's IPA. There have been changes at the rear, such as the loss of a small office at the end of the counter in 2002 and the reuse of a sitting room instead. At the rear right is the Green Room, added in 1906 (but modern fittings apart from, probably, the counter) and accessed from Valleyfield Street.

The snug as viewed from the main bar

The main bar looking towards the entrance

The door glass advertises Jeffrey's lager: lager was brewed in Britain from the 1880s

236

Edinburgh: city centre

West Register Street, EH2 2AA
0131 556 1884
www.caferoyal.org.uk
Grade A listed
LPA: Edinburgh

Café Royal

This famous Edinburgh pub has a truly stunning interior. The building, by architect Robert Paterson, dates from 1861 and opened as a showroom for gas and sanitary fittings but by 1863 had became the Café Royal Hotel. From the 1890s major alterations took place and much of what we see dates from 1900–1. The main space has six wonderful tiled paintings made by Doultons, designed by John Eyre and painted by Katherine Sturgeon and W. J. W. Nunn: they show six famous inventors; Benjamin Franklin, Michael Faraday, Robert Peel (calico printing), William Caxton, George Stephenson and James Watt. The counter was replaced in 1979 and a new tall gantry was installed in 2002. The fixed seating takes the form of a series of semi-circular areas against the outside walls. Beyond an ornate screen lies the Oyster Bar, an upmarket restaurant with more tiled murals plus eight stained-glass windows of British sportsmen, made by Ballantine & Gardiner of Edinburgh. It has a counter with small tiled panels and a mottled red marble counter: note also a revolving door from the 1920s. What is now called the Voodoo Bar(!) is a separate business entered up stairs on the west side of the building, and was refitted in 1923.

Three of the tiled panels depicting inventors and their inventions

Edinburgh: city centre

152–154 Rose Street, EH2 3JD
0131 226 1773
www.nicholsonspubs.co.uk/
kenilworthrosestreetedinburgh/
Grade A listed
LPA: Edinburgh

Kenilworth

237

The building originated about 1780 while the interior, by architect
Thomas Purves Marwick, dates from 1899 and was subject to
a very costly and careful restoration by Alloa Brewery in 1966.
It is one of four impressive pubs in Edinburgh with an island bar
(cf. Abbotsford [233] nearby). The walls are covered in blue and
white Minton tiles, topped off with rows of brown and cream tiles,
finishing some two-thirds up the double-height public bar, which
has a patterned plasterwork ceiling in turquoise and cream. There
is a massive mirror advertising Dryborough's ales of Edinburgh.
The pot-shelf and short partitioning attached to the bar are 1966
additions, which is also the date of the Scott Room, a small room
added down a new passage to the rear. Note the stained and leaded
glass windows on the front and side in the first-floor area. Listing
upgraded to A in 2008 as a result of survey work by CAMRA.

Tiles cover much of the walls:
in the centre the island servery

Edinburgh: city centre

1 Queensferry Street, EH2 4PA
0131 225 3549
Grade B listed
LPA: Edinburgh

H. P. Mathers Bar

238

This high-ceilinged, single-room pub is little changed in over 100 years.
It is on the ground floor of a five-storey building, designed in 1900 by
Sydney Mitchell & Wilson for the National Commercial Bank of
Scotland and the Caledonian United Services Club. The wine merchant
Hugh Mather took over and established the licensed premises in 1902.
In the porch there is floor-to-ceiling tiling and, within the pub itself,
the counter is original (but new top) as are the half-height panelling,

ceiling and frieze. The great feature is the towering gantry: its central parts are original although the side portions were added in the 1960s and it is not easy to spot the joins! The walls are adorned by a number of old brewery mirrors. A change in the 1960s relocated the ladies' toilet from the rear right corner to downstairs. The old water engine which dispensed beer by air pressure is still to be seen in the cellar and may be inspected at quiet times. Food consists of snacks.

Mathers Bar consists of a single space and has a fine gantry

Edinburgh: city centre
8 Young Street, EH2 4JB
0131 539 7119
www.oxfordbar.co.uk
Grade B listed
LPA: Edinburgh

Oxford Bar

239

This small, no-frills pub is something of an Edinburgh institution. At the front left is a tiny stand-up bar with no tables or chairs, just two sets of window seating for about four people. There is an old fireplace on the far left, partly covered up by the counter and thus predating the existing servery arrangements. The simple mirrored gantry may date from the late 19th century and has been added to with some basic shelving. Up three steps and through the doorway on the right is a sitting room with shutters. It also has a (possibly) 1950s brick fireplace and an old mirror promoting Murray's Pale Ale. One of the historic photos on the wall shows former landlord William Ross, who refused to serve women and Englishmen, and anyone ordering a lager would be instantly barred! Customers who remember him as a 'character' or … well, let's leave it! The pub was made famous after Ian Rankin based characters in the Inspector Rebus novels on customers and bar staff.

The small front bar at the
Oxford soon fills up

Edinburgh: Leith

7–9 Leith Walk, EH7 5QH

0131 555 2006

Grade A listed

LPA: Edinburgh

Central Bar

`240`

A down-to-earth drinkers' pub at the foot of Leith Walk and which
has one of Scotland's most stunning interiors. It was built in 1899
to designs by one of Scotland's leading pub architects, Peter Lyle
Henderson. This tall, nearly square space originally started life as
the bar for Leith's long-gone Central Station (closed 1972: see entries
111 and 196 for historic English station buffets). Either side are
entrance porches (with mosaic flooring and stained glass windows),
leading into a room in which the walls are completely covered with
Minton Hollins tiles. The side walls are notable for four tiled panels
of sporting scenes – yacht racing, hare-coursing, golf and shooting –
with tall, narrow mirrors between. The U-shaped counter backs on
to a stunning oak gantry which has glazed cupboards for cigars etc,
and sprouts the figures of four griffins. In the middle of the servery
there is an island gantry. On the left are four U-shaped seating areas.

The ceiling is papier-mâché with Jacobean detailing.Window screens with coloured glass bear the name of John Doig who was the first proprietor. At the back there were two sitting rooms originally but they are now converted to store rooms. Listing upgraded to A in 2008 as a result of survey work by CAMRA. Opens 9am Mon–Sat.

Hare coursing

The Central Bar consists of a single space which retains its fittings from the days when it was the Leith Station Buffet

Edinburgh: Newington

45–47 Ratcliffe Street, EH9 1SU

0131 667 7205

www.lesliesbaredinburgh.co.uk

Grade B listed

LPA: Edinburgh

Leslie's Bar

241

A magnificent island-bar pub of 1899 in a tenement, by architect P. L. Henderson. Its unique feature is the gantry-like structure on the left-hand side of the servery with its series of low, ticket booth-style windows for service. This arrangement is akin to snob screens in Victorian pubs in English cities which allowed customers a sense of privacy. On the left on entering is a small snug, separated from the lounge by a low panelled screen with semi-circular stained glass panels. At the far end of the counter is an elegant mahogany gantry. Other original features include a Lincrusta frieze, an ornate plaster cornice and decorative ceiling. The dado panelling came from a neighbouring house during a restoration in 1958. At the rear of the lounge is another snug, also of 1958. In 1971 a former shop was absorbed to become a sitting room and has a wide doorway and dado panelled walls that match the 1958 work. The window screens date from 2005. The eponymous John Leslie was the second licensee, from 1902 to 1924.

The lounge looking towards the rear of the pub

Prestonpans

227–229 High Street, EH32 9BE
01875 819922
www.prestoungrange.org/
gothenburg
Grade B listed
LPA: East Lothian

Prestoungrange Gothenburg

242

The 'Goth', as this superb pub is affectionately known, was built in 1908 for the East of Scotland Public Houses Trust, in Arts and Crafts style, and retains a wonderful interior. It was sold to the London-based Trust Houses Ltd in 1919. After a chequered late 20th-century history, it reopened following meticulous restoration in 2003 and won the CAMRA national conservation award. The public bar is a magnificent room with superbly designed features – low segmental arches at the sides with vertical struts, deep green Art Nouveau-style tiles and wall panelling. It has a servery in the centre which would form an island but for the tiny jug bar which joins it to the front entrance. To the left is an elegantly panelled lounge where the emphasis is on dining rather than drinking. A tiled spiral staircase leads to the upper floor where the historic features are limited to two fine fireplaces. The building has been extended at the rear to include a small brewery (opened 2004). The name comes from the Gothenburg system – still operating here – which originated in the Swedish city in 1865 to encourage temperance. Managers gained no benefit from alcohol sales but did so from food and non-alcoholic drinks. Profits above a certain percentage (usually 5%, as here) were devoted to projects for the benefit of the community. Here they go to the Prestoungrange Arts Festival which has funded the wall and ceiling paintings at the pub and other art works in the community.

The public bar where the ceiling decoration is modern work, paid for through the 'Gothenburg System' which is still active at this fine pub

West Calder

43 Main Street, EH55 8DL
Grade C listed
LPA: West Lothian

Railway Inn

243

Built around 1900, this corner-site pub has a U-shaped servery with a bar on either side of it. In the centre of the servery is the star attraction, an unusual openwork gantry, delicately detailed, with a two-storey superstructure and slender turned balusters. It has a wide opening in the middle to allow staff easy access from one side to the other. Originally the servery linked up the back wall, but a customer walkway has been created in recent times. Another significant survival, opposite the entrance, is the (now disused) tiny jug bar (or if you prefer the version of some regulars, specially built as the 'priests' hole' where clergy could sneak in undetected for a tipple – so are pub myths born!). A corridor leads to a large, fairly plain lounge. This, like the rest of the Railway, has wooden dado panelling. On the way there, the gents' offers a rather splendid and unusual marble urinal (plus old wall and floor tiling). Listed in 2008 as a result of survey work by CAMRA.

The gantry in the centre of the servery

Raising the Bar

The collaboration between CAMRA and English Heritage has been described on pp. 11–12. Similarly, CAMRA has been closely involved with Historic Scotland in achieving a better understanding and protection of Scotland's most important pub heritage. The catalyst for this was the launching in 2007 of CAMRA's pioneering book *Scotland's True Heritage Pubs*, which is still available, price £4.99, see p. 286. Its editor, Michael Slaughter, was convinced there were quite a number of Scottish pubs which really deserved to be protected by listing. Also apparent was that most listed pubs had either no or only brief descriptions of their interiors in the official record.

At the launch of the book Michael and Dave Gamston, Chair of CAMRA's Pub Heritage Group, produced compelling evidence that persuaded Historic Scotland's head of listing, Deborah Mays, to carry out a thematic review of public houses. It was undertaken by Louisa Humm, Inspector of Historic Buildings. After the review was completed she remarked: 'The thematic survey has served to emphasise how few good and complete historic pub interiors have survived in Scotland and how important it is to preserve those that remain. The majority of managers, licensees, barmen/women and even customers were very happy to let our inspectors roam around and were pleased that their pubs were being considered for listing. Several times customers pointed out features of interest and told us something about them People are generally pround of their local.' Completed in 2008, this important survey produced 11 new listings and 6 upgradings. Four pubs achieved new Grade A status, the very highest category (see p. 15): the Kenilworth, Edinburgh (237), Central Bar, Leith (240), Horse Shoe Bar, Glasgow (244), and the Feuars Arms, Dundee (254). Furthermore, 39 descriptions were revised to give full weight to the importance to the interior planning and fittings.

A further result of the project was the publication by Historic Scotland of a booklet, *Raising the Bar: an Introduction to Scotland's Historic Pubs* which has done much to increase awareness of the country's rich pub heritage. A downloadable copy is available at www.historic-scotland.gov.uk/ raising-the-bar-pubs-booklet.pdf. You can also search for listed pubs (and other buildings of course) at http://hsewsf.sedsh.gov.uk/ hslive/hbsearch.showadv.

Glasgow's Horse Shoe Bar (244) had its listing grade raised to A, the highest level

GREATER GLASGOW AND CLYDE VALLEY

Glasgow: city centre

17–19 Drury Street, G2 5AE

0141 248 6368

www.horseshoebar.co.uk

Grade A listed

LPA: Glasgow

🍺 🍴

⇌ Central

Horse Shoe Bar

244

A justifiably famous pub in the heart of Glasgow and one of the finest examples of Scotland's island-bar, open-plan pubs (cf. Abbotsford, Edinburgh [233]). It was built in 1870 and remodelled in 1885–7 by publican John Scouller, then again in 1901, when the partitions between sitting rooms and the bar were removed. At just over 104ft round the outer circumference, the counter is the second longest in the UK after the Falcon at Clapham Junction, London (57), which weighs in at a mighty 125ft. The initials 'JYW' in glazed screens on the counter and elsewhere refer to John Young Whyte who succeeded Scouller in 1923. The island gantry includes eight spirit casks on their sides (in use till the 1930s) with, unusually, two taps in each (cf. Central Bar, Renton [252]). On the side walls there are two horseshoe-shaped fireplaces: the similar features on the rear wall seem to have always been just ornamental. At the front is a clock with the twelve letters of 'The Horse Shoe' instead of numbers. The panelled walls have large bell-pushes towards the rear, mostly set in decorative panels. The skylight at the rear right was added in 1985. Listing upgraded to A in 2008 as a result of survey work by CAMRA.

The horseshoe motif is repeated many times: the initials JYW are of the owner from 1923

Glasgow: city centre
58 Bridge Street, G5 9HU
0141 429 4528
www.thelauriestonbar.com
Grade C listed
LPA: Glasgow
🍺 🍴
◉ Bridge Street

Laurieston Bar

245

This small, friendly pub has one of the most remarkable interiors in the UK. It is the most intact example of pub-building (in fact remodelling) from about 1960 and, thus, as important as a great Victorian pub – only very much rarer (see also 107, 135, 148 and 231)! Behind the frontage, with its black and white mosaic and distinctive lettering, traces of the Victorian building survive in three iron columns, floor tiling in the gents and the lower parts of the central gantry. Facing the Bridge Street entrance is a small off-sales, either side of which are the lounge (right) and public bar (left). The latter has fixed seating, a series of narrow, two-tiered fixed Formica tables and contemporary low chairs. The boarded bar counter (with Formica top) is a fairly simple affair, not unlike work of the 1930s, but the suspended structure over it and the ceiling panelling are quintessential 1960s work. There's even an original heated glass food display unit on the counter. The lounge is smarter, with more fixed seating, panelling and a number of bell-pushes. To complete the picture, Formica covers the walls in the loos. Listed in 2010 following a successful application by CAMRA. Food consists of tasty pies, bridies and peas. Listed in 2010 as a result of survey work by CAMRA.

The refitting of the Laurieston Bar about 1960 has, most unusually, remained intact ever since

Glasgow: city centre
1–3 Paisley Road West, G51 1LF
0141 429 3135
Grade B listed
LPA: Glasgow
◉ Shields Road

Old Toll Bar

246

'One of the most handsome bars in Glasgow' wrote the *Victualling Trades' Review* in 1893 when the Old Toll Bar reopened after a complete refit by its new owners. And so it remains today. There is now a single ground-floor bar although there used to be a jug and bottle department leading off Admiral Street (now incorporated into the main space). This has an enormously ebullient gantry incorporating two sets of four large vertical spirit casks either side of a central feature (a tier of smaller barrels in the recess below the large ones was removed some time ago). The counter has a modern polished granite top. On the panelled walls are four superb huge advertisement

The interior of the Old Toll Bar dates back to 1893: the granite counter top is modern

mirrors, painted and gilded by Forrest & Son of Glasgow, one of the largest suppliers of decorated mirrors in the 1890s. There are colourful painted windows on the inner doors and in the side entrance vestibule. Other Victorian features include a panelled ceiling, carved woodwork and mahogany panels above the seating and, low down in the servery, the mechanism and pressure dials associated with former beer dispense. Modern fittings in the downstairs lounge.

Glasgow: city centre

62 Glassford Street, G1 1UP
07773 973436
Grade B listed
LPA: Glasgow
≈ Argyle Street and Queen Street
◉ St Enoch

Steps Bar

247

This, with the Portland Arms (248) below, is one of Glasgow's two almost perfectly preserved Art Deco pubs. It was refitted in 1938 and is situated on the ground floor of a late 18th-century four-storey building; it has been owned by the same family for 40 years. Its name comes from the two steps in the frontage, which is clad in Vitrolite panelling and has frosted glass windows (one replaced in 2006). The interior is complete

With the Portland Arms, Shettleston (248), the Steps Bar is one of Glasgow's two good Art Deco pubs

What's distinctive about Scotland's pubs?

Scottish pubs differ markedly from those in England and Wales. They are commonly referred to as bars and, architecturally, they tend to be less ambitious than their southern counterparts. In larger towns and cities they are often located in the ground floor of tenement blocks and their façades may differ little from ordinary shop-fronts. Given a weaker system of brewery-ownership than across the border, there is a long tradition of naming bars after the owner or licensee.

Many Scottish pubs look unprepossessing. The Railway Tavern, Shettleston, Glasgow (249), is one such, yet within is a interesting, characterful interior

The English tendency a century ago to divide up pubs into numerous separate areas was much less marked in Scotland. From the mid-1880s, pressure from licensing magistrates to ensure good supervision led to many pubs being remodelled as single drinking spaces, often with an island servery in the centre: classic examples include the Abbotsford, Edinburgh (233) and the Horse Shoe Bar, Glasgow (244). Many pubs did possess other rooms, of course, and some had small snugs where customers were seated, and which were often termed sitting rooms (a name which spilled over into the north east of England). Excellent examples of sitting rooms can be found at the Portland

The ladies' snug at the Art Deco Portland Arms, Shettleston, Glasgow (248)

Arms, Shettleston, Glasgow (248), and the Clep Bar, Dundee (256).

A long and enthusiastic tradition of spirits drinking has left its mark in a number of pubs which still retain spirit casks in their bar-backs (or gantries to use the Scottish term). Excellent examples are at the Horse Shoe Bar and the Old Toll Bar (246) in Glasgow, the Bull Inn, Paisley (251), and the Central Bar, Renton (252). Water dispensers for diluting whisky can still be found on many a bar counter.

Frequently Scottish pubs have splendidly large, historic advertising mirrors, both built-in and hanging on the wall, which

Spirit casks survive in a number of gantries at pubs in this guide. This one is at the Central Bar, Renton (252).

ensure that no customer remains unaware of ABC's whisky or XYZ's ales. Particularly good examples can be found at the Abbotsford and Barony Bar (234) in Edinburgh, and the Old Toll Bar, Glasgow.

As in England and Wales, there was a great move to equip pubs with fine interiors at the end of the 19th century and the start of the next. Excellent examples can be found at the Café Royal, Edinburgh (236), Central Bar, Leith (240), and the Feuars Arms, Kirkcaldy (254), in addition to some other fine pubs already mentioned. Scotland also has a remarkable amount of Art Deco/Moderne work in its inter-war pub stock, most notably at the Steps Bar, (247) and the Portland Arms, Shettleston, Glasgow, the Clep Bar, Frews Bar (257), both in Dundee, and the magnificent work in parts of the Crook Inn, Tweedsmuir, Borders (p. 259). Intact pubs of the 1950s and 1960s are now almost non-existent anywhere, but Glasgow has one such rarity in the form of the Laurieston Bar (245). Such mid-20th-century pubs were often equipped with small fixed tables: these survive at the Steps, Clep and Laurieston Bars mentioned above.

Small fixed tables can be found in Scottish pubs from the interwar and postwar period. These, at the Laurieston Bar, Glasgow (245), date from about 1960

with sleek veneer-panelled walls, a back gantry of Australian walnut and the original counter. The hooped stall on the latter indicates an area for waiters, from the days when table service was provided in the sitting room at the rear left. This has more veneer panelling, original fixed seating and (of course) bell-pushes. A stained glass panel window depicts the Cunard liner RMS *Queen Mary*, built on the Clyde and launched in 1936: an aircraft flies above it. The only changes have been the replacement of floor coverings, the new gents' at the rear and the addition of a ladies' for the first time in the 1950s (hence the Formica-panelled walls as also found at the Laurieston Bar [245]).

Glasgow: Shettleston

1169 Shettleston Road, G32 7NB
0141 778 6657
Grade B listed
LPA: Glasgow
⇌ Shettleston

Portland Arms

248

Like the Steps Bar (247) above, this is a wonderful Art Deco survivor: it is also a good example Scotland's island bar pubs. Rebuilt in 1938, it is a single-storey structure designed by architects Thomas Sandilands & Macleod for a family that held it until 2006. There is banded veneer panelling to the oval bar counter, the shape of which is matched in the canopy above. In the centre of the servery stands an island gantry. All the walls are veneer-panelled and there are Art Deco fireplaces on the side walls, which also have their original fixed seating with wooden dividers and match strikers on them (match strikers also appear on the bar counter). Before the entrance door is a small 'Family Dept.' (jug and bottle) with a little hatch. Left is a small office (now a store). In each of the corners is a tiny sitting room with part-glazed partitioning, that on the right is labelled 'Ladies Room' and has a ladies' toilet leading off it. The only major changes since 1938 are the replacement of the floor covering and modernisation of the toilets. This is a popular drinkers' pub which gets packed when Celtic are playing at home.

Sleek elegance at the Art Deco, Portland Arms. One of the four snugs can be seen on the right. See the Steps Bar (247) for Glasgow's other important Art Deco pub

Glasgow: Shettleston

1410–1416 Shettleston Road,
G32 9AL (corner of Killin Street)
0141 778 2368
Grade C listed
LPA: Glasgow
⇌ Shettleston

Railway Tavern

249

A friendly, single-storey corner-site pub, outwardly plain but with a typical Glasgow island-bar arrangement and retaining its, probably, early 20th-century interior. The right-hand door leads into a self-contained 'family department' (off-sales). The main entrance is on the right and has a small vestibule inside. On the left is a long narrow bar fronting the street: on the right is an L-shaped drinking area running round the servery. Off this are a couple of sitting rooms and between them an annunciator box with three discs, which suggest there was originally an extra sitting room, now taken by the ladies' toilet. In the middle of the servery is a low island gantry with a couple of drawers predating the advent of the electronic till. There appears to have been a refit in the post war period, whence the mosaic floor and the loss of doors. Listed in 2012 following an application from CAMRA.

Screens still divide up the main bar space

Larkhall

3–5 London Road, ML9 1AQ
01698 883463
Grade C listed
LPA: South Lanarkshire

Village Tavern

250

Popular drinkers' pub in a late 19th-century sandstone building, last fitted out during inter-war times. The counter has ribbed panels, apart from the front section, probably suggests there was once a jug and bottle facing the entrance (cf. Portland Arms, Glasgow [248]). The modest island gantry (with space for staff to walk through the

central part) has an old till drawer that was in use up to 2000. There are panelled walls to picture-frame height, fixed slatted seats at the front and two old brewery mirrors. The cupboard in the far right corner (no. 5 on the door) was built for storing spirits. The rear room holds little interest apart from an old advertising mirror.

Looking towards the front of the Village Inn

What shaped Britain's pubs – 5: modern times

A few words to bring the story of the pub up to date. Time was when most pubs were owned by breweries, but legislation in 1989, under what are popularly known as the Beer Orders, forced the biggest owners to sell off any in excess of 2,000 in their tied estates. The idea was to stimulate competition – great in theory! But to meet this requirement, some brewers created separate pub-owning companies whilst others simply sold off the 'excess' estate. This latter development led to the extraordinary, unintended consequence of the formation of giant pub-owning companies ('pubcos'). The two largest of these, ironically, ended up with estates of nearly 10,000 each! The 2000s saw them struggling to service the debts incurred through these purchases and much dissatisfaction from struggling lessees who, after paying top price for leases, have been forced to buy beer at inflated prices through the pubcos who operate what is, to all intents and purposes, a tie. At the time of writing the government claims it is intending to take measures to ensure fairer trading practices by pubcos – time will tell. There are, however, still some vertically integrated brewers who retain a pub estate – major examples are Fullers, Greene King, Marstons and Shepherd Neame – but today the vast majority of pubs are no longer brewery-owned.

There are now fewer pubs than there were. Pubs have opened and closed over the centuries but, as at early 2013, the present alarming rate of closure is variously put at between twelve and eighteen a week. Pubs numbered about 66,000 in 2005 and the total is now down to 58,000 with 4,500 closing since 2008. Unsurprisingly, as pp. 256–9 shows, National Inventory pubs

Inside the Butchers Arms, Herne, Kent, the first of the new generation of micro-pubs – with (plastic) reminders of its former use   (Anthony Seminara)

are not immune from this attrition. The causes are many and various. At the individual level it may be down to poor management and inexperience but there are institutional factors at work too: economically hard times from the late 2000s which are still with us; rising prices due to swingeing increases in beer duty (it has risen 42 per cent between 2008 and 2012); the smoking ban which started in Scotland in 2006 and was applied to the rest of the UK in 2007, but which has affected some pubs more than others, especially in inner city, wet-led establishments; the availability of a bewildering variety of home entertainment which can be enjoyed with cheap alcohol from supermarkets; drink/driving legislation; and the avoidance of alcohol by some ethnic communities, which again particularly impacts on many inner city pubs.

But it is not all gloom. Some rural pubs are finding a route to viability through doubling up as post offices, shops, crèches, community centres or offering various other facilities, just as many used to combine pub-keeping with agriculture in times gone by (see p. 48). An interesting development is the way the wheel has come full circle in respect of size and, since about 2008, micro-pubs have been springing up in various parts of the country (see p. 47). More generally our pubs are now offering an unprecedented range of tasty real ale in what must surely be the golden age of beer drinking. With over one thousand breweries in this country – the highest number since the Second World War – the choice has never been better and real ale bucks the trend of declining beer sales overall. A synergy between micro-brewers and heritage pubs is suggested on p. 175. Real cider too is on the march with many new producers entering the market and many pubs stocking it.

Paisley

7 New Street, PA1 1XU

0141 849 0472

www.bullinnpaisley.co.uk

Grade A listed

LPA: Renfrewshire

Bull Inn

This fine pub was built in 1901 to designs by architect W. D. McLennan. Behind the stained glass front window, the interior has an Art Nouveau flavour with touches of classical detail. The (disused) narrow, right-hand door in the porch leads to a tiny, intact off-sales compartment. The other door leads to the panelled public bar which has an impressive back gantry down the right-hand side containing four large, elongated, upright whisky barrels and four smaller spirit casks. It also retains five (originally six) sets of four spirit cocks: these survivals of 'draft' spirit dispense are known at only four other pubs: the Haunch of Venison, Salisbury (188), Crown Bar, Belfast (266), Shipman's Northampton, and the Queen's Head ('Turner's Vault'), Stockport. Over the counter is the unusual device of six arched service areas. Moving further back, there is a glazed partition behind which are three delightful glazed snugs, one still with its door: each has its original fireplace but the seating has been replaced and the present glazing is modern. New toilets have replaced two snugs which used to lead off the top-lit area at the rear of the pub.

At the back of the Bull is a series of glazed snugs

Renton

123 Main Street, G82 4NL

01389 752088

Grade B listed

LPA: West Dunbartonshire

On the left is a jug and bottle compartment: the gantry houses old spirit casks

Central Bar

252

Built in 1893, this pub occupies the ground floor of a two-storey tenement. Behind the rather run-down frontage is an interesting interior. The panelled bar has a sweeping semi-circular counter and an elaborate ceiling and cornices. The gantry against the side wall houses spirit casks in each of its four bays: unusually, each has two taps (cf. Horse Shoe Bar, Glasgow [244]) and is, presumably, divided internally. There is also a free-standing central gantry within the servery for bottles, glasses etc. Opposite is a lovely mirror advertising Old Oak Tree whisky. On the left is an intact but disused jug and bottle compartment. At the rear were two sitting rooms (it seems that once there were two more on the right) both opened up to the bar: the left one has slatted seating but that to the right was recently opened out, and is devoid of seating.

KINGDOM OF FIFE

Kincardine

16 Forth Street, FK10 4LX

Grade C listed

LPA: Fife

Restricted opening hours

Railway Tavern

253

An amazing survivor: 200 years ago, this tucked-away terrace pub served drovers bringing their livestock south. It would have presented much the same plain appearance as now since the only sign that this is a pub are the words above the door, 'J. Dobie Licensee'. Three rooms are in public use (a fourth is now a store), all very simply appointed.

Above: the only advertisement that these are licensed premises.

The main bar

(Photos Michael Slaughter, 2004)

Entry is into a passage which has a hatch and a shelf for corridor drinking: it also has a working box for the bell-system, which can be used in the front right and left rear room to summon service. Note also the remains of two ceiling hooks – where drovers used to sling their hammocks. On the left is the public bar, one of the smallest in Scotland: its seating consists of just four double seats originally constructed by Alexanders, bus builders, of Falkirk! Listed in 2008 as a result of survey work by CAMRA. Opens 6.30pm and Sunday lunchtime.

Kirkcaldy

28 Bogies Wynd, KY1 2PH
01592 205577
Grade A listed
LPA: Fife

Feuars Arms

254

This fine interior dates from an Edwardian refit of 1902 and is especially notable for its display of ceramics. The pub now mainly consists of a large bar in an elongated U-shape, ranged around a 59ft-long counter. Originally this space was divided into two by a jug bar entered from Bogies Wynd, the footprint of which can be traced in the mosaic flooring which covers the whole of the present main bar: the jug bar door has been transplanted to the entrance of the gents'. At the back of the extensive servery is a semi-octagonal office with a glazed-in top (such publican's offices are very rare, especially outside London): in front of it stands a long-case clock. As for the amazing ceramics, brown

The pensive (or lascivious?) jester. The object of his interest is on p. 66

The fine Edwardian interior features extensive ceramic work. At the back of the servery is a publican's office

tiles cover the walls and the tall counter front, but pride of place goes to the two Doulton tiled panels featuring a jester, eyeing up a shepherdess a few feet away: each is, remarkably, a single tile. There are stained-glass windows with the arms of Scotland, England and Ireland, and also much etched glass. The gents' are worth a visit for the bizarre glass-sided Doulton cistern, a pair of marble-framed urinals, tiled walls and mosaic floor. At the rear left is a further room, refitted in modern times. Listing upgraded to A in 2008 as a result of survey work by CAMRA.

Leslie

203 High Street, KY6 3AZ
Grade C listed
LPA: Fife

Auld Hoose

255

This terraced drinkers' pub has been in the same family since 1933 and is interesting for an unspoilt, simple interior of a type that must have once been common in Scottish pubs. It has a bar on either side and between them, facing the entrance, a small screened-off jug bar and, to the right of this, a rather larger snug. The walls of the pub are panelled to full height even though this is not immediately obvious due to the application of modern paintwork. In the right-hand bar, behind a hinged window in the servery, are the mechanics of the electric air compressor that once dispensed the beer (the associated pressure dials were, sadly, removed recently but still languish at the back of the servery). In the corridor to the loos on the left is a mighty advertising mirror proclaiming 'Auld Hoose Luncheon Bar Fine Old Cameron Bridge Whisky'. At the rear is the 'Silver Pheasant' room, created in the 1960s by the present landlady's grandmother and still intact, displaying the taste of the day (not to mention the eponymous pheasant in a glass case). Advertisements in white enamelled letters (common a century ago) survive in several windows.

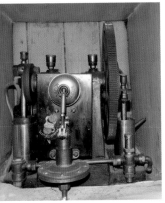

Part of the complex mechanism for raising beer in former days

Between the two bars are the screened-off snug and off-sales

TAYSIDE

Dundee

96–98 Clepington Road, DD3 7SW
01382 858953
Grade B listed
LPA: Dundee

Clep Bar   256

Behind the simple single-storey exterior is a truly superb survival, which gives a perfect impression of how small urban Scottish pubs were being built at the start of the Second World War. It was purpose-built, with two adjoining shops, in 1940–1 and probably designed by J. MacLellan Brown, the city architect. The layout of public bar, lounge, and jug and bottle is just as it was. The public bar has a projecting fireplace behind which are the tiny loos (entered from very narrow doors: the gents' still has original tiling) It has original three-quarter-height panelled walls, plus counter and gantry. The fixed bench seating has a number of solid wooden dividers and the fixed tables are original too. The delightful lounge also has partitions forming seating bays, more small fixed tables and panelling, together with leaded windows, including one advertising 'Bernard's Edinburgh Ales'. There are working bell-pushes and those in the lounge are still responded to. The off-sales on the right still opens occasionally.

The lounge with fixed tables, bell-pushes, hatch to the servery and dividers between the seating

Dundee

117 Strathmartine Road, DD3 7SD
Grade C listed
LPA: Dundee

Frews Bar   257

A three-roomed pub with a public bar (fitted out in 1915), flanked by an important pair of Art Deco lounges. The public bar has been amalgamated with a tiny snug on the right, by the removal of a short partition (evident in the floor). On the back of one of the pots that decorate the inglenook-style fireplace is written 'H & F Thomson

The Sporting Memories Lounge has sleek woodwork and a copper-fronted counter from the 1930s

Architect, Alex Fair Wood Carver, John Scott Joiner' and 'Mr Stewart Licence Holder 18th October 1915'. The back gantry with bevelled mirror panels may well date from 1915, although other fittings are more recent. The metal-framed windows are typical interwar work and the corner ones depict a plough (the old name of the pub) in stained glass. On the right is a lounge with stylish inter-war panelling, counter front and brass bell-pushes. At the rear is a second lounge which also retains its Art Deco fittings, including the copper-fronted counter, small fixed tables (cf. Clep Bar [256]) and other fittings. This, the 'Sporting Memories Lounge' is only open Friday nights, on Saturday, or by arrangement. The plethora of pictures and sporting memorabilia make it hard to appreciate the full effect of the 1930s work. Listed in 2008 as a result of survey work by CAMRA.

Dundee

165–167 Perth Road, DD2 1AS

01382 667783

www.speedwell-bar.co.uk

Grade B listed

LPA: Dundee

Speedwell Bar   258

The Speedwell has a lovely Edwardian interior, located at the bottom of a plain four-storey tenement, and was built in 1903 by the architects John Bruce & Son. It comprises two distinct parts. Immediately in front of, and to the right of the central entrance, is a large bar with an L-shaped servery which has a most impressive four-tier mirrored gantry (stocked, incidentally, with 160 malt whiskies). This bar is divided into two by a screen (with door) at the angle of the L. It is covered by an ornate Jacobean ceiling, and the left-hand area has a fine frieze. To the left of this main bar are a couple of rooms separated by a glazed screen. Both have wall-panelling, original fireplaces and bell-pushes but the seating is modern. The gents' toilets are definitely worth a look for their Edwardian lavatorial excellence of mosaic flooring, white tiling, Shanks' 'Odourless' urinals and cistern. At the Speedwell customers are welcome to bring in take-away food from local providers. Food consists of snacks.

The main bar, split in two by a low screen

Film and TV appearances

CHRIS WITT

We all know the camera can lie – and to good effect when some of our historic pubs appear in the movies or TV films. Take 'Rebus', for example, the redoubtable detective (played by Ken Stott) whose character was created by Ian Rankin for his novels whilst imbibing in the **Oxford Bar, Edinburgh** (239). Many of his characters were based on customers and staff there. How disconcerting, therefore, to discover that the STV series used the **Laurieston Bar, Glasgow** (245), as the Oxford was too small. Also filmed in the Laurieston was *Young Adam* (2003) starring Ewan McGregor and Tilda Swinton, based on the 1954 novel by Alexander Trocchi – so an appropriate, contemporary choice of venue.

The Black Friar (54) provided a backdrop in the James Ivory's adaptation of E.M. Forster's autobiographical novel.

The full-length film *Stone of Destiny* (2008), based on the 1950s true-life plot of Ian Hamilton to return the Stone of Scone to Scotland, had the conspirators regularly meeting in the **Portland Arms, Shettleston, Glasgow** (248), and then miraculously stepping outside the pub to a street scene in Edinburgh. More recently, the BBC TV mini-series *The Young James Herriott* (2011) used the **Central Bar, Renton** (252), to portray a typical Gorbals pub of the 1930s.

The 2012 TV film of Ian Rankin's novel *Doors Open*, starring Stephen Fry, is the most recent adaptation of his work and has an intriguing story involving art forgeries. The location, **Bennets Bar, Edinburgh** (235), was used because this was the first pub in Edinburgh in which Ian Rankin drank as a student.

London pubs have, unsurprisingly, featured in many film and TV productions – though not so many of our historic ones. Most notable has been the **Salisbury, WC2** (58), for the controversial film *Victim* (1961) with Dirk Bogarde and Sylvia Syms, in which the word 'homosexual' was first used on-screen; *Goodbye Mr Chips* (1969) starring Peter O'Toole, Petula Clark and Michael Redgrave; and *Travels With My Aunt* (1972) starring a young Maggie Smith. More recently *The Boat that Rocked* (2009), written and directed by Richard Curtis and starring Bill Nighy and Philip Seymour-Hoffman, has the main characters discussing their pirate radio station plans in the 1960s at the Salisbury.

The **Black Friar, EC4** (54), one of our most iconic pubs, featured in another risqué film *Maurice* (1987) and, allegedly, Michael Winner's production of *The Big Sleep* (1977). **Ye Olde Mitre** (63) was used for *Snatch* (2000) starring Mike Reid as Doug the Head in this gangster movie produced by Guy Ritchie, who puts in a micro-cameo appearance as a man reading a newspaper. *Deep Blue Sea* (2011) is based on the 1952 Terence Rattigan play and sees Tom Hiddleston and Rachel Weisz canoodling together in the pub whilst having an extra-marital affair!

Moving to Manchester and no, the Rovers Return was never an historic pub, but the **Peveril of the Peak** (106) is and was used in three episodes of the Granada TV detective series *Cracker* with Robbie Coltrane starring as the anti-hero criminal psychologist Fitz. Across to Yorkshire and the **Garden Gate, Leeds** (218), was heavily featured in *Room at the Top* (2012), the BBC4 remake of the 1959 film of the novel by John Braine. There are some good shots of the interior and the stained glass window in the doors clearly identifying the pub.

It is possible that some of our other historic pubs have featured on both the large and small screen – how fascinating to discover how, and why. Finally, *Odd Man Out*, Carol Reed's 1947 film starring James Mason as an IRA-like leader on the run: it used what looked like the stunning **Crown Bar, Belfast** (266); except it wasn't. A set was built to resemble the pub – which only goes to show that the camera can lie!

The Garden Gate, Leeds (218), featured in BBC4's *Room at the Top*. The smoke room

NORTHERN IRELAND

Mandeville Arms, Portadown, Co. Armagh
(Michael Slaughter, 2011)

CO. ANTRIM

Ballycastle

4 The Diamond, BT54 6AW
028 2076 2364
Grade B listed
LPA: Moyle

The tiny glazed snug with
its hatch to the servery
(Michael Slaughter, 2005)

Boyd Arms

259

This modest but elegant three-storey building is a former hotel. The right-hand front door leads into a corridor with a quarry-tiled floor, dado panelling, a couple of basic benches and narrow shelves for stand-up drinking. Note the annunciator box in the corridor showing where service was required, including what must have been letting bedrooms. The left-hand door leads to a typical, simple Irish bar stretching back from the street and which includes some Victorian or early 20th-century work, although the counter was revamped, probably in the 1950s or 1960s. Attached to the servery is a delightful tiny glazed snug with a little hatch through which drinks can be served. Across the corridor is another room but here the fittings, including the Victorian-style fireplace, are modern. The small room at the rear with a figure '2' over the doorway was refitted in 1998.

Ballycastle

71 Castle Street, BT54 6AS
028 2076 2975
www.houseofmcdonnell.
blogspot.co.uk
Grade B listed
LPA: Moyle
Restricted opening hours

House of McDonnell

260

Built in 1744, this is a great classic among Irish pubs and has been in the hands of the same family for fourteen generations since 1766. The interior was probably created around 1885. It shows a typical arrangement for a spirit-grocer's, where a shopping trip could be combined with one to the pub, until such 'mixed trading' was banned by law in 1923. The grocery part is at the front and has a panelled counter, black and white quarry-tiled floor and two large advertising mirrors.

The rear bar showing the spirit
casks set in the bar-back
(Michael Slaughter, 2005)

The screen formed the division between the two spheres of operation and behind it is a brown and cream quarry-tiled floor, panelled counter and an impressive bar-back fitting which houses two pairs of end-on spirit casks. On the rear wall a large mirror advertises Coleraine 'HC' whisky. Why HC? It stands for House of Commons, as Irish MPs in Victorian times are said to have been very partial to this brand (the 'e' to denote Irish whisk(e)y only became standard during the 20th century). A small snug leads off to the left and there is another small rear room. The lounge upstairs is only used at busy times. Open 2–11 Fri, Sat.

Ballyeaston

14 Ballyeaston Village, BT39 9SH
Not listed
LPA: Newton Abbey
Restricted opening hours

The lovely back fitting would be at home in a domestic living room: note the glass whiskey vats at the top
(Michael Slaughter, 2011)

Carmichael's

261

The rather forbidding grey exterior of the property conceals a basic, locals' village bar. On the left is the public bar where the counter has two rows of tiles at the top and bottom. The attractive, delicate bar-back fitting, said to have been introduced in 1937, has marquetry and balusters in the lower part, mirrored panels and a small central cupboard: it houses a pair of interesting McConnell's glass whiskey vats. The other room, across the hallway, is plainly appointed and brought into use on Saturdays if needed. The gents' is a basic affair and the ladies' is located at the bottom of the rear yard. Beer is only sold in bottles. Open 5–11 Sat only.

Bushmills

72–74 Main Street, BT57 8QD
028 2073 1240
Grade B listed
LPA: Moyle

The front bar and the advertising mirror in the bar-back
(Michael Slaughter, 2005)

Bush House

262

A three-room terraced pub where most of the interior work probably dates from just before WWII (or shortly afterwards). The small front bar has a bar-back with four advertising mirrors, panelling and terrazzo floor with a trough at the base of the panelled counter. The lounge at

the back has more terrazzo flooring, panelling and a bell-push which was still in use for service in 2005. The elegant mahogany fire-surround is said to have been brought in from the former Arcadia ballroom in Belfast. The old kitchen (rear left), complete with white glazed brick and 'Fairy Esse' cooker, was pressed into public use as the bell-pushes indicate. In recent years the wall separating the kitchen from the small front room was removed. The ladies' toilet penny-in-the-slot-device was still in use until the late 1990s. The out-buildings retain old equipment for bottling Guinness, but the rare traditional game of horseshoes, in which the aim is to land them on a pin, is no longer played in the yard at the insistence of the local health and safety officer – thanks for that!

Cushendun

2 Main Street, BT44 0PH

028 2176 1511

Grade B listed

LPA: Moyle

🍴

Restricted opening hours

Mary McBride's Bar 263

Originally this was a single tiny bar, first licensed in 1849 and, at just 5ft × 9ft 6ins, it was one of the smallest in all Ireland. It was owned by Robert McNeill, 1st (and last) Baron Cushendun, who died in 1934 having bequeathed the village to the Ulster Land Fund, which passed it to the National Trust in the 1990s. Mary McBride took over in the 1950s and died in 1983. She never drank herself and would not serve women. Her bar has very simple fittings – a plain counter, basic shelving for bottles and glasses and a bench round two walls. The floor tiles are modern replacements. One St Patrick's Day, 42 customers managed to cram themselves in. In the interests of viability, a new rear bar has been

The tiny, plain front bar
(Michael Slaughter, 2005)

created, together with the room on the right, converted from living quarters. These changes have taken away much of the overall sense of a basic, one-room Irish pub. That flavour can be recaptured at, say, McKee's in Dungannon, Co. Tyrone. Opens at 5pm Mon–Fri in winter.

CO. ARMAGH

Camlough
12 Main Street, BT35 7JG
028 3083 0515
Grade B listed
LPA: Newry & Mourne
Restricted opening hours

Carragher's Bar   264

A plain red frontage conceals one of the most important and complete pub interiors in the UK. The pub was originally built in 1862 and has been in the same family since 1888. It appears to have been refitted around 1890. Much of the main bar is taken up with snugs (p. 249) of the type found at the Crown Bar (266) and Fort Bar (267) in Belfast. Each has its own number and panels of stained glass in the doors. The bar-back is a seven-bay affair with mirrored strips and four spirit casks (two rum, two whiskey). There are also fine advertising mirrors and a late Victorian bar counter with a row of coloured tiles near the top. Note the copper heater, still in use, for making hot whiskey. The only real change has been the laying of attractive terrazzo flooring, perhaps in the 1920s: there is a spittoon trough in front of the counter. A door at the rear leads into a small room, also terrazzo-floored: beyond is a snooker room. The front windows are modern replacements of ones destroyed in the Troubles. Listed in 2008 following a successful application by CAMRA. Open 8–11 Tue–Sun (to gain access knock at the side door).

As in some other Irish pubs, a row of snugs face the servery (with its spirit casks)   (Michael Slaughter)

Portadown

1–3 Mandeville Street, BT62 3PB

028 3833 2070

Grade B listed

LPA: Craigavon

Mandeville Arms ('McConvilles')   265

Rebuilt in the 1890s, this is one of the great pub interiors of Northern Ireland. It was owned by the McConville family from 1865 to 2005. The decorated, mirrored bar-back incorporates four spirit casks; the counter has a typically Northern Irish fringe of tiles at the top and also another at the base. The most distinctive and, again, almost uniquely Northern Irish feature, is the survival of no less than ten snugs, including a 'ladies' snug at the front where female customers could quaff a quiet drink. Note the bell-pushes to order drinks and the tiny fixed tables on which to place them: some bell-pushes still work and the annunciator box is at the south end of the room. A colourful tiled floor, a fine plaster ceiling and lots of original stained glass complete the visual delight. Don't miss the wonderful cigar lighter, representing the Tichborne Claimant, an impostor whose attempts to prove he was the vanished Sir Roger Tichborne – the ninth wealthiest man in Britain – captivated public attention during two high-profile court cases in the 1870s. A second bar was added in 2008 but does not impact on the original one. Note the mighty lamp over the entrance – one of the best pub lamps anywhere.

A snug adjoins the back of the servery   (Michael Slaughter, 2011)

What's distinctive about Northern Ireland's pubs?

Pubs in Northern Ireland have more in common with those in Scotland than in England or Wales. Architecturally this means that they are generally unassuming; more like private houses or ordinary shops, rather than being distinctive, purpose-built structures. They are often spoken of as bars rather than pubs, and many take the name of the owner (or former owner), hence, in this guide, we have Carragher's Bar, Camlough (264), or Owen's Bar, Limavady (270).

The row of snugs at Carragher's Bar, Camlough (264) (Michael Slaughter)

At a few pubs (or bars!) a striking feature is a row of snugs down one side, parallel to, but at some remove from the servery. The grandest example is at the Crown Bar, Belfast (266) but they also occur at the Fort Bar, Belfast (267), Carragher's, and the Mandeville Arms, Portadown (265). There is no historic example of them on the mainland except for a relatively late example at the Cittie of Yorke in London (64), dating from 1924.

Ireland, like Scotland, has a long-standing tradition of spirits drinking, and many pubs were equipped with casks incorporated into the gantry (to use the local term for a bar-back), from which spirits and fortified wines were dispensed. None still function,

but they have been retained at various establishments, such as the House of McDonnell, Ballycastle (260), the Crown, Belfast, and Carragher's, Camlough.

Another distinctive feature is a decorative one. Some historic bar counters are embellished with bands of tiles, an attractive device which was not used elsewhere in the UK. Examples are at the Fort Bar, Belfast and the Mandeville Arms, Portadown.

An institutional difference between Northern Ireland and the mainland is (or rather was) the existence of the 'spirit-grocers' – that is, a place which doubled as a bar and a shop selling provisions. Hence you had the convenience of being able to get a drink on your

visit to buy the groceries, all under one roof. After the partition of Ireland such disreputable goings-on were outlawed in the North in 1923. However, traces of such arrangements can still be seen at the House of McDonnell, Ballycastle, and the Fort Bar, Belfast.

A word about beer and its service. Real ale is quite hard to come by in Northern Ireland and the only pub in this guide which sells it is the legendary Crown Bar in Belfast. Most beer is stout or lager, and the manufacturers thereof have seen fit to promote their products heavy-handedly with vast, tall fonts (often illuminated) which can look like a military line of defence. This is in complete contrast to historic arrangements when bar counters were unencumbered, and marks one of the less tasteful recent changes at pubs in the province.

And finally, Northern Ireland (and Ireland as a whole) is a wonderfully welcoming place, but visitors should remember its all-too-recent history of community tensions. The curious visitor, come to inspect an historic pub, may here or there be viewed with suspicion and should be alive to possible local sensitivities.

A mirror at the House of McDonnell, Ballycastle, Co. Antrim (260) advertising whisky: the spelling convention of Irish whiskey and Scottish whisky did not become firmly established until the 20th century   (Michael Slaughter)

BELFAST

City centre

46 Great Victoria Street, BT2 7BA
028 9024 3187
www.crownbar.com
Grade A listed
LPA: Belfast

Crown Bar

`266`

This, with Liverpool's Philharmonic (122) and Vines (123), is one of the UK's three most spectacular pubs. Built in the 1840s, it was refitted towards the end of the century. The outside, with its exotic tiling, gives a hint of the treasures within. On one side is the servery; on the other a row of small drinking booths with working bell-pushes which register at an ornate annunciator box halfway down the bar (booth J was removed in the 1970s). The booths are guarded by gryphons and lions bearing shields with Latin inscriptions which translate as 'True love of

The stunning interior at the Crown Bar rivals Liverpool's magnificent Philharmonic Dining Rooms
(Michael Slaughter, 2007)

country' and 'Fortune favours the brave'. The bar-back contains a series of casks and also two banks of taps to dispense spirits in times gone by (cf. Haunch of Venison, Salisbury [188]). The magnificent ceramic counter was made by Craven Dunnill and probably dates from around 1898: the pattern reappears at Burlington's, Lytham St Annes (48), and the Red Lion, Birmingham (172). Lighting is by 27 gas lights: these are modern replacements but add greatly to the atmosphere. In the porch, a mosaic crown gives rise to the saying that here you can trample on the British Crown with impunity! Owned since 1978 by the National Trust which has undertaken exemplary restoration work.

Plan based on the original kindly supplied by the National Trust

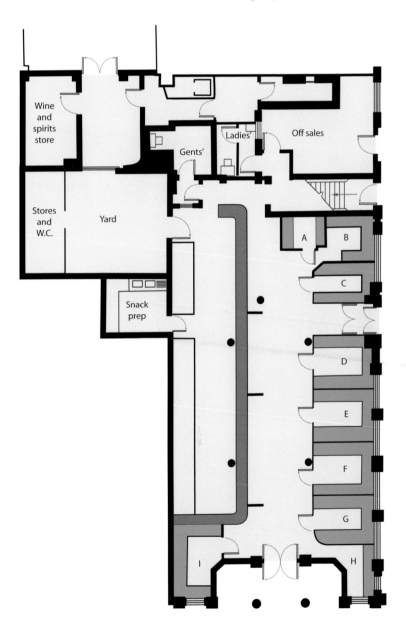

West

25–27 Springfield Road, BT12 7AB
Not listed
LPA: Belfast

Fort Bar ('Gilmartin's')   `267`

Like the Crown Bar (266), this pub retains a superb late Victorian interior. The seven-bay bar-back is spectacularly ornate (although altered by the addition in the 1970s of cask-ends all along). The counter has a typical Northern Irish fringe of tilework. There is a row of five snugs facing the servery, although originally there were more. Each has a number painted on a small glass pane in the door. No. 1 snug has been opened-up (it was situated on the rear right and traces on the black and white tiled floor indicate where it was). Snugs 7 and 8 were situated on the front left and were lost when the toilets were brought inside in, it is thought, the 1970s: their doors are now relocated to the left-hand side of the servery. On the rear left is what looks like a snug, but this was an area which is said to have sold groceries, a practice which would have ended in 1923 when the typically Irish institution of the spirit-grocers' (doubling as a grocer's and a bar) was made illegal.

Tiles line the top of the lavish bar counter, behind which is a highly ornamental bar-back with (largely concealed) spirit casks
(Michael Slaughter, 2002)

CO. FERMANAGH

Enniskillen
6 Church Street, BT74 7EJ
028 6632 2143
Grade B listed
LPA: Fermanagh
🍴

Blake's of the Hollow   268

This fine pub, which retains its Victorian layout and fittings, probably dates from a refurbishment of 1887. It was run by the same family from 1929 to 1996. The front bar is full of character, with the walls and ceiling being entirely wood-panelled. There are four large spirit casks in the bar-back; the old panelled counter has a rare white marble top (cf. 13, 45, 58, 111, 196 and 236), and a box high up on the right-hand wall shows where service was required by drinkers in other parts of the pub. The first of these is a tiny snug by the entrance which was, no doubt, used by ladies and other passers-by who wanted a drink without attracting general attention to the fact. At the far end of the servery is another snug with a venerable cast-iron fireplace. Further back still (and up a flight of steps) is the publican's office, still complete with the desk from where he could keep an eye on proceedings. Behind this is another snug and then a further larger room. At the rear, a massive 21st-century extension with a Gothic theme has been built on several levels and includes bars and a dining room.

Left: the snugs. Below: four large spirit casks
stand behind the counter at Blakes   (Michael Slaughter, 2005)

Irvinestown

38 Main Street, BT94 1GL
028 6862 1249
Not listed
LPA: Fermanagh
Restricted opening hours

The snug and its hatch to the
servery (Michael Slaughter, 2005)

Panelling covers the walls and
ceilings at the Central Bar, where
large spirit casks are in evidence
(Michael Slaughter, 2005)

Central Bar

269

Behind the modest façade of this popular town-centre pub lies a most impressive Victorian interior. It was refitted in 1895 and has been in the Reihill family since 1924. There is a typical tiny snug at the entrance for discreet drinking, then a high-ceilinged public bar with a huge Cantrell & Cochrane's mirror plus other smaller ones. This bar has not only panelled walls, but a panelled ceiling too. Behind the 25ft-long counter are four mighty barrels, which last dispensed spirits in 1953. On the left-hand wall is a bell and annunciator box for the staff in times past to see where table service was required (there is still a bell-push in the large lounge on the right). The spaces behind the public bar, including the former kitchen, have been brought into use in recent years. Open 4–11 Fri–Mon.

CO. LONDONDERRY

Limavady
50 Main Street, BT49 0EU
028 7772 2328
Grade B listed
LPA: Limavady

Owen's Bar

270

A real gem of a bar, opened in 1852 and refitted in 1929 although, with their conservative design, the fittings could easily be mistaken for earlier work. It has now been in the hands of the Owen family since 1960 and there has been no significant change since. A large square servery, with spirit casks in the back-fitting, takes up much of the main bar, but this is made up for by three further cosy rooms. There is a panelled corridor towards the rear and panelled ceilings in all except the rear left-hand room. At the front are two old etched windows. The Owen family have cherished the pub - for example, see the way the illuminated fridges are tucked under the counter and they have refused to encumber the counter with large, ugly, modern advertising founts which sprout up in most Northern Irish pubs. Closed Sun.

The square servery at Owen's   (Michael Slaughter, 2004)

Closed Pubs

CAMRA surveys reveal that, at any one time, around 2,000 UK pubs are 'in limbo' – closed for the time being but, not necessarily, gone forever. Not surprisingly, their numbers include several pubs on our National Inventory of Historic Pub Interiors. We are confident that some will return to active service under new owners who will appreciate the importance of their interiors. For others, the outlook is more gloomy. Most are in areas of towns and cities which are badly run down or where local custom has moved away, but a couple are in the country and one on a suburban housing estate.

However, we can report many real success stories from recent years, with heritage pubs coming back to life despite being effectively written off by their previous owners. Examples include the Victoria, Great Harwood, Lancashire (47), Bartons Arms, Birmingham (169), Garden Gate, Leeds (218), and, early in 2012, the Albion (now Albion Ale House), Conwy, in North Wales (225) and Crystal Fountain, Cannock, Staffordshire (148). Other pubs have been made viable by sensitive expansion – see the Best of Both Worlds feature on page 47. These pubs have all capitalised on their biggest asset – their historic interior – but have added other attractions, notably tasty real ale.

The photographs illustrating these pubs were taken between 2003 and 2012 and are all by Michael Slaughter.

The currently closed National Inventory pubs are as follows:

LONDON, GREATER

Barkingside
Doctor Johnson
Longwood Gardens, IG5 0EN
Grade II listed
LPA: Redbridge

London, Barkingside, Doctor Johnson: private bar

A large pub of 1938 in a sub-Georgian style for a large new housing estate. The layout of four rooms all served from a central servery is intact, as are most of the fittings, which have simple elegance, typical of 1930s pub-building. The corner room has a private bar with a quadrant-shaped counter.

St John's Wood
Crocker's Folly
24 Aberdeen Place, NW8 8JR
Grade II* listed
LPA: Westminster

London, St John's Wood, Crocker's Folly: the magnificent saloon

Built in 1898–9, this is one of the finest examples of late Victorian pub-building. Beyond the entrance is the magnificent 'Grand Saloon' with a marble counter top and lavish fireplace. The vast left-hand room was for billiards: the right-hand space was originally divided into several small compartments. The present name comes from the tale that Frank Crocker committed suicide on being ruined when the Great Central Railway's new terminus ended up at Marylebone, a mile away – not next door as he had expected. In fact this had always been the plan and Frank actually died of natural causes at the tender age of 41 in 1904.

MANCHESTER, GREATER

Manchester: Chorlton-on-Medlock
Mawson Hotel
78 Francis Street, M13 9SQ
Grade II listed
LPA: Manchester

Rebuilt in 1936–7 and hardly changed since. It has a drinking lobby and three other rooms plus an off-sales behind the servery. All retain their original fittings and

Manchester, Mawson Hotel: lobby bar

furnishings whilst the toilets display fine tiling and terrazzo floors. Statutorily listed in 2010 following a successful application by CAMRA.

NORTHUMBERLAND

Blyth
Kings Head
85 Bridge Street, NE24 3AE
Grade II listed
LPA: Northumberland

The right-hand room, which must have been refitted in late Victorian times, is astonishingly ornate. It has a U-shaped counter with a marble top, mosaic flooring and a lavishly decorated, almost square island-style fitting in the middle of the servery. Around the room is a dado of Victorian panelling with a row of bevelled mirrors above it.

Blyth, Kings Head: the fine Victorian right-hand room

WEST MIDLANDS

Birmingham: Digbeth
Woodman
106 Albert Street, B5 5LG
Grade II listed
LPA: Birmingham

Birmingham, Digbeth, Woodman: public bar

As this guide was going to press we learn that reopening is planned to take place at the end of May 2013. This is another of Birmingham's distinctive red brick and terracotta pubs and dates from 1896–7. On the street corner it has an L-shaped public bar which is tiled above a wooden dado. Behind is the smoke room and here there is more tiling above the level of the fixed seating. A tiled lobby on Albert Street leads to an attractive, small drinking area with a hatch to the servery. The third, plain room on the left was brought into public use relatively recently.

Birmingham: Handsworth
Red Lion
270 Soho Road, B21 9LX
Grade II* listed
LPA: Birmingham

Birmingham, Handsworth: Red Lion public bar

Closed Pubs

A fantastic pub of 1901 but one seriously at risk. It has a flamboyant, two-tone terracotta façade and contains a superb multi-room interior with a magnificent display of Minton tiling, including a series of tiled paintings in the corridor and a lavish staircase/hall. The narrow public bar along the front has a particularly lavish bar-back. At the rear is a smoke room and a coffee room.

Birmingham: Smethwick
Waterloo
Shireland Road, B66 4RQ
Grade II* listed
LPA: Birmingham

A flagship pub-hotel of 1907 for Mitchells & Butlers whose brewery was nearby. The interior features stunning tilework. The really spectacular room is the Grill Room in the basement: this was a restaurant and has an original grill and all-over tiling. It is understood there has been damage since it closed. It was sold in late 2012 but nothing is presently known of the new owner's intentions. Upgraded to II* in 1999 following joint CAMRA/English Heritage fieldwork.

Birmingham, Smethwick, Waterloo: the subterranean tiled grill room

YORKSHIRE: WEST

Bradford: city centre
Cock & Bottle
93 Barkerend Road, BD3 9AA
Grade II Listed
LPA: Bradford

With one of the finest interiors in the north of England, this late Victorian gem, a refurbishment of c.1900, is

Bradford, Cock & Bottle: public bar

rich in finely-worked joinery and glasswork of a quality equal to any of the grander drinking 'palaces' of that era. Its compartmented layout includes serveries with splendid bar fittings in two of its rooms and two delightful small snugs. Closed since 2011.

Leeds: Burley
Rising Sun
290 Kirkstall Road, LS4 2DN
Grade II listed
LPA: Leeds

Built around 1899, this is the least flamboyant of a surviving trio of Leeds drinking 'palaces' by local architect Thomas Winn (cf. Adelphi [216] and the nearby Cardigan Arms [215]). Though trading as a second-hand furniture shop since 2010, the old pub interior is largely in place. Statutorily listed in 1998 following CAMRA's pilot study of Leeds pubs for English Heritage.

Leeds, Burley, Rising Sun: smoke room

Leeds: Lower Wortley
Beech Hotel
Tong Road, LS12 1HX
Grade II listed
LPA: Leeds

Rebuilt in 1931 by Pontefract architects Garside
& Pennington for the Melbourne Brewery
(signage much in evidence). It has a spacious
front vault, a former off-sales (left) whilst beyond
the servery is a small smoke room. A large club
room lies beyond. Both back rooms lead off a
wall-tiled hallway-cum-foyer from the side
entrance. As at January 2013 the Beech had
been sold and news is awaited about its future.

Leeds, Lower Wortley, Beech Hotel: public bar

MID-WALES

Cemmaes Road (Powys)
Dovey Valley Hotel
SY20 8JZ
Grade II listed
LPA: Powys

As we go to press we learn that this small Victorian
former hotel has been sold and its future is not known.
There are two rooms, although only the plainly
furnished public bar is normally used. The smoke room
has a lovely mirror advertising Salt's Burton Ale, signed
by the maker, J. Baird of Glasgow. The furniture is a
real mixture with much of it suitable for a private living
room, which is a reminder that public houses were
often exactly that – ordinary houses licensed as public
places to enjoy a drink. Outside toilets.

SCOTLAND

BORDERS

Tweedsmuir
Crook Inn
ML12 6QN
Grade C listed
LPA: Scottish Borders

Some stunning Art Deco work of *c.*1936 is to be found
in the lobby and also the toilets, which have bright
vitreous wall panels. Of the same date, but a total
contrast, is Willie Wastle's Bar with its chunky rustic
woodwork. As at January 2013 the great news was
that the local community had raised the necessary
funds to purchase the building and to reopen it after
restoration work, which will take some 18 months.
This should enable visitors to once more experience
one of the most striking interiors in any British pub.
Follow progress at www.savethecrook.org.uk

Tweedsmuir, Crook Inn: ladies' toilets

Cemmaes Road, Dovey Valley Hotel: public bar

Fifty more to try

The 270 pubs in the main gazetteer of this guide are those identified by CAMRA's Pub Heritage Group as having interiors of outstanding national historic importance. As explained on p. 10, the Group has also compiled lists of pubs with rather less significant interiors, but ones which are nonetheless of special regional interest. These Regional Inventories contain too many pubs to list here and full details may be viewed at **www.heritagepubs.org.uk** where the drop-down menus allow easy searching by country, county, place and/or pub name. Here, however, is a short selection which you will probably enjoy visiting. It brings together a rich variety of pubs where, while not quite up to the demanding standards of the National Inventory, the floor layout has seen little change in the past half century or there are particular rooms or features of historic interest.

ENGLAND

Bristol, Nova Scotia, Hotwells, BS1 6XJ. Many late Victorian fixtures and fittings, including rare low screenwork to create a small snug.

Cambridgeshire, Newton, Queen's Head, CB22 7PQ. Timeless public bar and still-functioning jug & bottle in a country pub, little altered since 1963.

Cheshire, Wheelock, Commercial, CW11 3RR. Most of the 1930s refit within this Georgian building is intact.

Cornwall, Helston, Blue Anchor, TR13 8EL. A well-known home-brew pub retaining several small rooms and simple seating.

Derbyshire, Brassington, Olde Gate, DE4 4HJ. Three rooms of considerable character, especially the main bar with its superb inglenook fireplace.

Devon, Lydford, Castle Inn, EX20 4BH. A multi-room pub with slate floors and a number of high-backed settles.

Dorset, Bridport, George Hotel, DT6 3NQ. An unspoilt country town hotel with Victorian tiled floors, small rooms and a settle.

Dorset, Bournemouth, Cricketers Arms, BH1 4RN. The curved counters and bar-back date from an Edwardian refit, as does the baronial lounge with its stained glass skylight.

Durham, Durham City, Colpitts, DH1 4EG. Two bars with late Victorian fittings; intact off-sales.

Essex, Broads Green, Walnut Tree, CM3 1DT. A delightful snug retains its 1888 fittings. The public bar has changed only by the addition of a counter in 1962.

Hampshire, Braishfield, Newport Inn, SO51 0PL. A rare surviving example of a 1950s refit in the style of that era – a real time warp.

Herefordshire, Clodock, Cornewall Arms, HR2 0PD. Had separate rooms until 1960 but there is still much to admire including a tiny servery with old fittings.

Isle of Wight, Bonchurch, Bonchurch Inn, PO38 1NU. Converted in 1904 from outbuildings of the nearby manor house. Most fittings are at least 50 years old.

Kent, Faversham, Bear, ME13 7AG. Panelled corridor and three rooms from 1906 refit – some enlargement at rear into former living space.

Leicestershire, Leicester, Shakespeare's Head, LE1 5SH. Built in 1963 to a Moderne design with good-quality fittings in its three rooms and little changed since.

London, City, Jamaica Wine House, EC3V 9DS. Rebuilt in 1885 and featuring a unique layout of four narrow areas created by three screens at right angles to the counter.

London, Fleet Street, Tipperary, EC4Y 1HT. Refitted in 1895 with a fine mosaic floor, carved bar-back and panelling, the last inset with two vast glass advertising panels.

London, Forest Hill, Blythe Hill Tavern, SE23 1JB. Victorian local with 1920s interior in three separate rooms. Customers can cross the servery between two of them.

London, Hampstead, Holly Bush, NW3 6SG. Much altered and extended but some distinguished Victorian fittings such as the counter and bar-back remain.

London, Holborn, Seven Stars, WC2A 2JB. The central section is mostly the original Victorian scheme (in a much older building).

London, Kennington, Old Red Lion, SE11 4RS. A two-bar 'Brewer's Tudor' pub of 1929, still with many original fittings.

London, Soho, Coach & Horses, W1D 5DH. A largely intact interwar remodelling, displaying fine panelling plus rare spittoon troughs.

Manchester GTR, Marple, Hatters Arms, SK6 7AW. Terrace pub with three rooms and lobby bar dating from the 1930s.

Manchester, city centre, Castle Hotel, M4 1LE. A small pub whose star feature is the colourful Victorian ceramic counter front.

Manchester GTR, Rochdale, Healey Hotel, OL12 6LW. Most of a high-quality 1930s refurb is still present. Unusual Art Deco tiling in lobby.

Manchester GTR, Tottington, Towler, BL8 4AA. An early 20th-century pub with lobby bar, four rooms and many original fittings, notably the ceramic bar front.

Merseyside, Birkenhead, Crown Ale House, CH41 6JE. Particularly worth visiting for a rare Victorian bar-back which starts at 90 degrees along the left-hand wall.

Norfolk, Norwich, Gate House, NR5 8QJ. Tudor-style 1934 pub whose main bar resembles a baronial hall.

Northamptonshire, Northampton, Shipmans, NN1 2HG. The three-room Victorian layout is readily discernable. There is a rare set of spirit cocks on the bar-back.

Oxfordshire, Checkendon, Black Horse, RG8 0TE. A remote rural pub in same family hands from 1905 and little changed since, other than combining of two rooms.

Somerset, Kelston, Old Crown, BA1 9AQ. A coaching inn with possibly the only 'cash register' handpumps still used on a daily basis.

Staffordshire, Stoke-on-Trent, Burslem, Duke William, ST6 3AJ. Rebuilt c.1930 and pretty much intact. Fine glazed screenwork in lobby bar.

Sussex, East, Lewes, Lewes Arms, BN7 1YH. Retains a passageway with hatch and three of the original four rooms. Old counters, panelling and glazed panels.

Sussex, West, Southwick, Ship, BN42 2AD. Rare intact Watneys/Tamplins refit of 1963, although the public bar retains some 1930s fittings.

Tyne & Wear, Newcastle upon Tyne, Byker, Cumberland Arms, NE6 1LD. Some recent changes have taken place here but much from the 1898–9 rebuild can still be enjoyed.

Warwickshire, Five Ways, The Case is Altered, CV35 7JD. The low-beamed public bar was extended in the 1950s but maintains an older period charm.

West Midlands, Brierley Hill, Vine ('Bull & Bladder'), DY5 2TN. Famous four-roomed pub rebuilt in 1912, attached to Batham's brewery. The small front bar is the least-altered part.

Wiltshire, Ebbesbourne Wake, Horseshoe, SP5 5JF. A traditional village pub. Dado panelling, simple seating and casks stillaged behind the bar.

Yorkshire, North, Harrogate, Hales Bar, HG1 2RS. Rebuilt around 1827. The high-ceilinged saloon bar has gas lighting and late Victorian fittings.

Yorkshire, North, York, Black Swan, YO1 7PR. A medieval timber-framed house with a 17th-century staircase and other historic features. The décor in the rear Ingle Bar is mostly from the 1930s.

Yorkshire, North, York, Minster Inn, YO30 7BH. An Edwardian pub with an intact four-room and central corridor plan-form.

Yorkshire, South, Sheffield, White Lion, S2 4HT. The richly tiled central corridor, glazed snugs and front bar all date from an early 20th-century refit.

Yorkshire, West, Halifax, Big Six, HX1 3HG. Unusual layout and many interesting fittings, all of which can be dated to the late 1920s.

WALES

North East Wales, Gresford, Griffin, LL12 8RG. An early example (1947) of opening up a pub interior, using segmental archways and solid brick pillars.

West Wales, Cresswell Quay, Cresselly Arms, SA68 0TE. Little changed since 1896 and with beer still served from the jug.

SCOTLAND

Edinburgh and the Lothians, Musselburgh, Volunteer Arms ('Staggs'), EH21 6JE. The panelled public bar has its original counter and back gantry with huge polished spirit casks.

Greater Glasgow and Clyde Valley, Auldhouse, Auldhouse Arms, G75 9DW. The original core of the public bar and two sitting rooms survives despite later expansion.

Greater Glasgow and Clyde Valley, Uddingston, Rowan Tree, G71 7PF. Many of the impressive features (counter, gantry, panelling) date from a 1902–3 remodelling.

NORTHERN IRELAND

Co. Down, Killyleagh, Dufferin Arms, BT30 9QF. A former hotel, partly refitted in the 1960s, and with two tiny intact snugs.

Co. Tyrone, Moy, Tomney's Bar, BT71 7SG. A 300-year-old pub where the front and lounge bars are virtually unchanged since 1947.

Further reading

There is a vast literature about pubs. The following list is highly selective and aims to draw attention to the most useful and informative modern sources.

General

Geoff Brandwood, Andrew Davison and Michael Slaughter, *Licensed to Sell: the History and Heritage of the Public House*, English Heritage, Swindon, 2nd ed., 2011. A wide-ranging, accessible and richly illustrated history of the pub from earliest times to the present day.

Mark Girouard, *Victorian Pubs*, New Haven and London, Yale University Press, 1984 (reprint of 1975, first edition). A superbly researched, readable examination of the Victorian pub with much interesting information. Concentrates mainly on London but is of national application.

Geographically specific studies

In addition to the following –list, see the CAMRA guides advertised on pp. 285–6

Belfast. Gary Law, *Historic Pubs of Belfast*, Belfast, Appletree Press, 2002. A useful, compact guide.

Birmingham. Alan Crawford, Michael Dunn, and Robert Thorne, *Birmingham Pubs, 1880–1939*, Gloucester, Alan Sutton, 1989. A superb, compact study, including many fine pubs that have been lost.

Bradford. Paul Jennings, *The Public House in Bradford, 1770–1970*, Keele, Keele University, 1995. A scholarly yet readable study and of relevance beyond Bradford.

London. Geoff Brandwood & Jane Jephcote, *London Heritage Pubs*, St Albans, CAMRA, 2008. Covers the pubs on CAMRA's National and Regional Inventories.

North East England. Lynn F. Pearson, *The Northumbrian Pub: an Architectural History*, Morpeth, Sandhill Press, 1989. The definitive study of the architecture and arrangements of pubs in this region.

Northern Ireland. Cian Molloy, *The Story of the Irish Pub*, Dublin, Liffey Press, 2002. A wide-ranging study of pubs all over Ireland.

J. J. Tohill, *Pubs of the North*, privately printed, 1990. A gazetteer of the more significant Northern Irish pubs as they were around 1990

Scotland. Rudolph Kenna & Anthony Mooney, *People's Palaces: Victorian and Edwardian Pubs of Scotland*, Edinburgh, Paul Harris, 1983. A masterly survey of the golden age of pub-building in Scotland.

Games in or around the pub

Arthur R. Taylor, *Played at the Pub: the Pub Games of Britain*, Swindon: English Heritage, 2009. An excellent, comprehensive study, including many games few know exist.

Temperance

Brian Harrison, *Drink and the Victorians: the Temperance Question in England, 1815–1872*, Keele, Keele University, 2nd ed., 1994

Glossary

Ale: originally a fermented malt liquor, made without the use of hops. The term has been effectively interchangeable with 'beer' for at least 200 years.

Annunciator box: a device to indicate where service was required. Bell-pushes in 'better' rooms would activate moving disks on the box and sound a bell (see p.121 for an example).

Art Deco: a fashionable style between the two world wars in Europe and America. It relies on geometrical patterns and sleek lines. The name comes from the Exposition International des Arts-Décoratifs in Paris in 1924–5 which greatly enhanced its popularity.

Art Nouveau: a style relying on flowing lines and sinuous forms often based on nature and the human figure. It was popular from about 1890 until 1914, but more in Europe than the UK.

Bar-back: shelving, sometimes very ornately treated and incorporating mirrors, at the rear of a servery. Also known as a gantry in Scotland and Northern Ireland.

Bar parlour: as often, a term of some fluidity. In most parts of the country it implies a semi-public room where selected customers were admitted.

Beerhouse: a pub licensed to sell beer only.

Bottle and jug: see jug and bottle.

Brewers' Tudor: a style, especially popular between the world wars, drawing nostalgically upon the half-timbered architecture of the Tudor period.

Brewery tap: a brewery's nearest tied retail outlet.

Commercial room: a better-quality room in Midlands and northern pubs where commercial travellers and business people might gather and conduct transactions.

Drinking lobby/corridor: an area for almost exclusively stand-up drinking and found especially in the north. The lobby is very often an expanded corridor area with a bar counter: in corridors there is a hatch to the servery.

Gantry: Scottish and Northern Irish term for a bar-back (q.v.).

Improved public houses: inter-war ones built with the aim of making the pub respectable. They tended to be large, had a wide range of facilities, and sought to attract a better class of customer, including women.

Jug and bottle: small section of a pub, often with a separate entrance off the street, where drink could be purchased for consumption off the premises. Sometimes known as a jug bar.

Lounge: a better-quality pub-room.

Moderne: a fairly modest, simplified version of Art Deco.

News room: a term found especially in the north-west for a better room, where a quiet drink and the perusal of the press went hand in hand.

Pot-shelf: a shelf over the counter for housing glasses. They appear to be a late 20th-century development, and have profoundly and adversely affected the appearance of many pubs.

Private bar: a more select area than the public bar. The name suggests occupancy by a group of regulars known to one another.

Pubco: a pub-owning company with no brewing interests.

Public bar: the most basic pub room (also sometimes known as the vaults or simply as the bar): here drink was slightly cheaper than in the better rooms.

Quarry tile: plain, unglazed floor tiles, usually red and black.

Real ale: a term coined in the early 1970s to describe traditional beer, which undergoes a secondary fermentation and conditioning in the barrel (hence 'cask-conditioned' as opposed to 'keg' beers, which are brewery-conditioned).

Roadhouse: a (usually large) interwar pub beside a main road, often with extensive facilities to attract, for example, families and the new generation of motorists. See also improved public houses.

Saloon: a better class pub room.

Servery: the area from which drinks are dispensed.

Sitting room: another name for a (usually small) room in Scotland and the North East.

Smoke room: a better-class pub room.

Snob screens: small, swivelling translucent glazed panels at eye level that provided customers with a degree of privacy.

Snug: a small, intimate drinking space.

Spittoon (trough): A receptacle (or trough) for spit but no doubt accumulating cigar and cigarette ends, ash and other small refuse.

Stillage: a framework on which casks are mounted or 'stillaged' ready for service. Probably the name arises from the need for traditional beer to remain still for a period to allow it to clear.

Stillion: a fitting in the middle of a serving area with shelves and storage facilities.

Tap room: a common pub room but not, as the name might imply, connected to or within which drink was served or stored.

Tavern: originally a drinking house serving expensive wine, as well as food.

Teetotal: refusing all drinks containing alcohol.

Temperance: advocacy of drinking little or no alcohol. The earliest campaigners advocated moderation and boycotted only spirits: however, from 1832 increasing numbers became teetotal (q.v.).

Terracotta: hard-wearing, unglazed pottery.

Terrazzo: tiny pieces of marble set in concrete, rubbed down and polished.

Vault(s): as a pub room name, an alternative term for a public bar, especially in the north of England.

About the author

Geoff Brandwood is an architectural historian who became involved with CAMRA's historic pub interiors project in 1998. He was appointed as caseworker for a two-year, part-time project, jointly funded by CAMRA and English Heritage, to carry out a systematic review of the National Inventory pubs as they stood at that time, with a view to making recommendations on statutory listing and improving list descriptions (see also p. 12). He has written about historic pub interiors ever since in the pages of CAMRA's *What's Brewing* and *Beer* publications and he co-authored, with Andrew Davison and Michael Slaughter, English Heritage's best-selling book, *Licensed to Sell: the History and Heritage of the Public House*, published in 2004 and re-issued as a new edition in 2011. He has also written widely on church architecture, especially in the Victorian period, and is a past chairman of the Victorian Society.

Pub index

Bold type indicates pages with the National Inventory gazetteer entries
Italic type indicates pages with illustrations that are not part of the main gazetteer entries
* indicates pubs which are not part of CAMRA's National Inventory of Historic Pub Interiors

265

Geographical index

Bold type indicates pages with the National Inventory gazetteer entries
Italic type indicates pages with illustrations that are not part of the main gazetteer entries
* indicates pubs which are not part of CAMRA's National Inventory of Historic Pub Interiors

General index

Bold type indicates pages with illustrations

Record of visits

Bedfordshire

1. ☐ Cock, Broom
2. ☐ Painters Arms, Luton

Berkshire

3. ☐ Bell, Aldworth

Buckinghamshire

4. ☐ Swan, West Wycombe

Cambridgeshire

5. ☐ Hand & Heart, Peterborough

Cheshire

6. ☐ Travellers Rest, Alpraham
7. ☐ White Lion, Barthomley
8. ☐ Holly Bush, Bollington
9. ☐ Harrington Arms, Gawsworth
10. ☐ Hawk Inn, Haslington
11. ☐ Castle, Macclesfield
12. ☐ Bleeding Wolf, Scholar Green

Cornwall

13. ☐ Seven Stars, Falmouth

Cumbria

14. ☐ Pheasant, Bassenthwaite Lake
15. ☐ King's Head, Bootle
16. ☐ Blacksmiths Arms, Broughton Mills

Derbyshire

17. ☐ Olde Dolphin Inne, Derby
18. ☐ Duke of York, Elton
19. ☐ Crown Inn, Glossop
20. ☐ Holly Bush Inn, Makeney
21. ☐ Malt Shovel, Spondon
22. ☐ Three Stags' Heads, Wardlow Mires

Devon

23. ☐ Drewe Arms, Drewsteignton

24 ☐ Luppitt Inn, Luppitt

25 ☐ Bridge Inn, Topsham

Dorset

26 ☐ Vine, Pamphill

27 ☐ Square & Compass, Worth Matravers

County Durham

28 ☐ Milbank Arms, Barningham

29 ☐ Victoria, Durham

Essex

30 ☐ Old Ship, Aveley

31 ☐ Viper, Mill Green

32 ☐ Queen's Head, Tolleshunt D'Arcy

Gloucestershire and Bristol

33 ☐ Red Lion, Ampney St Peter

34 ☐ King's Head, Bristol

35 ☐ Five Mile House, Duntisbourne Abbots

36 ☐ Berkeley Arms, Purton

Hampshire

37 ☐ Red Lion, Southampton

38 ☐ Harrow, Steep

Herefordshire

39 ☐ Ye Olde Tavern, Kington

40 ☐ Sun, Leintwardine

41 ☐ Duke of York, Leysters

Hertfordshire

42 ☐ Green Dragon, Flaunden

Kent

43 ☐ Queen's Arms, Cowden Pound

44 ☐ Old House, Ightham Common

45 ☐ Red Lion, Snargate

Lancashire

46 ☐ Ye Horns Inn, Goosnargh

47 ☐ Victoria, Great Harwood

48 ☐ Burlington's Wine & Cocktail Bar, Lytham St Annes

49 ☐ Black Horse, Preston

Leicestershire

50 ☐ Three Horseshoes, Whitwick

Lincolnshire

51 ☐ Berkeley, Scunthorpe

Greater London – Inner

52 ☐ Victoria, Bayswater
53 ☐ Lord Nelson, Bermondsey
54 ☐ Black Friar, Blackfriars
55 ☐ Duke (of York), Bloomsbury
56 ☐ Corrib Bar, Camberwell
57 ☐ Falcon, Clapham Junction
58 ☐ Salisbury, Covent Garden
59 ☐ Tottenham, Fitzrovia
60 ☐ Olde Cheshire Cheese, Fleet Street
61 ☐ Dolphin, Hackney
62 ☐ Hope & Anchor, Hammersmith
63 ☐ Ye Olde Mitre, Hatton Garden
64 ☐ Cittie of Yorke, Holborn
65 ☐ Princess Louise, Holborn
66 ☐ Windsor Castle, Kensington
67 ☐ Black Lion, Kilburn
68 ☐ Prince Alfred, Maida Vale
69 ☐ Warrington, Maida Vale
70 ☐ Barley Mow, Marylebone
71 ☐ Elgin, Notting Hill
72 ☐ Red Lion, St James's
73 ☐ Hand & Shears, Smithfield
74 ☐ Viaduct Tavern, Smithfield
75 ☐ Argyll Arms, Soho
76 ☐ Dog & Duck, Soho
77 ☐ George, Southwark
78 ☐ Fox & Pheasant, West Brompton

Greater London – Outer

79 ☐ Fellowship Inn, Bellingham
80 ☐ Queens, Crouch End
81 ☐ Eastbrook, Dagenham
82 ☐ Herne Tavern, East Dulwich
83 ☐ Kings Arms, Hanwell
84 ☐ Salisbury, Harringay

85 ☐ Castle, Harrow-on-the-Hill

86 ☐ Half Moon, Herne Hill

87 ☐ Winchester, Highgate

88 ☐ Windermere, South Kenton

89 ☐ Kings Head, Tooting

90 ☐ Boleyn, Upton Park

91 ☐ Forester, West Ealing

Greater Manchester

92 ☐ Railway, Altrincham

93 ☐ Old White Lion, Bury

94 ☐ Grapes, Eccles

95 ☐ Lamb Hotel, Eccles

96 ☐ Royal Oak, Eccles

97 ☐ Stanley Arms, Eccles

98 ☐ Shakespeare, Farnworth

99 ☐ Plough, Gorton

100 ☐ Grapes, Heywood

101 ☐ Britons Protection, Manchester

102 ☐ Circus Tavern, Manchester

103 ☐ Hare & Hounds, Manchester

104 ☐ Marble Arch, Manchester

105 ☐ Mr Thomas's Chop House, Manchester

106 ☐ Peveril of the Peak, Manchester

107 ☐ Turnpike, Manchester

108 ☐ Royal Oak, Oldham

109 ☐ Cemetery Hotel, Rochdale

110 ☐ Coach & Horses, Salford

111 ☐ Station Buffet, Stalybridge

112 ☐ Alexandra, Stockport

113 ☐ Arden Arms, Stockport

114 ☐ Swan with Two Necks, Stockport

115 ☐ Nursery Inn, Stockport

116 ☐ White Lion, Westhoughton

117 ☐ Springfield, Wigan

Merseyside

118 ☐ Stork Hotel, Birkenhead

119 ☐ Crown Hotel, Liverpool

120 ☐ Lion Tavern, Liverpool

121 ☐ Peter Kavanagh's, Liverpool

122 ☐ Philharmonic Dining Rooms, Liverpool

123 ☐ Vines, Liverpool

124 ☐ Prince Arthur, Liverpool

125 ☐ Scotch Piper, Lydiate

126 ☐ Wheatsheaf, Sutton Leach

127 ☐ Volunteer Canteen, Waterloo

Norfolk

128 ☐ Red Lion, Kenninghall

Northumberland

129 ☐ Free Trade, Berwick-upon-Tweed

130 ☐ Star, Netherton

Nottinghamshire

131 ☐ Vale Hotel, Arnold

132 ☐ Olde Trip to Jerusalem, Nottingham

133 ☐ Five Ways, Nottingham

134 ☐ Test Match Hotel, West Bridgford

Oxfordshire

135 ☐ Fairview Inn, Oxford

136 ☐ North Star, Steventon

Shropshire

137 ☐ Cross Keys, Sellatyn

138 ☐ Loggerheads, Shrewsbury

139 ☐ Bull's Head, Telford

Somerset

140 ☐ Old Green Tree, Bath

141 ☐ Star Inn, Bath

142 ☐ Tucker's Grave Inn, Faulkland

143 ☐ Rose & Crown, Huish Episcopi

144 ☐ White Hart, Midsomer Norton

145 ☐ Seymour Arms, Witham Friary

Staffordshire

146 ☐ Butchers Arms, Audley

147 ☐ Coopers Tavern, Burton upon Trent

148 ☐ Crystal Fountain, Cannock

149 ☐ Anchor, High Offley

150 ☐ Red Lion, Rugeley

151 ☐ Coachmakers Arms, Stoke-on-Trent

152 ☐ Vine, Stoke-on-Trent

Suffolk

153 ☐ Cock, Brent Eleigh

154 ☐ Nutshell, Bury St Edmunds

155 ☐ Margaret Catchpole, Ipswich

156 ☐ King's Head, Laxfield

157 ☐ Butt & Oyster, Pin Mill

Sussex, East

158 ☐ King & Queen, Brighton

159 ☐ New Inn, Hadlow Down

160 ☐ General Havelock, Hastings

Sussex, West

161 ☐ Stag Inn, Ball's Cross

162 ☐ Blue Ship, The Haven

163 ☐ Royal Oak, Wineham

Tyne & Wear

164 ☐ Central, Gateshead

165 ☐ Crown Posada, Newcastle upon Tyne

166 ☐ Stag's Head, South Shields

167 ☐ Dun Cow, Sunderland

168 ☐ Mountain Daisy, Sunderland

West Midlands

169 ☐ Bartons Arms, Birmingham

170 ☐ Anchor, Birmingham

171 ☐ White Swan, Birmingham

172 ☐ Red Lion, Birmingham

173 ☐ Rose Villa Tavern, Birmingham

174 ☐ Villa Tavern, Birmingham

175 ☐ Black Horse, Birmingham

176 ☐ British Oak, Birmingham

177 ☐ Romping Cat, Bloxwich

178 ☐ Turf Tavern, Bloxwich

179 ☐ Shakespeare, Dudley

180 ☐ Old Swan, Netherton

181 ☐ Waggon & Horses, Oldbury

182 ☐ Manor Arms, Rushall

183 ☐ Beacon Hotel, Sedgley

184 ☐ Britannia, Upper Gornal

185 ☐ Horse & Jockey, Wednesbury

186 ☐ Vine, Wednesfield

Wiltshire

187 ☐ Bruce Arms, Easton Royal
188 ☐ Haunch of Venison, Salisbury

Worcestershire

189 ☐ Fleece, Bretforton
190 ☐ Bell & Cross, Clent
191 ☐ Cider House, Defford
192 ☐ Three Kings, Hanley Castle
193 ☐ Bush, Worcester
194 ☐ Punch Bowl, Worcester

Yorkshire, East

195 ☐ White Horse, Beverley
196 ☐ Station Buffet, Bridlington
197 ☐ Olde Black Boy, Hull
198 ☐ Olde White Harte, Hull
199 ☐ White Hart, Hull
200 ☐ Polar Bear, Hull

Yorkshire, North

201 ☐ Birch Hall Inn, Beck Hole
202 ☐ Three Horse Shoes, Boroughbridge
203 ☐ Zetland, Middlesbrough
204 ☐ New Inn, Selby
205 ☐ Royal Oak Hotel, Settle
206 ☐ Blue Bell, York
207 ☐ Golden Ball, York
208 ☐ Swan, York

Yorkshire, South

209 ☐ Coach & Horses, Barnburgh
210 ☐ Plough, Doncaster
211 ☐ Bath Hotel, Sheffield

Yorkshire, West

212 ☐ New Beehive Inn, Bradford
213 ☐ Three Pigeons, Halifax
214 ☐ King's Arms, Heath
215 ☐ Cardigan Arms, Leeds
216 ☐ Adelphi, Leeds
217 ☐ Whitelock's Ale House, Leeds
218 ☐ Garden Gate, Leeds
219 ☐ Old White Beare, Norwood Green

WALES

Glamorgan

220 ☐ Golden Cross, Cardiff

Mid-Wales

221 ☐ Crown & Anchor, Llanidloes

222 ☐ Lion Royal Hotel, Rhayader

North-East Wales

223 ☐ Fox, Ysceifiog

North-West Wales

224 ☐ Douglas Arms, Bethesda

225 ☐ Albion Ale House, Conwy

226 ☐ Red Lion Inn, Llansannan

West Wales

227 ☐ New Cross Inn, Court Henry

228 ☐ Dyffryn Arms, Pontfaen

SCOTLAND

Aberdeen and Grampian

229 ☐ Grill, Aberdeen

230 ☐ Fiddichside Inn, Craigellachie

Argyll and The Isles

231 ☐ Commercial, Lochgilphead

Edinburgh and the Lothians

232 ☐ Station Bar, Edinburgh

233 ☐ Abbotsford, Edinburgh

234 ☐ Barony Bar, Edinburgh

235 ☐ Bennets Bar, Edinburgh

236 ☐ Café Royal, Edinburgh

237 ☐ Kenilworth, Edinburgh

238 ☐ H.P. Mathers Bar, Edinburgh

239 ☐ Oxford Bar, Edinburgh

240 ☐ Central Bar, Edinburgh

241 ☐ Leslie's Bar, Edinburgh

242 ☐ Prestoungrange Gothenburg, Prestonpans

243 ☐ Railway Inn, West Calder

Greater Glasgow and Clyde Valley

244 ☐ Horse Shoe Bar, Glasgow
245 ☐ Laurieston Bar, Glasgow
246 ☐ Old Toll Bar, Glasgow
247 ☐ Steps Bar, Glasgow
248 ☐ Portland Arms, Glasgow
249 ☐ Railway Tavern, Glasgow
250 ☐ Village Tavern, Larkhall
251 ☐ Bull Inn, Paisley
252 ☐ Central Bar, Renton

Kingdom of Fife

253 ☐ Railway Tavern, Kincardine
254 ☐ Feuars Arms, Kirkcaldy
255 ☐ Auld Hoose, Leslie

Tayside

256 ☐ Clep Bar, Dundee
257 ☐ Frews Bar, Dundee
258 ☐ Speedwell Bar, Dundee

NORTHERN IRELAND

Co. Antrim

259 ☐ Boyd Arms, Ballycastle
260 ☐ House of McDonnell, Ballycastle
261 ☐ Carmichael's, Ballyeaston
262 ☐ Bush House, Bushmills
263 ☐ Mary McBride's Bar, Cushendun

Co. Armagh

264 ☐ Carragher's Bar, Camlough
265 ☐ Mandeville Arms, Portadown

Belfast

266 ☐ Crown Bar, Belfast
267 ☐ Fort Bar, Belfast

Co. Fermanagh

268 ☐ Blake's of the Hollow, Enniskillen
269 ☐ Central Bar, Irvinestown

Co. Londonderry

270 ☐ Owen's Bar, Limavady

Books for pub & beer lovers

CAMRA Books, the publishing arm of the Campaign for Real Ale, is the leading publisher of books on beer and pubs. Key titles include:

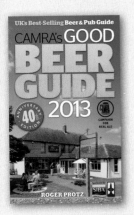

Good Beer Guide 2013

Edited by **ROGER PROTZ**

The *Good Beer Guide* is the only guide you will need to find the right pint, in the right place, every time. It's the original and best-selling independent guide to around 4,500 pubs throughout the UK. Now in its 40th year, this annual publication is a comprehensive and informative guide to the best real ale pubs in the UK, researched and written exclusively by CAMRA members and fully updated every year.

£15.99   ISBN 978 1 85249 290 8

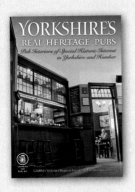

Yorkshire's Real Heritage Pubs

Edited by **DAVE GAMSTON**

This unique guide will lead you to over 120 pubs in Yorkshire and Humber which still have interiors or internal features of real historic significance. They range from simple rural 'time-warp' pubs to ornate Victorian drinking 'palaces' and include some of the more unsung pub interiors from the inter-war and later years that we take so much for granted. This is the first-ever guide of its kind for Yorkshire and it champions the need to celebrate, understand and protect the genuine pub heritage we have left.

£4.99   ISBN 978 1 85249 277 9

Real Heritage Pubs of Wales

Editors **MICHAEL SLAUGHTER** & **MICK DUNN**

An invaluable guide to over 100 pubs in Wales with historic interiors of real national significance, some of them stretching back a century or more, collected together for the first time in this book. The product of many years of surveying by volunteer members of CAMRA who are dedicated to preserving and protecting the UK's historic pub interiors.

£6.99   ISBN 978 1 85249 275 5

Scotland's True Heritage Pubs

Edited by **MICHAEL SLAUGHTER**

This unique guide will lead you to 115 Scottish pubs which have historic features of real national significance, many of which have altered little in the past 40 years or so. Some of the featured pubs are tiny, old-fashioned time-warp inns, others are magnificent Victorian drinking palaces and Art Deco masterpieces. There are also several quirky pubs, including one hidden away in a terrace.

£6.99   ISBN 978 1 85249 242 7

London Heritage Pubs – An inside story

GEOFF BRANDWOOD & **JANE JEPHCOTE**

The definitive guidebook to London's most unspoilt pubs. Raging from gloriously rich Victorian extravaganzas to unspoilt community street-corner locals, these pubs not only have interiors of genuine heritage value, they also have fascinating stories to tell. *London Heritage Pubs – An inside story* is a must for anyone interested in visiting and learning about London's magnificent pubs.

£14.99   ISBN 978 1 85249 247 2

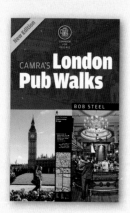

London Pub Walks

BOB STEEL

CAMRA's pocket-sized walking guide to London is back, this fantastic second edition is packed with fully updated routes, new pubs and pages of fresh content – including a bonus section of special tours around the city via public transport. Interlinking routes lead walkers from the heart of the British capital – Trafalgar Square, Big Ben, Fleet Street, the Southbank and Greenwich – to some of the most idyllic suburbs. Every walk features several excellent pubs that can be visited as part of the walk and details of their unique histories and the beers they offer.

£9.99   ISBN 978 1 85249 310 3

Great British Pubs

ADRIAN TIERNEY-JONES

Great British Pubs is a celebration of the British pub. This fully illustrated and practical book presents the pub as an ultimate destination – featuring pubs everyone should seek out and make a visit to. It recommends a selection of the very best pubs in various different categories, as chosen by leading beer writer Adrian Tierney-Jones. Every kind of pub is represented, with full-colour photography helping to showcase a host of excellent pubs from the seaside to the city and from the historic to the ultra-modern.

£14.99   ISBN 978 1 85249 265 6

A Campaign of Two Halves

Campaigning for Pub Goers & Beer Drinkers

CAMRA, the Campaign for Real Ale, is an independent not-for-profit, volunteer-led consumer group. We campaign tirelessly for good-quality real ale and pubs, as well as lobbying government to champion drinkers' rights and promote local pubs as centres of community life. As a CAMRA member you will have the opportunity to campaign to save pubs under threat of closure, for pubs to be free to serve a range of real ales at fair prices and for a reduction in beer duty that will help Britain's brewing industry survive.

Enjoying Real Ale & Pubs

CAMRA has over 147,000 members from all ages and backgrounds, brought together by a common belief in the issues that CAMRA deals with and their love of good quality British beer. From just £23 a year – that's less than a pint a month – you can join CAMRA and enjoy the following benefits:

Subscription to *What's Brewing*, our monthly colour newspaper, and *Beer*, our quarterly magazine, informing you about beer and pub news and detailing events and beer festivals around the country.

Free or reduced entry to over 160 national, regional and local beer festivals.

Money off many of our publications including the *Good Beer Guide*, the *Good Bottled Beer Guide* and *CAMRA's Great British Pubs*.

Access to a members-only section of our national website, **www.camra.org.uk**, which gives up-to-the-minute news stories and includes a special offer section with regular features.

Special discounts with numerous partner organisations and money off real ale in your participating local pubs as part of our Pubs Discount Scheme.

Log onto **www.camra.org.uk/joinus** for
CAMRA membership information.

CAMPAIGN
FOR
REAL ALE

The featured pubs in **Scotland** and **Northern Ireland**

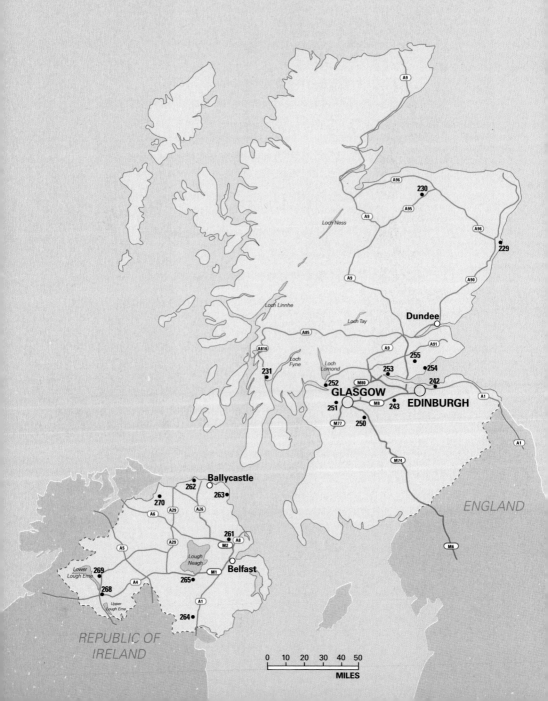

A9
A96
230
Loch Ness
A9
A95
A96
229
A9
A90
Loch Linnhe
Loch Tay
A85
Dundee
A816
A9
A91
Loch Fyne
Loch Lomond
255
231
253
254
A1
252
M80
242
GLASGOW
251
M8 243 EDINBURGH
M77 250
M74
A1
Ballycastle
262
263
270
A29 A26
M6
A6
ENGLAND
A29
261
A8
M2
A5
Lough
Neagh
M1
Belfast
Lower
Lough Erne 269
265
268
A4
A1
Upper
Lough Erne
264

REPUBLIC OF
IRELAND

0 10 20 30 40 50
MILES